CONTEMPORARY FORUM

AMERICAN SPEECHES on TWENTIETH-CENTURY ISSUES

EDITED BY

ERNEST J. WRAGE

BARNET BASKERVILLE

UNIVERSITY OF WASHINGTON PRESS *Seattle and London*

Copyright © 1962 by Ernest J. Wrage and Barnet Baskerville
Original hardcover edition published by Harper & Brothers, 1962
Washington Paperback edition, 1969
Library of Congress Catalog Card Number 62-10074
Printed in the United States of America

PREFACE

CONTEMPORARY FORUM contains speeches delivered in America in the twentieth century. Like its predecessor, *American Forum,* which emphasizes nineteenth-century speeches, *Contemporary Forum* also presents competing points of view on a series of critical issues, thus providing the substance and framework of an American forum as a venture in intellectual history through public address. This issue-centered approach recommends itself because it establishes secure linkages between the function of speech in a free society and the historical processes which speech shapes and by which it is shaped. Within this frame of reference, the history of public address may be pursued as a coherent discipline with the promise of substantial intellectual returns. As Vernon Parrington remarked when speaking of our formative centuries:

> No other path leads so directly and intimately into the heart of those old days as the thorny path of their theological and political controversies; and if one will resolutely pick his way amongst the thorns, he will have his reward in coming close to the men who debated earnestly over the plans and specifications of the Utopia that was to be erected in the free spaces of America. . . . The foundations of a later America were laid in vigorous polemics. . . .[1]

But what of the pertinence of such polemical materials in discovering life and thought of this later America? In the seventeenth and eighteenth centuries, the printed page was costly and scarce; perforce, opinion makers were preponderantly the talkers. Looking ahead to the dawn of the twentieth century, late nineteenth-century journalists, perhaps repelled by roving spellbinders, would occasionally dash off pieces, hopefully predicting that the printed word would eventually supplant the orator. Contrary to such predictions, of course, the spoken word has increased enormously in range and importance because of modern technology, mass media of communication, and the extension of democracy. As a consequence of increased human proximity—local, national, and international—problems have become more numerous, complex, and social in character, demanding wide con-

[1] "Introduction," *Main Currents in American Thought* (New York: Harcourt, Brace and Company, 1927), p. vii.

sultation and continuing persuasion for their solution. Hence the analysis of public discourse provides a sensitive cardiographic tracing of contemporary life forces.

The task of compiling an issue-centered anthology of contemporary speeches has involved more difficult decisions than were faced in the earlier collection. Answers to the same vexing questions—Which issues? Which speeches? Which speakers?—are here even more elusive, for the winnowing processes of history have not yet distinguished the permanent from the evanescent. Controversies in the public forum which in the heat of the moment seem of greatest magnitude may in cooler retrospect appear ephemeral and unimportant. Of the hazards in judging we are most painfully aware, and the hazards increase as we approach the present. Judgments, nevertheless, are unavoidable.

In selecting issues from among scores of questions aired in the American forum within the past sixty years, we have followed the broad currents of recent history to discover those points of tension that have forced the nation to come to terms with itself and with the world. We have also tried to make intelligent conjectures as to which of the public controversies are likely to inform tomorrow's readers about today's critical concerns. We are, of course, acutely aware of the omission of several issues of enormous consequence, such as conflicts between labor and management, mounting agricultural problems, control of atomic energy, disarmament, and the ominous "explosion" of populations. Such omissions result neither from oversight nor from choice, but simply from the limitations of space.

In selecting speeches, we were guided by the same criteria we used in *American Forum:* Are they representative statements in support of a position? Are they cogent, economical, relatively self-contained statements? Do they deal in essentials rather than tangential aspects? Do they convey the spirit of the occasion? In choosing speakers we have asked, Are they competent, accredited spokesmen for a particular position?

In response to suggestions from readers of *American Forum,* we have lengthened the essays introducing each unit. These essays are designed to furnish historical context and to supply interpretative accounts of public discourse on the topics. Bibliographical notes at the end of the book indicate sources of supplementary information: other speeches on the topic; more about the speakers themselves than can be offered in brief, identifying biographical notes; and more detailed historical background. The source of each speech text is clearly indicated in a footnote. We have tried scrupulously to obtain the most reliable texts available, drawing upon tape recordings, stenographic reports, government or other official documents, the press, and published collections of addresses. For textual references that may be unfamiliar to some readers, we have provided explanatory footnotes. Such notes are limited to items not readily available in standard reference books and to allusions that must be immediately comprehended for complete understanding.

When consulted about his biography, John Bright, the English statesman and parliamentary orator, remarked, "My life is in my speeches." Surely it is no overstatement to insist that one valid index to the life of America is the speeches of its public figures—statesmen, educators, clergymen, and other policy and opinion makers. *Contemporary Forum* presents thirty-two speeches by twenty-six speakers on nine issues of vital importance to twentieth-century America and the world. All but three of the texts are complete, and only relatively minor excisions were made in the three texts that are slightly shortened. All of these thirty-two speeches might have been heard by Americans now living; some will recall having heard many of them. In our judgment these speeches are likely to be of continuing interest not only to students of speech and literature, of social and political history, but to all who are invigorated by the drama of ideas in action.

We heartily thank colleagues who have made useful suggestions for this volume. We particularly wish to acknowledge our indebtedness for encouragement and direct assistance to Jo Baskerville, and to Naomi Wrage.

CONTENTS

Preface   v

Part One.   New Freedoms

THE PROGRESSIVE ERA   3

EUGENE VICTOR DEBS   *The Issue*   13
THEODORE ROOSEVELT   *The New Nationalism*   27
WOODROW WILSON   *First Inaugural Address*   40
ELIHU ROOT   *Business and Politics*   44

THE LEAGUE OF NATIONS DEBATE   51

HENRY CABOT LODGE   *In Opposition to the Proposed League of
Nations*   61
WOODROW WILSON   *In Support of the Proposed League of Nations*   76

MODERNISM VS. FUNDAMENTALISM IN RELIGION   87

HARRY EMERSON FOSDICK   *Shall the Fundamentalists Win?*   97
WILLIAM JENNINGS BRYAN   *Moses vs. Darwin*   107
JOHN GRESHAM MACHEN   *Christianity vs. Modern Liberalism*   120

Part Two.   The Great Divide

POLEMICS OF THE NEW DEAL ERA   133

FRANKLIN DELANO ROOSEVELT   *Address to the Commonwealth Club*   146
FRANKLIN DELANO ROOSEVELT   *First Inaugural Address*   157

FRANKLIN DELANO ROOSEVELT   *Fireside Chat on the Accomplish-
ments of the New Deal*   162
ALFRED EMANUEL SMITH   *Come Back to Your Father's House*   168
JOSEPH TAYLOR ROBINSON   *Jacob's Voice but Esau's Hands*   179
NORMAN MATTOON THOMAS   *Is the New Deal Socialism?*   188
HERBERT CLARK HOOVER   *A Holy Crusade for Liberty*   198

HIGHER EDUCATION AND SOCIAL CHANGE   206

JOHN DEWEY   *Education and New Social Ideals*   216
ROBERT MAYNARD HUTCHINS   *Education and Social Improvement*   220
WILLIAM H. COWLEY   *Fire Always Makes Room for Itself*   226

ISOLATIONISM VS. ONE WORLD   234

FRANKLIN DELANO ROOSEVELT   *The Arsenal of Democracy*   246
BURTON KENDALL WHEELER   *America's Present Emergency*   255
FRANKLIN DELANO ROOSEVELT   *Fourth Inaugural Address*   261

Part Three. Grave New World

THE COLD WAR ERA   265

ADLAI EWING STEVENSON   *There are No Gibraltars*   277
ROBERT ALPHONSO TAFT   *Our Misguided Foreign Policy*   285
JOSEPH RAYMOND MCCARTHY   *The Great Betrayal*   294
RALPH E. FLANDERS   *Colossal Innocence in the United States Senate*   301
HARRY S TRUMAN   *Valedictory*   305
DWIGHT DAVID EISENHOWER   *The Price of Peace*   313
JOHN FITZGERALD KENNEDY   *Inaugural Address*   317

TO SECURE THESE RIGHTS   321

THOMAS PICKENS BRADY   *Segregation and the South*   333
ROY WILKINS   *Deep South Crisis*   344

OUR UNFINISHED BUSINESS   352

ADLAI EWING STEVENSON   *The Political Relevance of Moral Principle*   355

Notes on Sources and Supplementary Reading   369

PART ONE

New Freedoms

THE PROGRESSIVE ERA

CHICAGO'S OLD COLISEUM rumbled with the unrelieved hubbub of milling and contentious delegates to the 1896 Democratic convention, while at the rostrum a succession of competing orators vainly belabored them with tired arguments on the money question. Spokesmen for bimetallism beseeched the delegates to sustain the majority report of the platform committee favoring expansion of currency through free and unlimited coinage of silver at a ratio of 16 to 1; the "goldbugs" urged fealty to the gold standard and adoption of a minority report. Control of the party was at stake and tension mounted as the closing speaker in the debate stepped forward. His voice overrode the noises below, penetrating even the acoustically dead recesses of the Coliseum: "I come to speak to you in defense of a cause as holy as the cause of liberty—the cause of humanity." A hush fell over the audience, and under the continuing spell of this handsome, superbly confident young delegate from Nebraska, minds and emotions meshed harmoniously as he lifted the money question from grubby economics to the high plane of religion and social justice. Facing the goldbugs, he confronted them with a constituency long neglected by the party of Jefferson and Jackson:

> When you come before us and tell us that we are about to disturb your business interests, we reply that you have disturbed our business interests by your course.
>
> We say to you that you have made the definition of a business man too limited in its application. The man who is employed for wages is as much a business man as his employer; the attorney in a country town is as much a business man as the corporation counsel in a great metropolis; the merchant at the cross-roads is as much a business man as the merchant of New York; the farmer who goes forth in the morning and toils all day—who begins in the spring and toils all summer—and who by the application of brains and muscle

3

to the natural resources of the country creates wealth is as much a
business man as the man who goes upon the board of trade and bets
upon the price of grain; the miners who go down a thousand feet
into the earth, or climb two thousand feet upon the cliffs, and bring
forth from their hiding places the precious metals to be poured into
the channels of trade are as much business men as the few financial
magnates who, in a back room, corner the money of the world. We
come to speak for this broader class of business men.

On he swept toward his peroration, pretested in the laboratories of rural politics:
"You shall not press down upon the brow of labor this crown of thorns, you
shall not crucify mankind upon a cross of gold." For just a moment the delegates
sat transfixed; then the "awful roar of 20,000 voices" crashed to the ceiling—
wildly cheering what remains today the most celebrated speech in convention
history. The next day the delegates nominated William Jennings Bryan, age
thirty-six, for President. In August the Populist party also nominated him to head
their ticket.

An indefatigable campaigner, Bryan covered over 18,000 miles to make more
than 600 speeches. His Republican opponent, William McKinley, remained se-
curely at home responding to delegations of well-wishers from his front porch
in Canton, Ohio. Eloquent though he was, Bryan's free silver fixation blurred
his broad social objectives, reduced his campaign to a monomania, and opened
him to concentrated attack by the Republican press and a small army of roving
spellbinders. Bryan's detractors pictured him as a knucklehead at best, at worst
a dupe of anarchists and communists. Young Theodore Roosevelt, for example,
gave Bryan the treatment at Utica, New York:

> As Mr. Bryan continues to talk on the stump his utterances grow
> wilder and wilder, until they can only properly be described as the
> ravings of a man whose folly even surpasses his capacity for harm.
> . . . Mr. Bryan is appealing more and more openly to the base ma-
> lignancy and hatred of those demagogues who strive to lead laboring
> men to ruin in order to wreak their vengeance on the thrifty and
> well-to-do. He advocates principles sufficiently silly and wicked to
> make them fit well in the mouth of the anarchist leader. For the
> government of Washington and Lincoln, for the system of orderly
> liberty bequeathed to us by our forefathers, he would substitute a
> red welter of lawlessness as fantastic and as vicious as the dream of a

European communist. . . . Instead of a government of the people, for the people, and by the people, which we now have, Mr. Bryan would substitute a government by the mob.[1]

Roosevelt pressed his point further, linking Bryan to unorthodox and controversial figures whom he depicted as reincarnated revolutionists. In Chicago, with arms flailing, he unloosed this sizzler: "Messrs. Bryan, Altgeld, Tillman, Debs, Coxey, and the rest have not the power to rival the deeds of Marat, Barrère, and Robespierre, but they are strikingly like the leaders of the Terror of France in mental and moral attitude. . . ."[2] Such talk made people jumpy, and scared off the upper and middling groups. Bryan's greatest strength came from the seriously aggrieved segments of the economy, particularly the near-bankrupt farmers; and though he lost, Bryan succeeded for the first time since Andrew Jackson in recalling the Democratic party to its historic mission as a people's party.

McKinley left the business oligarchy undisturbed, and with prosperity high in 1900, his renomination and election were assured. To the consternation of Mark Hanna, however, the Republican convention in an aberrant moment named Roosevelt as its Vice-Presidential candidate. Hanna thought Roosevelt was fine for cracking skulls of political opponents, but he shuddered at the mere possibility that this Rough Rider might become President through a fateful circumstance. "Don't you realize," he demanded, "that there's only one life between this madman and the White House?" In 1901 McKinley fell before an assassin's bullet.

Roosevelt's hyperthyroid attacks upon Bryan, an accredited precursor of the Progressive Era, make it ironic that his administration should usher in progressivism on a national scale which, taken with its ups and downs, lasted until the United States entered World War I. When Roosevelt came to office, zest for reform was spreading from agrarian regions to cities, from cities to state governments. In Wisconsin, Governor Robert M. La Follette was busily shaping a model state and the "Wisconsin Idea" was catching on.

---

[1] "The Enemies of American Honor," September 29, 1896. Hermann Hagedorn, ed., *The Works of Theodore Roosevelt, Memorial Edition* (New York: Charles Scribner's Sons, 1925, 24 vols.), XVI, pp. 392–393.

[2] "The Menace of the Demagogue," October 15, 1896. *Ibid.*, pp. 394–413. John Peter Altgeld, Governor of Illinois, had pardoned anarchists who were imprisoned for the Haymarket Riot, and had opposed Cleveland's use of Federal troops during the Pullman strike in Chicago; Benjamin ("Pitchfork Ben") Tillman, United States Senator from South Carolina, was a Populist agitator though he remained a Democrat; Eugene V. Debs, nationally known labor leader, had served a jail term for disobeying a Federal court injunction served during the recent Pullman strike; Jacob S. Coxey was celebrated for leading an army of unemployed in a march on Washington in 1894 to dramatize and urge his program of public works.

These twentieth-century progressives were under heavy obligations to the past —to Mugwumps, Populists, Social Gospelers, and suffragists; to Henry George, Edward Bellamy, Bryan, and a host of socially conscious agitators. But the new thrust for reform came from solid, middle-class, urban dwellers, and during a time of general prosperity at that. They were shocked out of their complacency by "muckraking" journalists who published exposés of seamy social and political life, and documentary reports on financial and industrial octopi ruthlessly squeezing out small enterprisers. Unless wrongs were redressed, the middle class faced attrition and might even be destroyed in some violent struggle ahead between plutocracy and the unpropertied, socially disaffected masses.

A conservative at heart, Roosevelt shared in the general anxiety of his class. Accordingly, he adopted reform as a countervailing force both to entrenched privilege and to the threat of proletarian uprisings. But he moved gingerly, giving the country the kind of realistic middle-of-the-road leadership that the middle class was prepared to follow. It was typical of him to administer verbal lashings to some few "malefactors of great wealth" while trying to woo the large body of honest conservatives to his Square Deal. As preacher-at-large, he flayed fat materialism and summoned Americans to emulate the heroic qualities of the pioneer and soldier. His speeches were laced with injunctions to public morality, and he uttered them with such resoluteness that they seemed novel and triumphant. He applauded "responsible" progressives but applied the lash to muckrakers who went too far and too fast.[3] Everything considered, his ambiguities notwithstanding, Roosevelt made substantial contributions to progressivism, particularly through creating a rhetorical environment favorable to its growth. He made reform exciting and quickened the national pulse; and as for Roosevelt personally, he was simply "dee-lighted" by the public's enthusiasm for the whole "bully" business.

Roosevelt came to reform in part through his fear of radicalism and his antipathy for radicals. He regarded Eugene Victor Debs, America's foremost Socialist, as an "undesirable citizen" and called his speeches "mere pieces of the literature of criminal violence." Debs reciprocated, and from his promontory in left field scolded workers for their infatuation with that cowboy in the White House, whom he regarded as a faker, a peddler of nostrums, an opportunist, and a lackey of capitalists. Roosevelt used reform to prevent radicalism from infecting the body politic; Debs campaigned to win workers to Socialism while fending off the petty

---

[3] See, for example, Roosevelt's speech, "The Man with the Muckrake," 1906. *Ibid.*, XVIII, pp. 571–581.

bourgeoisie who threatened to capture the Socialist party and divert it from its revolutionary aims.

Debs had come to Socialism through the labor movement. After holding important posts in the Brotherhood of Locomotive Firemen, he organized the American Railway Union in 1893 along lines of industrial unionism. In 1894 the fledgling union won a thumping victory over the powerful Great Northern Railroad. Almost immediately it was drawn into the ill-fated Pullman strike in Chicago and found itself pitted against an unbeatable combination of forces: The General Managers Association of railway companies, the Attorney General of the United States, the United States Army, the Federal courts, and a hostile press. The strike was broken, Debs was jailed for disobeying a court injunction, and the ARU was destroyed.

In jail Debs read up on Socialism, talked with Socialist visitors, and mulled over the Pullman episode from a Socialist's perspective. He left jail convinced that Socialist doctrine explained how the pieces fitted together. The ARU had been destroyed because capitalists could commandeer opinion makers and the United States Government itself; the real enemy of the workers and the downtrodden, he concluded, was the capitalist system; the story of the Pullman strike only dramatized the inexorability of the class struggle.

Having come to this view of things, Debs felt impelled to seek change through political action. He had supported Bryan and the Populists in 1896, thereby contributing inadvertently to Roosevelt's fusillade against Bryan; in 1900 Debs went over to Socialism. Between 1900 and 1920, he was the Socialist party's choice for President five times. His most spectacular campaign was in 1908, but his most spectacular results were obtained in 1912, when he received 5.99 percent of the votes cast. His last try was in 1920 as convict #9653 in Atlanta Penitentiary, where he was serving a ten-year sentence for having run afoul of the Espionage Acts of World War I.

Although Debs often spoke in a Marxist idiom, he had been influenced only superficially by Marx and other revolutionary importations. His was an indigenous radicalism, a native growth like that of Laurence Gronlund, Edward Bellamy, Henry Demarest Lloyd, and Upton Sinclair. He plunged into Socialism because he was repelled by a heartless and unjust economic system that fostered privilege and poverty and, in the process, destroyed man's essential humanity. Debs' Socialism was, essentially, based upon the philosophy of the heart and was never urged with greater spontaneity and fullness than in his speech of May 23, 1908. Debs was in Girard, Kansas, working on a Socialist sheet called the *Appeal to Reason,* when word came that he had again been nominated for the Presidency by the Socialist convention in Chicago. A few days later, his friend Fred Warren coaxed Debs to stroll to the town square to witness a carnival in progress, but instead of a carnival Debs found a crowd waiting to honor and hear him. His speech of May 23, now called "The Issue," comprises his indictment of capitalism and the substance of his social credo.

To Debs, Socialism meant a coöperative commonwealth wherein public ownership of the means of production would insure production for use, not profit, and an equitable distribution of wealth. Unmindful of personal costs, he devoted himself unswervingly to this model of society. As a crusader, he was easily the Socialist party's greatest asset, and among followers he inspired a hagiolatry. Even people unsympathetic to his goal, which included most Americans, were drawn to him by his manifest idealism, devotion to cause, personal charm, and fervent, evangelistic oratory. But even with benefit of Debs, the Socialist party's position in the Progressive Era was, at best, equivocal. In some measure the Socialists were the legatees of general ferment, but in the main they were regarded as a menace both by conservatives and by progressives, who were at one in their adherence to capitalism.

Roosevelt's political heir, William Howard Taft, piled up more votes than did Bryan and Debs together in the 1908 election. Out of office, Roosevelt took off on an African safari and European speaking tour. He returned a year later, and hardly had he unpacked his gear before he was off barnstorming. Two things fired him: his dissatisfaction with Taft's drift toward conservatism, and his reading of Herbert Croly's *The Promise of American Life,* published in 1909.

Croly's book offered an exposition of contemporary economic life, a critique of historical liberalism in the United States, and a manifesto for progressives. The modern age, Croly pointed out, was marked by large-scale economic organizations that comprised rival pressure blocs. These blocs served special interests, but in the Darwinian struggle the public interests were served inadequately or not at all. The times called for more government under the management of a strong executive who would rise above rival interests that ruled the legislative branch, and who would give effective expression to the national interests. Accordingly, Croly called upon liberals to abandon their attachment to Jefferson's archaic predilections for yeomanry and small government. Individual autonomy was a social myth; small enterprise must bow to inexorable economic forces that tended toward consolidation. More government was needed, not to break up indiscriminately the industrial combines in some vain attempt to restore Jacksonian individualism, as many liberals seemed to favor; but government must be strengthened to domesticate the economic Goliaths through social planning. To this end, Croly invoked the name of Alexander Hamilton, long considered the archenemy of liberals, urging a revival of Hamilton's doctrine of energetic government tempered by Jefferson's faith in political democracy. Croly called this fusion "the new nationalism," and he singled out Theodore Roosevelt as its foremost exemplar.

Roosevelt couldn't have agreed more. Indeed, his record and utterances while President gave credence to the body of Croly's argument. But the book did more for Roosevelt than to endorse his administration; it gave form to his thinking, pointed out new directions, and quickened his ambitions. And so, hot with the spirit of advanced progressivism, he set out on a 5000-mile western speaking tour in 1910. At Osawatomie, Kansas—a town with overtones from days of anti-slavery agitation—Roosevelt expounded "The New Nationalism," which "foretold the charter of the Progressive party of 1912." Liberals everywhere echoed the "yip and kyoodle" of the Osawatomie crowd; conservatives were aghast at Roosevelt's radicalism.[4] The fears of conservative Republicans were not baseless. Two years later Roosevelt stalked out of the Republican convention after an internecine struggle which Taft won, took his insurgent delegates with him, and founded an independent Progressive party popularly hailed as the Bull Moose party. Democrats nominated Woodrow Wilson, a reform-minded Governor of New Jersey, and as usual the Socialists named Eugene V. Debs.

The only real contest in 1912 was between Roosevelt and Wilson. Roosevelt swept through the land preaching his brand of progressivism under the banner of The New Nationalism; Wilson preached his brand under the label of The New Freedom. It was confusing. The root question dividing these two progressives, said Louis Brandeis, Wilson's advisor, was this: Should we have regulated competition or regulated monopoly?

Back in the days when he was President, Roosevelt had understood the public's apprehension over bigness in industry and finance; he had recognized that trust-busting was politically popular although, for the most part, economically and legally futile. Within a decade, however, he publicly shed his "rural Toryism." "Combinations in industry," he had asserted at Osawatomie in 1910, "are the result of an imperative economic law which cannot be repealed by political legis-

---

[4] *The Nation,* still a conservative organ, for example, denounced Roosevelt for "hiding behind Lincoln" while urging government by mob. The New Nationalism "makes progressives like Cummins and LaFollette look like moss-backed reactionaries, and Bryan himself appear pre-Adamite." Its "half-baked Rooseveltian Socialism" is the issue of the day. See vol. 91 (1910), pp. 205–256, *passim.*

lation. The effort at prohibiting all combination has substantially failed. The way out lies, not in attempting to prevent such combinations, but in completely controlling them in the interest of public welfare." And not only would he use government to regulate big industry, he would promote social legislation on a scale that looked to a later generation like the blueprint of a welfare state.

"There is one proposition upon which this campaign turns," said Wilson, "that monopoly is inevitable." He acknowledged the propriety, if not the inevitability, of some bigness in modern economic life; but he drew a line between natural and illegitimate developments. How did these monsters come into being in the first place? he asked. They were allowed to grow amidst conditions of unregulated competition. The job now is to break up trusts and monopolies and to keep new ones from being born. The proper role of government is to restore and guarantee conditions of real competition in the economy. Roosevelt's New Nationalism takes you down one road, Wilson told his audience in Sioux Falls, South Dakota, and The New Freedom takes you down another. "Choose your course, then, gentlemen, on the fifth of November. Adopt the great trusts into the family and depend upon your government to make them be good, or else take the course by which it will be impossible for them to live by anything except economy and brains. Let your government patronize them, or else put them on their mettle and let them survive, as all honest business ought to be able to survive, in the open competition of the market."[5]

As the campaign wore on, Wilson broadened his attack on The New Nationalism, insisting that a choice had to be made between two concepts of society and government. Roosevelt's paternalistic program of social welfare, he charged, would debauch free people and make them wards of the state. Wilson too held out the promise of social action, but in countering The New Nationalism, his model seemed to be some shadowy, bygone world of laissez faire.

Wilson won the election largely because Roosevelt had split the Republican party. His inaugural address on March 4, 1913, did much to allay doubts, particularly those of Roosevelt's followers, as to whether Wilson's heart really belonged to the twentieth-century progressives. The address was profoundly moving —lofty in moral tone, balanced yet refreshingly frank in its appraisal of social ills, and freighted with hints of statutory action to come. Throughout his first administration, continuing pressure from progressives in Congress helped to transform Wilson, the reluctant liberal, into a vigorous progressive, and in his speech

[5] John Wells Davidson, ed., *A Crossroads of Freedom* (New Haven: Yale University Press, 1956), p. 173.

accepting renomination in 1916 Wilson was justified in his appraisal of his first administration: "This record must equally astonish those who feared that the Democratic Party had not opened its heart to comprehend the demands of social justice. We have in four years come very near to carrying out the platform of the Progressive Party as well as our own; for we also are progressives." Out of the political alchemy of the times, The New Freedom underwent transformation until it emerged looking surprisingly like The New Nationalism. Progressivism was at high tide.

Dislodged from power, conservative businessmen and politicians were bewildered and resentful at being treated as pariahs and Philistines. Two weeks after Taft's defeat in 1912 Senator Elihu Root spoke with some bitterness at a banquet of the New York Chamber of Commerce. "There are hundreds of thousands of people, outside the great industrial communities, who think you are a den of thieves, and there are hundreds of thousands of people who think the manufacturers are not better than a set of confidence men."[6] Root was still smarting from the wounds inflicted by the campaign, and as Wilson's program unfolded his gloom deepened. Along with other conservatives, his nostalgia became acute for the good old days of a businessman's government.

Elihu Root came to government with a background in corporation law. He had been Secretary of War under both McKinley and Roosevelt, and during Roosevelt's second term he had served with high distinction as Secretary of State. Roosevelt greatly admired Root's ability and wavered between him and Taft as a likely successor to the Presidency. When Taft got the nod, Root entered the United States Senate in 1909. In the years that immediately followed, Root was overborne by the "ferment of new ideas." To counteract progressives, he "used his position in the Senate and as leader of the American bar to extol the old order, and this defense of conservatism was his most important contribution to the Progressive Era."[7]

Root was brainy and incisively articulate. Widely in demand, he spoke often and well in his campaign to mobilize conservatives and to start backfires against the spread of progressivism. Typical is his speech of 1915 called "Business and Politics," in which he reminded the Philadelphia Union League Club: "When we elected McKinley in 1896 and again in 1900, it was the businessmen of the United States who controlled the election," but alas, "The scepter has passed

[6] "The Spirit of Self-Government," November 21, 1912. *International Conciliation,* 44–63 (1911–1913), pp. 3–4.
[7] Richard Leopold, *Elihu Root and the Conservative Tradition* (Boston: Little, Brown and Company, 1954), p. 71.

from the businessman" and a hostile government is busily throttling him with regulatory commissions. To block the bureaucrats, Root urged businessmen to regain public confidence by creating a new image of themselves as the foremost agents of social progress. Root spoke with sincerity and feeling, for he genuinely admired the competence, expertise, and achievements of businessmen. Moreover, he was imbued with zeal for character building, and he regarded the emery wheel of competition as the best possible instrument for shaping responsible and self-reliant members of society.

But Root did not reject out of hand all political reforms that modified the established economic order here and there—particularly if they were carried out under conservative auspices. He did distrust, however, the use of government to promote the leveling process and all schemes to establish direct democracy through devices such as the initiative, referendum, and recall. To counter arguments of progressives for direct democracy, Root gave two lectures at Princeton University in 1913, entitled "Experiments in Government" and "Essentials of the Constitution." These lectures comprised a thoughtful conservative's restraint upon constitutional innovations of the Progressive Era and a forceful restatement of traditional constitutional theory based on limited, delegated, and distributed powers.

War ended the Progressive Era, and a recrudescence of conservatism marked the age of Harding, Coolidge, and Hoover. An elder statesman who had ridden out storms of the past, Root was listened to with respect. From the vantage point of the mid-twenties, he spoke in a serene and optimistic vein at a birthday dinner in his honor, observing that "wild enthusiasts may seek to disturb and destroy the order of our social life" but "they all pass." This was the long view. As for the present, ". . . there has been no period in the life of the American Republic in which she has been served by abler men, answering to higher standards of conduct, or more unselfish patriotism, than she is today."[8] Root had come home. The decade of the twenties gave apparent credibility to the revival of views about man, society, and government that had been shaped in the nineteenth century.

---

8 "American Ideals During the Past Half-Century," February 13, 1925, Union League Club, New York City. *International Conciliation*, 206–215 (1925), pp. 151–158.

The Issue

EUGENE VICTOR DEBS

Born, Terre Haute, Indiana, November 5, 1855; died, October 20, 1926. Educated in the public schools of Terre Haute. Active in the Brotherhood of Locomotive Firemen, to which he was elected secretary and treasurer in 1880; editor of the Locomotive Firemen's Magazine. *Member of Indiana state legislature, 1885. Organized American Railway Union, 1893, of which he was made president. Five times Socialist candidate for President of the United States in 1900, 1904, 1908, 1912, and 1920. Sentenced to Atlanta penitentiary in 1918 for violating sedition provision of the Espionage Acts. His sentence was commuted by President Harding in 1921.*

"I am opposed to capitalism because I love my fellow men. . . ."

C omrades, Ladies and Gentlemen: When I made inquiry a few moments ago as to the cause of this assembling I was told that it was the beginning of another street fair. I am quite surprised, and agreeably so, to find myself the central attraction. Allow me in the very beginning to express my heartiest appreciation of the more than kind and generous words which have been spoken here for me this afternoon. There are times when words—mere words—no matter how fitly chosen or well expressed—are almost meaningless. As the rosebud under the influence of sunshine and shower opens, so does my heart receive your benediction this afternoon.

Town square, Girard, Kansas, May 23, 1908. *Debs: His Life, Writings and Speeches* (Girard, Kansas: The Appeal to Reason, 1908), pp. 473–491.

I am a new resident of Girard; have been here but a comparatively short time, and yet I feel myself as completely at home among you, most of whom disagree with me upon very vital questions, as I do in the town in which I was born and reared and have lived all the days of my life. Since the day I first came here I have been treated with uniform kindness. I could not have been treated more hospitably anywhere. I have met practically all of your people, and all of them have taken me by the hand and treated me as cordially as if I had been neighbor and friend with them; and to say that I appreciate this is to express myself in hackneyed and unsatisfactory terms.

The honor to which reference has been made has come to me through no fault of my own. It has been said that some men are born great, some achieve greatness, and some have greatness thrust upon them. It is even so with what are called honors. Some men have honors thrust upon them. I find myself in that class. I did what little I could to prevent myself from being nominated by the convention now in session at Chicago, but the nomination sought me out, and in spite of myself I stand in your presence this afternoon the nominee of the Socialist party for the presidency of the United States.

Long, long ago I made up my mind never again to be a candidate for any political office within the gift of the people. I was constrained to violate that vow because when I joined the Socialist party I was taught that the desire of the individual was subordinate to the party will, and that when the party commanded it was my duty to obey. There was a time in my life when I had the vanities of youth, when I sought that bubble called fame. I have outlived it. I have reached that point when I am capable of placing an estimate upon my own relative insignificance. I have come to realize that there is no honor in any real sense of that term to any man unless he is capable of freely consecrating himself to the service of his fellow men.

To the extent that I am able to help those who are unable to help themselves, to that extent, and to that extent alone, do I honor myself and the party to which I belong. So far as the presidency of the United States is concerned, I would spurn it were it not that it conferred the power to serve the working class, and he who enters that office with any other conception of it prostitutes and does not honor that office.

Now, my friends, I am opposed to the system of society in which we live today, not because I lack the natural equipment to do for myself, but because I am not satisfied to make myself comfortable knowing that there are thousands upon thousands of my fellow men who suffer for the barest necessities of life. We were taught under the old ethic that man's business upon this earth was to look out for himself. That was the ethic of the jungle; the ethic of the wild beast. Take care of yourself, no matter what may become of your fellow man. Thousands of years ago the question was asked: "Am I my brother's keeper?" That question has never yet been answered in a way that is satisfactory to civilized society.

Yes, I am my brother's keeper. I am under a moral obligation to him that is inspired, not by any maudlin sentimentality, but by the higher duty I owe to myself. What would you think of me if I were capable of seating myself at a table and gorging myself with food and saw about me the children of my fellow beings starving to death?

Allow me to say to you, my fellow men, that nature has spread a great table bounteously for all of the children of men. There is room for all and there is a plate and a place and food for all, and any system of society that denies a single one the right and the opportunity to freely help himself to nature's bounties is an unjust and iniquitous system that ought to be abolished in the interest of a higher humanity and a civilization worthy of the name. And here let me observe, my fellow men, that while the general impression is that human society is stationary—a finality as it were—it is not so for a single instant. Underlying society there are great material forces that are in operation all of the circling hours of the day and night, and at certain points in the social development these forces outgrow the forms that hold them and these forms spring apart and then a new social system comes into existence and a new era dawns for the human race.

The great majority of mankind have always been in darkness. The overwhelming majority of the children of men have always been their own worst enemies. In every age of this world's history, the kings and emperors and czars and potentates, in alliance with the priests, have sought by all the means at their command to keep the people in darkness that they might perpetuate the power in which they riot and revel in luxury while the great mass are in a state of slavery and degradation, and he who has spoken out courageously against the existing order, he who has dared to voice the protest of the oppressed and downtrodden, has had to pay the penalty, all the way from Jesus Christ of Galilee down to Fred Warren of Girard.

Do you know, my friends, it is so easy to agree with the ignorant majority. It is so easy to make the people applaud an empty platitude. It takes some courage to face that beast called the Majority, and tell him the truth to his teeth! Some men do so and accept the consequences of their acts as becomes men, and they live in history—every one of them. I have said so often, and I wish to repeat it on this occasion, that mankind have always crowned their oppressors, and they have as uniformly crucified their saviors, and this has been true all along the highway of the centuries. It is true today. It will not always be so. When the great mass know the truth, they will treat an honest man decently while he lives and not crucify him, and then a thousand years afterward rear a monument above the dust of the hero they put to death.

I am in revolt against capitalism (and that doesn't mean to say, my friends, that I am hating you—not the slightest). I am opposed to capitalism because I love my fellow men, and if I am opposing you I am opposing you for what I believe to be your good, and though you spat upon me with contempt I should still oppose you to the extent of my power.

I don't hate the workingman because he has turned against me. I know the poor fellow is too ignorant to understand his self-interest, and I know that as a rule the workingman is the friend of his enemy and the enemy of his friend. He votes for men who represent a system in which labor is simply merchandise; in which the man who works the hardest and longest has the least to show for it.

If there is a man on this earth who is entitled to all the comforts and luxuries of this life in abundance it is the man whose labor produces them. If he is not, who is? Does he get them in the present system?

And, mark you, I am not speaking in a partisan sense this afternoon. I appreciate the fact that you have come here as republicans and democrats as well as Socialists to do me a personal honor, and I would be ungrateful, indeed, if I took advantage of such an occasion to speak to you in an offensive partisan sense. I wish to say in the broadest possible way that I am opposing the system under which we live today because I believe it is subversive of the best interests of the people. I am not satisfied with things as they are, and I know that no matter what administration is in power, even were it a Socialist administration, there will be no material change in the condition of the people until we have a new social system based upon the mutual economic interests of the whole people; until you and I and all of us collectively own those things that we collectively need and use.

That is a basic economic proposition. As long as a relatively few men own the railroads, the telegraph, the telephone, own the oil fields and the gas fields and the steel mills and the sugar refineries and the leather tanneries—own, in short, the sources and means of life—they will corrupt our politics, they will enslave the working class, they will impoverish and debase society, they will do all things that are needful to perpetuate their power as the economic masters and the political rulers of the people. Not until these great agencies are owned and operated by the people can the people hope for any material improvement in their social condition.

Is the condition fair today, and satisfactory to the thinking man?

According to the most reliable reports at our command, as I speak here this afternoon there are at least four millions of workingmen vainly searching for employment. Have you ever found yourself in that unspeakably sad predicament? Have you ever had to go up the street, begging for work, in a great city thronged with humanity—and, by the way, my friends, people are never quite so strange to each other as when they are forced into artificial, crowded and stifled relationship.

I would rather be friendless out on the American desert than to be friendless in New York or Chicago. Have you ever walked up one side of the street and come back on the other side, while your wife, Mary, was waiting at home with three or four children for you to report that you had found work? Quite fortunately for me I had an experience of similar nature quite early in my life. Quite fortunately because, had I not known from my own experience just what it is to have to beg for work, just what it is to be shown the door as if I were a very offensive intruder, had I not known what it is to suffer for the want of food, had I not seen every door closed and barred in my face, had I not found myself friendless and alone in the city as a boy looking for work, and in vain, perhaps I would not be here this afternoon. I might have grown up, as some others have who have been, as they regard themselves, fortunate. I might have waved aside my fellow men and said, "Do as I have done. If you are without work it is your own fault. Look at me; I am self-made. No man is under the necessity of looking for work if he is willing to work."

Nothing is more humiliating than to have to beg for work, and a system in which any man has to beg for work stands condemned. No man can defend it. Now the rights of one are as sacred as the rights of a million. Suppose you happen to be the one who has no work. This republic is a failure so far as you are concerned.

Every man has the inalienable right to work.

Here I stand, just as I was created. I have two hands that represent my labor power. I have some bone and muscle and sinew and some energy. I want to exchange the use of these for food and clothing and shelter. But between me and the tools with which work is done there stands a man artificially created. He says, "No, no!" Why not? "Because you cannot first make a profit for me."

Now, there has been a revolution in industry during the last fifty years, but the trouble with most people is that they haven't kept pace with it. They don't know anything about it and they are especially innocent in regard to it in the small western cities and states, where the same old conditions of a century ago still largely prevail. Your grandfather could help himself anywhere. All he needed was some cheap, simple primitive tools and he could then apply his labor to the resources of nature with his individual tools and produce what he needed. That era in our history produced our greatest men. Lincoln himself sprang from this primitive state of society. People have said, "Why, he had no chance. See how great he became." Yes, but Lincoln had for his comrades great, green-plumed forest monarchs. He could put his arms about them and hear their heart-throbs, as they whispered: "Go on, Abe, a great destiny awaits you." He was in partnership with nature. He associated with birds and bees and flowers, and he was in the fields and heard the rippling music of the laughing brooks and streams. Nature took him to her bosom and nourished him, and from his unpolluted heart there sprang his noble aspirations.

Had Lincoln been born in a sweatshop he would never have been heard of.

How is it with the babe that is born in Mott street, or in the lower Bowery, or in the east side of New York City? That is where thousands, tens of thousands and hundreds of thousands of babes are born who are to constitute our future generations.

I have seen children ten years of age in New York City who had never seen a live chicken. The babes there don't know what it is to put their tiny feet on a blade of grass. It is the most densely populated spot on earth.

You have seen your bee-hive—just fancy a human bee-hive of which yours is the miniature and you have the industrial hive under capitalism. If you have never seen this condition you are excusable for not being a Socialist. Come to New York, Chicago, San Francisco with me; remain with me just twenty-four hours, and then look into my face as I shall look into yours when I ask: "What about Socialism now?" These children by hundreds and thousands are born in sub-cellars, where a whole grown family is crowded together in one room, where modesty between the sexes is absolutely impossible. They are surrounded by filth and vermin. From their birth they see nothing but immorality and vice and crime. They are tainted in the cradle. They are inoculated by their surroundings and they are doomed from the beginning. This system takes their lives just as certainly as if a dagger were thrust into their quivering little hearts, and let me say to you that it were better for many thousands of them if they had never seen the light.

Now I submit, my friends, that such a condition as this is indefensible in the twentieth century. Time was when everything had to be done in a very primitive way, and most men had to work all their days, all their lives, to feed and shelter themselves. They had no time, they had no opportunity for higher development, and so they were what the world calls "illiterate." They had little chance. It took all their time and energy to feed the animal; but how is it today? Upon the average twenty men can today, with the aid of modern machinery, produce as much wealth as a thousand did a half century ago. Can you think of a single thing that enters into our daily existence that cannot be easily produced in abundance for all? If you can I wish you would do me the kindness to name it.

I don't know it all. I am simply a student of this great question, and I am serving as best I can and I know my eyes are ready for the light, and I thank that man, no matter what he be, who can add to the flame of the torch I bear. If there is a single thing that you can think of that cannot be produced in abundance, name it. Bread, clothing, fuel—everything is here.

Nature's storehouse is full to the surface of the earth. All of the raw materials are deposited here in abundance. We have the most marvelous machinery the world has ever known. Man has long since become master of the natural forces and made them work for him. Now he has but to touch a button and the wheels begin to spin and the machinery to whirr, and wealth is produced on every hand in increasing abundance.

Why should any man, woman or child suffer for food, clothing or shelter? Why? The question cannot be answered. Don't tell me that some men are too lazy to work. Suppose they are too lazy to work, what do you think of a social system that produces men too lazy to work? If a man is too lazy to work don't treat him with contempt. Don't look down upon him with scorn as if you were a superior being. If there is a man who is too lazy to work there is something the matter with him. He wasn't born right or he was perverted in this system.

You could not, if you tried, keep a normal man inactive, and if you did he would go stark mad. Go to any penitentiary and you will find the men there begging for the privilege of doing work.

I know by close study of the question exactly how men become idle. I don't repel them when I meet them. I have never yet seen the tramp I was not able to receive with open arms. He is a little less fortunate than I am. He is made the same as I am made. He is a child of the same Father. Had I been born in his environment, had I been subjected to the same things to which he was I would have been where he is.

Can you tell me why there wasn't a tramp in the United States in 1860? In that day, if some one had said "tramp," no one would have known what was meant by it. If human nature is innately depraved and men would rather ride on brake beams and sleep in holes and caves instead of comfortable beds, if they would do that from pure choice and from natural depravity, why were they not built that way fifty years ago? Fifty years ago capitalism was in its earlier stages. Fifty years ago work was still mainly done by hand, and every boy could learn a trade and every boy could master the tools and go to work. That is why there were no tramps. In fifty years that simple tool has become a mammoth machine. It gets larger and larger all the time. It has crowded the hand tool out of production. With the machine came the capitalist.

There were no capitalists, nor was there such a thing as capital before the beginning of the present system. Capitalists came with machinery. Up to the time that machinery supplanted the hand tool the little employer was himself a workingman. No matter what the shop or factory, you would find the employer working side by side with his men. He was a superior workman who got more orders than he could fill and employed others to help him, but he had to pay them the equivalent of what they produced because if he did not they would pack up their tools and go into business for themselves.

Now, the individual tool has become the mammoth machine. It has multiplied production by hundreds. The old tool was individually owned and used. The modern tool, in the form of a great machine, is social in every conception of it. Look at one of these giant machines. Come to the Appeal office and look at the press in operation. Here the progressive conception of the ages is crystallized. What individual shall put his hand on this social agency and say, "This is mine! He who would apply labor here must first pay tribute to me."

The hand tool has been very largely supplanted by this machine. Not many tools are left. You are still producing in a very small way here in Girard, but your production is flickering out gradually. It is but a question of time until it will expire entirely. In spite of all that can be said or done to the contrary production is organizing upon a larger and larger scale and becoming entirely co-operative. This has crowded out the smaller competitor and gradually opened the way for a new social order.

Your material interest and mine in the society of the future will be the same. Instead of having to fight each other like animals, as we do today, and seeking to glorify the brute struggle for existence—of which every civilized human being ought to be ashamed—instead of this, our material interests are going to be mutual. We are going to jointly own these mammoth machines, and we are going to operate them as joint partners and we are going to divide all the products among ourselves.

We are not going to send our surplus to the Goulds and Vanderbilts of New York. We are not going to pile up a billion of dollars in John D. Rockefeller's hands—a vast pyramid from the height of which he can look down with scorn and contempt upon the "common herd." John D. Rockefeller's great fortune is built upon your ignorance. When you know enough to know what your interest is you will support the great party that is organized upon the principle of collective ownership of the means of life. This party will sweep into power upon the issue of emancipation just as republicanism swept into power upon the abolition question half a century ago.

In the meantime, don't have any fear of us Socialists. We don't mean any harm! Many of you have been taught to look upon us as very dangerous people. It is amazing to what extent this prejudice has struck root. The capitalist press will tell you of a good many evil things that we Socialists are going to do that we never intend to do. They will tell you we are going to break up the home. Great heaven! What about the homes of the four million tramps that are looking for work today? How about the thousands and thousands of miserable shacks in New York and every great city where humanity festers? It would be a good thing if they were torn down and obliterated completely, for they are not fit for human habitation. No, we are not going to destroy the home, but we are going to make the home possible for the first time in history.

You may think you are very comfortable. Let me make you a little comparison. You may not agree with me. I don't expect you to and I don't ask you to. I am going to ask you to remember what I say this afternoon and perhaps before I am elected president of the United States you will believe what I say is true. Now there are those of you who are fairly comfortable under the present standard. Isn't it amazing to you how little the average man is satisfied with? You go out here to the edge of town and you find a small farmer who has a cabin with just room enough to keep himself and wife and two or three children, which has a mortgage on it, and he works early and late and gets just enough in net returns to keep him in working order, and he will deliver a lecture about the wonderful prosperity of the country.

He is satisfied, and that is his calamity.

Now, the majority of you would say that is his good fortune. "It is a blessing that he is satisfied." I want to see if I can show you that it is a curse to him and to society that he is satisfied.

If it had not been for the discontent of a few fellows who have not been satisfied with their condition you would still be living in caves. You never would have emerged from the jungle. Intelligent discontent is the mainspring of civilization.

Progress is born of agitation. It is agitation or stagnation. I have taken my choice.

This farmer works all day long, works hard enough to produce enough to live the life of a man; not of an animal, but of a man. Now there is an essential difference between a man and an animal. I admire a magnificent animal in any form except in the human form. Suppose you had everything that you could possibly desire, so far as your physical wants are concerned. Suppose you had a million to your credit in the bank, a palatial home and relations to suit yourself, but no soul capacity for real enjoyment. If you were denied knowing what sorrow is, what real joy is, what music is, and literature and sculpture, and all of those subtle influences that touch the heart and quicken the pulses and fire the senses, and so lift and ennoble a man that he can feel his head among the stars and in communion with God himself—if you are denied these, no matter how sleek or fat or contented you may be, you are still as base and as corrupt and as repulsive a being as walks God's green earth.

You may have plenty of money. The poorest people on this earth are those who have most money. A man is said to be poor who has none, but he is a pauper who has nothing else. Now this farmer, what does he know about literature? After his hard day's work is done, here he sits in his little shack. He is fed, and his animal wants are satisfied. It is at this time that a man begins to live. It is not while you work and slave that you live. It is when you have done your work honestly, when you have contributed your share to the common fund, that you begin to live. Then, as Whitman said, you can take out your soul; you can commune with yourself; you can take a comrade by the hand and you can look into his eyes and down into his soul, and in that holy communion you live. And if you don't know what that is, or if you are not at least on the edge of it, it is denied you to even look into the promised land.

Now this farmer knows nothing about the literature of the world. All its libraries are sealed to him. So far as he is concerned, Homer and Dante and Dickens might as well not have lived; Beethoven, Liszt and Wagner, and all those musicians whose art makes the common atmosphere blossom with harmony, never have been for this farmer. He knows nothing about poetry or art. Never rises above the animal plane upon which he is living. Within fifteen minutes after he has ceased to live he is forgotten; the next generation doesn't know his name, and the world doesn't know he ever lived. That is life under the present standard.

You tell me that is all the farmer is fit for? What do I propose to do for that farmer? Nothing. I only want him to know that he is robbed every day in the week, and if I can awaken him to the fact that he is robbed under the capitalist system he will fall into line with the Socialist movement, and will march to the polls on election day, and instead of casting his vote to fasten the shackles upon his limbs more firmly, he will vote for his emancipation. All I have to do is to show that farmer, that day laborer, that tramp, that they are victims of this system, that their interests are identical, that they constitute the millions and that the millions have the votes. The Rockefellers have the dollars, but we have the votes; and when we have sense enough to know how to use the votes we will have not only the votes but the dollars for all the children of men.

This seems quite visionary to some of you, and especially to those of you who know nothing about economics. I could not begin to tell you the story of social evolution this afternoon, of how these things are doing day by day, of how the world is being pushed into Socialism, and how it is bound to arrive, no matter whether you are for it or against it. It is the next inevitable phase of civilization. It isn't a scheme, it isn't a contrivance. It isn't anything that is made to order. The day is coming when you will be pushed into it by unseen hands whether you will or not. Nothing can be introduced until the people want it, and when the majority want it they will know how to get it.

I venture the prophecy that within the next five years you will be completely dispossessed. You are howling against the trusts, and the trusts are laughing at you. You keep on voting in the same old way and the trusts keep on getting what you produce. You say congress will give you some relief. Good heavens! Who will save us from congress? Don't you know that congress is made up almost wholly of trust lawyers and corporation attorneys? I don't happen to have the roll of this one, but with few exceptions they are all lawyers. Now, in the competitive system the lawyer sells himself to the highest bidder the same as the workingman does. Who is the highest bidder? The trust and corporation, of course. So the trust buys the best lawyer and the common herd gets the shyster.

Now it is a fact that politics is simply the reflex of economics. The material foundation of society determines the character of all social institutions—political, educational, ethical and spiritual. In exact proportion as the economic foundation of society changes the character of all social institutions changes to correspond to that basis. Half of this country was in favor of chattel slavery, and half was opposed to it, geographically speaking. Why was the church of the south in favor of chattel slavery? Why was the church of the north opposed to chattel slavery? The northern capitalist wasn't a bit more opposed to chattel slavery from any moral sense than was the southern plantation owner. The south produced cotton for the market by the hand labor of negro slaves. On the other hand, the north wasn't dependent upon cotton—could raise no cotton. In the north it was the small capitalist at the beginning of capitalism, who, with the machine, had begun to manufacture, and wanted cheap labor; and the sharper the competition the cheaper he could buy his labor. Now, chattel slavery to the southern plantation owner was the source of his wealth. He had to have slaves, and what the planta- tion owner had to have in economics the preacher had to justify in religion. As long as chattel slavery was necessary to the southern plantation owner, as long as that stage of the economic condition lasted, the preachers stood up in the pulpits of the south and said it was ordained of God, and proved it by the Bible. I don't know of any crime that the oppressors and their hirelings have not proven by the Bible.

Then competition between workers began as machines took the place of hand labor. Manufacturers wanted larger and larger bodies of labor and that competition spread out here to Kansas, and I have always felt when in Kansas that I stood on sacred soil. When I hear the name of Kansas I doff my hat in reverence. The free soilers came here, despised, hated and persecuted. They were the enemies of the human race. Why? Because they had hearts throbbing within their breasts. Because they looked with compassion upon the negro slave who received his wages in lashes applied to his naked back; who saw his crying wife torn from him and his children, pleading, snatched from his side and sold into slavery, while the great mass looked on just as the great mass is looking on today, and the preachers stood up in their pulpits and said: "It is all right. It is God-ordained." And whenever an abolitionist raised his head he was persecuted and hounded as if he had been a wild beast.

I heard this story from Wendell Phillips one evening. I never can forget it. How I wish he were here this afternoon! We sat together and he said: "Debs, the world will never know with what bitter and relentless persecution the early abolitionists had to contend."

Wendell Phillips was the most perfect aristocrat in the true sense I have ever seen; came nearest being a perfect man. And yet he was treated as if he had been the worst felon on earth. They went to his house one night to mob him, and why? Because he protested against sending a young negro girl back into slavery. They came to take her back, and the whole Commonwealth of Massachusetts said, "Take her back! Obey the law!" That is what they are everlastingly saying to us—"Obey the law!" Just above the door of the state house there was an inscription: "God bless the Commonwealth of Massachusetts." Wendell Phillips said: "If Massachusetts has become a slave hunter, if Massachusetts is in alliance with the slave catchers of the south, the inscription over that portal should be changed, and in place of 'God Bless the Commonwealth of Massachusetts' it should be: 'God Damn the Commonwealth of Massachusetts!' " God smiled in that same instant.

All of the slave catchers and holders, all of the oppressors of man, all of the enemies of the human race, all of the rulers of Siberia, where a large part of this earth's surface has been transformed into a hell—all have spoken in the name of the Great God and in the name of the Holy Bible.

There will be a change one of these days. The world is just beginning to awaken, and is soon to sing its first anthem of freedom. All the signs of the times are cheering. Twenty-five years ago there was but a handful of Socialists; today there are a half million. When the polls are closed next fall you will be astounded. The Socialist movement is in alliance with the forces of progress.

We are today where the abolitionists were in 1858. They had a million and a quarter of votes. There was dissension in the whig, republican and free soil parties, but the time had come for a great change, and the republican party was formed in spite of the bickerings and contentions of men. Lincoln made the great speech in that year that gave him the nomination and afterward made him president of the United States.

If you had said to the people in 1858, "In two years from now the republican party is going to sweep the country and seat the president," you would have been laughed to scorn. The Socialist party stands today where the republican party stood fifty years ago. It is in alliance with the forces of evolution, the one party that has a clear-cut, overmastering, overshadowing issue; the party that stands for the people, and the only party that stands for all the people. In this system we have one set who are called capitalists, and another set who are called workers; and they are at war with each other.

Now, we Socialists propose that society in its collective capacity shall produce, not for profit, but in abundance to satisfy human wants; that every man shall have the inalienable right to work and receive the full equivalent of all he produces; that every man may stand fearlessly erect in the pride and majesty of his own manhood.

Every man and every woman will then be economically free. They can, without let or hindrance, apply their labor, with the best machinery that can be devised, to all the natural resources, do the work of society and produce for all; and then receive in exchange a certificate of value equivalent to that of their production. Then society will improve its institutions in proportion to the progress of invention. Whether in the city or on the farm, all things productive will be carried forward on a gigantic scale. All industry will be completely organized. Society for the first time will have a scientific foundation. Every man, by being economically free, will have some time for himself. He can then take a full and perfect breath. He can enjoy life with his wife and children, because then he will have a home.

We are not going to destroy private property. We are going to establish private property—all the private property necessary to house man, keep him in comfort and satisfy his wants. Eighty per cent of the people in the United States have no property today. A few have got it all. They have dispossessed the people, and when we get into power we will dispossess them. We will reduce the workday and give every man a chance. We will go to the parks, and we will have music, because we will have time to play music and desire to hear it.

Is it not sad to think that not one in a thousand knows what music is? Is it not pitiable to see the poor, ignorant, dumb human utterly impervious to the divine influences of music? If humanity could only respond to the higher influences! And it would if it had time.

Release the animal, throw off his burden; give him a chance and he rises as if by magic to the plane of a man. Man has all of the divine attributes. They are in a latent state. They are not yet developed. It does not pay now to love music. Keep your eye on the almighty dollar and your fellow man. Get the dollar and keep him down. Make him produce for you. You are not your brother's keeper. Suppose he is poor! Suppose his wife is forced into prostitution! Suppose his child is deformed! And suppose he shuffles off by destroying himself! What is that to you?

But you ought to be ashamed. Take the standard home and look it in the face. If you know what that standard means, and you are a success, God help the failure!

Our conduct is determined by our economic relations. If you and I must fight each other to exist, we will not love each other very hard. We can go to the same church and hear the same minister tell us in good conscience that we ought to love each other, and the next day we approach some business transaction. Do we remember what the minister told us? No; it is gone until next Sunday. Six days in the week we are following the Golden Rule reversed. Now, when we approach a business transaction in competition, what is more natural than that we should try to get the better of it?—get the better of our fellow man?—cheat him if we can?

And if you succeed that fixes you as a business man. You have all the necessary qualifications. Don't let your conscience disturb you—that would interfere with business.

Competition was natural enough at one time, but do you think you are competing today? Many of you think you are competing. Against whom? Against Rockefeller? About as I would if I had a wheelbarrow and competed with the Sante Fe from here to Kansas City. That is about the way you are competing; but your boys will not have even that chance—if capitalism lives that long. You hear of the "late" panic. It is very late. It is going to be very late. This panic will be with us five years from now, and will continue till then.

I am not a prophet. I can no more penetrate the future than you can. I do study the forces that underlie society and the trend of evolution. I can tell by what we have passed through about what we will have in the future; and I know that capitalism can be abolished and the people put in possession. Now, when we have taken possession, and we jointly own the means of production, we will no longer have to fight each other to live; our interests, instead of being competitive, will be cooperative. We will work side by side. Your interest will be mine and mine will be yours. That is the economic condition from which will spring the humane social relation of the future.

When we are in partnership and have stopped clutching each other's throats, when we have stopped enslaving each other, we will stand together, hands clasped, and be friends. We will be comrades, we will be brothers, and we will begin the march to the grandest civilization the human race has ever known.

I did not mean to keep you so long this afternoon. I am sure I appreciate the patience with which you have listened to me. From the very depths of my heart I thank you, each of you—every man, woman and child—for this splendid testimonial, this beautiful tribute, which I shall remember with gratitude and love until memory empties its urn into forgetfulness.

The New Nationalism

THEODORE ROOSEVELT

*Born, New York City, October 27, 1858; died, Oyster Bay,
New York, January 6, 1919. Graduated from Harvard,
1880. Member of New York State Assembly, 1882–1884.
United States Civil Service Commissioner, 1889–1895. President of the Board of Police Commissioners of New York,
1895–1897. Assistant Secretary of the Navy, 1897–1898. Lieutenant Colonel of Rough Riders during Spanish-American
War, 1898. Republican Governor of New York, 1898–1900.
Elected Vice-President of the United States, 1900, succeeding to the Presidency upon the death of McKinley, 1901.
Re-elected President, 1904. After brief retirement, he re-
entered politics and sought Republican nomination for President in 1912; losing out to William Howard Taft, he
became nominee and unsuccessful candidate of the Progressive or Bull Moose party. Prominent as lecturer, historian,
essayist, cowboy, hunter, and explorer.*

"The citizens of the United States must effectively control
the mighty commercial forces which they have themselves
called into being."

W*e come here to-day* to commemorate one of the
epoch-making events of the long struggle for the
rights of man—the long struggle for the uplift of humanity. Our country—this
great Republic—means nothing unless it means the triumph of a real democracy,

Dedication of the John Brown Memorial Park, Osawatomie, Kansas, August 31, 1910.
Hermann Hagedorn, ed., *The Works of Theodore Roosevelt, Memorial Edition* (New York:
Charles Scribner's Sons, 1923–1925, 24 vols.), XIX, pp. 10–30.

the triumph of popular government, and, in the long run, of an economic system
under which each man shall be guaranteed the opportunity to show the best that
there is in him. That is why the history of America is now the central feature
of the history of the world; for the world has set its face hopefully toward our
democracy; and, O my fellow citizens, each one of you carries on your shoulders
not only the burden of doing well for the sake of your own country, but the
burden of doing well and of seeing that this nation does well for the sake of
mankind.

There have been two great crises in our country's history: first, when it was
formed, and then, again, when it was perpetuated; and, in the second of these
great crises—in the time of stress and strain which culminated in the Civil
War, on the outcome of which depended the justification of what had been done
earlier—you men of the Grand Army, you men who fought through the Civil
War, not only did you justify your generation, not only did you render life
worth living for our generation, but you justified the wisdom of Washington
and Washington's colleagues. If this Republic had been founded by them only
to be split asunder into fragments when the strain came, then the judgment of
the world would have been that Washington's work was not worth doing. It
was you who crowned Washington's work, as you carried to achievement the
high purpose of Abraham Lincoln.

Now, with this second period of our history the name of John Brown will
be forever associated; and Kansas was the theatre upon which the first act of
the second of our great national life dramas was played. It was the result of the
struggle in Kansas which determined that our country should be in deed as well
as in name devoted to both union and freedom; that the great experiment of
democratic government on a national scale should succeed and not fail. In name
we had the Declaration of Independence in 1776; but we gave the lie by our
acts to the words of the Declaration of Independence until 1865; and words
count for nothing except in so far as they represent acts. This is true everywhere;
but, O my friends, it should be truest of all in political life. A broken promise
is bad enough in private life. It is worse in the field of politics. No man is worth
his salt in public life who makes on the stump a pledge which he does not keep
after election; and, if he makes such a pledge and does not keep it, hunt him out
of public life. I care for the great deeds of the past chiefly as spurs to drive us
onward in the present. I speak of the men of the past partly that they may be
honored by our praise of them, but more that they may serve as examples for
the future.

It was a heroic struggle; and, as is inevitable with all such struggles, it had
also a dark and terrible side. Very much was done of good, and much also of
evil; and, as was inevitable in such a period of revolution, often the same man
did both good and evil. For our great good fortune as a nation, we, the people
of the United States as a whole, can now afford to forget the evil, or, at least,
to remember it without bitterness, and to fix our eyes with pride only on the

good that was accomplished. Even in ordinary times there are very few of us who do not see the problems of life as through a glass, darkly; and when the glass is clouded by the murk of furious popular passion, the vision of the best and the bravest is dimmed. Looking back, we are all of us now able to do justice to the valor and the disinterestedness and the love of the right, as to each it was given to see the right, shown both by the men of the North and the men of the South in that contest which was finally decided by the attitude of the West. We can admire the heroic valor, the sincerity, the self-devotion shown alike by the men who wore the blue and the men who wore the gray; and our sadness that such men should have had to fight one another is tempered by the glad knowledge that ever hereafter their descendants shall be found fighting side by side, struggling in peace as well as in war for the uplift of their common country, all alike resolute to raise to the highest pitch of honor and usefulness the nation to which they all belong. As for the veterans of the Grand Army of the Republic, they deserve honor and recognition such as is paid to no other citizens of the Republic; for to them the Republic owes its all; for to them it owes its very existence. It is because of what you and your comrades did in the dark years that we of to-day walk, each of us, head erect, and proud that we belong, not to one of a dozen little squabbling contemptible commonwealths, but to the mightiest nation upon which the sun shines.

I do not speak of this struggle of the past merely from the historic standpoint. Our interest is primarily in the application to-day of the lessons taught by the contest of half a century ago. It is of little use for us to pay lip-loyalty to the mighty men of the past unless we sincerely endeavor to apply to the problems of the present precisely the qualities which in other crises enabled the men of that day to meet those crises. It is half melancholy and half amusing to see the way in which well-meaning people gather to do honor to the men who, in company with John Brown, and under the lead of Abraham Lincoln, faced and solved the great problems of the nineteenth century, while, at the same time, these same good people nervously shrink from, or frantically denounce, those who are trying to meet the problems of the twentieth century in the spirit which was accountable for the successful solution of the problems of Lincoln's time.

Of that generation of men to whom we owe so much, the man to whom we owe most is, of course, Lincoln. Part of our debt to him is because he forecast our present struggle and saw the way out. He said:

"I hold that while man exists it is his duty to improve not only his own condition, but to assist in ameliorating mankind."

And again:

"Labor is prior to, and independent of, capital. Capital is only the fruit of labor, and could never have existed if labor had not first existed. Labor is the superior of capital, and deserves much the higher consideration."

If that remark was original with me, I should be even more strongly denounced as a Communist agitator than I shall be anyhow. It is Lincoln's. I am only quoting it; and that is one side; that is the side the capitalist should hear. Now, let the working man hear his side.

"Capital has its rights, which are as worthy of protection as any other rights. . . . Nor should this lead to a war upon the owners of property. Property is the fruit of labor; . . . property is desirable; is a positive good in the world."

And then comes a thoroughly Lincolnlike sentence:

"Let not him who is houseless pull down the house of another, but let him work diligently and build one for himself, thus by example assuring that his own shall be safe from violence when built."

It seems to me that, in these words, Lincoln took substantially the attitude that we ought to take; he showed the proper sense of proportion in his relative estimates of capital and labor, of human rights and property rights. Above all, in this speech, as in many others, he taught a lesson in wise kindliness and charity; an indispensable lesson to us of to-day. But this wise kindliness and charity never weakened his arm or numbed his heart. We cannot afford weakly to blind ourselves to the actual conflict which faces us to-day. The issue is joined, and we must fight or fail.

In every wise struggle for human betterment one of the main objects, and often the only object, has been to achieve in large measure equality of opportunity. In the struggle for this great end, nations rise from barbarism to civilization, and through it people press forward from one stage of enlightenment to the next. One of the chief factors in progress is the destruction of special privilege. The essence of any struggle for healthy liberty has always been, and must always be, to take from some one man or class of men the right to enjoy power, or wealth, or position, or immunity, which has not been earned by service to his or their fellows. That is what you fought for in the Civil War, and that is what we strive for now.

At many stages in the advance of humanity, this conflict between the men who possess more than they have earned and the men who have earned more than they possess is the central condition of progress. In our day it appears as the struggle of freemen to gain and hold the right of self-government as against the special interests, who twist the methods of free government into machinery for defeating the popular will. At every stage, and under all circumstances, the essence of the struggle is to equalize opportunity, destroy privilege, and give to the life and citizenship of every individual the highest possible value both to himself and to the commonwealth. That is nothing new. All I ask in civil life is what you fought for in the Civil War. I ask that civil life be carried on according to the spirit in which the army was carried on. You never get perfect justice, but the effort in handling the army was to bring to the front the men who could do the job. Nobody grudged promotion to Grant, or Sherman, or Thomas, or Sheridan, because they earned it. The only complaint was when a man got promotion which he did not earn.

Practical equality of opportunity for all citizens, when we achieve it, will have two great results. First, every man will have a fair chance to make of himself all that in him lies; to reach the highest point to which his capacities, unassisted by special privilege of his own and unhampered by the special privilege of others, can carry him, and to get for himself and his family substantially what he has earned. Second, equality of opportunity means that the commonwealth will get from every citizen the highest service of which he is capable. No man who carries the burden of the special privileges of another can give to the commonwealth that service to which it is fairly entitled.

I stand for the square deal. But when I say that I am for the square deal, I mean not merely that I stand for fair play under the present rules of the game, but that I stand for having those rules changed so as to work for a more substantial equality of opportunity and of reward for equally good service. One word of warning, which, I think, is hardly necessary in Kansas. When I say I want a square deal for the poor man, I do not mean that I want a square deal for the man who remains poor because he has not got the energy to work for himself. If a man who has had a chance will not make good, then he has got to quit. And you men of the Grand Army, you want justice for the brave man who fought, and punishment for the coward who shirked his work. Is not that so?

Now, this means that our government, National and State, must be freed from the sinister influence or control of special interests. Exactly as the special interests of cotton and slavery threatened our political integrity before the Civil War, so now the great special business interests too often control and corrupt the men and methods of government for their own profit. We must drive the special interests out of politics. That is one of our tasks to-day. Every special interest is entitled to justice—full, fair, and complete—and, now, mind you, if there were any attempt by mob-violence to plunder and work harm to the special interest, whatever it may be, that I most dislike, and the wealthy man, whomsoever he may be, for whom I have the greatest contempt, I would fight for him, and you would if you were worth your salt. He should have justice. For every special interest is entitled to justice, but not one is entitled to a vote in Congress, to a voice on the bench, or to representation in any public office. The Constitution guarantees protection to property, and we must make that promise good. But it does not give the right of suffrage to any corporation.

The true friend of property, the true conservative, is he who insists that property shall be the servant and not the master of the commonwealth; who insists that the creature of man's making shall be the servant and not the master of the man who made it. The citizens of the United States must effectively control the mighty commercial forces which they have themselves called into being.

There can be no effective control of corporations while their political activity remains. To put an end to it will be neither a short nor an easy task, but it can be done.

We must have complete and effective publicity of corporate affairs, so that the people may know beyond peradventure whether the corporations obey the law and whether their management entitles them to the confidence of the public. It is necessary that laws should be passed to prohibit the use of corporate funds directly or indirectly for political purposes; it is still more necessary that such laws should be thoroughly enforced. Corporate expenditures for political purposes, and especially such expenditures by public-service corporations, have supplied one of the principal sources of corruption in our political affairs.

It has become entirely clear that we must have government supervision of the capitalization, not only of public-service corporations, including, particularly, railways, but of all corporations doing an interstate business. I do not wish to see the nation forced into the ownership of the railways if it can possibly be avoided, and the only alternative is thoroughgoing and effective regulation, which shall be based on a full knowledge of all the facts, including a physical valuation of property. This physical valuation is not needed, or, at least, is very rarely needed, for fixing rates; but it is needed as the basis of honest capitalization.

We have come to recognize that franchises should never be granted except for a limited time, and never without proper provision for compensation to the public. It is my personal belief that the same kind and degree of control and supervision which should be exercised over public-service corporations should be extended also to combinations which control necessaries of life, such as meat, oil, and coal, or which deal in them on an important scale. I have no doubt that the ordinary man who has control of them is much like ourselves. I have no doubt he would like to do well, but I want to have enough supervision to help him realize that desire to do well.

I believe that the officers, and, especially, the directors, of corporations should be held personally responsible when any corporation breaks the law.

Combinations in industry are the result of an imperative economic law which cannot be repealed by political legislation. The effort at prohibiting all combination has substantially failed. The way out lies, not in attempting to prevent such combinations, but in completely controlling them in the interest of the public welfare. For that purpose the Federal Bureau of Corporations is an agency of first importance. Its powers, and, therefore, its efficiency, as well as that of the Interstate Commerce Commission, should be largely increased. We have a right to expect from the Bureau of Corporations and from the Interstate Commerce Commission a very high grade of public service. We should be as sure of the proper conduct of the interstate railways and the proper management of interstate business as we are now sure of the conduct and management of the national banks, and we should have as effective supervision in one case as in the other. The Hepburn Act, and the amendment to the act in the shape in which it finally passed Congress at the last session, represent a long step in advance, and we must go yet further.

There is a wide-spread belief among our people that, under the methods of making tariffs which have hitherto obtained, the special interests are too influential. Probably this is true of both the big special interests and the little special interests. These methods have put a premium on selfishness, and, naturally, the selfish big interests have gotten more than their smaller, though equally selfish, brothers. The duty of Congress is to provide a method by which the interest of the whole people shall be all that receives consideration. To this end there must be an expert tariff commission, wholly removed from the possibility of political pressure or of improper business influence. Such a commission can find the real difference between cost of production, which is mainly the difference of labor cost here and abroad. As fast as its recommendations are made, I believe in revising one schedule at a time. A general revision of the tariff almost inevitably leads to logrolling and the subordination of the general public interest to local and special interests.

The absence of effective State, and, especially, national, restraint upon unfair money-getting has tended to create a small class of enormously wealthy and economically powerful men, whose chief object is to hold and increase their power. The prime need is to change the conditions which enable these men to accumulate power which it is not for the general welfare that they should hold or exercise. We grudge no man a fortune which represents his own power and sagacity, when exercised with entire regard to the welfare of his fellows. Again, comrades over there, take the lesson from your own experience. Not only did you not grudge, but you gloried in the promotion of the great generals who gained their promotion by leading the army to victory. So it is with us. We grudge no man a fortune in civil life if it is honorably obtained and well used. It is not even enough that it should have been gained without doing damage to the community. We should permit it to be gained only so long as the gaining represents benefit to the community. This, I know, implies a policy of a far more active governmental interference with social and economic conditions in this country than we have yet had, but I think we have got to face the fact that such an increase in governmental control is now necessary.

No man should receive a dollar unless that dollar has been fairly earned. Every dollar received should represent a dollar's worth of service rendered—not gambling in stocks, but service rendered. The really big fortune, the swollen fortune, by the mere fact of its size acquires qualities which differentiate it in kind as well as in degree from what is possessed by men of relatively small means. Therefore, I believe in a graduated income tax on big fortunes, and in another tax which is far more easily collected and far more effective—a graduated inheritance tax on big fortunes, properly safeguarded against evasion and increasing rapidly in amount with the size of the estate.

The people of the United States suffer from periodical financial panics to a degree substantially unknown among the other nations which approach us in financial strength. There is no reason why we should suffer what they escape. It is of profound importance that our financial system should be promptly investigated, and so thoroughly and effectively revised as to make it certain that hereafter our currency will no longer fail at critical times to meet our needs.

It is hardly necessary for me to repeat that I believe in an efficient army and a navy large enough to secure for us abroad that respect which is the surest guaranty of peace. A word of special warning to my fellow citizens who are as progressive as I hope I am. I want them to keep up their interest in our internal affairs; and I want them also continually to remember Uncle Sam's interests abroad. Justice and fair dealing among nations rest upon principles identical with those which control justice and fair dealing among the individuals of which nations are composed, with the vital exception that each nation must do its own part in international police work. If you get into trouble here, you can call for the police; but if Uncle Sam gets into trouble, he has got to be his own policeman, and I want to see him strong enough to encourage the peaceful aspirations of other peoples in connection with us. I believe in national friendships and heartiest good-will to all nations; but national friendships, like those between men, must be founded on respect as well as on liking, on forbearance as well as upon trust. I should be heartily ashamed of any American who did not try to make the American Government act as justly toward the other nations in international relations as he himself would act toward any individual in private relations. I should be heartily ashamed to see us wrong a weaker power, and I should hang my head forever if we tamely suffered wrong from a stronger power.

Of conservation I shall speak more at length elsewhere. Conservation means development as much as it does protection. I recognize the right and duty of this generation to develop and use the natural resources of our land; but I do not recognize the right to waste them, or to rob, by wasteful use, the generations that come after us. I ask nothing of the nation except that it so behave as each farmer here behaves with reference to his own children. That farmer is a poor creature who skins the land and leaves it worthless to his children. The farmer is a good farmer who, having enabled the land to support himself and to provide for the education of his children, leaves it to them a little better than he found it himself. I believe the same thing of a nation.

Moreover, I believe that the natural resources must be used for the benefit of all our people, and not monopolized for the benefit of the few, and here again is another case in which I am accused of taking a revolutionary attitude. People forget now that one hundred years ago there were public men of good character who advocated the nation selling its public lands in great quantities, so that the nation could get the most money out of it, and giving it to the men who could cultivate it for their own uses. We took the proper democratic ground that the land should be granted in small sections to the men who were actually to till it and live on it. Now, with the water-power, with the forests, with the mines, we are brought face to face with the fact that there are many people who will go with us in conserving the resources only if they are to be allowed to exploit them for their benefit. That is one of the fundamental reasons why the special interests should be driven out of politics. Of all the questions which can come before this nation, short of the actual preservation of its existence in a great war, there is none which compares in importance with the great central task of leaving this land even a better land for our descendants than it is for us, and training them into a better race to inhabit the land and pass it on. Conservation is a great moral issue, for it involves the patriotic duty of insuring the safety and continuance of the nation. Let me add that the health and vitality of our people are at least as well worth conserving as their forests, waters, lands, and minerals, and in this great work the national government must bear a most important part.

I have spoken elsewhere also of the great task which lies before the farmers of the country to get for themselves and their wives and children not only the benefits of better farming, but also those of better business methods and better conditions of life on the farm. The burden of this great task will fall, as it should, mainly upon the great organizations of the farmers themselves. I am glad it will, for I believe they are all well able to handle it. In particular, there are strong reasons why the Departments of Agriculture of the various States, the United States Department of Agriculture, and the agricultural colleges and experiment stations should extend their work to cover all phases of farm life, instead of limiting themselves, as they have far too often limited themselves in the past, solely to the question of the production of crops. And now a special word to the farmer. I want to see him make the farm as fine a farm as it can be made; and let him remember to see that the improvement goes on indoors as well as out; let him remember that the farmer's wife should have her share of thought and attention just as much as the farmer himself.

Nothing is more true than that excess of every kind is followed by reaction; a fact which should be pondered by reformer and reactionary alike. We are face to face with new conceptions of the relations of property to human welfare, chiefly because certain advocates of the rights of property as against the rights of men have been pushing their claims too far. The man who wrongly holds that every human right is secondary to his profit must now give way to the advocate of human welfare, who rightly maintains that every man holds his property subject to the general right of the community to regulate its use to whatever degree the public welfare may require it.

But I think we may go still further. The right to regulate the use of wealth in the public interest is universally admitted. Let us admit also the right to regulate the terms and conditions of labor, which is the chief element of wealth, directly in the interest of the common good. The fundamental thing to do for every man is to give him a chance to reach a place in which he will make the greatest possible contribution to the public welfare. Understand what I say there. Give him a chance, not push him up if he will not be pushed. Help any man who stumbles; if he lies down, it is a poor job to try to carry him; but if he is a worthy man, try your best to see that he gets a chance to show the worth that is in him. No man can be a good citizen unless he has a wage more than sufficient to cover the bare cost of living, and hours of labor short enough so that after his day's work is done he will have time and energy to bear his share in the management of the community, to help in carrying the general load. We keep countless men from being good citizens by the conditions of life with which we surround them. We need comprehensive workmen's compensation acts, both State and national laws to regulate child labor and work for women, and, especially, we need in our common schools not merely education in book-learning, but also practical training for daily life and work. We need to enforce better sanitary conditions for our workers and to extend the use of safety appliances for our workers in industry and commerce, both within and between the States. Also, friends, in the interest of the working man himself we need to set our faces like flint against mob-violence just as against corporate greed; against violence and injustice and lawlessness by wage-workers just as much as against lawless cunning and greed and selfish arrogance of employers. If I could ask but one thing of my fellow countrymen, my request would be that, whenever they go in for reform, they remember the two sides, and that they always exact justice from one side as much as from the other. I have small use for the public servant who can always see and denounce the corruption of the capitalist, but who cannot persuade himself, especially before election, to say a word about lawless mob-violence. And I have equally small use for the man, be he a judge on the bench, or editor of a great paper, or wealthy and influential private citizen, who can see clearly enough and denounce the lawlessness of mob-violence, but whose eyes are closed so that he is blind when the question is one of corruption in business on a gigantic scale. Also remember what I said about excess in reformer and reactionary alike. If the reactionary man, who thinks of nothing but the rights of property, could have his way, he would bring about a revolution; and one of my chief fears in connection with progress comes because I do not want to see our people, for lack of proper leadership, compelled to follow men whose intentions are excellent, but whose eyes are a little too wild to make it really safe to trust them. Here in Kansas there is one paper which habitually denounces me as the tool of Wall Street, and at the same time frantically repudiates the statement that I am a Socialist on the ground that that is an unwarranted slander of the Socialists.

National efficiency has many factors. It is a necessary result of the principle of conservation widely applied. In the end it will determine our failure or success as a nation. National efficiency has to do, not only with natural resources and with men, but it is equally concerned with institutions. The State must be made efficient for the work which concerns only the people of the State; and the nation for that which concerns all the people. There must remain no neutral ground to serve as a refuge for lawbreakers, and especially for lawbreakers of great wealth, who can hire the vulpine legal cunning which will teach them how to avoid both jurisdictions. It is a misfortune when the national legislature fails to do its duty in providing a national remedy, so that the only national activity is the purely negative activity of the judiciary in forbidding the State to exercise power in the premises.

I do not ask for overcentralization; but I do ask that we work in a spirit of broad and far-reaching nationalism when we work for what concerns our people as a whole. We are all Americans. Our common interests are as broad as the continent. I speak to you here in Kansas exactly as I would speak in New York or Georgia, for the most vital problems are those which affect us all alike. The National Government belongs to the whole American people, and where the whole American people are interested, that interest can be guarded effectively only by the National Government. The betterment which we seek must be accomplished, I believe, mainly through the National Government.

The American people are right in demanding that New Nationalism, without which we cannot hope to deal with new problems. The New Nationalism puts the national need before sectional or personal advantage. It is impatient of the utter confusion that results from local legislatures attempting to treat national issues as local issues. It is still more impatient of the impotence which springs from overdivision of governmental powers, the impotence which makes it possible for local selfishness or for legal cunning, hired by wealthy special interests, to bring national activities to a deadlock. This New Nationalism regards the executive power as the steward of the public welfare. It demands of the judiciary that it shall be interested primarily in human welfare rather than in property, just as it demands that the representative body shall represent all the people rather than any one class or section of the people.

I believe in shaping the ends of government to protect property as well as human welfare. Normally, and in the long run, the ends are the same; but whenever the alternative must be faced, I am for men and not for property, as you were in the Civil War. I am far from underestimating the importance of dividends; but I rank dividends below human character. Again, I do not have any sympathy with the reformer who says he does not care for dividends. Of course, economic welfare is necessary, for a man must pull his own weight and be able to support his family. I know well that the reformers must not bring upon the people economic ruin, or the reforms themselves will go down in the ruin. But we must be ready to face temporary disaster, whether or not brought on by those who will war against us to the knife. Those who oppose all reform will do well to remember that ruin in its worst form is inevitable if our national life brings us nothing better than swollen fortunes for the few and the triumph in both politics and business of a sordid and selfish materialism.

If our political institutions were perfect, they would absolutely prevent the political domination of money in any part of our affairs. We need to make our political representatives more quickly and sensitively responsive to the people whose servants they are. More direct action by the people in their own affairs under proper safeguards is vitally necessary. The direct primary is a step in this direction, if it is associated with a corrupt-practices act effective to prevent the advantage of the man willing recklessly and unscrupulously to spend money over his more honest competitor. It is particularly important that all moneys received or expended for campaign purposes should be publicly accounted for, not only after election, but before election as well. Political action must be made simpler, easier, and freer from confusion for every citizen. I believe that the prompt removal of unfaithful or incompetent public servants should be made easy and sure in whatever way experience shall show to be most expedient in any given class of cases.

One of the fundamental necessities in a representative government such as ours is to make certain that the men to whom the people delegate their power shall serve the people by whom they are elected, and not the special interests. I believe that every national officer, elected or appointed, should be forbidden to perform any service or receive any compensation, directly or indirectly, from interstate corporations; and a similar provision could not fail to be useful within the States.

The object of government is the welfare of the people. The material progress and prosperity of a nation are desirable chiefly so far as they lead to the moral and material welfare of all good citizens. Just in proportion as the average man and woman are honest, capable of sound judgment and high ideals, active in public affairs—but, first of all, sound in their home life, and the father and mother of healthy children whom they bring up well—just so far, and no farther, we may count our civilization a success. We must have—I believe we have already—a genuine and permanent moral awakening, without which no wisdom of legislation or administration really means anything; and, on the other hand, we must try to secure the social and economic legislation without which any improvement due to purely moral agitation is necessarily evanescent. Let me again illustrate by a reference to the Grand Army. You could not have won simply as a disorderly and disorganized mob. You needed generals; you needed careful administration of the most advanced type; and a good commissary—the cracker line. You well remember that success was necessary in many different lines in order to bring about general success. You had to have the administration at Washington good, just as you had to have the administration in the field; and you had to have the work of the generals good. You could not have triumphed without that administration and leadership; but it would all have been worthless if the average soldier had not had the right stuff in him. He had to have the right stuff in him, or you could not get it out of him. In the last analysis, there-fore, vitally necessary though it was to have the right kind of organization and the right kind of generalship, it was even more vitally necessary that the average soldier should have the fighting edge, the right character. So it is in our civil life. No matter how honest and decent we are in our private lives, if we do not have the right kind of law and the right kind of administration of the law, we cannot go forward as a nation. That is imperative; but it must be an addition to, and not a substitution for, the qualities that make us good citizens. In the last analysis, the most important elements in any man's career must be the sum of those qualities which, in the aggregate, we speak of as character. If he has not got it, then no law that the wit of man can devise, no administration of the law by the boldest and strongest executive, will avail to help him. We must have the right kind of character—character that makes a man, first of all, a good man in the home, a good father, a good husband—that makes a man a good neighbor. You must have that, and, then, in addition, you must have the kind of law and the kind of administration of the law which will give to those qualities in the private citizen the best possible chance for development. The prime problem of our nation is to get the right type of good citizenship, and, to get it, we must have progress, and our public men must be genuinely progressive.

First Inaugural Address

WOODROW WILSON

Born, Staunton, Virginia, December 28, 1856; died, Washington, D.C., February 3, 1924. Graduated from Princeton, 1879; studied law at the University of Virginia, 1880. Admitted to the Georgia bar, 1882, and practiced law for one year. Received Ph.D. from Johns Hopkins, 1886. Taught history at Bryn Mawr, 1885–1888, and at Wesleyan, 1888–1890. Professor of jurisprudence and political economics at Princeton, 1890–1902. President of Princeton, 1902–1910. Governor of New Jersey, 1911–1912. As Democratic nominee, he was elected President of the United States in 1912 and 1916. Eloquent spokesman for reform, progressive principles, and the League of Nations.

"We have made up our minds to square every process of our national life again with the standards we so proudly set up at the beginning and have always carried at our hearts."

There has been a change of government. It began two years ago, when the House of Representatives became Democratic by a decisive majority. It has now been completed. The Senate about to assemble will also be Democratic. The offices of President and Vice-President have been put into the hands of Democrats. What does the change mean? That is the question that is uppermost in our minds today. That is the question I am going to try to answer, in order, if I may, to interpret the occasion.

Washington, D.C., March 4, 1913. *Inaugural Addresses of the Presidents of the United States,* House Document No. 540 (Washington: Government Printing Office, 1952), pp. 189–192.

It means much more than the mere success of a party. The success of a party means little except when the Nation is using that party for a large and definite purpose. No one can mistake the purpose for which the Nation now seeks to use the Democratic Party. It seeks to use it to interpret a change in its own plans and point of view. Some old things with which we had grown familiar, and which had begun to creep into the very habit of our thought and of our lives, have altered their aspect as we have latterly looked critically upon them, with fresh awakened eyes, have dropped their disguises and shown themselves alien and sinister. Some new things, as we look frankly upon them, willing to comprehend their real character, have come to assume the aspect of things long believed in and familiar, stuff of our own convictions. We have been refreshed by a new insight into our own life.

We see that in many things that life is very great. It is incomparably great in its material aspects, in its body of wealth, in the diversity and sweep of its energy, in the industries which have been conceived and built up by the genius of individual men and the limitless enterprise of groups of men. It is great, also, very great, in its moral force. Nowhere else in the world have men and women exhibited in more striking forms the beauty and the energy of sympathy and helpfulness and counsel in their efforts to rectify wrong, alleviate suffering, and set the weak in the way of strength and hope. We have built up, moreover, a great system of government, which has stood through a long age as in many respects a model for those who seek to set liberty upon foundations that will endure against fortuitous change, against storm and accident. Our life contains every great thing, and contains it in rich abundance.

But the evil has come with the good, and much fine gold has been corroded. With riches has come inexcusable waste. We have squandered a great part of what we might have used, and have not stopped to conserve the exceeding bounty of nature, without which our genius for enterprise would have been worthless and impotent, scorning to be careful, shamefully prodigal as well as admirably efficient. We have been proud of our industrial achievements, but we have not hitherto stopped thoughtfully enough to count the human cost, the cost of lives snuffed out, of energies overtaxed and broken, the fearful physical and spiritual cost to the men and women and children upon whom the dead weight and burden of it all has fallen pitilessly the years through. The groans and agony of it all had not yet reached our ears, the solemn, moving undertone of our life, coming up out of the mines and factories and out of every home where the struggle had its intimate and familiar seat. With the great Government went many deep secret things which we too long delayed to look into and scrutinize with candid, fearless eyes. The great Government we loved has too often been made use of for private and selfish purposes, and those who used it had forgotten the people.

At last a vision has been vouchsafed us of our life as a whole. We see the bad with the good, the debased and decadent with the sound and vital. With this vision we approach new affairs. Our duty is to cleanse, to reconsider, to restore, to correct the evil without impairing the good, to purify and humanize every process of our common life without weakening or sentimentalizing it. There has been something crude and heartless and unfeeling in our haste to succeed and be great. Our thought has been "Let every man look out for himself, let every generation look out for itself," while we reared giant machinery which made it impossible that any but those who stood at the levers of control should have a chance to look out for themselves. We had not forgotten our morals. We remembered well enough that we had set up a policy which was meant to serve the humblest as well as the most powerful, with an eye single to the standards of justice and fair play, and remembered it with pride. But we were very heedless and in a hurry to be great.

We have come now to the sober second thought. The scales of heedlessness have fallen from our eyes. We have made up our minds to square every process of our national life again with the standards we so proudly set up at the beginning and have always carried at our hearts. Our work is a work of restoration.

We have itemized with some degree of particularity the things that ought to be altered and here are some of the chief items: A tariff which cuts us off from our proper part in the commerce of the world, violates the just principles of taxation, and makes the Government a facile instrument in the hand of private interests; a banking and currency system based upon the necessity of the Government to sell its bonds fifty years ago and perfectly adapted to concentrating cash and restricting credits; an industrial system which, take it on all its sides, financial as well as administrative, holds capital in leading strings, restricts the liberties and limits the opportunities of labor, and exploits without renewing or conserving the natural resources of the country; a body of agricultural activities never yet given the efficiency of great business undertakings or served as it should be through the instrumentality of science taken directly to the farm, or afforded the facilities of credit best suited to its practical needs; watercourses undeveloped, waste places unreclaimed, forests untended, fast disappearing without plan or prospect of renewal, unregarded waste heaps at every mine. We have studied as perhaps no other nation has the most effective means of production, but we have not studied cost or economy as we should either as organizers of industry, as statesmen, or as individuals.

Nor have we studied and perfected the means by which government may be put at the service of humanity, in safeguarding the health of the Nation, the health of its men and its women and its children, as well as their rights in the struggle for existence. This is no sentimental duty. The firm basis of government is justice, not pity. These are matters of justice. There can be no equality or opportunity, the first essential of justice in the body politic, if men and women and children be not shielded in their lives, their very vitality, from the consequences of great industrial and social processes which they can not alter, control, or singly cope with. Society must see to it that it does not itself crush or weaken or damage its own constituent parts. The first duty of law is to keep sound the society it serves. Sanitary laws, pure food laws, and laws determining conditions of labor which individuals are powerless to determine for themselves are intimate parts of the very business of justice and legal efficiency.

These are some of the things we ought to do, and not leave the others undone, the old-fashioned, never-to-be-neglected, fundamental safeguarding of property and of individual right. This is the high enterprise of the new day: To lift everything that concerns our life as a Nation to the light that shines from the hearthfire of every man's conscience and vision of the right. It is inconceivable that we should do this as partisans; it is inconceivable we should do it in ignorance of the facts as they are or in blind haste. We shall restore, not destroy. We shall deal with our economic system as it is and as it may be modified, not as it might be if we had a clean sheet of paper to write upon; and step by step we shall make it what it should be, in the spirit of those who question their own wisdom and seek counsel and knowledge, not shallow self-satisfaction or the excitement of excursions whither they can not tell. Justice, and only justice, shall always be our motto.

And yet it will be no cool process of mere science. The Nation has been deeply stirred, stirred by a solemn passion, stirred by the knowledge of wrong, of ideals lost, of government too often debauched and made an instrument of evil. The feelings with which we face this new age of right and opportunity sweep across our heartstrings like some air out of God's own presence, where justice and mercy are reconciled and the judge and the brother are one. We know our task to be no mere task of politics but a task which shall search us through and through, whether we be able to understand our time and the need of our people, whether we be indeed their spokesmen and interpreters, whether we have the pure heart to comprehend and the rectified will to choose our high course of action.

This is not a day of triumph; it is a day of dedication. Here muster, not the forces of party, but the forces of humanity. Men's hearts wait upon us; men's lives hang in the balance; men's hopes call upon us to say what we will do. Who shall live up to the great trust? Who dares fail to try? I summon all honest men, all patriotic, all forward-looking men, to my side. God helping me, I will not fail them, if they will but counsel and sustain me!

Business and Politics

ELIHU ROOT

Born, Clinton, New York, February 15, 1845; died, New York City, February 7, 1937. Graduated from Hamilton College, 1865, and in law from New York University, 1867. Prominent in New York legal circles, and United States District Attorney, 1883–1885. Secretary of War, 1899–1904; Secretary of State, 1905–1909. Republican United States Senator from New York, 1909–1915. Member of the Permanent Court of Arbitration at the Hague; President, Carnegie Endowment for International Peace; Nobel Peace Prize, 1912. Advocated entry of United States into the League of Nations.

"If we permit a great body of bureaucracy to establish itself in control over the affairs of our daily lives, the most vital possession of a free people will be destroyed; that is, the independence of individual character."

It is very difficult to respond to such expressions as I have heard tonight, where my cooler judgment refuses to go in agreement, and where I know that a dispassionate stranger would withhold his approval. Such things as have been said within the past hour are, however, inexpressibly grateful to me, because they reveal the wealth of friendship and the partial judgment of affection.

I did not know until a few minutes ago of the purpose of The Union League to bestow this great honor upon me, in the gift of the medal of the League. I

Address at a reception in his honor, The Union League Club of Philadelphia, March 23, 1915. Robert Bacon and James B. Scott, eds., *Miscellaneous Addresses* (Cambridge: Harvard University Press, 1917), pp. 249–258. Reprinted by permission.

accept it with gratitude and deep appreciation which will continue during all of
my remaining life. We confer no titles of nobility in this republic, but we do
what is better: from the promptings of patriotic hearts we repay in double measure to overflowing, every debt which we think we owe to a public servant who
has commended himself to our judgment as Americans. No title could be worth
so much as your judgment; no office could be worth so much as your approval.
And it comes to me with all the more weight because I have a sentiment for
Philadelphia and its people, and for this club, that has continued through all
my active life. A throng of associations compels me as I come into this old club-
house to remember the good men, the strong men and the noble hearts that I
knew in days past who are here no more. When I remember how great a part
this organization has played in the strength and courage of this great land of
justice and liberty; when I remember how much I owe and my children and
children's children will owe to you, to realize that you are thanking me seems
almost too much to believe.

I had been thinking, as I came over in the train this afternoon, of my associations with Philadelphia, and I found, strangely enough, that of all the dear
friends I have known here, my mind went back constantly to McKinley. I recall
how, eighteen years ago, I came here upon a telegram to meet him, to talk
about the condition of things in Spain. I remember how he said, "There is danger
of war; there must not be war with Spain; there shall not be war with Spain. It
must be and it shall be prevented at all hazards." Then I thought of how little
any one man can do. The tendencies of the mighty eighty millions of people
moved on along the path of their destiny, and even that great and skillful man
with all the power of his high office could not prevent it. And I remember how,
a couple of years after, one of my first journeys as a member of his cabinet was
to come here to this club to be with him in one of those great receptions for
which you are so famous. And that led to reflection, not upon specific differences
between President McKinley and this Administration, between the legislation or
the policies of that time and this, but to reflection upon what in the retrospect
can be seen to have been a great nation-wide movement along the path of the
nation's unconscious purpose.

When we elected McKinley in 1896 and again in 1900, it was the business
men of the United States who controlled the election. It was the general, the
almost universal awakening of judgment on the part of men who carried on the
great production and commerce and transportation and finance in the business
of this mighty and prosperous country, which elected McKinley and inaugurated
and maintained the policies of his administration.

How great has been the change. The scepter has passed from the business man.
The distinguishing characteristic of recent years has been the conduct of the
government of the country by men who have but little concern with the business
of the country, by men who distrust the man of business, who suspect the man
of business. Measures relating to the great business and the small and multitudi-

nous business of the country have been framed and put into effect under influences which have rejected the voice of those whom they most immediately affect. The railroad man's testimony of what legislation there should be affecting railroads has been rejected, because he was a party in interest. The banker's testimony about finance has been rejected because he was a party in interest. The manufacturer's testimony about manufacturing has been rejected because he was a party in inter-est. The merchant's testimony about commerce has been rejected because he was a party in interest. The ship-owner's testimony about the merchant marine has been rejected because he was a party in interest. Knowledge of the business affairs of the country has disqualified men from taking any part in the conduct of the increasing participation of the government in the control and direction of business affairs.

Now, this has not been accidental. It is not a matter of individuals. It has not come because particular men have been elected to office and other particular men have failed. It has been a development of the feeling of the whole country; it has been to some degree sectional, but not in the old way. The men concerned in agriculture, in the main, have come to suspect and misunderstand the men concerned in business in the main. This is the distinguishing feature of this great change which has occurred since we elected McKinley.

It has had several causes. It has been partly because of the old hatred of wealth. Those parts of the country in which all of the people have been of comparatively small means have been filled with men who came to hate the rich in the great industrial communities in the North and East. Of course I need not tell you that this hatred of wealth is more than half mere vulgar worship of wealth. God knows that too much money does no man any good; too much money is more apt than not to ruin his children and invite for him kidney disease or hardening of the arteries.

But to the poor farmer on the prairies of the West or the cotton-fields of the South, it seems as if the rich men of the Eastern cities were living in heaven at his expense.

Another element of this change has been an entire or an almost entire failure of understanding of the processes, the conditions, the requirements and the results of the vast and complicated business by which the wealth of the country is created and maintained. Under simple conditions we all understood each other. Every man of the community understood in general about the life, the business and affairs of the other men in the same community. But life is so complicated now, the affairs of this great country are so involved, that there is very little real under-standing by one community of the affairs of another. How can the man who raises a crop of wheat in Dakota really understand the complicated machinery by which his wheat goes onto the breakfast table in Europe, and the price comes back to him? So, through a feeling of envy of the greater wealth of the East and North, of these industrial communities of which this city is a conspicuous example, and through misunderstandings, there has come about a feeling of adverse interest instead of the feeling of common interest that is so essential to the prosperity and perpetuity of a country. And that feeling has had its result in a series of laws and in the method of administering those laws. We have the Interstate Commerce Commission following every step taken by the great transportation companies. Understand, I am not now criticising these laws. I am citing them as elements—stating them as facts; but forming elements in a general condition to which they lead. We have the Interstate Commerce Commission keeping tab on the railroads. We have the Central Reserve Board of the Treasury Department and the office of the Comptroller of Currency following every move of the banks. We have the new Trade Commission which is empowered to go into your factories and mills and inquire into your personal affairs for the purpose of seeing whether you conform to that vague and indefinite standard which they are to apply to trade. We have the Internal Revenue Collector empowered to go into your personal affairs for the purpose of seeing whether your returns for the graduated income tax are full and complete. We have the Pure Food law, under which a vast range of production is subjected to inspection and regulation in the most minute detail. Everywhere, in every direction, supervision of business is the characteristic of the day.

And with the exercise of power over business under the Constitution as it is, comes the desire for enlargement of power, so we have proposals for amendments to the Constitution which will give to the national Government opportunity to extend and increase its control over the conduct of affairs in every state and in every locality. That finds its outlet first in matters that have much popularity. The proposal to amend the Constitution by putting in a prohibition amendment, is the first step toward national control of sumptuary laws directing what shall and shall not be done in every community; amendments to the Constitution in respect of the franchise, to direct who in every state shall or shall not have the right to the elective franchise. In general, the great industrial communities of the North and East are more and more being subjected to government control and regulation by the people of the parts of the country that know little of the business of the country.

I say the scepter has passed. The control has changed, and it is impossible to resist the conclusion that there lies the reason for the stagnation, the hesitation, the timidity, the unwillingness of American enterprise today. You cannot say it was the tariff alone. You cannot say it is the restrictions upon the trusts, the suits against the trusts or the great corporations which are called the trusts, alone. You cannot say it is the Clayton law or the Trade Commission law alone. But the men who are controlling the government of our country today are men who have been fighting the tariff so many years; have been fighting the trusts, or what they thought were the trusts—the great corporations—so long; have been fighting the railroad companies, the express companies and the telegraph companies so long; have been fighting the banks and the bankers so long, that when they come to administer the Government of the United States they cannot rid

themselves of an underlying hostility to American enterprise. Many of them are
good and sensible men, and patriotic American citizens—friends of mine and
friends of all of us. I have talked with them personally and they do not believe
it, but it is true. Underlying all their actions is an uneradicated but not unerad-
icable hostility to the men who they think have profited unduly by the tariff, to
the men who they think have unduly profited by the trusts, to the men who
they think have profited unduly by the control of the banking funds of the
country, and to the men who they think have made undue profits or dividends
out of the railroads and the enterprises that surround the proper administration
of a railroad. And the reason why business does not start is because way down in
the heart of Americans there is a doubt as to what is going to happen at the
hands of a hostile Government.

Now, what is going to be done about it? It is not something to be disposed
of by conquest. It is not something which we ought to be satisfied with disposing
of by mere votes. Merely electing a Republican President in 1916 ought not to
be enough. The country cannot live and prosper with such misunderstanding.
The people who are doing these things are honest and good Americans, but
they misunderstand a great part of the country. They do not realize that you
do your business in the city of Philadelphia on the same principles that they use
when they drive a load of wheat to the elevator or a load of potatoes to the
nearest town—upon no other principles, just as honestly and fairly. All the glamor
of occasional wealth and the magnitude of operations have blinded them to the
essential identity of the way in which they do their business and the way in
which you do yours. I say that this ought not to be permitted to continue; this
misunderstanding ought to be cleared away. It is a question, it is a serious question, it is a question again of preserving the Union, for we cannot live with that
kind of misunderstanding between the people of one section and the people of
other sections.

Now the first thing which is plain is that the business men of America, the
honest, reliable, good, fair citizens who are doing the great business of our country, should become vocal and take pains to see to it that they are no longer mis-
represented or misunderstood. What does an honest and fair man do when he
finds that somebody whose good opinion he respects, misunderstands him? He
does not try to shoot the other fellow or injure him; he tries to remove the misunderstanding, and that is what we ought to do. The business men of America
should wake up—get out of the condition of mind which they have been in for
some time past, in which they have taken all sorts of misrepresentations and
aspersions lying down. They should assert themselves; they should put upon foot
a campaign of education and instruction for a clearing of the air; so that all over
our broad land every American may come to respect every other American in
whatever business he may be engaged; so that American citizenship shall be
forever for the American citizen a title of respect and regard and brotherly affec-

tion. We ought to put an end to the condition in which a number of the people in our country feel no regret at the disasters of the people of other parts of the country. It is not an easy task, for this is a tremendous country. But if the men who elected McKinley will rise to the same standard of courage and determination that prevailed in 1896 and 1900, the task can be accomplished.

We have had missionaries of reform, missionaries of new theories, missionaries of every kind and character, except missionaries of good understanding. The business men of America should undertake their mission to make themselves understood by the people of America.

There is one other thing I want to say, and that is that all this regulation, and inspection, and inquiry into the affairs of the business man, present a danger that can be met in only one way. There is a tendency for the railroads to be afraid of the Interstate Commerce Commission, and for the banks to be afraid of the Central Reserve Board and the Comptroller of Currency, and for the express companies to be afraid of the Postmaster-General, and for the industrial establishments to be afraid of the new Trade Commission, and for the manufacturers of everything that comes under the Pure Food law to be afraid of the Department of Agriculture. It is a critical question for the people of the United States, whether that fear is going to control. For if it does, the power will be abused. There is only one way to meet that kind of power, and that is with courage.

What happens today or tomorrow is of little consequence. The tendencies of a nation are all that count. If we permit by cowardice or timidity; by cringing before official power—if we permit a great body of bureaucracy to establish itself in control over the affairs of our daily lives, the most vital possession of a free people will be destroyed; that is, the independence of individual character.

I grieve to see business halting, to see men out of work, to see honest people deprived of their income, to see the pains of contracting expenditure in the household, to see the unemployed on the street; but all of that is nothing compared with the danger that the people of the United States shall become subservient to power; all that is nothing compared with the danger that we lose all independence of individual character which has been built up through all the thousands of years of growth of Anglo-Saxon freedom. If we maintain that, nothing can prevail against us. If we lose it, we are slaves to the first conqueror. The subject is too high and too great for politics. I would not venture to treat it as a political question, for it goes to the very basis of the future of our beloved country.

It seems now that it is the important mission of the Republican party to reassert the individual independence, the individual rights, the individual integrity of the people of the United States. We are not justly subjects of suspicion. We are not justly subjects of condemnation. We are citizens of these great states, of these busy communities of industry. We are honest, free, true Americans, and we must not and we will not live in an atmosphere of suspicion and distrust. We will not be governed by men who look upon us as unfit to participate in government.

The mission of this Union League is not ended. Not only is eternal vigilance the price of liberty; eternal struggle is the price of liberty. You have again to strike with the weapons of your intelligence and your courage upon the battle-fields of public discussion, of public education and instruction; to strike and yet again to strike with all your power for the perpetuity of the Union, for the continuance of freedom, for the sure foundations of justice, for the memory of the great man who gave you birth as an organization. In your efforts you have my prayers, and always my grateful and affectionate remembrance.

THE LEAGUE OF NATIONS DEBATE

Woodrow Wilson's First Inaugural Address was devoted exclusively to domestic affairs. The new President interpreted his election as a mandate for reform— "to cleanse, to reconsider, to restore, to correct the evil without impairing the good, to purify and humanize every process of our common life. . . ." Wilson's first term in office, says Richard Hofstadter, produced "more positive legislation than any administration since the days of Alexander Hamilton."[1]

But the second Wilson administration was destined to be dramatically different from the first. Events abroad were to interrupt the legislative program of The New Freedom and transform the domestic reformer into a world statesman. Anticipating this change, Wilson was concerned almost exclusively in his Second Inaugural Address with America's relation to a world at war. After referring briefly to the domestic legislation of the previous four years, the President spoke ominously of "other matters . . . lying outside our own life as a nation and over which we had no control, but which, despite our wish to keep free of them, have drawn us more and more irresistibly into their own current and influence."

After the outbreak of hostilities in Europe in July, 1914, President Wilson, despite tremendous pressures from within and without the country, had been able to keep America technically neutral for nearly three years (the 1916 campaign was fought on the slogan "He kept us out of war"). But ultimately, when Germany announced her policy of unrestricted submarine warfare, Wilson, who had repeatedly proclaimed the principle of freedom of the seas, felt obliged, on April 2, 1917, to ask Congress for a declaration of war. "It is a fearful thing to lead this great peaceful people into war," he said, "but the right is more precious

---

[1] *The American Political Tradition* (New York: Vintage Books, 1959), p. 258. See also Arthur S. Link, *Woodrow Wilson and the Progressive Era* (New York: Harper & Brothers, 1954), pp. 229–30. Link, noting the temporary acceptance of progressivism by one of the major parties, states that "the Democratic Congressional majority had, by the fall of 1916, enacted almost every important plank in the Progressive platform of 1912."

than peace, and we shall fight for the things which we have always carried nearest our hearts. . . ." Among these he listed "a universal dominion of right by such a concert of free peoples as shall bring peace and safety to all nations, and make the world itself at last free." In the very act of leading his nation into war Woodrow Wilson was thinking ahead to the time when "a concert of free peoples" might eliminate the necessity for further wars.

There is ample evidence that long before his attention centered on *the* League, Wilson had been turning over in his mind the idea of *a* league to enforce peace. In his famous "Peace Without Victory" speech to the Congress of January 22, 1917, just a few months before America's entry into the war, he spoke of an "international concert" to hold the world at peace: "In every discussion of the peace that must end this war it is taken for granted that peace must be followed by some definite concert of power which will make it virtually impossible that any such catastrophe should ever overwhelm us again." Much earlier, on May 27, 1916, both Wilson and Henry Cabot Lodge (soon to become an implacable foe of the President and the League of Nations) spoke from the same platform to the League to Enforce Peace in Washington, D.C., and endorsed in principle some kind of international peace organization. While the war with Germany was still in progress, President Wilson laid before Congress and the world the "Fourteen Points," his prescription for a just and lasting peace. Point fourteen specified the establishment of "a general association of nations" to provide "mutual guarantees of political independence and territorial integrity to great and small states alike." And at the Metropolitan Opera House in New York just a few weeks before the armistice, Wilson again indicated the outlines of a just peace. It was necessary, he said, for all parties to the peace conference to come ready and willing to pay the price and to create "the only instrumentality by which it can be made certain that the agreements of the peace will be honored and fulfilled." That price, he made clear, is impartial justice for all concerned; that instrumentality a League of Nations—the most essential part of the peace settlement.

Throughout the world Woodrow Wilson's name was linked with the hope for an international organization for peace. His Fourteen Points were accepted by Germany and by the Allies as the basis for peace negotiations. Small wonder, then, that as the American President toured Europe in triumph after the armistice he should have interpreted the wild ovations he received as enthusiasm for a bright new world united under the banner of a League of Nations. "There was no mistaking the tone in the voices of those great crowds," he reported later. "It was not a tone of mere greeting; it was not a tone of mere generous welcome; it was the calling of comrade to comrade, the cries that come from men who say, 'We have waited for this day when the friends of liberty should come across the sea and shake hands with us, to see that a new world was constructed upon a new basis and foundation of justice and right.' " He had no way of knowing it at the time, but that month beginning December 14, 1918, when he waved to cheering thousands in Britain, Italy, and France, was to be the climax of his career, the brief moment when he was acknowledged everywhere as the greatest of the world leaders. What followed was bitter, frustrating, agonizing denouement. Less than a year later, the once buoyant figure in the flag-bedecked, crowd-engulfed automobile was a broken, half-paralyzed old man, surveying from a solitary wheelchair the wreckage of his noblest dream.

The story of how Woodrow Wilson's dream was shattered has been told many times; only its outlines may be sketched here.

Settling down to the serious business of treaty-making after the parades, the speeches, and the victory celebrations, Wilson found that his associates around the peace table did not share his idealism. William Allen White, who was in Paris to report the Peace Conference, noted the pervading influence of "unrestrained forces of amalgamated self-interest," and observed that "the air was filled with international horse-trading."[2] The existence of secret treaties among America's allies made prior to our entry into the war, the desire for vengeance and self-aggrandizement, the old European hatreds and rivalries, all forced Wilson into concessions and compromises which whittled down the Fourteen Points. The final treaty, though probably less punitive than it might have been without his influence for moderation and justice, fell far short of Wilson's ideal. He was adamant in his determination to incorporate the League Covenant into the treaty, however, hoping that the League of Nations would ultimately remedy the injustices. Publicly, the President was unwilling to admit the imperfections of the treaty, and Frederick Lewis Allen suggests that this was the source of Wilson's tragedy: "Having failed to embody his ideal in fact, he distorted the fact. He pictured the world to himself and to others, not as it was, but as he wished it to be."[3]

The first draft of the League Covenant was completed and laid before the peace conference on February 14, 1919. The following day its text was printed

---

[2] *The Autobiography of William Allen White* (New York: The Macmillan Company, 1946), p. 553.

[3] *Only Yesterday* (New York: Harper & Brothers, 1931), p. 28.

in American newspapers, prompting Senator Lodge's caustic request that "the terms of the league of nations, printed in all the newspapers, may be printed in the *Record* and also as a Senate document for convenience and use."[4] On the strength of a preliminary draft of the treaty appearing in the public press, then, debate in the Senate opened on *the* League months before an official copy had been placed before that body.

Returning to the United States in late February to sign the bills of the Sixty-fifth Congress and to discuss the Covenant with Congressional leaders, President Wilson encountered fierce hostility from the isolationist "irreconcilables" led by Senators William E. Borah, Hiram Johnson, and Robert M. La Follette, who were opposed to any kind of league for peace, and from the followers of Senator Lodge, who for personal and political reasons were opposed to a Wilson league. On the eve of the President's return to Paris, his opponents in the Senate united to issue a public vote of no confidence in the form of the notorious "round-robin" resolution. Conceived by Senator Brandegee, drawn up by Philander C. Knox, and signed by thirty-seven Republican Senators, this document was read to the Senate just before midnight on March 3 by Henry Cabot Lodge. It was designed to serve notice to the world that more than one third of the Senate (enough to defeat the treaty) would not approve "the constitution of the league of nations in the form now proposed to the peace conference." The resolution further proposed that "the urgent business of negotiating peace terms with Germany" be undertaken at once, and the discussion of a league of nations left for later consideration. Wilson replied in a speech in New York City on March 4 that he would tie the treaty and the League together so tightly that they could not be separated without destroying the entire structure.[5]

Shortly after the President's return to Paris, the president of Harvard University, Dr. A. Lawrence Lowell, and Senator Lodge engaged in a public debate on the Covenant of Paris in Symphony Hall, Boston—an event which attracted national attention.[6] Governor Calvin Coolidge, who presided, predicted that "wherever statesmen gather, wherever men love letters, this day's discussion will be read and pondered." In his opening statement Lodge professed devotion to

---

[4] *Congressional Record,* 65th Cong., 3rd Sess., vol. 57, pt. IV, p. 3407.

[5] The entire front page of *The New York Times* for March 5 was given over to a full text of Wilson's address, with headlines featuring this passage—an indication of the importance attached to the league issue at that time.

[6] The debate was held March 19, 1919, before a packed house of over three thousand persons, with thousands more in the roped-off area outside the auditorium. For a transcript see "Joint Debate on the Covenant of Paris," in *League of Nations,* vol. II, no. 2 (Boston: World Peace Foundation, April, 1919).

the idea of a league to secure peace, but itemized in detail the defects of the proposed Covenant. Lowell countered that the document under discussion was merely a preliminary draft. He agreed that it was defective, but he urged that the defects be removed and the Covenant ratified, intimating that his opponent seemed more interested in killing than correcting the proposed league. Elaborating upon one of Lodge's metaphors, Lowell said: "I agree fully with Senator Lodge that if you see a burglar entering your house you shoot him, but you shoot him not for the purpose of improving the burglar—it is because you do not wish to improve the burglar. Of course, if you look on this treaty as a burglar, shoot it; but for goodness' sake, say you are trying to shoot it and not that you are trying to improve it by destructive criticism."

Wilson, in Paris, had already concluded that Lodge was bent on shooting the burglar, and that it would be impossible to make any changes that would please him, but he did heed the suggestions of less hostile critics like William Howard Taft, Elihu Root, and Charles Evans Hughes. Incorporated in the revised Covenant presented to the Peace Conference in April were most of the changes recommended by these men during his February visit.

On June 28, 1919, the treaty of peace with Germany was signed at Versailles, and Wilson embarked for the United States, where, on July 10, in one of his most eloquent utterances, he presented to the Senate the treaty containing the Covenant of the League as its first twenty-six articles. It was immediately referred to the Senate Committee on Foreign Relations, nine of whose seventeen members had previously declared their opposition to the constitution of the League by signing the "round-robin" resolution. This committee was dominated by its able chairman, Henry Cabot Lodge.

Lodge, a Senator from Massachusetts since 1893, and one of the Senate's most distinguished members, had moved from minority leader to majority leader after the Republican victory of 1918. Patrician, urbane, son of one of New England's first families, a Harvard Ph.D., historian, biographer, former editor of the *North American Review,* he had for years been acknowledged "the scholar in politics."[7] His position as Republican floor leader and chairman of the Committee on Foreign Relations, his demonstrated skill as orator and parliamentarian, and his implacable opposition to Woodrow Wilson's League, made him the President's most formidable foe in the Senate.

[7] A newspaper correspondent had said of him in the campaign of 1883, "He is the gentleman and scholar in politics without the guilelessness and squeamishness of the said gentleman and scholar." Quoted in John A. Garraty, *Henry Cabot Lodge* (New York: Alfred A. Knopf, 1953), p. 72.

The enemies of the League represented their mission to be one of educating the public on the evils inherent in the treaty, centering their attack on Article X, under the terms of which signatories were pledged "to respect and preserve as against external aggression the territorial integrity and existing political independence of all members." But time was needed for this process of "education," so Lodge began by reading the entire text of the treaty aloud, a process which consumed two full weeks.[8] Then, while debate (which, as already noted, had actually begun in February, months before there was any official document to consider) proceeded on the Senate floor, the committee set to work to modify the treaty with a series of amendments and reservations.

On August 12, Senator Lodge delivered a major speech to the Senate, his first since Wilson had submitted the treaty.[9] It was a long speech, setting forth systematically and in detail his objections to the League, most of which he had advanced in earlier utterances. Lodge's conclusion was a ringing patriotic appeal: "I can never be anything else but an American, and I must think of the United States first . . . ," which evoked a wild demonstration from the galleries. Commenting acidly on talk of ideals, visions, and dreams, he said: "We are told that we shall 'break the heart of the world' if we do not take this league just as it stands. I fear that the hearts of the vast majority of mankind would beat on strongly and steadily and without any quickening if the league were to perish altogether."

As the summer wore on, and the tide of public opinion seemed to be turning against the League, Wilson decided to take his case to the people—"to clear away the mists . . . to remove the impressions, in order to check the falsehoods that have clustered around this great subject." In an 8000-mile tour that took him as far as the Pacific Coast, he delivered forty impassioned addresses in twenty-two days. The end came on September 25 at Pueblo, Colorado, where, after delivering what was perhaps the most moving address of the tour, he collapsed and was rushed back to Washington. His friend and secretary, Joseph Tumulty, reporting the impact of the Pueblo speech, said that as Wilson recalled his experience at the Suresnes cemetery "a great wave of emotion, such as I have never witnessed at a public meeting, swept through the whole amphitheatre."[10]

[8] As Lodge finished reading the 87,000-word document he found himself alone. The other Senators, and even his personal secretary, had departed. *The New York Times,* July 29, 1919, p. 1.

[9] Lodge includes as appendices to his *The Senate and the League of Nations* two of his major addresses from the league debate of 1919, those of February 28 and August 12. These were unquestionably his most important utterances during this debate. Because the earlier speech was based on a first draft of the Covenant, later revised, we have selected the August 12 speech for inclusion in this volume.

[10] *Woodrow Wilson As I Knew Him* (New York: Doubleday, Page and Co., 1921), p. 449.

Unfortunately for Wilson and for his cause, the United States Senate was not similarly moved by the President's eloquence. On November 19, 1919, the treaty was defeated, first with and subsequently without the Lodge reservations. The following March, after another prolonged debate, the treaty was again rejected by the Senate. Even in the face of so final and decisive a defeat, the President, who had said repeatedly that he had no doubts about the ultimate outcome, continued to hope. On October 3, 1920, he issued an appeal to the people to make the Presidential election a referendum on the League of Nations. The chief question being put to the voters, he said, was "Do you want your country's honor vindicated and the Treaty of Versailles ratified?" "The whole world will wait for your verdict in November as it would wait for an intimation of what its future is to be." The verdict (at least as interpreted by the Senate cabal) was no; the future was to be a generation of isolationism for the United States, and for the world another war more terrible than the first.

Why did Wilson, one of our most eloquent leaders, fail? Why did his countrymen reject his pleas for the League, and thus at the outset doom to destruction his grand design for a just and lasting peace? Many causes contributed to this the most tragic failure of his public life, not the least of which was the wave of public apathy, the weariness with idealism, which followed the Great Crusade. People were surfeited with talk of sacrifices, challenges, dreams and visions, and of service to mankind. They were more interested in getting back to the normal business of living than in assuming the role of "champions of liberty throughout the world." Added to this passivity was in some quarters an active xenophobia, a deep-set isolationist sentiment, a fear of involvement in Europe's troubles— which irreconcilables like Borah and Johnson were quick to exploit. Furthermore, although the League battle was not fought out strictly on party lines, it tended to be so, and there were obviously partisan efforts to discredit the Democratic President and his party.[11] Wilson was criticized for including only one Republican, Henry White, on the Peace Commission, and offended the entire Senate by failing to pick any Senator of either party to accompany him to Paris.

Chief responsibility for rejection of the League has sometimes been attributed to Senator Lodge. Although in 1915 Lodge had expressed approval of a league for peace, he soon became an outspoken critic of the league idea. After Wilson's

---

[11] Wilson himself was open to charges of partisanship. Perhaps the most striking example was his appeal to the voters on October 25, 1918, to elect a Democratic Congress "if you have approved of my leadership and wish me to be your unembarrassed spokesman in affairs at home and abroad. . . ." This ill-advised plea was quite naturally taken as an affront to the patriotism of Republican legislators.

"Peace Without Victory" address of January 22, 1917, he delivered a speech to
the Senate warning of the dangers of a league. He attempted to undercut Wilson's position at the Peace Conference by giving a memorandum to Henry White
indicating that the President did not have the support of the Senate or the
people, with the request that White present it to Clemenceau and other European
statesmen. In December, 1918, before any draft of the Covenant had been completed, he delivered a speech warning that the Senate had the power to reject
treaties. He participated in the preparation of the round-robin resolution in
March, 1919. After Wilson had laid the treaty before the Senate in July, Lodge
moved to refer it to the Foreign Relations Committee, where it was amended
and attenuated while Lodge and his followers carried on their campaign of
"public instruction." And during the summer and fall of 1919 the Republican
leader managed to hold together a tenuous coalition of reservationists and irreconcilables until in November the League was defeated.

Lodge denied any personal hostility toward President Wilson, but his private
letters, his many public utterances, and his own account of the whole affair,
The Senate and the League of Nations, render his denial unconvincing. He also
denied hostility to the League itself, taking the line that he was trying to perfect
the instrument and render it more acceptable to the United States. This denial
too is unconvincing. When in the debate with President Lowell he was asked point-
blank whether he would vote for the Covenant if it were amended to suit him,
his reply was evasive. And although he began his remarks that evening with an
expression of his ardent desire for an international league for peace, he closed
with a highly emotional, intensely nationalistic peroration—"I am an American.
. . . I have never had but one flag, never loved but one flag. I am too old to try
to love another, an international flag." In any enumeration of the factors leading
to the rejection of the Treaty of Versailles by the United States Senate, the persistent efforts of Henry Cabot Lodge can scarcely be overestimated.

But the supreme irony in the tragic frustration of Woodrow Wilson's dream
was the fact that he himself, through his very devotion to his cause, helped bring
about its destruction. It seems highly probable that there was sufficient pro-
League sentiment in the country and in the Senate itself to have brought about
ratification of the treaty with reservations. But the President, from first to last,
remained adamant on the subject of reservations. In a letter written November
18, 1919, the day before the final vote, he again urged his followers in the Senate
to vote against the resolution containing the Lodge reservations because "the
resolution in that form does not provide for ratification, but rather for the nulli-

fication of the treaty." Deferring to his wishes, the President's supporters voted against the treaty with reservations and, with the aid of the irreconcilables who wanted no league at all, defeated it. On the final vote, the irreconcilables voted with the Lodge reservationists to defeat the treaty without reservations.

Whether or not Wilson's course of action was justifiable, his motivations are clearly intelligible. He was accused of stubbornness in refusing to separate the Covenant from the treaty. But it must be remembered that the Fourteen Points, one of which called for a general association of nations, had originally been accepted as the basis for a peace settlement. It should be remembered also that Wilson felt that the peace treaty would be inoperative without the machinery of the League, and that he looked to the League to correct some of the injustices of the treaty.

Whether one regards Wilson's unwillingness to compromise on the matter of reservations as mere stubbornness or as high-minded adherence to principle depends somewhat on one's attitude toward the merits of his case. Throughout his life he had displayed a strong sense of duty and rectitude which was interpreted by some as strength of character, and which to others was simply irritating. But one cannot read the President's speeches and letters from 1918 to 1920 without being struck by the repetition of a theme which became an obsession to his sensitive spirit. He had been appalled at the applause following his war message, for it was as he said "a message of death for our young men." From that time on he was haunted by the ghosts of those men. As he stood amid the graves in Suresnes Cemetery on Memorial Day, 1919, it swept over him again, and he gave the clearest and most revealing statement of how he felt: "I beg you to realize the compulsion that I myself feel that I am under. . . . I sent these lads over here to die. Shall I—can I—ever speak a word of counsel which is inconsistent with the assurances I gave them when they came over? It is inconceivable." He spoke of the necessity he felt "to resist counsels that are hard to resist," and to stand steadfast, consecrated in the spirit of the dead men "who left me under eternal bonds of fidelity." Four months later at Pueblo, Colorado, Wilson recalled that day at Suresnes, expressing the wish that the foes of the League could visit the spot and feel as he had felt the moral obligation "not to go back on those boys," but to "make good their redemption of the world."

It was this "compulsion," this powerful sense of personal commitment and responsibility, that, rightly or wrongly, caused Woodrow Wilson to hold out to the end against reservations which might well have effected ratification of the treaty, but which in his mind constituted a betrayal of his trust. In the last scene of the last act of the drama, months after the November defeat and just before the final vote in March, 1920, he wrote a letter to Senator Gilbert M. Hitchcock, leader of pro-League forces in the Senate, giving his views on Article X. His views had not changed.

"For myself, I feel that I could not look the soldiers of our gallant armies in the face again if I did not do everything in my power to remove every obstacle that lies in the way of the adoption of this particular article of the Covenant, because we made these pledges to them as well as to the rest of the world, and it was to this cause they deemed themselves devoted in a spirit of crusaders. I should be forever unfaithful to them if I did not do my utmost to fulfill the high purpose for which they fought."

There is, of course, no way of knowing whether Wilson's dream of a just and lasting peace would have been brought closer to realization if the United States had joined the League of Nations. Nor can it be said that World War II came as a direct result of our failure to join, but there is no disputing the tragic accuracy of the President's prediction of subsequent events. "I can predict with absolute certainty," he said at Omaha in September, 1919, "that within another generation there will be another World War if the nations of the world do not concert the methods by which to prevent it." Precisely twenty years later, German tanks rolled into Poland and the world was again at war.

In Opposition to the Proposed League of Nations

HENRY CABOT LODGE

Born, Boston, Massachusetts, May 12, 1850; died, Cambridge, Massachusetts, November 9, 1924. Graduated from Harvard, 1871; LL.B., 1875; Ph.D. (Political Science), 1876. Admitted to Boston bar, 1876. Edited North American Review, *1873–1876, and* International Review *(with John T. Morse), 1880–1881. Author several volumes of history and biography. Republican member, Massachusetts House of Representatives, 1880–1881; United States House of Representatives, 1887–1893; United States Senate, 1893–1924. Senate majority leader, Chairman Foreign Relations Committee during League of Nations debate. As Senator, supported high protective tariff, strong navy, acquisition of Philippines; opposed free silver, woman suffrage, Eighteenth Amendment.*

"Internationalism . . . is to me repulsive. National I must remain, and in that way I, like all other Americans, can render the amplest service to the world."

*M*r. *President,* in the Essays of Elia, one of the most delightful is that entitled "Popular Fallacies." There is one very popular fallacy, however, which Lamb did not include in his list,

United States Senate, August 12, 1919. *Congressional Record*, 66th Cong., 1st Sess., vol. 58, pt. 4, pp. 3778–3784.

and that is the common saying that history repeats itself. Universal negatives are always dangerous, but if there is anything which is fairly certain, it is that history never exactly repeats itself. Popular fallacies, nevertheless, generally have some basis, and this saying springs from the undoubted truth that mankind from generation to generation is constantly repeating itself. We have an excellent illustration of this fact in the proposed experiment now before us, of making arrangements to secure the permanent peace of the world. To assure the peace of the world by a combination of the nations is no new idea. Leaving out the leagues of antiquity and of mediaeval times and going back no further than the treaty of Utrecht,[1] at the beginning of the eighteenth century, we find that at that period a project of a treaty to establish perpetual peace was brought forward in 1713 by the Abbé de Saint-Pierre.[2] The treaty of Utrecht was to be the basis of an international system. A European league or Christian republic was to be set up, under which the members were to renounce the right of making war against each other and submit their disputes for arbitration to a central tribunal of the allies, the decisions of which were to be enforced by a common armament. I need not point out the resemblance between this theory and that which under-lies the present league of nations. It was widely discussed during the eighteenth century, receiving much support in public opinion; and Voltaire said that the nations of Europe, united by ties of religion, institutions, and culture, were really but a single family.

[Lodge goes on to illustrate his thesis that "to assure the peace of the world by a combination of the nations is no new idea." He refers to the plans of Napoleon and of the Emperor Alexander, and particularly to the treaty of Paris (November 20, 1815) between defeated France and Great Britain, Russia, Austria, and Prussia. From this combination of powers, allegedly formed to maintain peace in Europe, developed the "Holy Alliance" which became an instrument of reaction and oppression.]

. . . .

I have taken the trouble to trace in the merest outline the development of the Holy Alliance, so hostile and dangerous to human freedom, because I think it carries with it a lesson for us at the present moment, showing as it does what may come from general propositions and declarations of purposes in which all the world agrees. Turn to the preamble of the covenant of the league of nations now before us, which states the object of the league. It is formed "in order to promote international cooperation and to achieve international peace and security by the acceptance of obligations not to resort to war, by the prescription of open,

[1] The "Peace of Utrecht" consisted of a series of treaties made in 1713 at the conclusion of the War of the Spanish Succession, putting an end to French expansion and signalizing the rise of the British Empire.
[2] Charles Irénée Castel, Abbé de Saint-Pierre (1658–1743), French social philosopher. Author of *Projet de paix perpetuelle* (1713), in which he described an international court and a league of states.

just, and honorable relations between nations, by the firm establishment of the understandings of international laws as the actual rule of conduct among governments and by the maintenance of justice and a scrupulous respect for all treaty obligations in the dealings of organized peoples with one another."

No one would contest the loftiness or the benevolence of these purposes. Brave words, indeed! They do not differ essentially from the preamble of the treaty of Paris, from which sprang the Holy Alliance. But the covenant of this league contains a provision which I do not find in the treaty of Paris, and which is as follows:

The assembly may deal at its meetings with any matter within the sphere of action of the league or affecting the peace of the world.

There is no such sweeping or far-reaching provision as that in the treaty of Paris, and yet able men developed from that treaty the Holy Alliance, which England, and later France were forced to abandon and which, for 35 years, was an unmitigated curse to the world. England broke from the Holy Alliance and the breach began three years after it was formed, because English statesmen saw that it was intended to turn the alliance—and this league is an alliance—into a means of repressing internal revolutions or insurrections. There was nothing in the treaty of Paris which warranted such action, but in this covenant of the league of nations the authority is clearly given in the third paragraph of article 3, where it is said:

The assembly may deal at its meetings with any matter within the sphere of action of the league or affecting the peace of the world.

No revolutionary movement, no internal conflict of any magnitude can fail to affect the peace of the world. The French Revolution, which was wholly internal at the beginning, affected the peace of the world to such an extent that it brought on a world war which lasted some 25 years. Can anyone say that our Civil War did not affect the peace of the world? At this very moment, who would deny that the condition of Russia, with internal conflicts raging in all parts of that great Empire, does not affect the peace of the world and therefore come properly within the jurisdiction of the league? "Any matter affecting the peace of the world" is a very broad statement which could be made to justify almost any interference on the part of the league with the internal affairs of other countries. That this fair and obvious interpretation is the one given to it abroad is made perfectly apparent in the direct and vigorous statement of M. Clemenceau in his letter to Mr. Paderewski, in which he takes the ground in behalf of the Jews and other nationalities in Poland that they should be protected, and where he says that the associated powers would feel themselves bound to secure guaranties in Poland "of certain essential rights which will afford to the inhabitants the necessary protection, whatever changes may take place in the internal constitution of the Polish Republic." He contemplates and defends interference with the internal affairs of Poland—among other things—in behalf of a complete religious freedom, a purpose with which we all deeply sympathize. These promises of the French prime minister are embodied in effective clauses in the treaties with Germany and with Poland and deal with the internal affairs of nations, and their execution is intrusted to the "principal allied and associated powers"; that is, to the United States, Great Britain, France, Italy, and Japan. This is a practical demonstration of what can be done under article 3 and under article 11 of the league covenant, and the authority which permits interference in behalf of religious freedom, an admirable object, is easily extended to the repression of internal disturbances which may well prove a less admirable purpose. If Europe desires such an alliance or league with a power of this kind, so be it. I have no objection, provided they do not interfere with the American Continents or force us against our will but bound by a moral obligation into all the quarrels of Europe. If England, abandoning the policy of Canning, desires to be a member of a league which has such powers as this, I have not a word to say. But I object in the strongest possible way to having the United States agree, directly or indirectly, to be controlled by a league which may at any time, and perfectly lawfully and in accordance with the terms of the covenant, be drawn in to deal with internal conflicts in other countries, no matter what those conflicts may be. We should never permit the United States to be involved in any internal conflict in another country, except by the will of her people expressed through the Congress which represents them.

With regard to wars of external aggression on a member of the league the case is perfectly clear. There can be no genuine dispute whatever about the meaning of the first clause of article 10. In the first place, it differs from every other obligation in being individual and placed upon each nation without the intervention of the league. Each nation for itself promises to respect and preserve as against external aggression the boundaries and the political independence of every member of the league. Of the right of the United States to give such a guaranty I have never had the slightest doubt, and the elaborate arguments which have been made here and the learning which has been displayed about our treaty with Granada, now Colombia, and with Panama, were not necessary for me, because, I repeat, there can be no doubt of our right to give a guaranty to another nation that we will protect its boundaries and independence. The point I wish to make is that the pledge is an individual pledge. We have, for example, given guaranties to Panama and for obvious and sufficient reasons. The application of that guaranty would not be in the slightest degree affected by 10 or 20 other nations giving the same pledge if Panama, when in danger, appealed to us to fulfill our obligation. We should be bound to do so without the slightest reference to the other guarantors. In article 10 the United States is bound on the appeal of any member of the league not only to respect but to preserve its independence and its boundaries, and that pledge, if we give it, must be fulfilled.

There is to me no distinction whatever in a treaty between what some persons are pleased to call legal and moral obligations. A treaty rests and must rest, except where it is imposed under duress and securities and hostages are taken for its fulfillment, upon moral obligations. No doubt a great power impossible of coercion can cast aside a moral obligation if it sees fit and escape from the performance of the duty which it promises. The pathway of dishonor is always open. I, for one, however, cannot conceive of voting for a clause of which I disapprove because I know it can be escaped in that way. Whatever the United States agrees to, by that agreement she must abide. Nothing could so surely destroy all prospects of the world's peace as to have any powerful nation refuse to carry out an obligation, direct or indirect, because it rests only on moral grounds. Whatever we promise we must carry out to the full, "without mental reservation or purpose of evasion." To me any other attitude is inconceivable. Without the most absolute and minute good faith in carrying out a treaty to which we have agreed, without ever resorting to doubtful interpretations or to the plea that it is only a moral obligation, treaties are worthless. The greatest foundation of peace is the scrupulous observance of every promise, express or implied, of every pledge, whether it can be described as legal or moral. No vote should be given to any clause in any treaty or to any treaty except in this spirit and with this understanding.

I return, then, to the first clause of article 10. It is, I repeat, an individual obligation. It requires no action on the part of the league, except that in the second sentence the authorities of the league are to have the power to advise as to the means to be employed in order to fulfill the purpose of the first sentence. But that is a detail of execution, and I consider that we are morally and in honor bound to accept and act upon that advice. The broad fact remains that if any member of the league suffering from external aggression should appeal directly to the United States for support the United States would be bound to give that support in its own capacity and without reference to the action of other powers because the United States itself is bound, and I hope the day will never come when the United States will not carry out its promises. If that day should come, and the United States or any other great country should refuse, no matter how specious the reasons, to fulfill both in letter and spirit every obligation in this covenant, the United States would be dishonored and the league would crumble into dust, leaving behind it a legacy of wars. If China should rise up and attack Japan in an effort to undo the great wrong of the cession of the control of Shantung to that power, we should be bound under the terms of article 10 to sustain Japan against China, and a guaranty of that sort is never invoked except when the question has passed beyond the stage of negotiation and has become a question for the application of force. I do not like the prospect. It shall not come into existence by any vote of mine.

Article 11 carries this danger still further, for it says:

Any war or threat of war, whether immediately affecting any of the members of the league or not, is hereby declared a matter of concern to the whole league, and the league shall take any action that shall be deemed wise and effectual to safeguard the peace of nations.

"Any war or threat of war" means both external aggression and internal disturbance, as I have already pointed out in dealing with article 3. "Any action" covers military action, because it covers action of any sort or kind. Let me take an example, not an imaginary case, but one which may have been overlooked because most people have not the slightest idea where or what a King of the Hejaz is. The following dispatch appeared recently in the newspapers:

HEJAZ AGAINST BEDOUINS

The forces of Emir Abdullah recently suffered a grave defeat, the Wahabis attacking and capturing Kurma, east of Mecca. Ibn Savond is believed to be working in harmony with the Wahabis. A squadron of the royal air force was ordered recently to go to the assistance of King Hussein.

Hussein I take to be the Sultan of Hejaz. He is being attacked by the Bedouins, as they are known to us, although I fancy the general knowledge about the Wahabis and Ibn Savond and Emir Abdullah is slight and the names mean but little to the American people. Nevertheless, here is a case of a member of the league—for the King of Hejaz is such a member in good and regular standing and signed the treaty by his representatives, Mr. Rustem Haidar and Mr. Abdul Havi Aouni.

Under article 10, if King Hussein appealed to us for aid and protection against external aggression affecting his independence and the boundaries of his kingdom, we should be bound to give that aid and protection and to send American soldiers to Arabia. It is not relevant to say that this is unlikely to occur; that Great Britain is quite able to take care of King Hussein, who is her fair creation, reminding one a little of the Mosquito King, a monarch once developed by Great Britain on the Mosquito Coast of Central America. The fact that we should not be called upon does not alter the right which the King of Hejaz possesses to demand the sending of American troops to Arabia in order to preserve his independence against the assaults of the Wahabis or Bedouins. I am unwilling to give that right to King Hussein, and this illustrates the point which is to me the most objectionable in the league as it stands—the right of other powers to call out American troops and American ships to go to any part of the world, an obligation we are bound to fulfill under the terms of this treaty. I know the answer well—that of course they could not be sent without action by Congress. Congress would have no choice if acting in good faith, and if under article 10 any member of the league summoned us, or if under article 11 the league itself summoned us, we should be bound in honor and morally to obey. There would be no escape except by a breach of faith, and legislation by Congress under those circumstances would be a mockery of independent action. Is it too much to ask that provision should be made that American troops and American ships should never be sent anywhere or ordered to take part in any conflict except after the deliberate action of the American people, expressed according to the Constitution through their chosen representatives in Congress?

Let me now briefly point out the insuperable difficulty which I find in article 15. It begins: "If there should arise between members of the league any dispute likely to lead to a rupture." "Any dispute" covers every possible dispute. It therefore covers a dispute over tariff duties and over immigration. Suppose we have a dispute with Japan or with some European country as to immigration. I put aside tariff duties as less important than immigration. This is not an imaginary case. Of late years there has probably been more international discussion and negotiation about questions growing out of immigration laws than any other one subject. It comes within the definition of "any dispute" at the beginning of article 15. In the eighth paragraph of that article it is said that "if the dispute between the parties is claimed by one of them, and is found by the council to arise out of a matter which, by international law, is solely within the domestic jurisdiction of that party, the council shall so report and shall make no recommendation as to its settlement." That is one of the statements, of which there are several in this treaty, where words are used which it is difficult to believe their authors could have written down in seriousness. They seem to have been put in for the same purpose as what is known in natural history as protective coloring. Protective coloring is intended so to merge the animal, the bird, or the insect in its background that it will be indistinguishable from its surroundings and difficult, if not impossible, to find the elusive and hidden bird, animal, or insect. Protective coloring here is used in the form of words to give an impression that we are perfectly safe upon immigration and tariffs, for example, because questions which international law holds to be solely within domestic jurisdiction are not to have any recommendation from the council, but the dangers are there just the same, like the cunningly colored insect on the tree or the young bird crouching motionless upon the sand. The words and the coloring are alike intended to deceive. I wish somebody would point out to me those provisions of international law which make a list of questions which are hard and fast within the domestic jurisdiction. No such distinction can be applied to tariff duties or immigration, nor indeed finally and conclusively to any subject. Have we not seen the school laws of California, most domestic of subjects, rise to the dignity of a grave international dispute? No doubt both import duties and immigration are primarily domestic questions, but they both constantly involve and will continue to involve international effects. Like the protective coloration, this paragraph is wholly worthless unless it is successful in screening from the observer the existence of the animal, insect, or bird which it is desired to conceal. It fails to do so and the real object is detected. But even if this bit of deception was omitted—and so far as the question of immigration or tariff questions are concerned it might as well be—the ninth paragraph brings the important point clearly to the front.

Immigration, which is the example I took, cannot escape the action of the league by any claim of domestic jurisdiction; it has too many international aspects.

Article 9 says:

The council may, in any case under this article, refer the dispute to the assembly.

We have our dispute as to immigration with Japan or with one of the Balkan States, let us say. The council has the power to refer the dispute to the assembly. Moreover the dispute shall be so referred at the request of either party to the dispute, provided that such request be made within 14 days after the submission of the dispute to the council. So that Japan or the Balkan States, for example, with which we may easily have the dispute, ask that it be referred to the assembly and the immigration question between the United States and Jugoslavia or Japan as the case may be, goes to the assembly. The United States and Japan or Jugoslavia are excluded from voting and the provision of article 12, relating to the action and powers of the council, apply to the action and powers of the assembly provided, as set forth in article 15, that a report made by the assembly "if concurred in by the representatives of those members of the league represented on the council and of a majority of the other members of the league, exclusive in each case of the representatives of the parties to the dispute, shall have the same force as a report by the council concurred in by all the members thereof other than the representatives of one or more of the parties to the dispute." This course of procedure having been pursued, we find the question of immigration between the United States and Japan is before the assembly for decision. The representatives of the council, except the delegates of the United States and of Japan or Jugoslavia, must all vote unanimously upon it as I understand it, but a majority of the entire assembly, where the council will have only seven votes, will decide. Can anyone say beforehand what the decision of that assembly will be, in which the United States and Jugoslavia or Japan will have no vote? The question in one case may affect immigration from every country in Europe, although the dispute exists only for one, and in the other the whole matter of Asiatic immigration is involved. Is it too fanciful to think that it might be decided against us? For my purpose it matters not whether it is decided for or against us. An immigration dispute or a dispute over tariff duties, met by the procedure set forth in article 15, comes before the assembly of delegates for a decision by what is practically a majority vote of the entire assembly. That is something to which I do not find myself able to give my assent. So far as immigration is concerned, and also so far as tariff duties, although less important, are concerned, I deny the jurisdiction. There should be no possibility of other nations deciding who shall come into the United States, or under what conditions they shall enter. The right to say who shall come into a country is one of the very highest attributes of sovereignty. If a nation cannot say without appeal who shall come within its gates and become a part of its citizenship it has ceased to be a sovereign nation.

It has become a tributary and a subject nation, and it makes no difference whether it is subject to a league or to a conqueror.

If other nations are willing to subject themselves to such a domination, the United States, to which many immigrants have come and many more will come, ought never to submit to it for a moment. They tell us that so far as Asiatic emigration is concerned there is not the slightest danger that that will ever be forced upon us by the league, because Australia and Canada and New Zealand are equally opposed to it. I think it highly improbable that it would be forced upon us under those conditions, but it is by no means impossible. It is true the United States has one vote and that England, if you count the King of the Hejaz, has seven—in all eight—votes; yet it might not be impossible for Japan and China and Siam to rally enough other votes to defeat us; but whether we are protected in that way or not does not matter. The very offering of that explanation accepts the jurisdiction of the league, and personally, I cannot consent to putting the protection of my country and of her workingmen against undesirable immigration, out of our own hands. We and we alone must say who shall come into the United States and become citizens of this Republic, and no one else should have any power to utter one word in regard to it.

Article 21 says:

Nothing in this covenant shall be deemed to affect the validity of international engagements, such as treaties of arbitration or regional understandings like the Monroe doctrine for securing the maintenance of peace.

This provision did not appear in the first draft of the covenant, and when the President explained the second draft of the convention to the peace conference he said:

Article 21 is new.

And that was all he said. No one can question the truth of the remark, but I trust I shall not be considered disrespectful if I say that it was not an illuminating statement. The article was new, but the fact of its novelty, which the President declared, was known to everyone who had taken the trouble to read the two documents.

. . . .

Let me now deal with the article itself. We have here some protective coloration again. The Monroe doctrine is described as a "regional understanding" whatever that may mean. The boundaries between the States of the Union, I suppose, are "regional understandings," if anyone chooses to apply to them that somewhat swollen phraseology. But the Monroe doctrine is no more a regional understanding than it is an "international engagement." The Monroe doctrine was a policy declared by President Monroe. Its immediate purpose was to shut out Europe from interfering with the South American Republics, which the

Holy Alliance designed to do. It was stated broadly, however, as we all know, and went much further than that. It was, as I have just said, the corollary of Washington's declaration against our interfering in European questions. It was so regarded by Jefferson at the time and by John Quincy Adams, who formulated it, and by President Monroe, who declared it. It rested firmly on the great law of self-preservation, which is the basic principle of every independent State.

It is not necessary to trace its history or to point out the extensions which it has received or its universal acceptance by all American statesmen without regard to party. All Americans have always been for it. They may not have known its details or read all the many discussions in regard to it, but they knew that it was an American doctrine and that, broadly stated, it meant the exclusion of Europe from interference with American affairs and from any attempt to colonize or set up new States within the boundaries of the American Continent. I repeat it was purely an American doctrine, a purely American policy, designed and wisely designed for our defense. It has never been an "international engagement." No nation has ever formally recognized it. It has been the subject of reservation at international conventions by American delegates. It has never been a "regional understanding" or an understanding of any kind with anybody. It was the declaration of the United States of America, in their own behalf, supported by their own power. They brought it into being, and its life was predicated on the force which the United States could place behind it. Unless the United States could sustain it it would die. The United States has supported it. It has lived—strong, efficient, respected. It is now proposed to kill it by a provision in a treaty for a league of nations.

The instant that the United States, who declared, interpreted, and sustained the doctrine, ceases to be the sole judge of what it means, that instant the Monroe doctrine ceases and disappears from history and from the face of the earth. I think it is just as undesirable to have Europe interfere in American affairs now as Mr. Monroe thought it was in 1823, and equally undesirable that we should be compelled to involve ourselves in all the wars and brawls of Europe. . . .

Another point in this covenant where change must be made in order to protect the safety of the United States in the future is in article 1, where withdrawal is provided for. This provision was an attempt to meet the very general objection to the first draft of the league, that there was no means of getting out of it without denouncing the treaty; that is, there was no arrangement for the withdrawal of any nation. As it now stands it reads that—

Any member of the league may, after two years' notice of its intention to do so, withdraw from the league, provided that all its international obligations and all its obligations under this covenant shall have been fulfilled at the time of its withdrawal.

The right of withdrawal is given by this clause, although the time for notice, two years, is altogether too long. Six months or a year would be found, I think, in most treaties to be the normal period fixed for notice of withdrawal. But whatever virtue there may be in the right thus conferred is completely nullified by the proviso. The right of withdrawal cannot be exercised until all the international obligations and all the obligations of the withdrawing nations have been fulfilled. The league alone can decide whether "all international obligations and all obligations under this covenant" have been fulfilled, and this would require, under the provisions of the league, a unanimous vote so that any nation desiring to withdraw could not do so, even on the two years' notice, if one nation voted that the obligations had not been fulfilled. Remember that this gives the league not only power to review all our obligations under the covenant but all our treaties with all nations for every one of those is an "international obligation."

Are we deliberately to put ourselves in fetters and be examined by the league of nations as to whether we have kept faith with Cuba or Panama before we can be permitted to leave the league? This seems to me humiliating to say the least. The right of withdrawal, if it is to be of any value whatever, must be absolute, because otherwise a nation desiring to withdraw could be held in the league by objections from other nations until the very act which induces the nation to withdraw had been completed; until the withdrawing nation had been forced to send troops to take part in a war with which it had no concern and upon which it did not desire to enter. It seems to me vital to the safety of the United States not only that this provision should be eliminated and the right to withdraw made absolute but that the period of withdrawal should be much reduced. As it stands it is practically no better in this respect than the first league draft which contained no provision for withdrawal at all, because the proviso here inserted so encumbers it that every nation to all intents and purposes must remain a member of the league indefinitely unless all the other members are willing that it should retire. Such a provision as this, ostensibly framed to meet the objection, has the defect which other similar gestures to give an impression of meeting objections have, that it apparently keeps the promise to the ear but most certainly breaks it to the hope.

I have dwelt only upon those points which seem to me most dangerous. There are, of course, many others, but these points, in the interest not only of the safety of the United States but of the maintenance of the treaty and the peace of the world, should be dealt with here before it is too late. Once in the league the chance of amendment is so slight that it is not worth considering. Any analysis of the provisions of this league covenant, however, brings out in startling relief one great fact. Whatever may be said, it is not a league of peace; it is an alliance, dominated at the present moment by five great powers, really by three, and it has all the marks of an alliance. The development of international law is neglected. The court which is to decide disputes brought before it fills but a small place. The conditions for which this league really provides with the utmost care are political conditions, not judicial questions, to be reached by the executive council and the assembly, purely political bodies without any trace of a judicial character about them. Such being its machinery, the control being in the hands of political appointees whose votes will be controlled by interest and expediency, it exhibits that most marked characteristic of an alliance—that its decisions are to be carried out by force. Those articles upon which the whole structure rests are articles which provide for the use of force; that is, for war. This league to enforce peace does a great deal for enforcement and very little for peace. It makes more essential provisions looking to war than to peace, for the settlement of disputes.

Article 10 I have already discussed. There is no question that the preservation of a State against external aggression can contemplate nothing but war. In article 11, again, the league is authorized to take any action which may be necessary to safeguard the peace of the world. "Any action" includes war. We also have specific provisions for a boycott, which is a form of economic warfare. The use of troops might be avoided but the enforcement of a boycott would require blockades in all probability, and certainly a boycott in its essence is simply an effort to starve a people into submission, to ruin their trade, and, in the case of nations which are not self-supporting, to cut off their food supply. The misery and suffering caused by such a measure as this may easily rival that caused by actual war. Article 16 embodies the boycott and also, in the last paragraph, provides explicitly for war. We are told that the word "recommends" has no binding force; it constitutes a moral obligation, that is all. But it means that if we, for example, should refuse to accept the recommendation, we should nullify the operation of article 16 and, to that extent, of the league. It seems to me that to attempt to relieve us of clearly imposed duties by saying that the word "recommend" is not binding is an escape of which no nation regarding the sanctity of treaties and its own honor would care to avail itself. The provisions of article 16 are extended to States outside the league who refuse to obey its command to come in and submit themselves to its jurisdiction; another provision for war.

Taken altogether, these provisions for war present what to my mind is the gravest objection to this league in its present form. We are told that of course nothing will be done in the way of warlike acts without the assent of Congress. If that is true, let us say so in the covenant. But as it stands there is no doubt whatever in my mind that American troops and American ships may be ordered to any part of the world by nations other than the United States, and that is a proposition to which I for one can never assent. It must be made perfectly clear that no American soldiers, not even a corporal's guard, that no American sailors, not even the crew of a submarine, can ever be engaged in war or ordered anywhere except by the constitutional authorities of the United States. To Congress is granted by the Constitution the right to declare war, and nothing that would take the troops out of the country at the bidding or demand of other nations should ever be permitted except through congressional action. The lives of Americans must never be sacrificed except by the will of the American people expressed through their chosen Representatives in Congress. This is a point upon which no doubt can be permitted.

. . . .

It has been reiterated here on this floor, and reiterated to the point of weariness, that in every treaty there is some sacrifice of sovereignty. That is not a universal truth by any means, but it is true of some treaties and it is a platitude which does not require reiteration. The question and the only question before us here is how much of our sovereignty we are justified in sacrificing. In what I have already said about other nations putting us into war I have covered one point of sovereignty which ought never to be yielded, the power to send American soldiers and sailors everywhere, which ought never to be taken from the American people or impaired in the slightest degree. Let us beware how we palter with our independence. We have not reached the great position from which we were able to come down into the field of battle and help to save the world from tyranny by being guided by others. Our vast power has all been built up and gathered together by ourselves alone. We forced our way upward from the days of the Revolution, through a world often hostile and always indifferent. We owe no debt to anyone except to France in that Revolution, and those policies and those rights on which our power has been founded should never be lessened or weakened. It will be no service to the world to do so and it will be of intolerable injury to the United States. We will do our share. We are ready and anxious to help in all ways to preserve the world's peace. But we can do it best by not crippling ourselves.

I am as anxious as any human being can be to have the United States render every possible service to the civilization and the peace of mankind, but I am certain we can do it best by not putting ourselves in leading strings or subjecting our policies and our sovereignty to other nations. The independence of the United States is not only more precious to ourselves but to the world than any single possession. Look at the United States to-day. We have made mistakes in the past. We have had shortcomings. We shall make mistakes in the future and fall short of our own best hopes. But none the less is there any country to-day on the face of the earth which can compare with this in ordered liberty, in peace, and in the largest freedom? I feel that I can say this without being accused of undue boastfulness, for it is the simple fact, and in making this treaty and taking on these obligations all that we do is in a spirit of unselfishness and in a desire for the good of mankind. But it is well to remember that we are dealing with nations every one of which has a direct individual interest to serve and there is grave danger in an unshared idealism. Contrast the United States with any country on the face of the earth to-day and ask yourself whether the situation of the United States is not the best to be found. I will go as far as anyone in world service, but the first step to world service is the maintenance of the United States. You may call me selfish if you will, conservative or reactionary, or use any other harsh adjective you see fit to apply, but an American I was born, an American I have remained all my life. I can never be anything else but an American, and I must think of the United States first, and when I think of the United States first in an arrangement like this I am thinking of what is best for the world, for if the United States fails the best hopes of mankind fail with it. I have never had but one allegiance—I cannot divide it now. I have loved but one flag and I cannot share that devotion and give affection to the mongrel banner invented for a league. Internationalism, illustrated by the Bolshevik and by the men to whom all countries are alike provided they can make money out of them, is to me repulsive. National I must remain, and in that way I, like all other Americans, can render the amplest service to the world. The United States is the world's best hope, but if you fetter her in the interests and quarrels of other nations, if you tangle her in the intrigues of Europe, you will destroy her power for good and endanger her very existence. Leave her to march freely through the centuries to come as in the years that have gone. Strong, generous, and confident, she has nobly served mankind. Beware how you trifle with your marvelous inheritance, this great land of ordered liberty, for if we stumble and fall, freedom and civilization everywhere will go down in ruin.

We are told that we shall "break the heart of the world" if we do not take this league just as it stands. I fear that the hearts of the vast majority of mankind would beat on strongly and steadily and without any quickening if the league were to perish altogether. If it should be effectively and beneficently changed the people who would lie awake in sorrow for a single night could be easily gathered in one not very large room, but those who would draw a long breath of relief would reach to millions.

We hear much of visions and I trust we shall continue to have visions and dream dreams of a fairer future for the race. But visions are one thing and visionaries are another, and the mechanical appliances of the rhetorician designed to give a picture of a present which does not exist and of a future which no man can predict are as unreal and shortlived as the steam or canvas clouds, the angels suspended on wires, and the artificial lights of the stage. They pass with the moment of effect and are shabby and tawdry in the daylight. Let us at least be real. Washington's entire honesty of mind and his fearless look into the face of all facts are qualities which can never go out of fashion and which we should all do well to imitate.

Ideals have been thrust upon us as an argument for the league until the healthy mind, which rejects cant, revolts from them. Are ideals confined to this deformed experiment upon a noble purpose, tainted as it is with bargains, and tied to a peace treaty which might have been disposed of long ago to the great benefit of the world if it had not been compelled to carry this rider on its back? *"Post equitem sedet atra cura,"* Horace tells us, but no blacker care ever sat behind any rider than we shall find in this covenant of doubtful and disputed interpretation as it now perches upon the treaty of peace.

No doubt many excellent and patriotic people see a coming fulfillment of noble ideals in the words "League for Peace." We all respect and share these aspirations and desires, but some of us see no hope, but rather defeat, for them in this murky covenant. For we, too, have our ideals, even if we differ from those who have tried to establish a monopoly of idealism. Our first ideal is our country, and we see her in the future, as in the past, giving service to all her people and to the world. Our ideal of the future is that she should continue to render that service of her own free will. She has great problems of her own to solve, very grim and perilous problems, and a right solution, if we can attain to it, would largely benefit mankind. We would have our country strong to resist a peril from the West, as she has flung back the German menace from the East. We would not have our politics distracted and embittered by the dissensions of other lands. We would not have our country's vigor exhausted or her moral force abated by everlasting meddling and muddling in every quarrel, great and small, which afflicts the world. Our ideal is to make her ever stronger and better and finer, because in that way alone, as we believe, can she be of the greatest service to the world's peace and to the welfare of mankind.

In Support of the Proposed League of Nations

WOODROW WILSON

(*For biographical sketch, see p. 40.*)

"In order to clear away the mists . . . in order to check the falsehoods . . . I want to tell you a few very simple things about the treaty and the Covenant."

M<sup>r. *Chairman and Fellow Countrymen:* It is with a great deal of genuine pleasure that I find myself in Pueblo, and I feel it a compliment that I should be permitted to be the first speaker in this beautiful hall. One of the advantages of this hall, as I look about, is that you are not too far away from me, because there is nothing so reassuring to men who are trying to express the public sentiment as getting into real personal contact with their fellow citizens. I have gained a renewed impression as I have crossed the continent this time of the homogeneity of this great people to whom we belong. They come from many stocks, but they are all of one kind. They come from many origins, but they are all shot through with the same principles and desire the same righteous and honest things. I have received a more inspiring impression this time of the public opinion of the United States than it was ever my privilege to receive before.

The chief pleasure of my trip has been that it has nothing to do with my personal fortunes, that it has nothing to do with my personal reputation, that it has nothing to do with anything except great principles uttered by Americans of all sorts and of all parties which we are now trying to realize at this crisis of the

Pueblo, Colorado, September 25, 1919. *Addresses of President Wilson, September 4 to September 25, 1919,* Senate Document No. 120 (Washington: Government Printing Office, 1919), pp. 359–370.

affairs of the world. But there have been unpleasant impressions as well as pleasant impressions, my fellow citizens, as I have crossed the continent. I have perceived more and more that men have been busy creating an absolutely false impression of what the treaty of peace and the Covenant of the League of Nations contain and mean. I find, moreover, that there is an organized propaganda against the League of Nations and against the treaty proceeding from exactly the same sources that the organized propaganda proceeded from which threatened this country here and there with disloyalty, and I want to say—I cannot say too often —any man who carries a hyphen about with him carries a dagger that he is ready to plunge into the vitals of this Republic whenever he gets ready.[1] If I can catch any man with a hyphen in this great contest I will know that I have got an enemy of the Republic. My fellow citizens, it is only certain bodies of foreign sympathies, certain bodies of sympathy with foreign nations that are organized against this great document which the American representatives have brought back from Paris. Therefore, in order to clear away the mists, in order to remove the impressions, in order to check the falsehoods that have clustered around this great subject, I want to tell you a few very simple things about the treaty and the Covenant.

Do not think of this treaty of peace as merely a settlement with Germany. It is that. It is a very severe settlement with Germany, but there is not anything in it that she did not earn. Indeed, she earned more than she can ever be able to pay for, and the punishment exacted of her is not a punishment greater than she can bear, and it is absolutely necessary in order that no other nation may ever plot such a thing against humanity and civilization. But the treaty is so much more than that. It is not merely a settlement with Germany; it is a readjustment of those great injustices which underlie the whole structure of European and Asiatic society. This is only the first of several treaties. They are all constructed upon the same plan. The Austrian treaty follows the same lines. The treaty with Hungary follows the same lines. The treaty with Bulgaria follows the same lines. The treaty with Turkey, when it is formulated, will follow the same lines. What are those lines? They are based upon the purpose to see that every government dealt with in this great settlement is put in the hands of the people and taken out of the hands of coteries and of sovereigns who had no right to rule over the people. It is a people's treaty, that accomplishes by a great sweep of practical justice the liberation of men who never could have liberated themselves, and the power of the most powerful nations has been devoted not to their aggrandizement but to the liberation of people whom they could have put under their control if they had chosen to do so. Not one foot of territory is demanded by the conquerors, not one single item of submission to their authority is demanded by them. The men who sat around that table in Paris knew that the time had come when the people were no longer going to consent to live

---

[1] The reference is to so-called "hyphenated Americans," those with foreign backgrounds and parentage (i.e., German-Americans, Japanese-Americans, etc.).

under masters, but were going to live the lives that they chose themselves, to live under such governments as they chose themselves to erect. That is the fundamental principle of this great settlement.

And we did not stop with that. We added a great international charter for the rights of labor. Reject this treaty, impair it, and this is the consequence to the laboring men of the world, that there is no international tribunal which can bring the moral judgments of the world to bear upon the great labor questions of the day. What we need to do with regard to the labor questions of the day, my fellow countrymen, is to lift them into the light, is to lift them out of the haze and distraction of passion, of hostility, out into the calm spaces where men look at things without passion. The more men you get into a great discussion the more you exclude passion. Just so soon as the calm judgment of the world is directed upon the question of justice to labor, labor is going to have a forum such as it never was supplied with before, and men everywhere are going to see that the problem of labor is nothing more nor less than the problem of the elevation of humanity. We must see that all the questions which have disturbed the world, all the questions which have eaten into the confidence of men toward their governments, all the questions which have disturbed the processes of industry, shall be brought out where men of all points of view, men of all attitudes of mind, men of all kinds of experience, may contribute their part to the settlement of the great questions which we must settle and cannot ignore.

At the front of this great treaty is put the Covenant of the League of Nations. It will also be at the front of the Austrian treaty and the Hungarian treaty and the Bulgarian treaty and the treaty with Turkey. Every one of them will contain the Covenant of the League of Nations, because you cannot work any of them without the Covenant of the League of Nations. Unless you get the united, concerted purpose and power of the great Governments of the world behind this settlement, it will fall down like a house of cards. There is only one power to put behind the liberation of mankind, and that is the power of mankind. It is the power of the united moral forces of the world, and in the Covenant of the League of Nations the moral forces of the world are mobilized. For what purpose? Reflect, my fellow citizens, that the membership of this great League is going to include all the great fighting nations of the world, as well as the weak ones. It is not for the present going to include Germany, but for the time being Germany is not a great fighting country. All the nations that have power that can be mobilized are going to be members of this League, including the United States. And what do they unite for? They enter into a solemn promise to one another that they will never use their power against one another for aggression; that they never will impair the territorial integrity of a neighbor; that they never will interfere with the political independence of a neighbor; that they will abide by the principle that great populations are entitled to determine their own destiny and that they will not interfere with that destiny; and that no matter what differences arise amongst them they will never resort to war without first having done

one or other of two things—either submitted the matter of controversy to arbitration, in which case they agree to abide by the result without question, or submitted it to the consideration of the council of the League of Nations, laying before that council all the documents, all the facts, agreeing that the council can publish the documents and the facts to the whole world, agreeing that there shall be six months allowed for the mature consideration of those facts by the council, and agreeing that at the expiration of the six months, even if they are not then ready to accept the advice of the council with regard to the settlement of the dispute, they will still not go to war for another three months. In other words, they consent, no matter what happens, to submit every matter of difference between them to the judgment of mankind, and just so certainly as they do that, my fellow citizens, war will be in the far background, war will be pushed out of that foreground of terror in which it has kept the world for generation after generation, and men will know that there will be a calm time of deliberate counsel. The most dangerous thing for a bad cause is to expose it to the opinion of the world. The most certain way that you can prove that a man is mistaken is by letting all his neighbors know what he thinks, by letting all his neighbors discuss what he thinks, and if he is in the wrong you will notice that he will stay at home, he will not walk on the street. He will be afraid of the eyes of his neighbors. He will be afraid of their judgment of his character. He will know that his cause is lost unless he can sustain it by the arguments of right and of justice. The same law that applies to individuals applies to nations.

But, you say, "We have heard that we might be at a disadvantage in the League of Nations." Well, whoever told you that either was deliberately falsifying or he had not read the Covenant of the League of Nations. I leave him the choice. I want to give you a very simple account of the organization of the League of Nations and let you judge for yourselves. It is a very simple organization. The power of the League, or rather the activities of the League, lie in two bodies. There is the council, which consists of one representative from each of the principal allied and associated powers—that is to say, the United States, Great Britain, France, Italy, and Japan, along with four other representatives of smaller powers chosen out of the general body of the membership of the League. The council is the source of every active policy of the League, and no active policy of the League can be adopted without a unanimous vote of the council. That is explicitly stated in the Covenant itself. Does it not evidently follow that the League of Nations can adopt no policy whatever without the consent of the United States? The affirmative vote of the representative of the United States is necessary in every case. Now, you have heard of six votes belonging to the British Empire. Those six votes are not in the council. They are in the assembly, and the interesting thing is that the assembly does not vote. I must qualify that statement a little, but essentially it is absolutely true. In every matter in which the assembly is given a voice, and there are only four or five, its vote does not count unless concurred in by the representatives of all the nations represented on the council,

so that there is no validity to any vote of the assembly unless in that vote also
the representative of the United States concurs. That one vote of the United
States is as big as the six votes of the British Empire. I am not jealous for advantage, my fellow citizens, but I think that is a perfectly safe situation. There
is no validity in a vote, either by the council or the assembly, in which we do
not concur. So much for the statements about the six votes of the British Empire.

Look at it in another aspect. The assembly is the talking body. The assembly
was created in order that anybody that purposed anything wrong should be subjected to the awkward circumstance that everybody could talk about it. This is
the great assembly in which all the things that are likely to disturb the peace of
the world or the good understanding between nations are to be exposed to the
general view, and I want to ask you if you think it was unjust, unjust to the
United States, that speaking parts should be assigned to the several portions of
the British Empire? Do you think it unjust that there should be some spokesman
in debate for that fine little stout Republic down in the Pacific, New Zealand?
Do you think it was unjust that Australia should be allowed to stand up and
take part in the debate—Australia, from which we have learned some of the
most useful progressive policies of modern time, a little nation only five million
in a great continent, but counting for several times five in its activities and in
its interest in liberal reform? Do you think it unjust that that little Republic
down in South Africa, whose gallant resistance to being subjected to any outside
authority at all we admired for so many months and whose fortunes we followed
with such interest, should have a speaking part? Great Britain obliged South
Africa to submit to her sovereignty, but she immediately after that felt that it
was convenient and right to hand the whole self-government of that colony over
to the very men whom she had beaten. The representatives of South Africa in
Paris were two of the most distinguished generals of the Boer Army, two of the
realest men I ever met, two men that could talk sober counsel and wise advice,
along with the best statesmen in Europe. To exclude General Botha and General
Smuts from the right to stand up in the parliament of the world and say something concerning the affairs of mankind would be absurd. And what about
Canada? Is not Canada a good neighbor? I ask you, Is not Canada more likely
to agree with the United States than with Great Britain? Canada has a speaking
part. And then, for the first time in the history of the world, that great voiceless
multitude, that throng hundreds of millions strong in India, has a voice, and I
want to testify that some of the wisest and most dignified figures in the peace
conference at Paris came from India, men who seemed to carry in their minds
an older wisdom than the rest of us had, whose traditions ran back into so many
of the unhappy fortunes of mankind that they seemed very useful counselors as
to how some ray of hope and some prospect of happiness could be opened to its
people. I for my part have no jealousy whatever of those five speaking parts in
the assembly. Those speaking parts cannot translate themselves into five votes
that can in any matter override the voice and purpose of the United States.

Let us sweep aside all this language of jealousy. Let us be big enough to know the facts and to welcome the facts, because the facts are based upon the principle that America has always fought for, namely, the equality of self-governing peoples, whether they were big or little—not counting men, but counting rights, not counting representation, but counting the purpose of that representation. When you hear an opinion quoted you do not count the number of persons who hold it; you ask, "Who said that?" You weigh opinions, you do not count them, and the beauty of all democracies is that every voice can be heard, every voice can have its effect, every voice can contribute to the general judgment that is finally arrived at. That is the object of democracy. Let us accept what America has always fought for, and accept it with pride that America showed the way and made the proposal. I do not mean that America made the proposal in this particular instance; I mean that the principle was an American principle, proposed by America.

When you come to the heart of the Covenant, my fellow citizens, you will find it in Article X, and I am very much interested to know that the other things have been blown away like bubbles. There is nothing in the other contentions with regard to the League of Nations, but there is something in Article X that you ought to realize and ought to accept or reject. Article X is the heart of the whole matter. What is Article X? I never am certain that I can from memory give a literal repetition of its language, but I am sure that I can give an exact interpretation of its meaning. Article X provides that every member of the League covenants to respect and preserve the territorial integrity and existing political independence of every other member of the League as against external aggression. Not against internal disturbance. There was not a man at that table who did not admit the sacredness of the right of self-determination, the sacredness of the right of any body of people to say that they would not continue to live under the Government they were then living under, and under Article XI of the Covenant they are given a place to say whether they will live under it or not. For following Article X is Article XI, which makes it the right of any member of the League at any time to call attention to anything, anywhere, that is likely to disturb the peace of the world or the good understanding between nations upon which the peace of the world depends. I want to give you an illustration of what that would mean.

You have heard a great deal—something that was true and a great deal that was false—about that provision of the treaty which hands over to Japan the rights which Germany enjoyed in the Province of Shantung in China. In the first place, Germany did not enjoy any rights there that other nations had not already claimed. For my part, my judgment, my moral judgment, is against the whole set of concessions. They were all of them unjust to China, they ought never to have been exacted, they were all exacted by duress from a great body of thoughtful and ancient and helpless people. There never was any right in any of them. Thank God, America never asked for any, never dreamed of asking for any. But when Germany got this concession in 1898, the Government of the United States made no protest whatever. That was not because the Government of the United States was not in the hands of high-minded and conscientious men. It was. William McKinley was President and John Hay was Secretary of State—as safe hands to leave the honor of the United States in as any that you can cite. They made no protest because the state of international law at that time was that it was none of their business unless they could show that the interests of the United States were affected, and the only thing that they could show with regard to the interests of the United States was that Germany might close the doors of Shantung Province against the trade of the United States. They, therefore, demanded and obtained promises that we could continue to sell merchandise in Shantung. Immediately following that concession to Germany there was a concession to Russia of the same sort, of Port Arthur, and Port Arthur was handed over subsequently to Japan on the very territory of the United States. Don't you remember that when Russia and Japan got into war with one another the war was brought to a conclusion by a treaty written at Portsmouth, N.H., and in that treaty without the slightest intimation from any authoritative sources in America that the Government of the United States had any objection, Port Arthur, Chinese territory, was turned over to Japan? I want you distinctly to understand that there is no thought of criticism in my mind. I am expounding to you a state of international law. Now, read Articles X and XI. You will see that international law is revolutionized by putting morals into it. Article X says that no member of the League, and that includes all these nations that have demanded these things unjustly of China, shall impair the territorial integrity or the political independence of any other member of the League. China is going to be a member of the League. Article XI says that any member of the League can call attention to anything that is likely to disturb the peace of the world or the good understanding between nations, and China is for the first time in the history of mankind afforded a standing before the jury of the world. I, for my part, have a profound sympathy for China, and I am proud to have taken part in an arrangement which promises the protection of the world to the rights of China. The whole atmosphere of the world is changed by a thing like that, my fellow citizens. The whole international practice of the world is revolutionized.

But you will say, "What is the second sentence of Article X? That is what gives very disturbing thoughts." The second sentence is that the council of the League shall advise what steps, if any, are necessary to carry out the guarantee of the first sentence, namely, that the members will respect and preserve the territorial integrity and political independence of the other members. I do not know any other meaning for the word "advise" except "advise." The council advises, and it cannot advise without the vote of the United States. Why gentlemen should fear that the Congress of the United States would be advised to do something that it did not want to do I frankly cannot imagine, because they cannot even be advised to do anything unless their own representative has participated in the advice. It may be that that will impair somewhat the vigor of the League, but, nevertheless, the fact is so, that we are not obliged to take any advice except our own, which to any man who wants to go his own course is a very satisfactory state of affairs. Every man regards his own advice as best, and I dare say every man mixes his own advice with some thought of his own interest. Whether we use it wisely or unwisely, we can use the vote of the United States to make impossible drawing the United States into any enterprise that she does not care to be drawn into.

Yet Article X strikes at the taproot of war. Article X is a statement that the very things that have always been sought in imperialistic wars are henceforth forgone by every ambitious nation in the world. I would have felt very lonely, my fellow countrymen, and I would have felt very much disturbed if, sitting at the peace table in Paris, I had supposed that I was expounding my own ideas. Whether you believe it or not, I know the relative size of my own ideas; I know how they stand related in bulk and proportion to the moral judgments of my fellow countrymen, and I proposed nothing whatever at the peace table at Paris that I had not sufficiently certain knowledge embodied the moral judgment of the citizens of the United States. I had gone over there with, so to say, explicit instructions. Don't you remember that we laid down fourteen points which should contain the principles of the settlement? They were not my points. In every one of them I was conscientiously trying to read the thought of the people of the United States, and after I uttered those points I had every assurance given me that could be given me that they did speak the moral judgment of the United States and not my single judgment. Then when it came to that critical period just a little less than a year ago, when it was evident that the war was coming to its critical end, all the nations engaged in the war accepted those fourteen principles explicitly as the basis of the armistice and the basis of the peace. In those circumstances I crossed the ocean under bond to my own people and to the other governments with which I was dealing. The whole specification of the method of settlement was written down and accepted beforehand, and we were architects building on those specifications. It reassures me and fortifies my position to find how before I went over men whose judgment the United States has often trusted were of exactly the same opinion that I went abroad to express. Here is something I want to read from Theodore Roosevelt:

The one effective move for obtaining peace is by an agreement among all the great powers in which each should pledge itself not only to abide by the decisions of a common tribunal but to back its decisions by force. The great civilized nations should combine by solemn agreement in a great world league for the peace of righteousness; a court should be established. A changed and amplified Hague court would meet the requirements, composed of representatives from each nation, whose representatives are sworn to act as judges in each case and not in a representative capacity.

Now there is Article X. He goes on and says this:

The nations should agree on certain rights that should not be questioned, such as territorial integrity, their right to deal with their domestic affairs, and with such matters as whom they should admit to citizenship. All such guarantee each of their number in possession of these rights.

Now, the other specification is in the Covenant. The Covenant in another portion guarantees to the members the independent control of their domestic questions. There is not a leg for these gentlemen to stand on when they say that the interests of the United States are not safeguarded in the very points where we are most sensitive. You do not need to be told again that the Covenant expressly says that nothing in this Covenant shall be construed as affecting the validity of the Monroe Doctrine, for example. You could not be more explicit than that. And every point of interest is covered, partly for one very interesting reason. This is not the first time that the Foreign Relations Committee of the Senate of the United States has read and considered this Covenant. I brought it to this country in March last in a tentative, provisional form, in practically the form that it now has, with the exception of certain additions which I shall mention immediately. I asked the Foreign Relations Committees of both Houses to come to the White House and we spent a long evening in the frankest discussion of every portion that they wished to discuss. They made certain specific suggestions as to what should be contained in this document when it was to be revised. I carried those suggestions to Paris, and every one of them was adopted. What more could I have done? What more could have been obtained? The very matters upon which these gentlemen were most concerned were, the right of withdrawal, which is now expressly stated; the safeguarding of the Monroe Doctrine, which is now accomplished; the exclusion from action by the League of domestic questions, which is now accomplished. All along the line, every suggestion of the United States was adopted after the Covenant had been drawn up in its first form and had been published for the criticism of the world. There is a very true sense in which I can say this is a tested American document.

I am dwelling upon these points, my fellow citizens, in spite of the fact that I dare say to most of you they are perfectly well known, because in order to meet the present situation we have got to know what we are dealing with. We are not dealing with the kind of document which this is represented by some gentlemen to be; and inasmuch as we are dealing with a document simon-pure in respect of the very principles we have professed and lived up to, we have got to do one or other of two things—we have got to adopt it or reject it. There is no middle course. You cannot go in on a special-privilege basis of your own. I take it that you are too proud to ask to be exempted from responsibilities which the other members of the League will carry. We go in upon equal terms or we do not go in at all; and if we do not go in, my fellow citizens, think of the tragedy of that result—the only sufficient guarantee to the peace of the world withheld! Ourselves drawn apart with that dangerous pride which means that we shall be ready to take care of ourselves, and that means that we shall maintain great

standing armies and an irresistible navy; that means we shall have the organization of a military nation; that means we shall have a general staff, with the kind
of power that the general staff of Germany had: to mobilize this great manhood
of the Nation when it pleases, all the energy of our young men drawn into the
thought and preparation for war. What of our pledges to the men that lie dead
in France? We said that they went over there not to prove the prowess of America
or her readiness for another war but to see to it that there never was such a war
again. It always seems to make it difficult for me to say anything, my fellow
citizens, when I think of my clients in this case. My clients are the children; my
clients are the next generation. They do not know what promises and bonds I
undertook when I ordered the armies of the United States to the soil of France,
but I know, and I intend to redeem my pledges to the children; they shall not
be sent upon a similar errand.

Again and again, my fellow citizens, mothers who lost their sons in France
have come to me and, taking my hand, have shed tears upon it not only, but
they have added, "God bless you, Mr. President!" Why, my fellow citizens, should
they pray God to bless me? I advised the Congress of the United States to create
the situation that led to the death of their sons. I ordered their sons oversea.
I consented to their sons being put in the most difficult parts of the battle line,
where death was certain, as in the impenetrable difficulties of the forest of Ar-
gonne. Why should they weep upon my hand and call down the blessings of
God upon me? Because they believe that their boys died for something that
vastly transcends any of the immediate and palpable objects of the war. They
believe, and they rightly believe, that their sons saved the liberty of the world.
They believe that wrapped up with the liberty of the world is the continuous
protection of that liberty by the concerted powers of all civilized people. They
believe that this sacrifice was made in order that other sons should not be called
upon for a similar gift—the gift of life, the gift of all that died—and if we did
not see this thing through, if we fulfilled the dearest present wish of Germany
and now dissociated ourselves from those alongside whom we fought in the war,
would not something of the halo go away from the gun over the mantelpiece,
or the sword? Would not the old uniform lose something of its significance?
These men were crusaders. They were not going forth to prove the might of the
United States. They were going forth to prove the might of justice and right,
and all the world accepted them as crusaders, and their transcendent achievement
has made all the world believe in America as it believes in no other nation organized in the modern world. There seems to me to stand between us and the rejection or qualification of this treaty the serried ranks of those boys in khaki, not
only these boys who came home, but those dear ghosts that still deploy upon the
fields of France.

My friends, on last Decoration Day I went to a beautiful hillside near Paris,
where was located the cemetery of Suresnes, a cemetery given over to the burial
of the American dead. Behind me on the slopes was rank upon rank of living

American soldiers, and lying before me upon the levels of the plain was rank upon rank of departed American soldiers. Right by the side of the stand where I spoke there was a little group of French women who had adopted those graves, had made themselves mothers of those dear ghosts by putting flowers every day upon those graves, taking them as their own sons, their own beloved, because they had died in the same cause—France was free and the world was free because America had come! I wish some men in public life who are now opposing the settlement for which these men died could visit such a spot as that. I wish that the thought that comes out of those graves could penetrate their consciousness. I wish that they could feel the moral obligation that rests upon us not to go back on those boys, but to see the thing through, to see it through to the end and make good their redemption of the world. For nothing less depends upon this decision, nothing less than the liberation and salvation of the world.

You will say, "Is the League an absolute guarantee against war?" No; I do not know any absolute guarantee against the errors of human judgment or the violence of human passion, but I tell you this: With a cooling space of nine months for human passion, not much of it will keep hot. I had a couple of friends who were in the habit of losing their tempers, and when they lost their tempers they were in the habit of using very unparliamentary language. Some of their friends induced them to make a promise that they never would swear inside the town limits. When the impulse next came upon them, they took a street car to go out of town to swear, and by the time they got out of town they did not want to swear. They came back convinced that they were just what they were, a couple of unspeakable fools, and the habit of getting angry and of swearing suffered great inroads upon it by that experience. Now, illustrating the great by the small, that is true of the passions of nations. It is true of the passions of men however you combine them. Give them space to cool off. I ask you this: If it is not an absolute insurance against war, do you want no insurance at all? Do you want nothing? Do you want not only no probability that war will not recur, but the probability that it will recur? The arrangements of justice do not stand of themselves, my fellow citizens. The arrangements of this treaty are just, but they need the support of the combined power of the great nations of the world. And they will have that support. Now that the mists of this great question have cleared away, I believe that men will see the truth, eye to eye and face to face. There is one thing that the American people always rise to and extend their hand to, and that is the truth of justice and of liberty and of peace. We have accepted that truth and we are going to be led by it, and it is going to lead us, and through us the world, out into pastures of quietness and peace such as the world never dreamed of before.

MODERNISM VS. FUNDAMENTALISM
IN RELIGION

THE RELIGIOUS controversy between liberalism and orthodoxy after World War I furnishes striking parallels to the great controversy of a century before. Between 1815 and 1830, the Congregational Church of New England was split by the Unitarian movement, and the "faith once delivered to the saints" was thrown on the defensive by the heretical doctrines of William Ellery Channing, Ralph Waldo Emerson, Theodore Parker, and others.[1] In the 1920s religious orthodoxy was once again threatened by innovations that called into question what had long been regarded as eternal and unchanging truth. This time the attack came from two directions: religious modernists, armed with the higher criticism, discounted supernatural aspects of religion and disparaged Biblical literalism; and scientists advanced an evolutionary hypothesis that seemed to contradict the Biblical account of creation and therefore to weaken faith in the infallibility of the Holy Scriptures.

This renewal of religious disputation was in some measure part of a general postwar reaction—the desire to return to "normalcy" in religion as in other fields, a longing for the old securities, and a resentment of experimentation, innovation, and disturbing new ideas. Science had achieved an immense prestige, and many devout Christians associated science with materialism, secularism, and loss of spiritual values. Believing that religious faith was being undermined, they sought solace in orthodox creeds. Some fundamentalists took refuge in unyielding obscurantism, rejecting outright the discoveries of science whenever they came into conflict with a literal interpretation of the Bible. Modernists, on the other hand, wished to

---

[1] For the details of this controversy see "Religious Liberalism vs. Orthodoxy," in Wrage and Baskerville, *American Forum: Speeches on Historic Issues, 1788–1900* (New York: Harper & Brothers, 1960), pp. 75–113.

adapt Christian principles to changing social conditions, and to reconcile the new knowledge with the old faith.

Between 1909 and 1912 twelve pamphlets called *The Fundamentals* were published under orthodox auspices as a bulwark against mounting unbelief. These articles outlined the basic tenets of evangelical religion, the so-called "Five Points of Fundamentalism": (1) the infallibility and supernatural origin of the Bible, (2) the virgin birth of Jesus, (3) Christ's vicarious atonement, (4) His miraculous resurrection, and (5) His second coming. Through the cooperation of two wealthy California laymen *The Fundamentals* were sent free of charge "to every pastor, evangelist, missionary, theological student, Sunday School superintendent, YMCA and YWCA secretary in the English-speaking world." Nearly three million copies were ultimately distributed in this country and abroad.

The appearance of *The Fundamentals* marked the beginnings of an organized movement against "liberal" religion. After the war the fundamentalists moved from defense to militant attack through such organizations as Defenders of the Christian Faith, The Bible Crusaders of America, The Bible League of North America, and, most important and longest-lived, The World's Christian Fundamentals Association, founded in 1919 by William Bell Riley. The Bible schools, notably Moody Bible Institute in Chicago and its sister institution on the West Coast, The Bible Institute of Los Angeles, were convenient bases of operation for the innumerable crusades, mass meetings, rallies, conventions, and conferences which continued throughout the 1920s. From these and similar sources flowed a river of religious tracts, printed sermons, weekly and monthly church periodicals, books, and pamphlets, extolling the old-time religion and excoriating evolutionists, modernists, and other heretics.

Liberals made prompt reply. One of the pivotal episodes in the modernist-fundamentalist controversy was a sermon preached by Harry Emerson Fosdick on May 21, 1922, in the First Presbyterian Church of New York City. Dr. Fosdick, widely known as an eloquent liberal clergyman, had become increasingly disturbed by fundamentalist intolerance. His sermon "Shall the Fundamentalists Win?" was a protest against attempts to drive liberals out of the churches, and a plea for a spirit of tolerance and conciliation which would enable fundamentalists and liberals to remain amicably within the Christian fellowship.[2] Fosdick

---

[2] William Ellery Channing's Baltimore sermon "Unitarian Christianity" (1819) offers an interesting parallel. Channing's sermon, like Fosdick's, was an appeal for tolerance and understanding. Each man sought to clarify the liberal position and to allay, rather than to incite, controversy. Yet each sermon in its time provoked an extended controversy. Both sermons were widely circulated in print, both elicited numerous replies from eminent conservatives, and each

called attention to the great mass of available new knowledge—knowledge about the origin and laws of the universe, knowledge about human history, and particularly about the development of other religions—and stressed the need to reconcile and adjust Christian faith to this new knowledge: "The new knowledge and the old faith cannot be left antagonistic or even disparate, as though a man on Saturday could use one set of regulative ideas for his life and on Sunday could change gears to another altogether. We must be able to think our modern life clear through in Christian terms and to do that we also must be able to think our Christian life clear through in modern terms."

After suggesting certain applications of this principle to three of the "fundamentals"—the virgin birth, the inspiration of the Bible, and the second coming of Christ—Fosdick closed with a plea for a proper sense of proportion, an ability to distinguish between "little matters" and "colossal issues." It is almost unforgivable, he asserted, "that men should tithe mint and anise and cummin, and quarrel over them, when the world is perishing for the lack of the weightier matters of the law, justice, and mercy, and faith."

"If ever a sermon failed to achieve its object," Fosdick wrote in his autobiography, "mine did. It was a plea for good will, but what came of it was an explosion of ill will, for over two years making headline news of a controversy that went the limit of truculence."[3] The sermon in pamphlet form came to the attention of Ivy Lee, an advertising man and a liberal Presbyterian layman. With Fosdick's permission, Lee divided the sermon into sections, provided captions, cut out parts of the conciliatory introduction and conclusion, retitled it "The New Knowledge and the Christian Faith," and circulated it to a nation-wide audience. The gathering storm now broke in fury.

The first reply came from Clarence E. Macartney, a Presbyterian minister of Philadelphia, in an article entitled "Shall Unbelief Win?"[4] Though uncompromising in tone, this article was free from the hostility of later utterances. Praising the sermon's lucidity of thought, charm of style, and freedom from bigotry and arrogance, Macartney nevertheless branded Fosdick's views as "subversive of the Christian Faith." He regarded this candid sermon as clear evidence of the impossibility of a reconciliation between the evangelical and modernist positions. One, he affirmed, must be wrong and the other right; both cannot possibly be

elevated its author to a place of leadership in the liberal movement. Cf. Wrage and Baskerville, *American Forum,* pp. 82–98.

[3] Harry Emerson Fosdick, *The Living of These Days* (New York: Harper & Brothers, 1956), p. 145.

[4] *The Presbyterian,* XCII (July 13, 1922; July 20, 1922).

right. Taking up in turn Fosdick's liberal views regarding the "fundamentals," Macartney sought to refute each by reference to the authority of the Bible and eminent theologians. He was particularly incensed by the liberal rejection of the atonement: "Our chief complaint against the rationalist and the modernist is not their writings and sayings about the deity of our Lord, the Bible, the Second Advent, but their rejection of the one great truth of Christianity, that through his death we have remission of our sins and are justified with God." Fosdick's remarks likening disputes over doctrinal matters to petty quarrels over mint, anise, and cummin, he called "an almost unpardonable flippancy on the part of one who speaks as a teacher of Christianity." Macartney denied the existence of any fundamentalist conspiracy to put liberals out of the church. He assured Fosdick and his associates that they need not worry about excommunication, for "in the minds of thousands upon thousands of Christians, they are already *out* of the church, and no act of an ecclesiastical court could make the fact more real." The Philadelphia minister closed with a prayer that they might be brought back in.

But the Reverend Mark A. Matthews of Seattle, Washington, offered no prayers for the re-entry of liberals into the fold. In fact, as the battle became more heated, he expressed the hope that Dr. Fosdick, a Baptist, would yield to the importunings of some of his followers and join the Presbyterian Church, for then he could be tried for heresy and officially ousted. Matthews, a former Moderator of the General Assembly, and pastor of what was said to be the largest Presbyterian church in the country, was precisely the kind of militant fundamentalist whom Fosdick had described in his sermon as driving stakes "to mark out the deadline of doctrine around the church, across which no one is to pass except on terms of agreement." He regarded modernists as enemies of Christ, as "old, rank heretics in present day clothes." For a true Christian to compromise with, even to tolerate, such heretics was unthinkable.

Sunday after Sunday from his Seattle pulpit Matthews hurled his short, stinging, unequivocal sermons—anathemas against the forces of Antichrist, exhortations to salvation through the Blood of the Lamb.[5] As Lyman Beecher, exactly one hundred years before, had replied to Channing's liberal manifesto with a defense of the evangelical system, so Matthews, taking the same text, Jude 3, replied to Fosdick with a plea to the orthodox to contend for the faith once delivered to the saints.[6] "There have been no amendments, no additions, no sub-

[5] Mark A. Matthews, *Gospel Sword Thrusts* (New York: Fleming H. Revell Co., 1924).
[6] *Ibid.*, pp. 94–99.

tractions from this supernatural faith. It is the creed delivered by Almighty God to those who are born again through the blood of Jesus Christ. There can be no other creed God will sanction, that the Church should hold, or that individuals should teach. All modifications come from the enemies of Christ, the rationalist enemies of Christ." Between heresy and orthodoxy, between rationalistic forces and real Christianity, Matthews insisted, there could never be peace or unity. "The battle must be fierce, the contention must be strenuous. . . ."

Although most fundamentalist speaking and writing struck much the same note, some few, such as the Reverend J. Gresham Machen, spoke in the restrained tones of the scholar. Machen was a member of the faculty of Princeton Theological Seminary, author of several books, and an able polemicist who spoke forcefully without resorting to emotionalism.[7] Like Matthews, Machen believed modernism to be antagonistic to Christianity; like Matthews he brooked no compromise: one side or the other must win. But Machen was no obscurantist. He showed tolerance of, but not agreement with, those who stood firm on an infallible Bible, closing their minds to everything which seemed to contradict its literal interpretation.[8]

Machen rejected the catch phrases of liberalism, such as "the fatherhood of God and the brotherhood of man," and "Christianity is a life, not a doctrine." He opposed attempts at reconciliation between Christianity and science on the ground that they relinquished the distinguishing characteristics of Christianity. To remove everything from Christianity that could be objected to in the name of science was, he felt, to capitulate to the enemy. For Machen the great distinguishing feature of Christianity was *the redemptive power of Christ,* and he continually differentiated "that great redemptive religion called Christianity" from "that modern non-redemptive religion" called modernism or liberalism. " 'Christ died'—that is history; 'Christ died for our sins'—that is doctrine. Without these two elements, joined in an absolutely indissoluble union, there is no Christianity."[9]

A host of other conservative spokesmen joined Macartney, Matthews, and Machen in their attack on Fosdick in particular and modernism in general. Throughout the controversy Dr. Fosdick's congregation remained loyal while

---

[7] Machen's sermon, "Christianity vs. Modern Liberalism," is not typical of the variety of fundamentalist sermons that Fosdick criticized. Although stanchly orthodox, Machen won intellectual respect from his critics along with approval from supporters.

[8] *Christianity and Liberalism* (New York: The Macmillan Company, 1923), p. 9. This book is a more extensive treatment of the topics discussed in the sermon, "Christianity vs. Modern Liberalism."

[9] *Ibid.,* p. 27.

fundamentalists from coast to coast blasted at him in print and from the pulpit. It grated on some that Fosdick, a Baptist, should occupy a Presbyterian pulpit, accept his salary from a Presbyterian congregation, and attack the official doctrine of the Presbyterian Church. In 1923, Fosdick submitted his resignation after the Presbyterian General Assembly noted with disfavor his deviation from the five points of fundamentalist doctrine, but his congregation refused to accept it.

During 1924 the controversy became more widespread and more vituperative. Liberals within and without the church rallied to Fosdick; fundamentalists in various denominations joined the attack. The 1924 session of the General Assembly, yielding to the urgings of Fosdick's influential friends, offered him the option of joining the Presbyterian Church and accepting its doctrines. This compromise was acceptable to both sides: Fosdick's friends were pleased that they had made it possible for him to remain at First Church; his enemies welcomed the prospect of having him within reach of ecclesiastical courts. Fosdick, however, declined the invitation and resigned his pulpit, explaining to his devoted congregation: "I must not do what for me would be a disingenuous and fictitious thing, under the guise of taking solemn vows."[10] But his resignation marked not the end but the enlargement and extension of Fosdick's ministry. For the next twenty years, at the Park Avenue Baptist Church, later known as the Riverside Church, Dr. Fosdick led immense audiences in "an adventure into unrestricted inter-denominationalism." Through his numerous books and his nationally broadcast radio sermons he reached millions with his liberal religious message. Having driven him out of the Presbyterian Church the fundamentalists had won a battle but lost the war.

As the fundamentalist-modernist doctrinal conflict reached its climax in the Fosdick affair, a second climactic episode was building on another front—a contest between evolution and fundamentalist religion.

In March, 1925, Tennessee made it illegal for any teacher in any public-supported school of the state "to teach any theory that denies the story of the Divine Creation of man as taught in the Bible and to teach instead that man has descended from a lower order of animals." This law was challenged by John T. Scopes, a high school biology teacher in Dayton, Tennessee. Clarence Darrow was engaged to defend Scopes; William Jennings Bryan joined attorneys for the prosecution. The Dayton "Monkey Trial," every bizarre detail of which was carried by newspaper and telegraph around the world, turned into "a duel to the

---

[10] Fosdick, *op. cit.,* p. 174.

death," as Bryan called it, between religion and science—or, more accurately, between the Biblical literalism of the fundamentalists and the new scientific knowledge.

The fundamentalists' fight against modernism, launched with the publication of *The Fundamentals* in 1909, and their conflict with the evolutionists were, of course, closely related battles, fought concomitantly and often against the same foes. Most modernist preachers were also evolutionists, though many evolutionists, notably scientists and college professors, were not concerned with religious disputation, but with the right to teach the truth as they saw it.[11] Unquestionably the foremost fundamentalist soldier on both fronts was William Jennings Bryan. As a prominent Presbyterian layman he had led the attack on Dr. Fosdick in the 1923 General Assembly, and he had by his speeches and writings established himself nationally as the leader of the anti-evolutionist forces.

The centuries-old conflict between science and religion had been sharpened in the nineteenth century by the publication of two books by Charles Darwin, *The Origin of Species* (1859) and *The Descent of Man* (1871). During the final quarter of the century one of the favorite topics of discussion in the journals, on lecture platforms, in Chautauqua tents, and in the pulpit was the question of the relation between religion and science—could a reconciliation between the two be effected, or were they, as some affirmed, irreconcilably opposed in a battle to the death?[12] But by the end of World War I, except in rural areas relatively untouched by the new knowledge, and among less-educated ministers and laymen, the conflict had been largely resolved in favor of science, or in some less literal interpretation of the Genesis story which softened apparent inconsistencies with the Darwinian hypothesis.

Bryan's entry into the controversy in the early 1920s gave great impetus to the anti-evolutionist cause and served to focus attention once again on the subject. By this time his political career was behind him, but on lecture tours around the country he was impressed by deteriorating moral standards, particularly among the young. Speaking on college campuses, he found that the miracles were called into question, that where religion and science conflicted, it was religion that was

[11] For example, Professor Henry Fairfield Osborn pointed out that "Evolution is in no sense a part of modernism; it goes back to the wise, learned, and observant founders of Christianity in Western Europe." He believed evolution to be a universal principle in nature, accepted by Augustine, Kingsley, and contemporary Catholic clergymen. *Evolution and Religion* (New York: Charles Scribner's Sons, 1923), Foreword.

[12] One dramatic example was the running debate between agnostic Robert Ingersoll and New York minister T. DeWitt Talmage. Wrage and Baskerville, *American Forum*, pp. 283–312.

abandoned, and that "a brute doctrine" was being substituted for a priceless faith. He became convinced, as Mrs. Bryan explained later, "that the teaching of evolution as a fact instead of a theory caused the students to lose faith in the Bible; first, in the story of creation, and later in other doctrines which underlie the Christian religion."[13] Bryan's position, as clearly revealed in his speeches, was indistinguishable from that expressed by fundamentalist George McCready Price in his striking aphorism: "No Adam, no fall; no fall, no atonement; no atonement, no Saviour. Accepting Evolution, how can we believe in a fall?"

From the time he entered the fight until his sudden death following the Dayton trial, Bryan waged relentless warfare against those who would undermine Christian faith, and he was never long out of the headlines. Month after month the newspapers chronicled his speeches denouncing evolution and evolutionists in New York's Hippodrome, at Chicago's Moody Church, at great universities, in small Bible colleges, at fundamentalist conventions, and before Southern legislatures pondering anti-evolution bills. He supplied less facile fundamentalists with serviceable phrases: "It's more important to know the Rock of Ages than the age of rocks"; "I would rather believe in God and reason from God down, than to believe in dirt and reason from dirt up"; "It's better for one to know that he is close to the Heavenly Father, than to know how far the stars in the heavens are apart."

Early in February, 1922, national attention was drawn to a debate in the Kentucky legislature over a bill to prohibit the teaching of evolution. Bryan, believed to be behind the Kentucky campaign, was lambasted in the newspapers, then invited by *The New York Times* to air his views on evolution in their columns.[14] In a systematic presentation of his position—of which his other writings and speeches on the subject were merely repetitions and amplifications—Bryan listed his chief objections to Darwinism: (1) it is a hypothesis, and a hypothesis is nothing more than a guess; (2) it has not one syllable in the Bible to support it; (3) there is not the slightest shred of scientific evidence to support it;[15] (4) it resorts to absurd explanations which tax human credulity; and (5) it destroys faith in religion, the only basis of morals.

Subsequent issues of the Sunday *Times* carried replies to Bryan by eminent

[13] *The Memoirs of William Jennings Bryan* (Philadelphia: John C. Winston Co., 1925), p. 479.

[14] "God and Evolution," *The New York Times,* February 26, 1922, sec. VII, p. 1.

[15] Bryan never grasped the idea of gradual evolution. The fact that no example could be found of one species in the act of evolving into another was to him sufficient proof of the falsity of the theory.

scientists and clergymen. Henry Fairfield Osborn, President of the American Museum of Natural History, attempted to show that Darwin's hypothesis, supported by a flood of proof, had become universally accepted.[16] Harry Emerson Fosdick, shocked by Bryan's "sincere but appalling obscurantism," branded his identification of "hypothesis" and "guess" as "a sophistry so shallow and palpable that one wonders at his hardihood in risking it."[17] Regarding Bryan's skepticism about evolution of species, Professor Edwin Grant Conklin of Princeton observed: "Apparently Mr. Bryan demands to see a monkey or an ass transformed into a man, though he must be familiar enough with the reverse process." Conklin went on to ridicule "the Hotspurs who demand that evolution be re-enacted 'while they wait.' "[18]

In January, 1923, speaking in Moody Church before a reported audience of 5000, Bryan delivered his address on "Moses vs. Darwin."[19] Here he clearly revealed that his principal quarrel with Darwinism was that it tended to destroy faith in the accuracy of the Bible. The greatest of all issues, he said, is whether the Bible is true or false, the Word of God or the work of man. If the Holy Bible —the only source of our conception of God, the only account of Christ, the only guide to conduct—is found fallible, then the whole structure of Christianity comes crashing down. "If the Bible is not the Word of God it has practiced a fraud on hundreds of millions of people for nineteen centuries." The speaker left no doubt as to where he stood: "I am for the Bible against all those that oppose it."

In his role as defender of the Bible against its foes, Bryan had taken a leading part in several of the numerous campaigns to pass state legislation making it illegal "to teach any theory that denies the story of the Divine creation of man as taught in the Bible." Copies of his lecture "Is the Bible True?" distributed to the Tennessee legislature both before and after the introduction of an anti-evolution bill, were thought to have been helpful in securing its passage.[20] When, in order to provide a test case, John Scopes violated the law, Bryan was the obvious choice to assist in the prosecution.

The story of the Scopes trial has provided grist for novel, stage, film, and television. It became fundamentalism's last massive stand in the 1920s. Since Scopes

[16] "Evolution and Religion," *The New York Times,* March 5, 1922, sec. VII, p. 2.
[17] "A Reply to Mr. Bryan in the Name of Religion," *The New York Times,* March 12, 1922, sec. VII, p. 2.
[18] "Bryan and Evolution," *The New York Times,* March 5, 1922, sec. VII, p. 14.
[19] *The New York Times,* January 9, 1923, p. 6. This report quotes Bryan as calling Dr. Fosdick "the most altitudinous higher critic I know of," although no such statement appears in the text reprinted in this volume from the *Moody Church News.*
[20] Bryan, *Memoirs,* p. 481.

had admittedly violated the law, the principal point at issue was the constitutionality of the law itself. But the legal issue was soon forgotten as Darrow concentrated his efforts upon discrediting Bryan and his "fool ideas." And when the
Peerless Leader was humiliated by the merciless cross-examination of Clarence
Darrow, almost literally before the eyes of the whole world, his followers and
his cause shared in the humiliation. Bryan was denied even the climactic moment
of glory to which he had looked forward—the chance to deliver his speech of
summation, which he felt was "the mountain-peak of my life's efforts." After the
decision to dispense with summary speeches at the trial, he entrusted his man-
uscript to the editor of the Chattanooga *Daily News,* who subsequently made the
text public. This last speech, a lengthy repetition of the arguments and illustra-
tions he had been presenting for years, was published on page 1 of *The New
York Times,* Wednesday, July 29, 1925, together with an account of his funeral.

After Bryan's death, lesser men made attempts to carry on in his place, but
none was successful. With the spread of knowledge and national preoccupation
with other issues, altercations between fundamentalists and modernists, evolutionists and anti-evolutionists, were driven farther and farther back in the pages
of the daily newspapers. Declining interest in this controversy may have reflected
a corresponding decline in the importance of old-time religion in the daily life
of the people. It is possible that militant defense of the "fundamentals" seemed
a less important matter than it once had. It is possible also that more and more
Americans were coming to agree with Dudley Field Malone, a counsel for
Scopes' defense, who speaking in reply to Bryan's last address said: "Infidelity
will not come from the study of science or of constantly revealed facts. Infidelity
will come to haunt the aisles of faith only when children grown to maturity
realize that they have been denied access to full knowledge by any church or
dogma. If God be God, He will not be disturbed by the truth."[21]

---

[21] *The New York Times,* September 20, 1925, p. 23.

Shall the Fundamentalists Win?

HARRY EMERSON FOSDICK

Born, Buffalo, New York, May 24, 1878. Graduated from Colgate University, 1900, and from Union Theological Seminary, 1904. Ordained Baptist minister, 1903; pastor First Church, Montclair, New Jersey, 1904–1915. Taught homiletics and practical theology, Union Theological Seminary, 1908–1946. Pastor First Presbyterian Church, New York City, 1918–1925; Park Avenue Baptist Church (later Riverside Church), 1926–1946. Radio sermons broadcast nationally. Among his numerous books are: The Meaning of Prayer (1915), The Meaning of Faith (1917), The Modern Use of the Bible (1924), Adventurous Religion (1926), Successful Christian Living (1937), A Faith for Tough Times (1952) *and* The Living of These Days (1956).*

"As I plead thus for an intellectually hospitable, tolerant, liberty-loving church, I am of course thinking primarily about this new generation."

*T*his morning we are to think of the Fundamentalist controversy which threatens to divide the American churches, as though already they were not sufficiently split and riven. A scene, suggestive for our thought, is depicted in the fifth chapter of the Book of the Acts, where the Jewish leaders hale before them Peter and others of the apostles

The First Presbyterian Church, New York City, May 21, 1922. Based on a stenographic report by Margaret Renton, the text was furnished by Harry Emerson Fosdick and is reproduced with his permission.

because they had been preaching Jesus as the Messiah. Moreover, the Jewish leaders propose to slay them, when in opposition Gamaliel speaks: "Refrain from these men, and let them alone: for if this counsel or this work be of men, it will be overthrown: but if it is of God ye will not be able to overthrow them; lest haply ye be found even to be fighting against God."

One could easily let his imagination play over this scene and could wonder how history would have come out if Gamaliel's wise tolerance could have controlled the situation. For though the Jewish leaders seemed superficially to concur in Gamaliel's judgment, they nevertheless kept up their bitter antagonism and shut the Christians from the synagogue. We know now that they were mistaken. Christianity, starting within Judaism, was not an innovation to be dreaded; it was the finest flowering out that Judaism ever had. When the Master looked back across his racial heritage and said, "I came not to destroy, but to fulfill," he perfectly described the situation. The Christian ideas of God, the Christian principles of life, the Christian hopes for the future, were all rooted in the Old Testament and grew up out of it, and the Master himself, who called the Jewish temple his Father's house, rejoiced in the glorious heritage of his people's prophets. Only, he did believe in a living God. He did not think that God was dead, having finished his words and works with Malachi. He had not simply a historic, but a contemporary God, speaking now, working now, leading his people now, from partial into fuller truth. Jesus believed in the progressiveness of revelation and these Jewish leaders did not understand that. Was this new gospel a real development which they might welcome or was it an enemy to be cast out? And they called it an enemy and excluded it. One does wonder what might have happened had Gamaliel's wise tolerance been in control.

We, however, face today a situation too similar and too urgent and too much in need of Gamaliel's attitude to spend any time making guesses at suppositious history. Already all of us must have heard about the people who call themselves the Fundamentalists. Their apparent intention is to drive out of the evangelical churches men and women of liberal opinions. I speak of them the more freely because there are no two denominations more affected by them than the Baptists and the Presbyterians. We should not identify the Fundamentalists with conservatives. All Fundamentalists are conservatives, but not all conservatives are Fundamentalists. The best conservatives can often give lessons to the liberals in true liberality of spirit, but the Fundamentalist program is essentially illiberal and intolerant. The Fundamentalists see, and they see truly, that in this last generation there have been strange new movements in Christian thought. A great mass of new knowledge has come into man's possession: new knowledge about the physical universe, its origin, its forces, its laws; new knowledge about human history and in particular about the ways in which the ancient peoples used to think in matters of religion and the methods by which they phrased and explained their spiritual experiences; and new knowledge, also, about other religions and the strangely similar ways in which men's faiths and religious practices have developed everywhere.

Now, there are multitudes of reverent Christians who have been unable to keep this new knowledge in one compartment of their minds and the Christian faith in another. They have been sure that all truth comes from the one God and is his revelation. Not, therefore, from irreverence or caprice or destructive zeal, but for the sake of intellectual and spiritual integrity, that they might really love the Lord their God not only with all their heart and soul and strength, but with all their mind, they have been trying to see this new knowledge in terms of the Christian faith and to see the Christian faith in terms of this new knowledge. Doubtless they have made many mistakes. Doubtless there have been among them reckless radicals gifted with intellectual ingenuity but lacking spiritual depth. Yet the enterprise itself seems to them indispensable to the Christian Church. The new knowledge and the old faith cannot be left antagonistic or even disparate, as though a man on Saturday could use one set of regulative ideas for his life and on Sunday could change gear to another altogether. We must be able to think our modern life clear through in Christian terms and to do that we also must be able to think our Christian life clear through in modern terms.

There is nothing new about the situation. It has happened again and again in history, as, for example, when the stationary earth suddenly began to move and the universe that had been centered in this planet was centered in the sun around which the planets whirled. Whenever such a situation has arisen, there has been only one way out: the new knowledge and the old faith had to be blended in a new combination. Now, the people in this generation who are trying to do this are the liberals, and the Fundamentalists are out on a campaign to shut against them the doors of the Christian fellowship. Shall they be allowed to succeed?

It is interesting to note where the Fundamentalists are driving in their stakes to mark out the deadline of doctrine around the church, across which no one is to pass except on terms of agreement. They insist that we must all believe in the historicity of certain special miracles, preeminently the virgin birth of our Lord; that we must believe in a special theory of inspiration—that the original documents of the scripture, which of course we no longer possess, were inerrantly dictated to men a good deal as a man might dictate to a stenographer; that we must believe in a special theory of the atonement—that the blood of our Lord, shed in a substitutionary death, placates an alienated deity and makes possible welcome for the returning sinner; and that we must believe in the second coming of our Lord upon the clouds of heaven to set up a millennium here, as the only way in which God may bring history to a worthy denouement. Such are some of the stakes which are being driven, to mark a deadline of doctrine around the church.

If a man is a genuine liberal, his primary protest is not against holding these opinions, although he may well protest against their being considered the fundamentals of Christianity. This is a free country and anybody has a right to hold these opinions or any others, if he is sincerely convinced of them. The question is: Has anybody a right to deny the Christian name to those who differ with him on such points and to shut against them the doors of the Christian fellowship? The Fundamentalists say that this must be done. In this country and on the foreign field they are trying to do it. They have actually endeavored to put on the statute books of a whole state binding laws against teaching modern biology. If they had their way, within the church they would set up in Protestantism a doctrinal tribunal more rigid than the pope's. In such an hour, delicate and dangerous, where feelings are bound to run high, I plead this morning the cause of magnanimity and liberality and tolerance of spirit. I would, if I could reach their ears, say to the Fundamentalists about the liberals what Gamaliel said to the Jews, "Refrain from these men, and let them alone: for if this counsel or this work be of men, it will be overthrown: but if it is of God ye will not be able to overthrow them; lest haply ye be found even to be fighting against God."

That we may be entirely candid and concrete and may not lose ourselves in any fog of generalities, let us this morning take two or three of these Fundamentalist items and see with reference to them what the situation is in the Christian churches. Too often we preachers have failed to talk frankly enough about the differences of opinion which exist among evangelical Christians, although everybody knows that they are there. Let us face this morning some of the differences of opinion with which somehow we must deal.

We may as well begin with the vexed and mooted question of the virgin birth of our Lord. I know people in the Christian churches, ministers, missionaries, laymen, devoted lovers of the Lord and servants of the gospel, who, alike as they are in their personal devotion to the Master, hold quite different points of view about a matter like the virgin birth. Here, for example, is one point of view: that the virgin birth is to be accepted as historical fact; it actually happened; there was no other way for a personality like the Master to come into this world except by a special biological miracle. That is one point of view, and many are the gracious and beautiful souls who hold it. But, side by side with them in the evangelical churches is a group of equally loyal and reverent people who would say that the virgin birth is not to be accepted as an historic fact.

To believe in virgin birth as an explanation of great personality is one of the familiar ways in which the ancient world was accustomed to account for unusual superiority. Many people suppose that only once in history do we run across a record of supernatural birth. Upon the contrary, stories of miraculous generation are among the commonest traditions of antiquity. Especially is this true about the founders of great religions. According to the records of their faiths, Buddha and Zoroaster and Lao-Tse and Mahavira were all supernaturally born. Moses, Confucius and Mohammed are the only great founders of religion in history to

whom miraculous birth is not attributed. That is to say, when a personality arose
so high than men adored him, the ancient world attributed his superiority to some
special divine influence in his generation, and they commonly phrased their faith
in terms of miraculous birth. So Pythagoras was called virgin born, and Plato,
and Augustus Caesar, and many more. Knowing this, there are within the evangelical churches large groups of people whose opinion about our Lord's coming
would run as follows: those first disciples adored Jesus—as we do; when they
thought about his coming they were sure that he came specially from God—as
we are; this adoration and conviction they associated with God's special influence
and intention in his birth—as we do; but they phrased it in terms of a biological
miracle that our modern minds cannot use. So far from thinking that they have
given up anything vital in the New Testament's attitude towards Jesus, these
Christians remember that the two men who contributed most to the church's
thought of the divine meaning of the Christ were Paul and John, who never even
distantly allude to the virgin birth.

Here in the Christian churches are these two groups of people and the question
which the Fundamentalists raise is this: Shall one of them throw the other out?
Has intolerance any contribution to make to this situation? Will it persuade anybody of anything? Is not the Christian church large enough to hold within her
hospitable fellowship people who differ on points like this and agree to differ
until the fuller truth be manifested? The Fundamentalists say not. They say
that the liberals must go. Well, if the Fundamentalists should succeed, then out
of the Christian church would go some of the best Christian life and consecration
of this generation—multitudes of men and women, devout and reverent Christians, who need the church and whom the church needs.

Consider another matter on which there is a sincere difference of opinion between evangelical Christians: the inspiration of the Bible. One point of view is
that the original documents of the scripture were inerrantly dictated by God to
men. Whether we deal with the story of creation or the list of the dukes of
Edom or the narratives of Solomon's reign or the Sermon on the Mount or the
thirteenth chapter of first Corinthians, they all came in the same way and they
all came as no other book ever came. They were inerrantly dictated; everything
there—scientific opinions, medical theories, historical judgments, as well as spiritual insights—is infallible. That is one idea of the Bible's inspiration. But side
by side with those who hold it, lovers of the Book as much as they, are multitudes
of people who never think about the Bible so. Indeed, that static and mechanical
theory of inspiration seems to them a positive peril to the spiritual life. The
Koran similarly has been regarded by Mohammedans as having been infallibly
written in heaven before it came to earth. But the Koran enshrines the theological and ethical ideas of Arabia at the time when it was written. God an oriental
monarch, fatalistic submission to his will as man's chief duty, the use of force
on unbelievers, polygamy, slavery—they are all in the Koran. The Koran was
ahead of the day when it was written, but, petrified by an artificial idea of inspira-

tion, it has become a millstone about the neck of Mohammedanism.

When one turns from the Koran to the Bible, he finds this interesting situation. All of these ideas, which we dislike in the Koran, are somewhere in the Bible. Conceptions from which we now send missionaries to convert Mohammedans are to be found in the Book. There one can find God thought of as an oriental monarch; there, too, are patriarchal polygamy, and slave systems, and the use of force on unbelievers. Only in the Bible these elements are not final; they are always being superseded; revelation is progressive. The thought of God moves out from oriental kingship to compassionate fatherhood; treatment of unbelievers moves out from the use of force to the appeals of love; polygamy gives way to monogamy; slavery, never explicitly condemned before the New Testament closes, is nevertheless being undermined by ideas that in the end, like dynamite, will blast its foundations to pieces. Repeatedly one runs on verses like this: "It was said to them of old time. . . . but I say unto you"; "God, having of old time spoken unto the fathers in the prophets by divers portions and in divers manners, hath at the end of these days spoken unto us in his Son"; "The times of ignorance therefore God overlooked; but now he commandeth men that they should all everywhere repent"; and over the doorway of the New Testament into the Christian world stand the words of Jesus: "When he, the spirit of truth is come, he shall guide you into all the truth." That is to say, finality in the Koran is behind; finality in the Bible is ahead. We have not reached it. We cannot yet compass all of it. God is leading us out toward it. There are multitudes of Christians, then, who think, and rejoice as they think, of the Bible as the record of the progressive unfolding of the character of God to his people from early primitive days until the great unveiling in Christ; to them the Book is more inspired and more inspiring than ever it was before; and to go back to a mechanical and static theory of inspiration would mean to them the loss of some of the most vital elements in their spiritual experience and in their appreciation of the Book.

Here in the Christian church today are these two groups, and the question which the Fundamentalists have raised is this: Shall one of them drive the other out? Do we think the cause of Jesus Christ will be furthered by that? If he should walk through the ranks of this congregation this morning, can we imagine him claiming as his own those who hold one idea of inspiration and sending from him into outer darkness those who hold another? You cannot fit the Lord Christ into that Fundamentalist mold. The church would better judge his judgment. For in the middle west the Fundamentalists have had their way in some communities and a Christian minister tells us the consequence. He says that all the educated people are looking for their religion outside the churches.

Consider another matter upon which there is a serious and sincere difference of opinion between evangelical Christians: the second coming of our Lord. The second coming was the early Christian phrasing of hope. No one in the ancient world had ever thought, as we do, of development, progress, gradual change, as God's way of working out his will in human life and institutions. They thought

of human history as a series of ages succeeding one another with abrupt sudden-
ness. The Graeco-Roman world gave the names of metals to the ages—gold,
silver, bronze, iron. The Hebrews had their ages too—the original paradise in
which man began, the cursed world in which man now lives, the blessed messianic kingdom some day suddenly to appear on the clouds of heaven. It was the
Hebrew way of expressing hope for the victory of God and righteousness. When
the Christians came they took over that phrasing of expectancy and the New
Testament is aglow with it. The preaching of the apostles thrills with the glad
announcement, "Christ is coming!"

In the evangelical churches today there are differing views of this matter. One
view is that Christ is literally coming, externally on the clouds of heaven, to set
up his kingdom here. I never heard that teaching in my youth at all. It has
always had a new resurrection when desperate circumstances came and man's
only hope seemed to lie in divine intervention. It is not strange, then, that during
these chaotic, catastrophic years there has been a fresh rebirth of this old phrasing
of expectancy. "Christ is coming!" seems to many Christians the central message
of the gospel. In the strength of it some of them are doing great service for the
world. But unhappily, many so over-emphasize it that they outdo anything the
ancient Hebrews or the ancient Christians ever did. They sit still and do nothing
and expect the world to grow worse and worse until he comes.

Side by side with these to whom the second coming is a literal expectation,
another group exists in the evangelical churches. They, too, say, "Christ is coming!" They say it with all their hearts; but they are not thinking of an external
arrival on the clouds. They have assimilated as part of the divine revelation the
exhilarating insight which these recent generations have given to us, that development is God's way of working out his will. They see that the most desirable
elements in human life have come through the method of development. Man's
music has developed from the rhythmic noise of beaten sticks until we have in
melody and harmony possibilities once undreamed. Man's painting has developed
from the crude outlines of the cavemen until in line and color we have achieved
unforeseen results and possess latent beauties yet unfolded. Man's architecture has
developed from the crude huts of primitive men until our cathedrals and business
buildings reveal alike an incalculable advance and an unimaginable future. Development does seem to be the way in which God works. And these Christians,
when they say that Christ is coming, mean that, slowly it may be, but surely, his
will and principles will be worked out by God's grace in human life and institutions, until "he shall see of the travail of his soul and shall be satisfied."

These two groups exist in the Christian churches and the question raised by
the Fundamentalists is: Shall one of us drive the other out? Will that get us
anywhere? Multitudes of young men and women at this season of the year are
graduating from our schools of learning, thousands of them Christians who may
make us older ones ashamed by the sincerity of their devotion to God's will on
earth. They are not thinking in ancient terms that leave ideas of progress out.

They cannot think in those terms. There could be no greater tragedy than that the Fundamentalists should shut the door of the Christian fellowship against such.

I do not believe for one moment that the Fundamentalists are going to succeed. Nobody's intolerance can contribute anything to the solution of the situation which we have described. If, then, the Fundamentalists have no solution of the problem, where may we expect to find it? In two concluding comments let us consider our reply to that enquiry.

The first element that is necessary is a spirit of tolerance and Christian liberty. When will the world learn that intolerance solves no problems? This is not a lesson which the Fundamentalists alone need to learn; the liberals also need to learn it. Speaking, as I do, from the viewpoint of liberal opinions, let me say that if some young, fresh mind here this morning is holding new ideas, has fought his way through, it may be by intellectual and spiritual struggle to novel positions, and is tempted to be intolerant about old opinions, offensively to condescend to those who hold them and to be harsh in judgment on them, he may well remember that people who held those old opinions have given the world some of the noblest character and the most memorable service that it ever has been blessed with, and that we of the younger generation will prove our case best, not by controversial intolerance, but by producing, with our new opinions, something of the depth and strength, nobility and beauty of character that in other times were associated with other thoughts. It was a wise liberal, the most adventurous man of his day—Paul the apostle—who said, "Knowledge puffeth up, but love buildeth up."

Nevertheless, it is true that just now the Fundamentalists are giving us one of the worst exhibitions of bitter intolerance that the churches of this country have ever seen. As one watches them and listens to them, he remembers the remark of General Armstrong of Hampton Institute: "Cantankerousness is worse than heterodoxy." There are many opinions in the field of modern controversy concerning which I am not sure whether they are right or wrong, but there is one thing I am sure of: courtesy and kindliness and tolerance and humility and fairness are right. Opinions may be mistaken; love never is.

As I plead thus for an intellectually hospitable, tolerant, liberty-loving church, I am of course thinking primarily about this new generation. We have boys and girls growing up in our homes and schools, and because we love them we may well wonder about the church which will be waiting to receive them. Now, the worst kind of church that can possibly be offered to the allegiance of the new generation is an intolerant church. Ministers often bewail the fact that young people turn from religion to science for the regulative ideas of their lives. But this is easily explicable. Science treats a young man's mind as though it were really important. A scientist says to a young man: "Here is the universe challenging our investigation. Here are the truths which we have seen, so far. Come, study with us! See what we already have seen and then look further to see more, for science is an intellectual adventure for the truth." Can you imagine any man who is worth while turning from that call to the church, if the church seems to him to say: "Come and we will feed you opinions from a spoon. No thinking is allowed here except such as brings you to certain specified, predetermined conclusions. These prescribed opinions we will give you in advance of your thinking; now think, but only so as to reach these results." My friends, nothing in all the world is so much worth thinking of as God, Christ, the Bible, sin and salvation, the divine purposes for humankind, life everlasting. But you cannot challenge the dedicated thinking of this generation to these sublime themes upon any such terms as are laid down by an intolerant church.

The second element which is needed if we are to reach a happy solution of this problem is a clear insight into the main issues of modern Christianity and a sense of penitent shame that the Christian church should be quarreling over little matters when the world is dying of great needs. If, during the war, when the nations were wrestling upon the very brink of hell and at times all seemed lost, you chanced to hear two men in an altercation about some minor matter of sectarian denominationalism, could you restrain your indignation? You said, "What can you do with folks like this who, in the face of colossal issues, play with the tiddledywinks and peccadillos of religion?" So, now, when from the terrific questions of this generation one is called away by the noise of this Fundamentalist controversy, he thinks it almost unforgivable that men should tithe mint and anise and cummin, and quarrel over them, when the world is perishing for the lack of the weightier matters of the law, justice, and mercy, and faith.

These last weeks, in the minister's confessional, I have heard stories from the depths of human lives where men and women were wrestling with the elemental problems of misery and sin—stories that put upon a man's heart a burden of vicarious sorrow, even though he does but listen to them. Here was real human need crying out after the living God revealed in Christ. Consider all the multitudes of men who so need God, and then think of Christian churches making of themselves a cockpit of controversy when there is not a single thing at stake in the controversy on which depends the salvation of human souls. That is the trouble with this whole business. So much of it does not matter! And there is one thing that does matter—more than anything else in all the world—that men in their personal lives and in their social relationships should know Jesus Christ.

Just a week ago I received a letter from a friend in Asia Minor. He says that they are killing the Armenians yet; that the Turkish deportations still are going on; that lately they crowded Christian men, women and children into a conventicle of worship and burned them together in the house where they had prayed to their Father and to ours. During the war, when it was good propaganda to stir up our bitter hatred against the enemy we heard of such atrocities, but not now! Two weeks ago, Great Britain, shocked and stirred by what is going on in Armenia, did ask the Government of the United States to join her in investigating the atrocities and trying to help! Our government said that it was not any of our business at all. The present world situation smells to heaven! And now, in the presence of colossal problems, which must be solved in Christ's name and for Christ's sake, the Fundamentalists propose to drive out from the Christian churches all the consecrated souls who do not agree with their theory of inspiration. What immeasurable folly!

Well, they are not going to do it; certainly not in this vicinity. I do not even know in this congregation whether anybody has been tempted to be a Fundamentalist. Never in this church have I caught one accent of intolerance. God keep us always so and ever increasing areas of the Christian fellowship: intellectually hospitable, open-minded, liberty-loving, fair, tolerant, not with the tolerance of indifference as though we did not care about the faith, but because always our major emphasis is upon the weightier matters of the law.

Moses vs. Darwin

WILLIAM JENNINGS BRYAN

Born, Salem, Illinois, March 19, 1860; died, Dayton, Ten-
nessee, July 26, 1925. Graduated from Illinois College, 1881,
and Union College of Law, Chicago, 1883. Practiced law,
Jacksonville, Illinois; moved, 1887, to Lincoln, Nebraska.
United States Representative, 1891–1895. Unsuccessful Dem-
ocratic candidate for United States Senate, 1894, and for
Presidency, 1896, 1900, 1908. Edited weekly Commoner,
1901–1913. Secretary of State under Wilson; resigned June,
1915. A perennial Chautauqua lecturer, his most famous
lecture was "The Prince of Peace." Devoted final years to
a defense of religious fundamentalism; appeared for the
prosecution in Scopes trial in Tennessee, 1925; died shortly
after close of trial.

"It makes a wonderful difference whether a man traces his
ancestry to the jungle or to the throne of God."

I appreciate very much the opportunity of speaking in
this hall on this subject to this audience. Mr. Moody
was one of the first evangelists I ever heard. I do not know of anyone whom I
have heard preach who had more influence on my thought, my feeling, and my
life than Dwight L. Moody. And therefore I always come with pleasure into
the institution to which his name has been given.

The question that is the largest in the world, the greatest issue before the

Moody Church, Chicago, Illinois, January 8, 1923. Text is based upon a stenographic report
unchanged by Bryan and printed in *The Moody Church News*, VIII, no. 1 (January, 1923),
1–3, 6–7.

world today is not determined by political conventions. While I regard government as a very important thing, I long since learned that the most important things of life are not touched by the government. Why, my friends, if a man's ideas are not what they ought to be he can be miserable under any form of government, and if they are what they ought to be he will be happy under any form of government. Government touches only a part of the life; religion touches all of the life. Government touches only that part of man's existence which is spent on earth and if we are right in our belief, that is but an infinitely small part of an infinitely large circle.

The largest questions in the world today are not being discussed at Paris. They are beyond all questions of government, and the greatest issues in the world today transcend in importance any question of politics in this country, and any question of international politics. The greatest of all the issues is whether the Bible is true or false. More rests upon it than upon any other subject or any other issue. I will prove it to you—whether the Bible is true or false, whether it is the Word of God or the work of man. If the Bible is the work of man it will fall. If it can be convicted of being the work of man, it is the greatest impostor that this world ever saw. If the Bible is not the Word of God, it has practiced a fraud on hundreds of millions of people for nineteen centuries. If it is not true, it not only should be rejected, but driven out of society. And if they can convict this Bible of being a fraud don't think it is going to be retained for its literary merit. If it is convicted of fraud it will not have the value that it would have had had it not claimed to be the Word of God; if it is His revealed will to men, it cannot die. Why is this issue so important? Because the civilized world has but one conception of God, and that is the Bible conception. Why is it so important? Because it gives the only account of Christ. Because it is the only guide that we can rely on as an infallible guide or light for our feet and light to our path. This Bible, I say, if it is true, gives us a conception of God. It gives an explanation of Christ, and it gives us an infallible guide, the only standard that we have. I want to show you how important this Bible is.

I affirm that belief in God is the most fundamental of all thoughts, that a belief in God underlies civilization. Let me show you what rests upon belief in God, before I take up that which menaces belief in God. If belief in God is an immaterial thing, you will not be concerned whether anything menaces it or not. But if it is essential to society as I believe it is, and necessary to civilization, then anything that menaces belief in God is the most destructive thing in the world. Let me show you: First, a consciousness of God's presence in the life. That is the most comforting thing that a human being knows, and he can't have it unless he believes in God. My friends, there is no human being who does not recognize the finiteness of man, and time and again we come into the presence of conditions that make us see how small we are. If there is anybody who has an exaggerated idea of his own power let him go to the death bed of one who is near and dear to him and let him stand there as the life ebbs away, and see how small and helpless he is in the presence of death. There are conditions that we cannot understand. But we can fall back on the strong arms of the infinite and when we approach the end of life, if our hearts have been inclined about great causes and we feel the powers of the body slipping away, and we feel the lethargy stealing over our mind, and the eyes grow dim and darkness gathers, and we know that the end is near, into whose hands can we entrust ourselves, except into the hands of the One who gave our powers and faculties to us? There is nothing that will take the place of a consciousness of God's presence and you can't have it unless you believe in God.

What next? A sense of responsibility to God. That is the most potent influence that acts upon human life. In all the journey from the cradle to the grave there is no restraining path that approaches the consciousness of responsibility to God. You can't build society or civilization on but one thing, and that is morality. And there is only one thing upon which morality is built and that is religion. And religion rests on God.

Third, unless you believe in God you will not pray. You must not only believe in God, but in a personal God. If it were possible to wipe out of every human heart and mind all thought of God, and with it all thought of prayer—if it were possible to conceive of a situation where after tonight no human heart anywhere would ever be raised again in gratitude to God and in appeal for forgiveness of sin and in petition for guidance, if never human heart again was open to divine suggestion, and no human being ever cared what God thought, or had any desire to do His will, can you imagine the chaos that would follow?

Without a belief in God there can be no belief in a future life with its awards and punishment. If there be no God, then death ends all. What shall we substitute in hours of temptation for the belief that at the Judgment Day men must render an account of the deeds done in the flesh? And unless there be a God the world must wait in vain for the coming of a universal brotherhood. We trace our kinship with each other to the common Father of us all. If there is no Father, there is no brother. There are only two attitudes that a human being can assume when he deals with his fellowmen. One is the attitude of a brother, when he is restrained by the ties of kinship. There is only one other. What is it? The attitude of a brute, when he devours with the hunger of a beast.

If there be no God there can be no Son of God as Saviour of the world. Have you thought what it would mean to get Christ out of the world? It is an idle question. Christ is so interwoven with everything that is good that He cannot be taken out of the world. We could not take Him out if we tried. There will never be a movement for the uplifting of mankind that will not be inspired by the thought of the Man of Galilee. He is the great Fact of history. There is no other fact to be mentioned in comparison. He is the great Figure of all time.

If there is no God, then there is no Bible, the Word of God. Unless there is a Heavenly Father with a will to reveal there can be no revealed will of God. What would it mean to take the Bible out of the world? I believe the Bible has done more for civilization than all the other books combined. Let me present it this way: If we had to choose between the Bible and all the other books that have been written, I think it would be infinitely better to let all other books go and keep the Bible alone and build the world anew on God's Word. That may seem like a strong statement, but I am just beginning. I have a proposition stronger than that. But I did not want to spring that first!

I have always been on the defensive, but I have been aggressively so. I am always defending the things that are old and time honored. But when I want to defend something I always attack the enemy who attacks the thing I defend, and fight the battle on his territory. Knowing that we have this Bible to defend, and knowing from whom, I am going to shell the position of the enemy and bring him out from under cover. And I have a proposition to make, and I submit it and am ready to defend it. I challenge any professor in any college in the United States that draws his pay from the public treasury (I am not extending this challenge to all colleges—just those supported by taxation. We have some colleges supported by endowments that don't preach the Bible and you can't make them do it until the money runs out), but I am speaking of public institutions. I want some professor who is drawing his salary from the taxes of the people to answer it if he dares. I know lots of them believe it, but they won't answer it. Here is the proposition: There are three verses in the first chapter of Genesis that mean more to man than all the books that man has ever written in all the libraries of the world. Is that strong enough? And we have all the rest of the Bible besides. The first verse of the three is the first verse of the first chapter of Genesis, "In the beginning God created heaven and earth." I affirm that is the only sentence ever written upon which you can stand and explain the origin of life and defend the explanation. Search your libraries. Read all the books man has ever written and find out from any other source the origin of life. Life is the one important thing in all the world. And that is the only verse that tells us how life began. We give the atheist too much latitude. We let him ask all the questions. Do you know of any reason why the atheist should be given the childish task of asking questions? A five-year-old child can ask questions that no grown person can answer. Why should we let the atheist run around like a child asking questions that they can't answer themselves? The Christian might just as well admit that any question that denies infinite knowledge cannot be answered by his finite mind. If we say to the atheist, "We will take turn about asking questions. We will ask one and you will ask one." Isn't that fair? Well, what is his question? There is only one, "Where do you begin?" And our answer is, *We begin where the Bible begins.* And where does the Bible begin? "In the beginning." Where else could it begin? In the beginning God, all-wise, all-powerful and all-loving. Yes, we begin with the first great Cause sufficient for anything that can come thereafter.

Having answered the atheist's first question it is now our turn and we ask our first question. It is the same as his, "Where do you begin?" And then his trouble begins. Why should an atheist ask you where you begin unless he has a starting point? It is just as necessary that an atheist shall have a beginning point for his philosophy as that a Christian shall. Where does the atheist begin? Have you ever heard of any of them going back farther than we do? They can't begin with God because they deny there is one, and they can't go back of God because there is nothing there. In the beginning, God. I have never known one to go back farther than the Nebular Hypothesis, and it begins some distance on this side of the beginning. And then the hypothesis begins by assuring that two things existed that the hypothesis does not try to explain. It begins by assuming that matter is here. Where did it come from? They don't know. When did it come? They don't know. How did it come? They don't know. They just say it is here. They say that they assume it was divided into particles infinitely fine. Why not finer? And they assume that each particle was separated from every other particle. And after they have it all divided they cannot bring it together, so they have to assume that force existed. Where did it come from? They don't know. When did it come, and how? They don't know. They say, "Let us suppose that matter and force are here." Why have I not a right to suppose? *I would rather believe in God and reason from God down than to believe in dirt and reason from dirt up.*

These fellows say I don't know anything. They try to rule me out on an intellectual qualification. I know more than they think I do. I know this: that in all the books in all the libraries ever written there are only two lines of reasoning about the creation. One is from God down and the other is from inanimate matter up, and I assert that our line of reasoning from God down is more reasonable than theirs. It is more rational. I affirm that there has never been suggested by anybody at any time, anywhere, a substitute for the first verse of the first chapter of Genesis that was as rational and easy to understand, as easy to believe, as easy to explain and as easy to defend. It is the only solid rock in all the world.

The first verse gives the origin of life. What is the second? It is the twenty-fourth. That is the verse where Moses states as God's Word God's Law governing reproduction. If life is to exist on this earth it must reproduce, and if life is to be reproduced it must be reproduced according to law. I affirm that that is the only sentence in the whole world that states the greatest scientific fact in the world, and that is the law which governs life's continuity on earth. My friends, we don't call Moses a scientist, and yet all the scientists together have never given the world as much science that is important as Moses gave in one sentence when he gave God's law of reproduction according to time. That is the greatest scientific fact in the world. It is the basis of all our conclusions. You can bring together all the other facts of science or cases of science and all of them melted into one do not mean as much to man as the law of continuity of life. And that law has never been violated. They have never found one living thing in plant life or animal life that has reproduced except according to kind, and man, being a little lower than the angels, man with all his power, has never yet been able to coerce a single living species to violate God's law and cross the line of species.

The only thing that in nineteen hundred years has really menaced the fundamental fact of God and religion is the attempt to substitute a man's guess for the
law of God. And they have found nothing yet to support the man's guess. The
first verse gives us the law of life. The second gives us the law of continuity.
And what is the third verse? It is the 26th. That is the verse that gives you the
only explanation of man's presence on the earth. I affirm that no man has ever
been able to guess the riddle of life. No man has ever been able to explain why
man is here. How can he without revelation? Man comes into this world without
his own volition. He has not one word to say, as to the age in which he will be
born or the land in which he will first see the light or the race of which he will
be a member, or the family environment that will surround him in his youth.
He is here absolutely by chance, and when he comes he does not know how long
he will stay, and he can't insure himself for one hour against disease or death.
And yet he is commander-in-chief of all that is. Try to solve the riddle if you
can, without revelation. You will find the explanation in the 26th verse. My
friends, when a man finds out that he is a child of a King, when he finds out
that God, after making all other things made him in his own image, and gave
him the earth as his inheritance, when he finds that out and knows that he is
part of a plan and is here for a purpose, he realizes that his highest duty, and
it ought to be his greatest pleasure, is to try to find out God's will concerning him
and do it. For when he seeks to know God's will he finds it. God says all these
things are yours, but obey. Obey, and I have linked your happiness to your virtue.
Obey, and I have linked your success to your righteousness. Obey, and I have
made it possible for you to rise up to and live upon that exalted plane to which
I invite all My children.

Now let the atheists, the agnostics, the professors get to work and give us
something more important. And besides these three verses we have the rest of
the Bible as well. We have the consolation of the Psalms. We have the inspiration of the prophets. We have the instruction that comes from God's dealing
with his chosen people. We have the history of Jesus and His atoning blood.
We have a code of morality to stand for all time. We have a gospel for every
human being. If the Bible is true, you ought to defend it.

What menaces the Bible? You say there are some hypocrites in the church.
Yes, there are, but they can't overthrow the Bible. The Bible overthrows them.
You call them hypocrites because they don't live up to the Bible. You say there
are good people outside the church. They are only good because they borrowed
their morality from the church without the honesty to give the church the credit.
The two greatest hindrances to the church are people inside who get their
morality outside and people outside who get their morality inside. But that can't
destroy the church or the Bible. There is only one thing that in nineteen centuries has seriously menaced the Bible and belief in God, and that is a man's
guess. Darwin gets the credit for his hypothesis, but his grandfather before him

had some ideas that the Bible was not entirely true, and that man may not have come by special act from God. You can go all the way back in history and you will find suggestions that there were Greeks who held a brute origin for man. But Darwin gets the credit for it because he attempted to explain how it came about.

The *Dearborn Independent* sent out to a number of presidents of colleges and universities and asked several questions, among them two, the first one, "Do biologists now contend that man came up from the ape line?" and the second, "Did Darwin think so?" And I think all of them answered who believe in evolution, that they do not now contend that man came up from the ape line. They say the modern thought is that he came up from the same tree but by a different branch. And all but two of them say they don't understand that Darwin ever taught that man came up through the ape line. It looks like they did not read Darwin, and they probably got their information from somebody who had gotten theirs from somebody else. They deny Darwin said it, and yet it is there in black and white. He not only had us coming up from the ape, but he had us coming up from European instead of American apes. But what interests me is that we have shaken off the ape's tale [*sic*]. It is much easier to believe that man came from a monkey, or a gorilla than to believe he came by another line and then destroyed the line. I think it is perfectly fair that when a man comes out and says that we are descendants of animals that he shall give us his family tree before he tells us about ours.

There are three objections that I have to Darwin's doctrine. The first is that it is not true. But that is not the most important objection. There are lots of lies that are not worth fooling about. It is the most ridiculous thing proposed seriously by sober men. But that is not the greatest objection, because there are lots of funny things that you need not worry about. But it is destructive. I want first to show you that it isn't true. I want to show you that people sometimes use words that they don't understand. And when they understand them they quit using them. I venture to assert that there is not one man who says he is an evolutionist who knows what evolution means. I say this because I have had them try to explain it and they show that they do not understand. I affirm that no evolutionist has ever given an illustration of evolution, because nothing has ever evolved so far as we know, and until they find something that evolves they can't illustrate evolution. They don't know what the word hypothesis means. Yet they all talk about it. What do you suppose it means? It means a man's guess. Go to the dictionary and you will find that guess is given as a synonym for hypothesis. If Darwin had called it a guess it would not have lasted a year. It has stayed sixty years as a hypothesis. One of these professors sits behind a desk with glasses on and hurls "hypothesis" at a student and it knocks him senseless. Why doesn't he call it a guess? Darwin guessed that about two hundred million years ago one or a few germs of life appeared on this planet. That is Darwin's hypothesis, although his son put it at fifty-seven million. Why do you suppose the son could not guess as much as the father? Why, he hadn't guessed as long. And some still younger have guessed twenty-four million, and some very old have put it as high as two hundred. Darwin said there were one or a few germs. I read a book on evolution in which the author said every living animal came from one germ and that every living thing in the vegetable world came from one germ, and every living thing in the animal world came from one germ. And back of those two germs there was one germ from which these two came. Oh, what a day in which to live when one germ would have two children, one an animal and the other a vegetable. Darwin guessed that one or a few germs appeared. When he was a young man he said God put them here. After a while he apologized for it, and he used the word appeared because it did not indicate where they came from or how. He guessed that they appeared and they began to reproduce. Some scientists say they could not have done it. And I would rather guess with them than with Darwin. Some guessed that if a few had appeared they would have died before they could have reproduced. They just kept on, according to Darwin, until finally we have between two and three million species. I am so conservative that I put it at one million. I know that we have a million distinct species in the animal and vegetable kingdom, and Darwin's guess is that every one of the million species came by slow and gradual change from one or a few invisible germs of life that appeared two hundred million years ago. Isn't that plain enough? If it were true that two hundred million years ago there were a few germs which appeared and began to reproduce and continued changing gradually until we have a million species, our contention is that every square foot of the earth's surface would teem with conclusive proof of the change. We say that it is not true. Why? Because they have investigated for sixty years and they have examined millions of species from insects so small that they have to examine them through a microscope, and they have yet to find the first living thing that was not perfect, for there is not a single one in transition from one species to another. Isn't it absurd, my friends, to say that everything changed when they can't find anything that changed?

If any of you think I am taking any risk when I announce this subject I want to tell you that if Darwin's descendants ever sue me for slandering their ancestors, there will be a great trial. And if the case is called for trial, and the sheriff goes to the door and says, "Oh, yes, oh, yes, all the witnesses of Darwin will come into court," and not a one will come. And the judge will say, "Mr. Bryan, as the burden of proof is on the plaintiff, and as they have presented no evidence, you need not call your witnesses." But I tell him I want to call them anyway. Then I will take an alphabetical list of all the species, a million of them. I will bring them all into court, and I will ask them one question and they will answer in concert. I will say, "Do any of you species know of any change in your family?" And every one will say, "Not in my family." With no witnesses on one side and a million on the other, that is the way the case will stand. I tell you that there is no scientist on earth who will stand before a body of scientists and show where any species ever developed into any other, and yet they want you to believe that all species have come by slow and gradual change by the operation of resident or interior forces without any aid from above.

There was a meeting the other day of the American Society for the Advancement of Science. They met at Cambridge, and passed a resolution declaring that they believed in organic evolution of plants, animals and man, and protested against any legislation that would prevent it being taught in the schools. And that Society had a meeting in Toronto a year ago, and on the 28th day of December a man named Bateson came on the scene from England at the invitation of this Society. The papers said they had eleven thousand members. This man Bateson came at their invitation and spoke to them at Toronto on the 28th day of December, and he discussed evolution and his speech was published in "Science," a magazine published in New York that bears that name, and in that speech Bateson said to those scientists that he would give them every effort that had ever been made to find the origin of species, and he took up every effort and traced it from the beginning to end, and told them that *never in one single case had the experiment succeeded*. He said, "We have faith in evolution, but we have our doubts about the origin of species." There is no evolution unless it accounts for the species. And he says we have faith in evolution but have our doubts about the origin of the species. "But don't be discouraged," he adds, "we may find it tomorrow." That is optimism.

Out in Nebraska somebody found a tooth, just one tooth, no jaw bone, no skull, no skeleton, just a tooth. But the man who discovered it took it to New York and showed it to Professor Osborn, the head of the museum there. And he called in some other spirits like-minded and they held a postmortem examination on an extinct animal, and solemnly decided that that tooth came from an animal nearer to man than any other animal. They had about settled down to that belief when somebody found a skull of a monkey-man in Africa. And he thought that came from the animal nearest to man. And it looks as if the scientific world was going to be divided by a controversy between a tooth on one side and the skull of a monkey on the other. I think they are wasting lots of time, but if there is going to be a fight, if it is Nebraska against Africa, I'm for Nebraska. I love every foot of its land. And I love the people even better than before the last election. And if it has got to be a fight between Nebraska and Africa, count me for the tooth.

Isn't it ridiculous for learned men to get so excited about a tooth or a skull? When a fellow wakes up with the idea that he has brute blood in his veins he is so interested in tracing his family tree that he will *go around the world to see a skeleton when he would not go across the street to save a soul*. You can't interest these men in the saving of souls, but they are very much interested in a five-toed horse. There is one fact that is worth all the resemblances in the world, and that is that you can't find a species that ever changed, and if they can't find where two species in the plant life came one from the other or the two from a common ancestor, why do they try to drag man from his high state down to a brute level?

People have said, "Do you mean to say there is no evidence upon which to believe this evolutionary hypothesis?" No, absolutely none. "Well," they say, "how on earth can these intelligent men believe it if it is not true?" You can't go to a penitentiary in the United States but what you will find college graduates there, and yet we have got men teaching in our schools who believe all you have to do is to train the mind. If they understood the Bible they would know that "out of the heart are the issues of life." They would know that "as a man think-eth in his heart so is he." When the heart goes wrong it takes the mind with it. There isn't an ounce of love in all the minds in the world. There is no morality in the human mind. The mind is a mental machine. It works for its master, and the master is the heart. And the mind of a trained man will work just as willingly for a burglar as it will to plan service to society.

These men are mind-worshippers. They are trying to substitute education for religion. Evolution flatters the mind of a vain man. The evolutionist says to the student, "You can't understand the Bible. There are the miracles. You can't understand them. Let me give you something that makes everything plain. Evolu-tion is the law, and when you understand evolution you understand everything." It is flattering to the mind, and some of our minds are susceptible to flattery. But it is something else. I think it is a lazy man's theology, and it is acceptable and attractive to a lazy man. It is the laziest theory that any man ever proposed. If a man believed his ancestors were animals all he has to do on Sunday morning is to stand in front of a cage of animals and speculate on how far he has come. But *if he is a Christian he has got to go to church and consider how far he has to go before he is perfect.* Christianity is no lazy man's job. There never was a religion that stirred to energy like Christianity does. It tells us that every human being is traveling every day and every moment up or down, either rising to the highest place that God has made possible or sinking to the lowest level that man can reach. Christianity gives us an ideal within sight of the weakest and lowliest and yet so high that the best are kept with their faces turned upward. Evolution chills hope and courage and ambition. If you will take a book on psychology written by a believer in Darwin you will find he tells you that man is just a bundle of brute instincts, and it isn't your fault if you do wrong. *It makes a wonderful difference whether a man traces his ancestry to the jungle or to the throne of God.* If our ideals are below us we are living down. If they are above us we strive to climb up.

I want for a moment to speak of the absurdity of it. I realize that right here I am going to deal with the most important of the objections, and therefore I am going to be brief. I want to say to you that this is not only untrue—this hypothesis that links man to the animal—but it is explained by explanations that are more fantastic and unreal and absurd than anything that you can find in any book of fiction—more fantastic than the Arabian Nights. I want to tell you of a few of them and then you will understand why these fellows don't like to have someone talk before their students who exposes their ridiculous position. It is all right for them to make fun of Jonah, but they don't like to have any one make fun of them. There is nothing in the Bible that can be made the object of ridicule like the guesses that they give. The first I take from Darwin. Do you know Darwin thought man's brain was superior to woman's brain? Poor Darwin! If he had lived fifty years longer he would have taken it back. . . . I am telling you what the professors teach to your children, and they do it without a smile. Do you know that they actually believe that the eye came by development; that God did not make man as he is, but according to Darwin everything we have came from things invisible, and through a process of change. This is the explanation of how the eye came to be: There was a time when no animal had an eye, and at that time one day a little animal without eyes discovered a piece of pigment or freckle on the skin. And when the rays of the sun in traveling over the body of the animal came to this piece of pigment they began to converge there more than elsewhere, and they made it hotter there, irritated the skin and brought out a nerve. Out of the nerve came an eye.

Do you know a man by the name of Fosdick? He wrote a book on faith. Look on page one hundred forty-four. I will give you almost the exact words. He says that evolutionists tell you that if man has an eye it is because the light waves beat upon the skin and eyes came out to answer. If he has ears it is because sound waves were there and the ears came out to hear. He says that evolutionists say that everything has come out in response to environment. Think of it, my friends. If the light waves beat on the skin, why did not eyes come out all over? And yet men can believe that and teach it when they cannot believe the miracles of the Bible.

But the chief objection to this belief is that it is destructive. Mark my words. I do not say that everyone who believes Darwinism and takes it seriously loses his religious life. That is what they say we say, but they know that is not our objection. We say the tendency is to undermine faith in God. When I tell you I believe in quarantining against small pox I do not say that everybody that takes small pox dies, and we quarantine against it not because everybody dies, but because some do. I am opposed to Darwinism not only because it is untrue, not only because it is absurd, but my principal objection is because it is dangerous. More than five per cent who take it in college die of it. In the first place it killed Darwin, and that ought to be enough. Darwin began life a Christian. His father wanted him to become a minister, and he was not pleased when he turned aside to study science. When Darwin was a boy he believed all that was Christian. If you doubt it read his letters written just before he died. We quote the Bible as authority, and so did he. But before he died he said he believed there never had been any revelation. He discarded the Bible as the Word of God by inspiration given, and with it he discarded Christ. He brings man down to a brute level and then judges man by brute standards, and shuts the door of heaven against it.

If there is any atheist who wants to quote Darwin, I can quote too. Let him do it, but let no minister quote Darwin, unless he tells his congregation what Darwinism did to Darwin.

A teacher in Bryn Mawr College in Pennsylvania says he does not believe in a personal God and a personal immortality. When the students come to graduate forty-five per cent of them tell him that they have discarded the cardinal principles of the Christian faith. The reason they do it is because they have come under the influence of the cultured—men who are their instructors. That is what Leuba says and what he is teaching in Bryn Mawr College. But you don't have to go to Darwin or to Leuba for evidence. You can just go to the parents who send their children to college, and have them tell you, "I sent my boy or my girl a Christian and they came back an atheist."

I believe in freedom of conscience. I believe any man can be an atheist. He has a right to be. He has just as much right to be an atheist as any man has the right to be a Christian in this land. That is the law, and I will help to enforce it as the law. I want freedom of conscience myself, and I shall do what I can to prevent any law that will rob another of the same right. They say we are trying to suppress free speech. We believe in the right of the atheist to teach atheism. We believe in the right of the agnostic to teach agnosticism, just as much as we believe in the right of the Christian to teach Christianity. We give them every right we ask for ourselves. Is the time coming in this country when the atheist and the agnostic have higher rights than the Christian? A Christian has to build his own college. We have them all over, Catholic, Methodist, Baptist, Lutheran Colleges. Every denomination in this land builds its own college. Those who want them, go down in their pockets for the money to build them. And they put above the door the kind of instruction given so that those who send their children there will know what the child is going to learn. All we ask is that the atheist and the agnostic shall do the same. Let them go down in their pockets and build atheistic colleges, hire atheistic teachers, to teach atheism to atheistic children. But there are no atheistic colleges. There are no agnostic colleges. Why? Because the atheist and the agnostic can draw public salary and propagate his theory. We have not the slightest doubt but when the American people find what is going on in the schools they will tend to the matter very quickly. If there ever was a time when we can't afford to allow the faith of people in God and in the Bible to be destroyed it is now.

We have come out of a war, the bloodiest war that the world ever saw. We look back and we find that thirty million human lives were lost, and three hundred millions of dollars in property were destroyed, and the debts of the world are three times as great. We find that the world has been bearing the devil's burden, and it can't bear it any longer. To whom shall they turn? There is only One. That is the One reared in the carpenter shop. Whose yoke is easy and Whose burden is light. And remember it wasn't ignorant men who brought the world to ruin. It was college graduates who built the dreadnaughts, and it was scientists who mixed the gases and made the liquid fire. It was wise men who made the war so hellish that the world was about to commit suicide. *Darwin's God was nowhere.* Darwin's Bible was nothing. Darwin's Christ was nothing. No man aspiring to be God can save the world. It requires a God condescending to be a man. Evolution would rob Christ of the glory of the virgin birth, and would rob Him of the majesty of His Deity, and the triumph of His resurrection. We need the Christ Whose blood has colored the stream of time, Whose philosophy fits every human need, that is the Christ of whom the Bible tells.

I am glad to come, and in this great city and under the auspices of this organization, and in this tabernacle and before this magnificent audience, I am glad to plead with the world to get back to God. I believe in a real God, and when the world comes back to God it will be looking for the Word of God and it will find it in the Bible, the revealed will of God. There it will find the story of Christ, the only Hope, Whose teachings can solve all the problems that vex our hearts and perplex the world. I am for the Bible against all those that oppose it.

Christianity vs. Modern Liberalism

JOHN GRESHAM MACHEN

Born, Baltimore, Maryland, July 28, 1881; died, Bismarck, North Dakota, January 1, 1937. Graduated from Johns Hopkins, 1901; M.A., Princeton University, 1904; B.D., Princeton Theological Seminary, 1905. Ordained Presbyterian Ministry, 1914. Taught New Testament Literature and Exegesis, Princeton Theological Seminary, 1906–1929. Fought with liberal faction in Presbyterian Church in mid-twenties, left Princeton to become Professor of New Testament, Westminster Theological Seminary, Philadelphia. Found Presbyterian Board of Foreign Missions too liberal; set up independent board, 1933. Suspended from ministry for defiance of church authorities, 1936; established independent body, later called Orthodox Presbyterian Church. Author, The Origin of Paul's Religion (*1921*), Christianity and Liberalism (*1923*), The Virgin Birth of Christ (*1930*).

"It is the fundamental business of the Christian church today to set forth the teaching of Christianity truly and plainly in opposition to the teachings of the modern rivals of Christianity."

I will read a few verses from the First Epistle to the Corinthians, fifteenth chapter, beginning with the first

verse:—

Chicago, Illinois, at the Founders' Week Conference, Moody Bible Institute, February 5–9, 1923. Text is based upon a stenographic report published in *The Moody Bible Institute Monthly*, XXIII (April, 1923), pp. 349–352.

Moreover, brethren, I declare unto you the gospel which I preached unto you, which also ye have received, and wherein ye stand;

By which also ye are saved, if ye keep in memory what I preached unto you, unless ye have believed in vain.

For I delivered unto you first of all that which I also received, how that Christ died for our sins according to the scriptures;

And that he was buried and that he rose again the third day according to the scriptures:

And that he was seen of Cephas, then of the twelve:

After that, he was seen of above five hundred brethren at once; of whom the greater part remain unto this present, but some are fallen asleep.

After that he was seen of James; then of all the apostles.

And last of all he was seen of me also, as of one born out of due time.

For I am the least of the apostles, that am not meet to be called an apostle, because I persecuted the church of God.

But by the grace of God I am what I am; and his grace which was bestowed upon me was not in vain; but I laboured more abundantly than they all; yet not I, but the grace of God which was with me.

Therefore whether it were I or they, so we preach, and so ye believed.

In the time allotted me this afternoon I shall not try to settle the religious issue of the day, but try to be bold enough to present that issue as briefly and clearly as I can, that you may be aided in settling it for yourself.

But presenting the issue sharply and clearly is by no means a popular business at present. There are many people at the present time who, as Dr. Francis L. Patton has aptly put it, prefer to fight their intellectual battles in what may be called a condition of "low visibility."

Presenting the issue sharply is regarded by them as an impious proceeding. May it not discourage contributions to mission boards? May it not prevent church consolidation and cause a poor showing in church statistics?

But for my part I am glad to tell you that my sympathies are with those men, whether conservatives or radicals, who have a passion for light. The type of religion which delights in the pious sound of traditional phrases regardless of their meaning and shrinks from controversial matters, will never stand amid the shocks of life.

When you get beneath the traditional phraseology used everywhere today to the real underlying issue, you discover that that great redemptive religion called Christianity is being attacked within the church by a totally different type of religious thought and life, which is only the more opposed to Christianity because it is making use of traditional Christian phraseology. That modern non-redemptive religion which is attacking Christianity at its root is called by various names. It is called Modernism. It is called Liberalism.

All such names are unsatisfactory; the latter in particular is question-begging, because the movement is regarded as liberal only by its friends. To those opposed to it it seems to involve a narrow attention to certain facts, and a closing of the eyes to others that are equally vital.

But by whatever name the movement may be called, the root of the movement is found in Naturalism, and by that I mean the denial of any entrance of the creative power of God, as sharply distinguished from his works in nature at the beginnings of Christianity.

When I use the term "Naturalism" it is in a different way from that in which it is used by the philosophers, but in that non-philosophic sense it expresses fairly well what is really at the root of that which is called by a degradation of the original noble term, "liberal religion."

What then are the teachings of modern Naturalism as over against the teachings of Christianity? At the beginning of the discussion we are met with an objection which goes to the very roots of the matter. People will tell us that teachings are unimportant. They will tell us that even if the teachings of modern naturalistic Liberalism are entirely different from the teachings of Christianity, yet the two may turn out to be fundamentally the same, because teachings and doctrines are unimportant. All creeds they tell us are equally good for they all spring from Christian experience.

Well now, my friends, whether the objection is well founded or not, we ought to observe exactly what the objection means. I will tell you what it means, it means that we are falling back into a fundamental skepticism, because if all creeds are equally true, then since the creeds are contradictory one to another, it follows with inexorable logic that all are equally false, or at least equally uncertain. To say that all creeds are equally true is the same as to say that all creeds are equally false or equally uncertain; and when you say that creeds make little difference provided there be a unitary Christian experience, you are falling back into agnosticism which fifty or seventy-five years ago was regarded as the deadliest enemy of the Christian church. That enemy has not been made a friend, but has been made only more dangerous, by being received within our walls.

Christianity they will tell us is a life and not a doctrine. Now that seems to be a devout and pious utterance, but it is radically false all the same, and to see that it is false you do not need even to be a Christian, you need have just common sense and common honesty. For when you say that Christianity is this or that, you are making an assertion in the sphere of history. You are not saying what you think ought to be true, but what you think actually is a fact. When people say that Christianity is this or that—some have ventured the absurd assertion that Christianity is Democracy—when you say Christianity is this or that, you are making an assertion in the sphere of history. It is just like saying that the Roman Empire under Nero was a free democracy. It is possible that the Roman Empire under Nero might have been a great deal better if it had been a free democracy, but the question is whether as a matter of fact it was a free democracy or not. So when you say that Christianity is a life, not a doctrine, you are making an assertion in the sphere of history, because Christianity is an historical phenomenon exactly like the Roman Empire, like the kingdom of Prussia or the United States of America.

Now before you can determine whether Christianity is this or that, you have to go back to the beginning of the Christian movement. At the beginning of the life of every corporation is the incorporation paper, commonly called the charter, and in this paper are set forth the objects of the corporation. It is conceivable that other objects may be more desirable than those set forth in the incorporation paper, but if the directors use the name and resources of that particular corporation to pursue these other objects, they are going *ultra vires*[1] of the corporation. It is the same fundamentally with Christianity. It is conceivable that after further investigation we may have fresh views about it. It is conceivable that the founders of the Christian movement were wrong, and that we in the twentieth century can better their program. It is conceivable that they had no right to legislate for all subsequent generations. That is a matter for us to determine in the light of the evidence, but at any rate the founders of the Christian movement did have an inalienable right to legislate for all generations that should choose to bear this name of Christian.

Therefore, if you would honestly determine what can bear the name Christian, you have to go back to the beginnings of the Christian movement. Now the beginnings of the movement constitute a fairly definite historical phenomenon; there is a certain agreement as to what Christianity at its inception was, possible even between Christians and non-Christians, because we have certain sources of information which are admitted to come from the first Christian generation, like the passage we read today—sources which give us definite information about the beginnings of Christianity.

The Christian movement began a few days after the death of Jesus of Nazareth. I can see no good historical justification for calling anything that existed before the death of Jesus of Nazareth, Christianity. At any rate, to be cautious, I will say that if Christianity existed before that time it existed only in a preliminary stage. Evidently after the death of Jesus of Nazareth there was a strange new beginning among His disciples, and that new beginning began the movement which caused the spread of the Christian religion out into the world.

Now, what was the character of the movement at its beginning? For one thing, it was not merely a life as distinguished from a doctrine. Do not misunderstand me. It certainly was a strange new kind of life; anybody who came into contact with those early Christians recognized that they were living an entirely different sort of life from the people around them. It is perfectly clear that the first Christians were living a new type of life, a life of strange purity and strange unselfishness.

But how was that type of life produced? I will tell you the way modern leaders of the church would have expected it to be produced. They would have expected the first Christian missionaries to go forward and say: "We have been

[1] Beyond power; exceeding legal authority.

in contact with a wonderful person, namely, Jesus of Nazareth, and our lives have been changed by that contact. We call upon you, our hearers, to submit yourselves to the contagion through us with the life of Jesus of Nazareth."

That is just what people are saying today. That is what modern men would have expected the first Christian missionaries to say, but as a matter of historical fact they said nothing of the kind. They produced a new type of life not by exhortation, not by the contagion of personal influence, but by the proclamation of a piece of news: they produced it by the account of something that had recently happened.

That seemed a strange thing to the people of those days—to change men's lives not by telling them to be good, but by giving them an account of things that had happened. It seems strange today, it is what Paul called the foolishness of the message. It seemed to be an absolutely foolish way of trying to change the lives of men, but to the historian it is perfectly plain that that is the way they went at it.

Do you want me to tell you what the first Christian movement was in Jerusalem? They did not say, "Submit yourselves to the spell of Jesus Christ and be children of God the way Jesus was a Son of God," but they said, "Christ died for our sins according to the scriptures; he was buried; he has been raised on the third day according to the scriptures." It was an account of things that had happened and an account of the meaning of the happenings, and when you get those historical facts with the meaning of the facts you have Christian doctrine. Christ died—that is history. Christ died for our sins—that is doctrine. We have that at the very basis of all Christian work; it was there in Christianity in the first century, and today Christianity, as then, is founded upon the account of something that happened.

What I mean can be summed up in the first chapter of Acts—the eighth verse —"Ye shall be my witnesses in Jerusalem, in all Judea, and Samaria, and unto the uttermost part of the earth."

Now it is a complete misinterpretation of these words if you say that the witness is merely to what Christ has done for you in your own souls. That is not the way the words are meant. Paramount is the witness to the plain historical fact of the resurrection of Christ. If there is some skeptic here, I do not need to argue with him about the historical value of the book of Acts, or whether Jesus really spoke these words, because all historians, whether Christians or not, ought to admit that it is a good summary of what the Christian movement at its very beginning was; it was a campaign of witnessing, an account of historical facts; Christ died; He was buried; He has been raised.

Well then, if the Christian worker is fundamentally a witness, it is important, despite modern impressions about it, that the Christian worker should tell the truth. When a witness gets up on the witness stand it makes little difference what the cut of his coat is, or whether his sentences are nicely turned; the important thing is that he should tell the truth, the whole truth and nothing but the truth. That is the important thing for the Christian preacher and Christian worker today. Do not misunderstand me. It is a sad thing if you tell the truth with your lips and if your life belies your message, because then the more true the message the greater your sin, for you are bringing despite upon the truth. On the other hand, it is a sad thing when a man uses the gifts God has given him in order to proclaim things which are false. Therefore, the first thing is that we should tell the story which is at the basis of Christianity and tell it straight, and full, and plain.

It *does* make a vast deal of difference what our teachings are, and it is the fundamental business of the Christian church today to set forth the teaching of Christianity truly and plainly in opposition to the teachings of the modern rivals of Christianity. And the chief modern rival of Christianity is not Mohammedanism or Buddhism, but naturalistic Liberalism, which is almost dominant in our large ecclesiastical bodies today.

What then, briefly, are the teachings of Christianity over against the teachings of Liberalism? We have just said that Christianity is an account of something that happened, not something that always was true, but something that happened about 1900 years ago, when God saved man through the atoning death of the Lord Jesus Christ.

But before you can understand that gospel, that account of something that happened, you must know first something of God, and second something about man. These are the two great presuppositions of the gospel message, and it is these presuppositions, as well as the gospel message, to which modern Liberalism is diametrically opposed.

It is opposed to Christianity in its view of God, and in its attitude toward God. Now in the Christian view of God there are many elements, but one element is absolutely fundamental, and gives consistency to all the rest. It is the awful transcendence of God, the awful separateness of God; and it is that element in the Christian presentation of God upon which despite is being cast everywhere in the modern liberal church, because it regards God as fundamentally just another name for the great process of nature as it is. We find ourselves in the midst of a vast process, and to that vast process is applied the name of God. That is what people mean by the immanence of God.

Now do not misunderstand me. God according to the Christian view is immanent in the world. God is everywhere—"closer to us than breathing"—but immanent in the world not because He is identified with the world but because He is the Creator of it and upholds the things which He has made. The fundamental thing in the Christian notion of God is the sharp distinction between all created things and the Creator who is the explanation of all mysteries.

It is strange that men can call that a new vision of God which obscures the distinction between God and man, and involves God even in the sin of the world! How men can call such a view of God a new revelation is strange, because pantheism as it is called, is just as old as the hills, and has always been with us to blight the religious life of man. Modern Liberalism even when not consistently pantheistic, is at any rate pantheizing since it seeks to obliterate the sharp distinction between God and man, and involves God in the sin of mankind. Very different is the holy and living God of the Bible and of Christian faith!

In the second place, modern Liberalism differs from Christianity in its view of man. It differs because it obliterates the distinction between man and God in the way I have said, but it differs in a more fundamental manner still. At the very basis of modern Liberalism in the church is a loss of the consciousness of sin. You can examine the religious literature of the present day, the Sunday-school lesson helps and the sermons, and you will find that the characteristic thought through the whole of them is a profound satisfaction with human goodness. The modern preacher has no words too strong to express his scorn of the Christian view of the awfulness of sin.

A few months ago I stopped in a distant city and went to what seemed to be the leading church. It was the day when the new Sunday-school teachers were inducted into their office; and the preacher preached a sermon about Christian education and told his people, especially those who were to train the young, that formerly there had been a terrible view that children were lost in sin and needed a Redeemer. And he got a laugh from his congregation by quoting the old theologians about the awfulness of sin under which all men were born in this world and the need of redemption in order to escape the righteous judgment of God. He said, "People really used to believe that all children were born in sin and needed the Saviour, Jesus, but we have learned in these days that it is our duty as Christian teachers merely by the teaching of Jesus to draw out the good that is already in them."

The question arose in my mind why he quoted the theologians, why he indulged simply in the vulgar ridicule of them, when he wanted to cast ridicule upon the doctrine of the retributive justice of God; because he could have raised a better laugh if he had quoted the words of Jesus!

Jesus said more awful things about the terribleness of sin and the retributive justice of God than any man, and it is exceedingly strange how men at the present time who claim to have Jesus as Master (they speak of him always as "the Master," but they do not speak of him as Lord or Saviour), who claim to have Jesus as their authority in the sphere of religion, will proceed in the same breath to cast despite upon the things which are at the very center of His teaching, and at the very center of Christianity, as is the awfulness of the guilt of sin.

Do you want me to tell you what the fundamental fault with the church today is? It is this—the modern preacher, whether in the Sunday-school class, or in the home or in the pulpit, is feverishly engaged in an absolutely impossible task. He is engaged in calling the "righteous" to repentance, in trying to bring men into the church, and at the same time permit them to retain their pride in their own goodness. Even our Lord did not succeed in calling the righteous to repentance, and probably we shall be no more successful than He. At the very basis of Christian preaching is the mystery of the consciousness of sin and that is produced by the Holy Spirit, and when a man comes under the conviction of sin his whole attitude is changed.

These are the two presuppositions of the Christian message—the Christian view of the awful holiness of God and the Christian view of the terrible guilt of sin. God could only bring sinful man into His presence through the atoning death of Jesus Christ our Lord, but the account of that gospel is found in the Bible and with regard to the Bible modern Liberalism differs fundamentally from Christianity.

The Christian view of the Bible of course makes the contents of the Bible absolutely unique. You might have all the ideas of the Bible in some other book, but you would have no Christianity; because Christianity is an account not merely of things that always were true, but an account of something that happened, and unless the thing really happened then we are still hopeless under the guilt of sin. It all depends upon the question whether, as a matter of fact, the eternal Son of God did take our sins upon Him and die instead of us on the cross.

According to the Christian view of the Bible it not only contains an account of something that happened, but contains a true account, and thus there is added to the Christian doctrine of revelation the Christian doctrine of the inspiration of the Word of God, and upon that doctrine despite is everywhere being cast today. Men are always talking about the "mechanical" view of inspiration, which makes the Biblical writers little more than stenographers. But as a matter of fact the Christian doctrine of inspiration does not deny the human characteristics of the biblical writers, nor display any lack of interest in the human means that these writers had for gathering their information, but it holds that by the Spirit of God these writers were preserved from the errors which are found in other books, and thus gave to us the only infallible rule of faith and practice.

But what does modern Liberalism substitute for the authority of the Bible? Sometimes a totally false impression is produced that it substitutes the authority of Jesus.

That is altogether false, because when asked what they consider the authority of Jesus, we discover that modern Liberalism rejects a great many of the recorded words of Jesus. It does not believe that Jesus ever spoke some of them, because in His recorded words in the gospels are some things most hateful to it. Modern Liberalism says that not everything recorded of Jesus in the Gospels was spoken by Jesus, and we must sort out the words which were spoken by Him and reject the rest.

But suppose we press it further. We shall discover that even in the reduced Jesus of modern liberal reconstruction there are some things abhorrent to the Liberal church, and modern Liberals if pinned down to it will say that they do not believe everything Jesus said was true, but they will say they are still Christians, they are still His followers, because they still hold to the central life purpose of Jesus.

Well, what was the central life purpose of Jesus? According to the Gospel of Mark the central life purpose of Jesus is found in His atoning death. "The Son of man came not to be ministered unto, but to minister, and give his life a ransom for (instead of) many."

These words are of course abhorrent to the Liberal church. But when you ask what the central life purpose of Jesus was, you will find you are in the mire of dispute, and that they will accept as authoritative only a few of the sayings of Jesus, not because they are His sayings, but because they happen to agree with their own opinions. The real authority of the modern Liberal is not Jesus, but it is, as men say, "Christian experience."

But what do you mean by Christian experience? What do you mean by Christian experience as authority? Surely you do not mean merely a majority vote of the organized Church. Do you mean, then, individual experience? But this is endlessly diverse, and therefore what you will have substituted for the true authority of the Word of God, is no authority at all but the shifting emotions of sinful men.

But people say what a foolish thing it is to depend upon a book! *It all depends upon the book,* my friends. The Reformation of the sixteenth century was founded upon the authority of a Book! May that Book again set aflame the world, and may the present bondage give place again to the glorious freedom of the sons of God!

When you come to the contents of the Bible everything points to the central figure—Jesus Christ. What is thought of Christ, first, by the modern Liberal church and second, by Christian men?

At this point a further perplexity arises, for ask the modern Liberal preacher his view of Christ, and he will say with great conviction, "I believe in the deity of Christ, I believe that Jesus is God."

We hear much like that today. People say, "Why, after all, this great preacher is most orthodox because he believes in the deity of Christ, and those who are objecting to his presence as a leader in the church, are mere uncharitable heresy hunters."

Do you not see, my friends, that, when they say Jesus is God, the value of that utterance depends upon what they mean by God? That little word "God" is not a bit more beautiful than any other English word. The value of it depends altogether upon what you mean by it, and when the modern Liberal preacher says he believes Christ is God, he may mean God exists in all the world, God exists wherever life pulsates through humanity, and only appears fuller and plainer than any other place in the life of Jesus.

That is what is often meant, and of course that is very far from the Christian

faith. Very often when he says Jesus is God, he means to use the term in this
way: "We have given up," he says, "the old notion that there is a Creator and
Ruler of the world. We know nothing about that—that is metaphysical. The
word 'God' is useful merely as expressing the highest object of men's desires."
So when they say Jesus is God they do not mean that Jesus is the supreme ruler
of the world, but simply that Jesus, though a man like the rest of men, is the
highest thing we know.

Such men are further removed from the Christian faith than Unitarians. Uni-
tarians at least believe in God, whereas these men speak highly of Jesus, call
Jesus God, only because they think low of God, not because they think high of
Jesus.

In another way also such men are inferior to Unitarians, inferior in the plain
matter of honesty. When they say, Jesus is God, the truthfulness of that utterance
depends altogether upon the audience addressed. I do not mean to deny that such
Liberal preachers do believe in the very core of their hearts that Jesus is God,
they certainly mean that. But the great trouble is, they know perfectly well those
words are going to be taken by the simple minded hearers whom they address in
a way totally different from the way in which they mean it. They are offending
therefore against the fundamental principle of truthfulness of language. The
assertion, "I believe that Jesus is God," is truthful before an audience of theologi-
cally trained persons who understand the modern way of thinking about God,
but if it be addressed to a simple minded people, then the language is untruthful
and all the best motives in the world cannot possibly excuse it. Nothing can
possibly excuse language which is not in accordance with facts.

Liberalism is different from Christianity also as to salvation. What is the way
of salvation according to the Christian account? Two aspects are be distinguished.
In the first place, the basis of it all is in the atoning death of Christ. According
to Christian belief that is a very simple thing. Men talk about the theory of the
atonement as though it were a subtle thing, but you can put it in words of one
syllable. We deserve eternal death. The Lord Jesus Christ, because he loved us,
died instead of us on the Cross.

That certainly is not incomprehensible. It is mysterious in its depth of grace,
but it is a thing that a child can understand. Do you want me to tell you what
is difficult? It is not the simple Bible presentation of the death of Christ, but the
manifold modern effort to get rid of that simple presentation of the Cross in the
interests of human pride.

The modern liberals pour out the vials of their scorn upon the Bible presentation of the Cross of Christ. They speak of it with disgust as involving a "trick"
intended to placate an "alienated God." Thus they pour out their scorn upon a
thing so holy that in the presence of it the Christian heart melts in gratitude too
deep for words.

People talk about Christian experience. My friends, where can Christian experience be found if not at the Cross of Christ, at that blessed place where a man knows that in a great mystery the guilt of his sin was taken by the Holy One, and borne instead of him on the Cross?

The very nerve of the Christian view of the Cross is that God Himself makes the sacrifice for our salvation. Where can love be found except at the Cross of Christ, the one who died, the just for the unjust? "For God so loved the world that he gave his only begotten Son." There, and there alone, is to be found the love that is love indeed.

This work of Christ is applied by the Holy Spirit of God in the new birth. You will hear very little about the new birth in modern preaching. Modern missionaries will tell you, you must give up the thought of winning individual converts in mission lands. For the new birth they are inclined to substitute "the social gospel." But at the very centre of Christianity are the words "Ye must be born again."

That is the work of the Spirit of God, the application of the work of Christ. But in applying the work of Christ the Spirit makes use of faith. People who have found salvation know what it means.

Liberals talk about faith in Jesus, but they mean simply admiration of Jesus. They talk about it as if the basis of the Christ life were "make Jesus Master in your life." The Y.M.C.A., in recent years, has put the declaration of purpose to live the Christ life as somehow being on a par with the reception of the salvation which is found in the Cross of Christ. I do not see but that that is the exact opposite of faith. That means that you are trusting in your own works. Faith means not that you *do* something, but that you *receive* first the gracious gift of God. When the Lord Jesus has died for you you accept it without work of your own. You accept the gracious thing He did. And then by God's help the good life follows.

Christianity is fighting a great battle today. It is one of three great crises in the history of the Christian church. One came in the second century when Christianity was almost engulfed by paganism in the church in the form of Gnosticism. There was another in the middle ages when legalism was almost dominant in the church, similar to the modern legalism which appears in the Liberal church. Christianity today is fighting a great battle, but I, for my part, am looking for ultimate victory. God will not desert His church.

PART TWO

The Great Divide

POLEMICS OF THE NEW DEAL ERA

HERBERT HOOVER came to the Presidency in the autumn of Coolidge prosperity, and a golden glow was still on the land. "We in America are nearer to the final triumph over poverty than ever before in the history of any land," he optimistically predicted when accepting the nomination. "We shall soon with the help of God be in sight of the day when poverty will be banished from this nation." There were problems, to be sure, but they could be solved within the "American System," by which Hoover meant a free market economy and decentralized political rule. The ultimate ideal, in his own aphorism, was "Self-government by the people outside of Government."

In office Hoover took an active, diagnostic interest in the health of the nation as a whole. He established commissions to study conditions of the body politic and disseminate factual reports to civic groups and local governments for their guidance in programs of social improvement. After Coolidge's apathy, Hoover's spirit of inquiry created a lively stir and provoked talk about an emerging age of "voluntary socialism." Within months after Hoover's inauguration, however, the national economy was in convulsion. In October, 1929, the stock market began to act crazily. Nothing organic, was the diagnosis, just a temporary upset. Events proved otherwise, and when Hoover left office in 1933 paralysis had spread to the extremities.

Throughout his term, however, Hoover had stoutly insisted that the American System was fundamentally sound and that its economic spasms, largely traceable to the last war and its repercussions, particularly in Europe, would pass in good time. He recalled that our economic history was pocked by depressions of varying depths from which we had always recovered with renewed vitality. And as before, deflation must run its natural course before the life forces inherent in the system would reinvigorate the organism. Yet the severity of this depression, he conceded, called for unprecedented action by the Federal Government. Heretofore, Presidents had always stood aloof and let economic eruptions blow themselves out, and Hoover justified his departure from the hands-off tradition only as a temporary expedient to mitigate the effects of the depression and to speed recovery. As he put it in a 1932 campaign speech: "In times of emergency, when forces are running beyond control of individuals or other cooperative action, beyond the control of local communities and of States, then the great reserve powers of the Federal Government shall be brought into action to protect the community. But when these forces have ceased there must be a return to State, local and individual responsibility."[1]

Hoover's program of "temporary" positive measures, while considerable, proved inadequate to counteract this, the worst crisis in the history of capitalism. Moreover, Hoover himself was pathetically ill-cast for the dynamic leadership demanded by the times. Unquestionably a man of intelligence and rectitude, he was also shy, diffident, and excessively sensitive to criticism. His distaste for politics rendered him incapable of interpreting his program successfully or even communicating convincingly a sense of action. His somber speeches offered no tonic to the despairing millions. Indeed, much of the opprobrium that attached itself to Hoover's name originated in his preachments on rugged individualism and in his opposition to a Federal "dole" lest it sap the spirit of self-reliance. People who sold apples on street corners dubbed them Hoover apples; shacks that sprang up near city dumps were called Hoovervilles; rugged individualism was jeeringly turned into ragged individualism. After World War I, when Hoover ended his tenure as head of the American relief organizations, he was esteemed and honored throughout the world as the great humanitarian; now, scarcely more than a decade later, destitute countrymen cursed his name.

Renominated by Republicans, Hoover's campaign in 1932 was funereal. His ideas were tired, his style lackluster, his delivery muffled. Conversely, Franklin Roosevelt flew to Chicago in a mood of high adventure to accept in person the nomination from the Democratic convention. Standing before exuberant delegates, he declared in ringing tones: "The appearance before a National Convention of its nominee for President, to be formally notified of his selection, is unprecedented and unusual, but these are unusual times. I have started out on the tasks that lie ahead by breaking the absurd tradition that a candidate should remain in professed ignorance of what has happened for weeks until he is formally notified of that event many weeks later." This was but a symbol, he added, of "other foolish traditions that need to be broken." His personal guarantee con-

---

[1] "The Consequences of the Proposed New Deal," *Addresses Upon the American Road* (New York: Charles Scribner's Sons, 1938), p. 5.

tained a new phrase: "I pledge you, I pledge myself, to a new deal for the American people."

With equal buoyancy, Roosevelt talked up his proposed New Deal in twenty-seven major campaign speeches, most of which focused sharply on specific problems and solutions. His most broadly philosophical campaign speech was given to the Commonwealth Club in San Francisco on September 23. This speech, which had been in the works since August but was not put in final form until the morning Roosevelt delivered it, was originally prepared by Adolf Berle; but, like so many of Roosevelt's speeches, by the time it reached the final draft it had become a collaborative effort by the candidate and his brain trusters.[2] In this speech Roosevelt advanced a view of American history that marked the end of rugged individualism. The new era required "an economic constitutional order" to cope with economic anarchy, distribute wealth more equitably, and insure social health. Franklin Roosevelt's Commonwealth Address foreshadowed the outlines of the New Deal much as Theodore Roosevelt's "New Nationalism" of 1910 paved the way and provided a charter for the Progressive party in 1912.

Looking back on the 1932 campaign, Raymond Moley, Roosevelt's chief advisor at the time, wrote that "We had, half-unconsciously, created a new kind of political oratory. Each speech contained a well-matured exposition of policy. And if those sections of each speech were put together, they formed in combination a sweeping program of reform and experiment."[3] By and large the political pundits failed to put the pieces together properly, or what is more likely, they liberally discounted what they heard as so much more campaign oratory. But the man with most at stake, Herbert Hoover, did take Roosevelt's speeches seriously, perceived their coherence, and from them predicted what the country was in for if the Democrats won. In his last major campaign speech, Hoover pointed out that "This campaign is more than a contest between two men. It is more than a contest between two parties. It is a contest between two philosophies of government." Reaffirming his faith in the American System, Hoover drew upon Roosevelt's Commonwealth Address to warn that the proposed New Deal was the antithesis of the historic American view and spirit upon which our greatness depended. He spoke forebodingly of the "enormous expansion of the Federal Government" in prospect: "My countrymen, the proposals of our opponents represent a profound change in American life—less in concrete proposal, bad as that may be, than by implication and evasion. Dominantly in their spirit they represent

[2] Raymond Moley, *After Seven Years* (New York: Harper & Brothers, 1939), pp. 57–59; Samuel Rosenman, *Working With Roosevelt* (New York: Harper & Brothers, 1952), p. 171.

[3] Moley, *op. cit.*, p. 62.

a radical departure from the foundations of 150 years which have made this coun-try the greatest nation in the world. This election is not a mere shift from the ins to the outs. It means deciding the direction our Nation will take over a cen-tury to come."[4]

Repudiated at the polls, Hoover had the unenviable job during the interregnum of presiding over a nation that tobogganed toward disaster. In the closing days of his Administration, banks shuttered their windows and suspended operations. On March 4, 1933, people huddled around radios with desperate intensity. Unable though they were to see the wire-taut muscles in Roosevelt's face while he deliv-ered his inaugural speech, their response to his confident voice and message turned despair into hope edged with excitement. "This great Nation will endure as it has endured, will revive and prosper," affirmed the new President. "So, first of all, let me assert my firm belief that the only thing we have to fear is fear itself—nameless, unreasoning, unjustified terror which paralyzes needed efforts to convert retreat into advance." At bottom, the present crisis was a failure in social philosophy. "Restoration calls, however, not for changes in ethics alone. The Nation asks for action, and action now." Should the normal processes of government be inadequate to the needs of a stricken nation, "I shall ask the Con-gress for the one remaining instrument to meet the crisis—broad Executive power that would be given to me if we were in fact invaded by a foreign foe." To closet the specter of dictatorship, Roosevelt added, "We do not distrust the future of essential democracy."

Roosevelt himself had written the first draft of his inaugural speech on Feb-ruary 27 at his home in Hyde Park, and a final draft was made on March 3, the day before the inauguration. Never before in all human history had a speech been heard by so many people; never before had an address produced such an immediate, widespread, or profound impact upon a nation's psychology. A new mood of hopeful expectation had been achieved through the alchemy of a man, his message, his rhetoric, and the far-flung radio audience.

The first one hundred days of the new Administration were unprecedented. The immediate job was to reopen and shore up the banks. The manner and spirit with which this job was tackled geared the Congress for a flood of admin-istration measures. Within eight hours, Congress introduced and passed an Emer-gency Banking Act; the President signed it the same day. On March 12, in his first radio fireside chat, Roosevelt gave the country an elementary lesson in bank-

---

[4] Madison Square Garden, October 31, 1932. "Consequences of the Proposed New Deal," *op. cit.*, pp. 1–19.

ing, explaining the nature of the crisis and how the Government was meeting it. The fireside chat proved to be a brilliant invention because of Roosevelt's keen appreciation of the value of communication, his gift for the popular idiom, and his incomparable radio voice and personality. Through the fireside chat he made the affairs of government warm, interesting, and personal; he created a public opinion on issues to which few congressmen dared remain indifferent. The fireside chat was Roosevelt's supreme achievement, thought Gerald W. Johnson, for it "gave him the power to accomplish all his other works."

Backed by public opinion, Roosevelt launched a gigantic program for relief, recovery, and reform. Fifteen breath-taking months later, he took to the microphone to clarify the objectives of the New Deal, lest they be lost in a chaos of new legislation and alphabetical agencies. But his fireside chat on the accomplishments of the New Deal was not simply a schoolmaster's exposition. The New Deal faced a popular referendum in November, and the President wanted to be dead sure that the much touted "forgotten man" of the Hoover era didn't forget where his interests lay when he stepped into a voting booth. "Are you better off than you were last year?" he pointedly asked every John Doe. And to silence grumblers that he was taking the country down some collectivist road, Roosevelt offered an analogical anodyne. The modernizing of government, he averred, was comparable to plans under way for modernizing the White House without altering its classic lines.

Public approval expressed itself in bulging White House mailbags after the fireside chat and in a sweeping victory at the polls in November; but, at the very crest of his success, Roosevelt's New Deal inexplicably foundered, then bogged down seriously. The President was hesitant, uncertain about his next steps. Since "Recovery had proceeded far enough to end despair, but not far enough to restore satisfaction," as Arthur Schlesinger, Jr., remarks, the critics began to swarm. Early in 1935, the British journalist and historian H. G. Wells reported:

> I came to America against head-winds in early March, and I arrived amidst a tornado of angry voices. Things conspired to give an unfavorable impression of all that had been done in the past year. Then the radio had been dominated by the President, and a certain hopeful imaginative generosity prevailed; now, so far as the discussion of public affairs went, the air carried a chorus of utterances of a quality that dear old Sanderson of Oundle would have called "raucous." What did these raucous voices amount to and were they and

not those broader intimations really going to determine the general quality of the American effort?[5]

What indeed? New Dealers nervously wondered how much substance lay behind the raucous voices of Father Charles E. Coughlin, the radio priest of Royal Oak, Michigan, and Senator Huey P. Long of Louisiana, the two panacea makers who at the moment seemed most threatening.

Since the early 1930s Coughlin had been peppering bankers, capitalists, Communists in his weekly broadcasts, or more personally pillorying Herbert Hoover, Bernard Baruch, J. P. Morgan, and others as custodians of a bankrupt order. Originally a New Dealer, Coughlin coined the slogan "Roosevelt or Ruin." In 1934 he began taking pot shots at the New Deal, and by 1936 he converted his slogan into "Roosevelt *and* Ruin." Late in 1934, Coughlin hammered together a platform he called "Social Justice," consisting of sixteen rickety, slippery planks designed to support Christian capitalism or, as he put it, "production for use at a profit." His weekly broadcasts in behalf of Social Justice seem crankish in today's cold print, but the effect of his rolling Irish brogue and richly inflected voice suggested the advent of a new Messiah. Coughlin's fan mail exceeded Roosevelt's, and most of the envelopes contained folding money.

Huey P. Long loomed as an even more formidable rebel, since he had already established a political machine and a regional following. An upstart politician in the 1920s, Long became Governor of Louisiana, parading under a slogan redolent of William Jennings Bryan: "Every man a king but no one wears a crown." Long had grown up in the parish of Winn, a caldron of social rebellion, and he was richly endowed with the motives and attributes of a demagogue—lust for power backed by cunning intelligence, a knack for improvising, command of the vernacular, ready recourse to Scriptural authority, and a talent for gaudy platform showmanship. He became a national figure via the United States Senate, where he played a maddeningly disruptive role while using his position to snare followers for his "Share Our Wealth" scheme. When the New Deal faltered in 1934, Long's hopes for a third party quickened. Accordingly he stepped up his campaign for progressive taxation on fortunes beyond one million dollars, which would become confiscatory after the eighth million. These tax revenues would be used to guarantee every "deserving family" five thousand dollars, education for the young, and pensions for the aged. Jobs would be made plentiful by reducing the work week and year. Long's nationally broadcast speeches for redistribu-

[5] *The New America: The New World* (New York: The Macmillan Company, 1935), p. 25.

tion of wealth beguiled the stricken of the land with high hopes for security while skipping lightly over the means by which to achieve them. The plausibility of Long's scheme originated in one of the hard facts of life, *viz.,* the nation did suffer from maldistribution of wealth. If his antics and crackpot scheme offended people who ate regularly, hungry people were shocked by current New Deal programs for destroying crops and little pigs in order to shore up a profit system that left human beings destitute.

Long and Coughlin fished in the same muddy waters of social discontent, but each continued to use his own bait. On Capitol Hill there was widespread concern lest an alliance between these agitators and their followers might cost the Democratic party the election in 1936. This anxiety erupted on the night of March 4, 1935, when General Hugh Johnson, until recently the head of the National Recovery Administration, used the occasion of a dinner in his honor to discredit Long and Coughlin in the hope of forestalling a coalition between them. An ex-cavalryman, Johnson was a specialist in the eloquence of the barrackroom. The theme and tone of his speech were essentially this: "Two Pied Pipers have come to Hamelin Town. You can laugh at Father Coughlin—you can snort at Huey Long—but the country was never under greater menace." Johnson's speech, spiced with anticlericalism, initiated one of the most spectacular political vendettas of the century.

Long was stung into immediate reprisals. The next day in the Senate he stripped down to his pink shirt and unloosed a tirade against Franklin "Deela-no" Roosevelt and his lackeys for selling out to the same financial overlords who had ruled Hoover, particularly Bernard Baruch. Senator Joseph Robinson, the majority leader, had suffered too long from the indignities of the Kingfish, as Long was popularly known. "Mr. President," Robinson began, "the Senate and the galleries have just witnessed a demonstration of egotism, of arrogance, of ignorance, that is seldom displayed in the Senate of the United States and which requires a measure of talent possessed only by the Senator from Louisiana." Following Robinson's tongue lashing, Long yelled threateningly, "Beware! Beware! If things go on like they've been going on you won't be here." In the course of the Donnybrook, the Kingfish accused some of his fellow Senators of plotting his murder in the Senate chamber; they in turn charged him with disgracing the Senate by planting his armed bodyguard in the galleries. So it went, and the next day offered more of the same, with Long insisting that "the President has told the administration Senators to turn on the heat from all sides." He stood ready "to face the burning."

Surrounded by three bodyguards in the studio, the Kingfish took to the radio on March 7 to reply to General Johnson. After a few swipes at the General, he invested thirty of his forty-five minutes in pushing his Share Our Wealth program. It was a shrewd pitch, since the highly publicized Senate fracas guaranteed him an audience comparable in size and spirit to a heavyweight championship fight, plus ample newspaper coverage the next day. A few days later, on March 11, Coughlin uncorked an epithet-drenched radio attack upon "moneychangers" in general and their "chocolate soldier" champion in particular. With his speech the sensational week-long "slanging match" came to an end.

Roosevelt knew that Long and Coughlin, sustained by real economic grievances, were political threats. Consequently, their guerilla warfare drove him off dead center and toward the left, as he admitted, in order "to steal Long's thunder." In the summer of 1935, Congress passed four important measures—the Wealth Tax, the Social Security Act, the Public Utility Holding Act, and the National Labor Relations Act—all of which endeared the New Deal to large blocs of its beneficiaries and undercut critics of Roosevelt's inaction. At the same time, the leftward veering of the "Second New Deal" further alienated businessmen and others committed to economic orthodoxy.

One of the dissident blocs was the American Liberty League, which was organized in 1934 and financed by discontented millionaires. Because it was a rich man's club offering only a return to traditionalism, the Liberty League lacked popular appeal. Hence, when Alfred E. Smith, once popular Governor of New York and the Democratic candidate for President in 1928, agreed to speak to a Liberty League dinner at the Mayflower Hotel in Washington, D.C., and simultaneously to a nation-wide radio audience, it looked as if the League had finally recruited its spokesman for the masses. As a prelude, the Democratic candidate for President in 1924, John W. Davis, spoke to the New York Bar Association on the day before the Mayflower event, warning that the United States was plunging toward dictatorship under the New Deal. The next night, January 24, excitement among the two thousand guests at the Mayflower ran so high that Jouett Shouse, the chairman, splintered his gavel trying to settle the audience. Smith, employing his well-remembered speaking tactic, invited his audience to "look at the record"—the Administration's record of broken promises. Put the platforms of the Democratic and Socialist parties side by side, he challenged; then strike out the party names and compare the planks. The experiment would show, Smith predicted, a callous disregard for the 1932 Democratic platform and striking similarity between Socialist promises and New Deal performance. "There can be but one capital," he warned ominously. "Washington or Moscow."

"It was perfect," exclaimed Pierre S. Du Pont, after the speech, but John L. Lewis, talking to a convention of miners, called Smith a "jibbering political jackanapes." Without adjudicating between these polarities of opinion, *The New York Times* regarded the Smith attack as the worst blow yet suffered by the New Deal. Four days later Senator Joseph Robinson replied to Smith on behalf of the Administration.[6] Robinson had been Smith's Vice-Presidential running mate in 1928, and his rebuke was therefore the more stinging. Recalling the liberal proposals Smith had once espoused, Robinson charged him with political irresponsibility ill-concealed by a flimsy façade of rationalizations. Obviously Smith had abandoned his brown derby for the high hat, jibed Robinson.

The 1936 political campaign was on. Senator William Borah of Idaho spoke in Brooklyn on January 28 and announced himself a candidate for President on the Republican ticket. He urged domestic liberalism and denounced old guard Republicans, monopoly, and intervention in foreign affairs. On January 29, thirty-five hundred Democrats met in a "grass roots convention" in Macon, Georgia, to block the renomination of Roosevelt and to denounce with fine impartiality the New Deal, Negro equality, and Karl Marx. Governor Eugene Talmadge, snapping his red galluses, called for a "holy war" against the Communists in Washington; and Gerald L. K. Smith, pushing Long's Share Our Wealth program, invoked the ghost of Huey Long, who had been assassinated the previous September, to join the convention. Out in Topeka, Kansas, Governor Alfred M. Landon made his opening bid for the Republican nomination for President in a nation-wide radio speech, describing himself as a "constitutional liberal."

"The air rings, the newspapers are filled with the politics of bedlam," Norman Thomas wryly observed on February 2 in a radio talk intended to set the record straight after Smith's Mayflower speech. Twice Socialist candidate for President and the most brilliant political debater on the national scene, Thomas proceeded to expose Smith's ignorance of Socialism and to ridicule the notion that the New Deal was doing the work of the Socialists. "Roosevelt did not carry out the Socialist platform," he quipped, "unless he carried it out on a stretcher." Commendable as were recent social gains, the New Deal was no model of the co-operative commonwealth for which Eugene V. Debs once had campaigned and to which Thomas now devoted his energies. More disturbing still, the New Deal

---

[6] Robinson was "armed with a speech" by Charles Michelson, the Democratic party's publicity man, and with "additional notes from Cordell Hull," according to Arthur M. Schlesinger, Jr., *The Age of Roosevelt: The Politics of Upheaval* (Boston: Houghton Mifflin Company, 1960), III, p. 519.

tended to foster state capitalism, thus rendering the country vulnerable to an eventual Fascist takeover. Moscow was no joke, but it was the shadow of Berlin that stretched ominously over the land. Thomas' critique exhibited apprehensions typical of parties of the left over the gathering forces of Fascism at home and abroad.[7]

When the Republicans held their national convention in June, 1936, they bowed to political necessities as they compromised old conservatism in their party platform and gravitated toward Governor Alfred Landon, "the Kansas Coolidge," who combined a record of fiscal orthodoxy with progressive leanings. But when Herbert Hoover walked out on the convention platform on June 10, the convention exploded. There had been misgivings about inviting Hoover to speak, so much was he the public's symbol of the depression; but the glum Hoover of 1932 had become a man transformed by his mission. He blistered the New Deal for its chaos, its moral bankruptcy, and its collectivist skewings; he called for a holy crusade of liberty and liberation. When he had finished, the prolonged ovation and cries of "We want Hoover" looked like a stampede in the making and prompted the worried chairman, Bertrand Snell, to say that the former President had left for New York when, in fact, he sat in a nearby room, happy in his vindication and still hopeful that the ovation would be translated into a nomination. The Republicans nominated Landon, but Hoover represented a past to which the delegates in their hearts wished to return.

The Democratic convention was merely a ratifying ceremony for Roosevelt and Garner. The Socialists again chose Norman Thomas, and the Communists took Earl Browder, who urged a popular front among liberals and waged largely an anti-Landon campaign. The Union party, with William Lemke of North Dakota as its nominee, was the political creature of Father Coughlin, Dr. Francis Townsend, and the remnants of Huey Long's movement held together by Gerald L. K. Smith.

When the votes were counted in November, the impressive New Deal sweep made it abundantly clear that the United States had crossed a great divide in its political and social outlook. Only Maine and Vermont were left on the receding slopes. Yet within months the political coalitions that had sustained the New Deal began to splinter. The rout of the opposition in November had been too

[7] With benefit of the long, retrospective view, Thomas' attitude toward the New Deal has become more benign, and he acknowledges that appraisal made in the 1930's suffered somewhat from campaign heat. A splendid review of his thought as revealed in his speeches and comments is a recording by Thomas on his seventy-fifth birthday, "Norman Thomas Reminisces" (New Rochelle, New York: Spoken Arts, Inc., 1959).

complete, and Roosevelt himself stimulated political in-fighting, first by his abortive attempt to pack the Supreme Court in 1937, and then his attempt in 1938 to purge Congress of recalcitrant Democrats. Some new economic measures were enacted, but many basic problems continued to plague the economy and stubbornly resisted New Deal treatment. Nearly nine million workers still had not been absorbed by private industry. Roosevelt wanted desperately to balance the budget and was forever frustrated in his attempts. Perforce, "pump priming" became the accepted because necessary mode of sustaining the economy. By the end of 1938, it was evident that the New Deal had lost its forward thrust, that it was through as an instrument of innovation and creativity. Roosevelt himself signaled the end of the pioneering stage when he addressed Congress on January 4, 1939: "We have now passed the period of internal conflict in the launching of our program of social reform. Our full energies may now be released to invigorate the processes of recovery in order to preserve our reforms, and to give every man and woman who wants to work a real job at a living wage."

Although the New Deal had run its course in a half dozen years, its impact upon America was profound and permanent. The old faith in rugged individualism and minimal government was obsolete. In the new conception, government had a positive responsibility for social and economic welfare. In some measure this was acknowledged by the Republican platform and Presidential candidate in 1936; it was made incontrovertibly explicit by Wendell Willkie, the Republican nominee in 1940. In his acceptance address, Willkie said pointedly that "by 1929 the concentration of private power had gone further than it should ever go in a democracy."

> I believe that the forces of free enterprise must be regulated. I am opposed to business monopolies.
>
> I believe in collective bargaining, by representatives of labor's own free choice, without interference and in full protection of those obvious rights. I believe in the maintenance of minimum standards for wages and of maximum standards for hours. I believe that such standards should constantly rise.
>
> I believe in the Federal regulation of interstate utilities, of securities markets, and of banking. I believe in Federal pensions, in adequate old age benefits and in unemployment allowances.
>
> I believe that the Federal government has a responsibility to equalize the lot of the farmer with that of the manufacturer. If this cannot

be done by parity of prices, other means must be found—with the least possible regimentation of the farmer's affairs.

I believe in the encouragement of cooperative buying and selling, and in the full extension of rural electrification.

The purpose of all such measures is indeed to obtain a better distribution of wealth and earning power of this country.

But I do not base my claim to liberalism solely on my faith in such reforms. American liberalism does not consist merely in reforming things. It consists in making things.[8]

In this and other campaign speeches, Willkie adopted the bulk of New Deal social measures and sought to reconcile them with traditional faith in free enterprise. In short, he endorsed a mixed economy in which government was assigned a positive function.

Truman's Fair Deal constituted a further commitment to the welfare state. When, in 1952, the Republicans rejected their natural ideological leader, Robert A. Taft, and nominated General Dwight D. Eisenhower, hunger for office after twenty years of political starvation was the overriding consideration. But in choosing Eisenhower and his "middle way" they guaranteed further domestication of the essential features of the New Deal. As Eisenhower put it in a 1952 campaign speech: "Now, ladies and gentlemen, this middle way today starts off with certain very definite assumptions. It assumes that all Americans of all parties have now accepted and will forever support what we call social gains, the security people are entitled to in their old age and to make certain they are adequately cared for, insurance against unemployment, equal opportunities for everybody regardless of race, religion, where he was born or what is his national origin." Itemizing still other social gains he would preserve, Eisenhower concluded: "No one counts that thing [sic] a political issue any more. That is part of America."[9] To be sure, conservatives wishing to turn back the clock have not acquiesced in Eisenhower's conclusion, but neither have they been able to muster effective support either within or outside the major parties. Nor have radicals succeeded in wooing voters to take a sharp leftward swing.

Early in the 1930s, many Americans yielded to an insurrectionary mood. Grave doubts about the contemporary relevance of democracy to the needs of modern society came to the surface; revolutionary upheavals abroad seemed portentous.

---

[8] For complete text, see *The New York Times,* August 18, 1940, p. 33.
[9] *Vital Speeches of the Day,* XVIII (1951–1952), p. 677.

Above all, Roosevelt and the New Deal changed the mood of the nation and revived confidence in its ability to cope with its severest problems through parliamentary means. Indeed, out of the turbulent polemics of the era emerged a strengthened democracy—socially conscious, responsive, and responsible.

Address to the Commonwealth Club

FRANKLIN DELANO ROOSEVELT

Born, Hyde Park, New York, January 30, 1882; died, Warm Springs, Georgia, April 12, 1945. Graduated from Harvard, 1904. Attended Columbia Law School, and admitted to New York bar, 1907. Democratic member, New York Senate, 1911–1913. Assistant Secretary of Navy, 1913–1920. Democratic candidate for Vice-President of the United States, 1920. Stricken with polio in 1921, he recovered sufficiently to re-enter politics and be elected Governor of New York, 1928; re-elected, 1930. As Democratic candidate, he was elected to four terms as President of the United States in 1932, 1936, 1940, and 1944.

"As I see it, the task of Government in its relation to business is to assist the development of an economic declaration of rights, an economic constitutional order."

I count it a privilege to be invited to address the Commonwealth Club. It has stood in the life of this city and State, and, it is perhaps accurate to add, the Nation, as a group of citizen leaders interested in fundamental problems of Government, and chiefly concerned with achievement of progress in Government through nonpartisan means.

The privilege of addressing you, therefore, in the heat of a political campaign, is great. I want to respond to your courtesy in terms consistent with your policy.

I want to speak not of politics but of government. I want to speak not of parties, but of universal principles. They are not political, except in that large

The Commonwealth Club of California, San Francisco, September 23, 1932. *The New York Times,* September 24, 1932, p. 6. Reprinted by permission of *The New York Times.*

sense in which a great American once expressed a definition of politics—that nothing in all of human life is foreign to the science of politics.

I do want to give you, however, a recollection of a long life spent, for a large part, in public office. Some of my conclusions and observations have been deeply accentuated in these past few weeks. I have traveled far—from Albany to the Golden Gate. I have seen many people, and heard many things, and today, when, in a sense, my journey has reached the half-way mark, I am glad of the opportunity to discuss with you what it all means to me.

Sometimes, my friends, particularly in years such as these, the hand of discouragement falls upon us. It seems that things are in a rut, fixed, settled, that the world has grown old and tired and very much out of joint. This is the mood of depression, of dire and weary depression.

But then we look around us in America, and everything tells us that we are wrong. America is new. It is in the process of change and development. It has the great potentialities of youth, and particularly is this true of the great West, and of this coast, and of California.

I would not have you feel that I regard this in any sense a new community. I have traveled in many parts of the world, but never have I felt the arresting thought of the change and development more than here, where the old, mystic East would seem to be near to us, where the currents of life and thought and commerce of the whole world meet us. This factor alone is sufficient to cause man to stop and think of the deeper meaning of things when he stands in this community.

But, more than that, I appreciate that the membership of this club consists of men who are thinking in terms beyond the immediate present, beyond their own immediate tasks, beyond their own individual interests. I want to invite you, therefore, to consider with me in the large some of the relationships of government and economic life that go deep into our daily lives, our happiness, our future and our security.

The issue of Government has always been whether individual men and women will have to serve some system of government or economics, or whether a system of government and economics exists to serve individual men and women. This question has persistently dominated the discussion of government for many generations. On questions relating to these things men have differed, and for time immemorial it is probable that honest men will continue to differ.

The final word belongs to no man; yet we can still believe in change and in progress. Democracy, as a dear old friend of mine in Indiana, Meredith Nicholson, has called it, is a quest, a never-end seeking for better things, and in the seeking for these things and the striving for them, there are many roads to follow. But, if we map the course of these roads, we find that there are only two general directions.

When we look about us, we are likely to forget how hard people have worked to win the privilege of Government. The growth of the national governments of

Europe was a struggle for the development of a centralized force in the nation, strong enough to impose peace upon ruling barons. In many instances the victory of the central government, the creation of a strong central government, was a haven of refuge to the individual. The people preferred the master far away to the exploitation and cruelty of the smaller master near at hand.

But the creators of national government were perforce ruthless men. They were often cruel in their methods, but they did strive steadily toward something that society needed and very much wanted—a strong central State, able to keep the peace, to stamp out civil war, to put the unruly nobleman in his place, and to permit the bulk of individuals to live safely.

The man of ruthless force had his place in developing a pioneer country, just as he did in fixing the power of the central government in the development of the nations. Society paid him well for his services and its development. When the development among the nations of Europe, however, had been completed, ambition and ruthlessness, having served their term, tended to overstep their mark.

There came a growing feeling that government was conducted for the benefit of a few who thrived unduly at the expense of all. The people sought a balancing —a limiting force. There came gradually, through town councils, trade guilds, national parliaments, by constitution and by popular participation and control, limitations on arbitrary power.

Another factor that tended to limit the power of those who ruled was the rise of the ethical conception that a ruler bore a responsibility for the welfare of his subjects.

The American colonies were born in this struggle. The American Revolution was a turning point in it. After the Revolution the struggle continued and shaped itself in the public life of the country. There were those who, because they had seen the confusion which attended the years of war for American independence, surrendered to the belief that popular Government was essentially dangerous and essentially unworkable. They were honest people, my friends, and we cannot deny that their experience had warranted some measure of fear.

The most brilliant, honest and able exponent of this point of view was Hamilton. He was too impatient of slow-moving methods. Fundamentally he believed that the safety of the Republic lay in the autocratic strength of its government, that the destiny of individuals was to serve that government, and that fundamentally a great and strong group of central institutions, guided by a small group of able and public-spirited citizens, could best direct all government.

But Mr. Jefferson, in the summer of 1776, after drafting the Declaration of Independence, turned his mind to the same problem and took a different view. He did not deceive himself with outward forms. Government to him was a means to an end, not an end in itself; it might be either a refuge and a help or a threat and a danger, depending on the circumstances. We find him carefully analyzing the society for which he was to organize a government: "We have no paupers. The great mass of our population is of laborers, our rich who cannot live without labor, either manual or professional, being few and of moderate wealth. Most of the laboring class possess property, cultivate their own lands, have families and from the demand for their labor, are enabled to exact from the rich and the competent such prices as enable them to feed abundantly, clothe above mere decency, to labor moderately and raise their families."

These people, he considered, had two sets of rights, those of "personal competency" and those involved in acquiring and possessing property. By "personal competency" he meant the right of free thinking, freedom of forming and expressing opinions, and freedom of personal living, each man according to his own lights. To insure the first set of rights, a Government must so order its functions as not to interfere with the individual. But even Jefferson realized that the exercise of the property rights might so interfere with the rights of the individual that the Government, without whose assistance the property rights could not exist, must intervene, not to destroy individualism, but to protect it.

You are familiar with the great political duel which followed; and how Hamilton and his friends, building toward a dominant, centralized power, were at length defeated in the great election of 1800 by Mr. Jefferson's party. Out of that duel came the two parties, Republican and Democratic, as we know them today.

So began, in American political life, the new day, the day of the individual against the system, the day in which individualism was made the great watchword of American life.

The happiest of economic conditions made that day long and splendid. On the Western frontier, land was substantially free. No one who did not shirk the task of earning a living was entirely without opportunity to do so. Depressions could, and did, come and go; but they could not alter the fundamental fact that most of the people lived partly by selling their labor and partly by extracting their livelihood from the soil, so that starvation and dislocation were practically impossible. At the very worst there was always the possibility of climbing into a covered wagon and moving West where the untilled prairies afforded a haven for men to whom the East did not provide a place. So great were our natural resources that we could offer this relief not only to our own people, but to the distressed of all the world. We could invite immigration from Europe and welcome it with open arms. Traditionally, when a depression came a new section of land was opened in the West. And even our temporary misfortune served our manifest destiny.

It was in the middle of the nineteenth century that a new force was released and a new dream created. The force was what is called the industrial revolution, the advance of steam and machinery and the rise of the forerunners of the modern industrial plant.

The dream was the dream of an economic machine, able to raise the standard of living for everyone; to bring luxury within the reach of the humblest; to annihilate distance by steam power and later by electricity, and to release everyone from the drudgery of the heaviest manual toil.

It was to be expected that this would necessarily affect government. Heretofore, government had merely been called upon to produce conditions within which people could live happily, labor peacefully, and rest secure. Now it was called upon to aid in the consummation of this new dream.

There was, however, a shadow over the dream. To be made real it required use of the talents of men of tremendous will and tremendous ambition, since by no other force could the problems of financing and engineering and new developments be brought to a consummation.

So manifest were the advantages of the machine age, however, that the United States fearlessly, cheerfully and, I think, rightly accepted the bitter with the sweet. It was thought that no price was too high to pay for the advantages which we could draw from a finished industrial system. The history of the last half century is accordingly in large measure a history of a group of financial Titans, whose methods were not scrutinized with too much care, and who were honored in proportion as they produced the results, irrespective of the means they used. The financiers who pushed the railroads to the Pacific were always ruthless, often wasteful, and frequently corrupt; but they did build railroads, and we have them today.

It has been estimated that the American investor paid for the American railway system more than three times over in the process; but despite this fact the net advantage was to the United States. As long as we had free land, as long as population was growing by leaps and bounds, as long as our industrial plants were insufficient to supply our own needs, society chose to give the ambitious man free play and unlimited reward, provided only that he produced the economic plant so much desired.

During this period of expansion there was equal opportunity for all, and the business of government was not to interfere but to assist in the development of industry.

This was done at the request of business men themselves. The tariff was originally imposed for the purpose of "fostering our infant industry," a phrase I think the older among you will remember as a political issue not so long ago.

The railroads were subsidized, sometimes by grants of money, oftener by grants of land. Some of the most valuable oil lands in the United States were granted to assist the financing of the railroad which pushed through the Southwest.

A nascent merchant marine was assisted by grants of money, or by mail subsidies, so that our steam shipping might ply the seven seas.

Some of my friends tell me that they do not want the Government in business. With this I agree, but I wonder whether they realize the implications of the past.

For while it has been American doctrine that the government must not go into business in competition with private enterprises, still it has been traditional, particularly in Republican administrations, for business urgently to ask the government to put at private disposal all kinds of government assistance. The same man who tells you that he does not want to see the government interfere in business—and he means it and has plenty of good reasons for saying so—is the first to go to Washington and ask the government for a prohibitory tariff on his product.

When things get just bad enough—as they did two years ago—he will go with equal speed to the United States Government and ask for a loan. And the Reconstruction Finance Corporation is the outcome of it.

Each group has sought protection from the Government for its own special interests without realizing that the function of Government must be to favor no small group at the expense of its duty to protect the rights of personal freedom and of private property of all its citizens.

In retrospect we can now see that the turn of the tide came with the turn of the century. We were reaching our last frontier; there was no more free land and our industrial combinations had become great uncontrolled and irresponsible units of power within the State.

Clear-sighted men saw with fear the danger that opportunity would no longer be equal; that the growing corporation, like the feudal baron of old, might threaten the economic freedom of individuals to earn a living. In that hour our antitrust laws were born.

The cry was raised against the great corporations. Theodore Roosevelt, the first great Republican Progressive, fought a Presidential campaign on the issue of "trust busting" and talked freely about malefactors of great wealth. If the Government had a policy it was rather to turn the clock back, to destroy the large combinations and to return to the time when every man owned his individual small business.

This was impossible. Theodore Roosevelt, abandoning the idea of "trust busting," was forced to work out a difference between "good" trusts and "bad" trusts. The Supreme Court set forth the famous "rule of reason" by which it seems to have meant that a concentration of industrial power was permissible if the method by which it got its power, and the use it made of that power, were reasonable.

Woodrow Wilson, elected in 1912, saw the situation more clearly. Where Jefferson had feared the encroachment of political power on the lives of individuals, Wilson knew that the new power was financial. He saw, in the highly centralized economic system, the despot of the twentieth century, on whom great masses of individuals relied for their safety and their livelihood, and whose irresponsibility and greed (if they were not controlled) would reduce them to starvation and penury.

The concentration of financial power had not proceeded as far in 1912 as it has today, but it had grown far enough for Mr. Wilson to realize fully its implications. It is interesting, now, to read his speeches. What is called "radical" today (and I have reason to know whereof I speak) is mild compared to the campaign of Mr. Wilson. "No man can deny," he said, "that the lines of endeavor have more and more narrowed and stiffened; no man who knows anything about the development of industry in this country can have failed to observe that the larger kinds of credit are more and more difficult to obtain unless you obtain them upon terms of uniting your efforts with those who already control the industry of the country, and nobody can fail to observe that every man who tries to set himself up in competition with any process of manufacture which has taken place under the control of large combinations of capital will presently find himself either squeezed out or obliged to sell and allow himself to be absorbed."

Had there been no World War—had Mr. Wilson been able to devote eight years to domestic instead of to international affairs—we might have had a wholly different situation at the present time. However, the then distant roar of European cannon, growing ever louder, forced him to abandon the study of this issue. The problem he saw so clearly is left with us as a legacy; and no one of us on either side of the political controversy can deny that it is a matter of grave concern to the government.

A glance at the situation today only too clearly indicates that equality of opportunity as we have known it no longer exists. Our industrial plant is built. The problem just now is whether, under existing conditions, it is not overbuilt.

Our last frontier has long since been reached, and there is practically no more free land. More than half of our people do not live on the farms or on lands and cannot derive a living by cultivating their own property.

There is no safety valve in the form of a Western prairie to which those thrown out of work by the Eastern economic machines can go for a new start. We are not able to invite the immigration from Europe to share our endless plenty. We are now providing a drab living for our own people.

Our system of constantly rising tariffs has at last reacted against us to the point of closing our Canadian frontier on the north, our European markets on the east, many of our Latin-American markets to the south, and a goodly proportion of our Pacific markets on the west, through the retaliatory tariffs of those countries.

It has forced many of our great industrial institutions, who exported their surplus production to such countries, to establish plants in such countries, within the tariff walls. This has resulted in the reduction of the operation of their American plants and opportunity for employment.

Just as freedom to farm has ceased, so also the opportunity in business has narrowed. It still is true that men can start small enterprises, trusting to native shrewdness and ability to keep abreast of competitors; but area after area has been preempted altogether by the great corporations, and even in the fields which still have no great concerns the small man starts under a handicap.

The unfeeling statistics of the past three decades show that the independent business man is running a losing race. Perhaps he is forced to the wall; perhaps he cannot command credit; perhaps he is "squeezed out," in Mr. Wilson's words, by highly organized corporate competitors, as your corner grocery man can tell you.

Recently a careful study was made of the concentration of business in the United States. It showed that our economic life was dominated by some 600-odd corporations who controlled two-thirds of American industry. Ten million small business men divided the other third. More striking still, it appeared that, if the process of concentration goes on at the same rate, at the end of another century we shall have all American industry controlled by a dozen corporations and run by perhaps a hundred men. Put plainly, we are steering a steady course toward economic oligarchy, if we are not there already.

Clearly, all this calls for a re-appraisal of values. A mere builder of more industrial plants, a creator of more railroad systems, an organizer of more corporations, is as likely to be a danger as a help.

The day of the great promoter or the financial Titan, to whom we granted anything if only he would build or develop, is over. Our task now is not discovery or exploitation of natural resources or necessarily producing more goods.

It is the soberer, less dramatic business of administering resources and plants already in hand, of seeking to reestablish foreign markets for our surplus production, of meeting the problem of underconsumption, of adjusting production to consumption, of distributing wealth and products more equitably, of adapting existing economic organizations to the service of the people. The day of enlightened administration has come.

Just as in older times the central Government was first a haven of refuge and then a threat, so now in a closer economic system the central and ambitious financial unit is no longer a servant of national desire but a danger. I would draw the parallel one step farther. We did not think because national government had become a threat in the eighteenth century that therefore we should abandon the principle of national government. Nor today should we abandon the principle of strong economic units called corporations merely because their power is susceptible of easy abuse. In other times we dealt with the problem of an unduly ambitious central government by modifying it gradually into a constitutional democratic government. So today we are modifying and controlling our economic units.

As I see it, the task of Government in its relation to business is to assist the development of an economic declaration of rights, an economic constitutional order. This is the common task of statesman and business man. It is the minimum requirement of a more permanently safe order of things.

Happily, the times indicate that to create such an order not only is the proper policy of government, but it is the only line of safety for our economic structures as well.

We know now that these economic units cannot exist unless prosperity is uniform—that is, unless purchasing power is well distributed throughout every group in the nation. That is why even the most selfish of corporations for its own interest would be glad to see wages restored and unemployment aided and to bring the Western farmer back to his accustomed level of prosperity and to assure a permanent safety to both groups.

That is why some enlightened industries themselves endeavor to limit the freedom of action of each man and business group within the industry in the common interest of all; why business men everywhere are asking a form of organization which will bring the scheme of things into balance, even though it may in some measure qualify the freedom of action of individual units within the business.

The exposition need not further be elaborated. It is brief and incomplete, but you will be able to expand it in terms of your own business or occupation without difficulty.

I think everyone who has actually entered the economic struggle—which means everyone who was not born to safe wealth—knows in his own experience and his own life that we have now to apply the earlier concepts of American government to the conditions of today.

The Declaration of Independence discusses the problem of government in terms of a contract. Government is a relation of give and take—a contract, perforce, if we would follow the thinking out of which it grew. Under such a contract rulers were accorded power, and the people consented to that power on consideration that they be accorded certain rights. The task of statesmanship has always been the re-definition of these rights in terms of a changing and growing social order. New conditions impose new requirements upon government and those who conduct government.

I held, for example, in proceedings before me as Governor, the purpose of which was the removal of the Sheriff of New York, that under modern conditions it was not enough for a public official merely to evade the legal terms of official wrongdoing. He owed a positive duty as well. I said, in substance, that if he had acquired large sums of money, he was, when accused, required to explain the sources of such wealth. To that extent this wealth was colored with a public interest. I said that public servants should, even beyond private citizens, in financial matters be held to a stern and uncompromising rectitude.

I feel that we are coming to a view, through the drift of our legislation and our public thinking in the past quarter century, that private economic power is, to enlarge an old phrase, a public trust as well. I hold that continued enjoyment of that power by any individual or group must depend upon the fulfillment of that trust. The men who have reached the summit of American business life know this best; happily, many of these urge the binding quality of this greater social contract.

The terms of that contract are as old as the Republic, and as new as the new economic order.

Every man has a right to life; and this means that he has also a right to make a comfortable living. He may by sloth or crime decline to exercise that right, but it may not be denied him. We have no actual famine or dearth; our industrial and agricultural mechanism can produce enough and to spare. Our government, formal and informal, political and economic, owes to everyone an avenue to possess himself of a portion of that plenty sufficient for his needs, through his own work.

Every man has a right to his own property; which means a right to be assured to the fullest extent attainable, in the safety of his savings. By no other means can men carry the burdens of those parts of life which in the nature of things afford no chance of labor—childhood, sickness, old age.

In all thought of property, this right is paramount; all other property rights must yield to it.

If, in accord with this principle, we must restrict the operations of the speculator, the manipulator, even the financier, I believe we must accept the restriction as needful not to hamper individualism but to protect it.

These two requirements must be satisfied, in the main, by the individuals who claim and hold control of the great industrial and financial combinations which dominate so large a part of our industrial life. They have undertaken to be not business men but princes—princes of property. I am not prepared to say that the system which produces them is wrong. I am very clear that they must fearlessly and competently assume the responsibility which goes with the power. So many enlightened business men know this that the statement would be little more than a platitude were it not for an added implication.

This implication is, briefly, that the responsible heads of finance and industry, instead of acting each for himself, must work together to achieve the common end.

They must, where necessary, sacrifice this or that private advantage, and in reciprocal self-denial must seek a general advantage. It is here that formal government—political government, if you choose—comes in.

Whenever in the pursuit of this objective the lone wolf, the unethical competitor, the reckless promoter, the Ishmael or Insull, whose hand is against every man's, declines to join in achieving an end recognized as being for the public welfare, and threatens to drag the industry back to a state of anarchy, the government may properly be asked to apply restraint.

Likewise, should the group ever use its collective power contrary to the public welfare, the government must be swift to enter and protect the public interest.

The government should assume the function of economic regulation only as a last resort, to be tried only when private initiative, inspired by high responsibility, with such assistance and balance as government can give, has finally failed. As yet there has been no final failure, because there has been no attempt; and I decline to assume that this nation is unable to meet the situation.

The final term of the high contract was for liberty and the pursuit of happiness.

We have learned a great deal of both in the past century. We know that individual liberty and individual happiness mean nothing unless both are ordered in the sense that one man's meat is not another man's poison.

We know that the old "rights of personal competency"—the right to read, to think, to speak, to choose and live a mode of life—must be respected at all hazards.

We know that liberty to do anything which deprives others of those elemental rights is outside the protection of any compact, and that government in this regard is the maintenance of a balance, within which every individual may have a place if he will take it; in which every individual may find safety if he wishes it; in which every individual may attain such power as his ability permits, consistent with his assuming the accompanying responsibility.

All this is a long, slow task. Nothing is more striking than the simple innocence of the men who insist, whenever an objective is present, on the prompt production of a patent scheme guaranteed to produce a result.

Human endeavor is not so simple as that. Government includes the art of formulating a policy, and using the political technique to attain so much of that policy as will receive general support; persuading, leading, sacrificing, teaching always, because the greatest duty of a statesman is to educate.

But in the matters of which I have spoken we are learning rapidly in a severe school. The lessons so learned must not be forgotten even in the mental lethargy of a speculative upturn.

We must build toward the time when a major depression cannot occur again; and if this means sacrificing the easy profits of inflationist booms, then let them go; and good riddance.

Faith in America, faith in our tradition of personal responsibility, faith in our institutions, faith in ourselves demands that we recognize the new terms of the old social contract.

We shall fulfill them, as we fulfilled the obligation of the apparent Utopia which Jefferson imagined for us in 1776, and which Jefferson, Roosevelt and Wilson sought to bring to realization.

We must do so, lest a rising tide of misery, engendered by our common failure, engulf us all.

But failure is not an American habit; and in the strength of great hope we must all shoulder our common load.

First Inaugural Address

FRANKLIN DELANO ROOSEVELT

(*For biographical sketch, see p. 146.*)

"So, first of all, let me assert my firm belief that the only thing we have to fear is fear itself. . . ."

This is a day of national consecration, and I am certain that my fellow Americans expect that on my induction into the Presidency I will address them with a candor and a decision which the present situation of our Nation impels. This is preeminently the time to speak the truth, the whole truth, frankly and boldly. Nor need we shrink from honestly facing conditions in our country today. This great Nation will endure as it has endured, will revive and will prosper. So, first of all, let me assert my firm belief that the only thing we have to fear is fear itself—nameless, unreasoning, unjustified terror which paralyzes needed efforts to convert retreat into advance. In every dark hour of our national life a leadership of frankness and vigor has met with that understanding and support of the people themselves which is essential to victory. I am convinced that you will again give that support to leadership in these critical days.

In such a spirit on my part and on yours we face our common difficulties. They concern, thank God, only material things. Values have shrunken to fantastic levels; taxes have risen; our ability to pay has fallen; government of all kinds is faced by serious curtailment of income; the means of exchange are frozen in the currents of trade; the withered leaves of industrial enterprise lie on every

Washington, D.C., March 4, 1933. *Congressional Record,* 73rd Cong., Special Sess., vol. 77, pt. I, pp. 5–6. The first eight words in the above text, jotted down by Mr. Roosevelt immediately prior to delivery, do not appear in the *Congressional Record*. Since they were a part of the address as delivered, the editors have added them to the official text.

side; farmers find no markets for their produce; the savings of many years in thousands of families are gone.

More important, a host of unemployed citizens face the grim problem of existence, and an equally great number toil with little return. Only a foolish optimist can deny the dark realities of the moment.

Yet our distress comes from no failure of substance. We are stricken by no plague of locusts. Compared with the perils which our forefathers conquered because they believed and were not afraid, we have still much to be thankful for. Nature still offers her bounty, and human efforts have multiplied it. Plenty is at our doorstep, but a generous use of it languishes in the very sight of the supply. Primarily this is because the rulers of the exchange of mankind's goods have failed, through their own stubbornness and their own incompetence, have admitted their failure, and abdicated. Practices of the unscrupulous money changers stand indicted in the court of public opinion, rejected by the hearts and minds of men.

True they have tried, but their efforts have been cast in the pattern of an outworn tradition. Faced by failure of credit, they have proposed only the lending of more money. Stripped of the lure of profit by which to induce our people to follow their false leadership, they have resorted to exhortations, pleading tearfully for restored confidence. They know only the rules of a generation of self-seekers. They have no vision, and when there is no vision the people perish.

The money changers have fled from their high seats in the temple of our civilization. We may now restore that temple to the ancient truths. The measure of the restoration lies in the extent to which we apply social values more noble than mere monetary profit.

Happiness lies not in the mere possession of money; it lies in the joy of achievement, in the thrill of creative effort. The joy and moral stimulation of work no longer must be forgotten in the mad chase of evanescent profits. These dark days will be worth all they cost us if they teach us that our true destiny is not to be ministered unto but to minister to ourselves and to our fellow men.

Recognition of the falsity of material wealth as the standard of success goes hand in hand with the abandonment of the false belief that public office and high political position are to be valued only by the standards of pride of place and personal profit; and there must be an end to a conduct in banking and in business which too often has given to a sacred trust the likeness of callous and selfish wrongdoing. Small wonder that confidence languishes, for it thrives only on honesty, on honor, on the sacredness of obligations, on faithful protection, on unselfish performance; without them it can not live.

Restoration calls, however, not for changes in ethics alone. This Nation asks for action, and action now.

Our greatest primary task is to put people to work. This is no unsolvable problem if we face it wisely and courageously. It can be accomplished in part by direct recruiting by the Government itself, treating the task as we would treat the emergency of a war, but at the same time, through this employment, accomplishing greatly needed projects to stimulate and reorganize the use of our natural resources.

Hand in hand with this we must frankly recognize the overbalance of population in our industrial centers and, by engaging on a national scale in a redistribution, endeavor to provide a better use of the land for those best fitted for the land. The task can be helped by definite efforts to raise the values of agricultural products and with this the power to purchase the output of our cities. It can be helped by preventing realistically the tragedy of the growing loss through foreclosure of our small homes and our farms. It can be helped by insistence that the Federal, State, and local Governments act forthwith on the demand that their cost be drastically reduced. It can be helped by the unifying of relief activities which to-day are often scattered, uneconomical, and unequal. It can be helped by national planning for and supervision of all forms of transportation and of communications and other utilities which have a definitely public character. There are many ways in which it can be helped, but it can never be helped merely by talking about it. We must act and act quickly.

Finally, in our progress toward a resumption of work we require two safeguards against a return of the evils of the old order; there must be a strict supervision of all banking and credits and investments; there must be an end to speculation with other people's money, and there must be provision for an adequate but sound currency.

These are the lines of attack. I shall presently urge upon a new Congress in special session detailed measures for their fulfillment, and I shall seek the immediate assistance of the several States.

Through this program of action we address ourselves to putting our own national house in order and making income balance outgo. Our international trade relations, though vastly important, are in point of time and necessity secondary to the establishment of a sound national economy. I favor as a practical policy the putting of first things first. I shall spare no effort to restore world trade by international economic readjustment, but the emergency at home can not wait on that accomplishment.

The basic thought that guides these specific means of national recovery is not narrowly nationalistic. It is the insistence, as a first consideration, upon the interdependence of the various elements in and parts of the United States—a recognition of the old and permanently important manifestation of the American spirit of the pioneer. It is the way to recovery. It is the immediate way. It is the strongest assurance that the recovery will endure.

In the field of world policy I would dedicate this Nation to the policy of the good neighbor—the neighbor who resolutely respects himself and, because he does so, respects the rights of others—the neighbor who respects his obligations and respects the sanctity of his agreements in and with a world of neighbors.

If I read the temper of our people correctly, we now realize as we have never realized before our interdependence on each other; that we can not merely take but we must give as well; that if we are to go forward, we must move as a trained and loyal army willing to sacrifice for the good of a common discipline, because without such discipline no progress is made, no leadership becomes effective. We are, I know, ready and willing to submit our lives and property to such discipline, because it makes possible a leadership which aims at a larger good. This I propose to offer, pledging that the larger purposes will bind upon us all as a sacred obligation, with a unity of duty hitherto evoked only in time of armed strife.

With this pledge taken, I assume unhesitatingly the leadership of this great army of our people dedicated to a disciplined attack upon our common problems.

Action in this image and to this end is feasible under the form of government which we have inherited from our ancestors. Our Constitution is so simple and practical that it is possible always to meet extraordinary needs by changes in emphasis and arrangement without loss of essential form. That is why our constitutional system has proved itself the most superbly enduring political mechanism the modern world has produced. It has met every stress of vast expansion of territory, of foreign wars, of bitter internal strife, of world relations.

It is to be hoped that the normal balance of executive and legislative authority may be wholly adequate to meet the unprecedented task before us. But it may be that an unprecedented demand and need for undelayed action may call for temporary departure from that normal balance of public procedure.

I am prepared under my constitutional duty to recommend the measures that a stricken nation in the midst of a stricken world may require. These measures, or such other measures as the Congress may build out of its experience and wisdom, I shall seek, within my constitutional authority, to bring to speedy adoption.

But in the event that the Congress shall fail to take one of these two courses, and in the event that the national emergency is still critical, I shall not evade the clear course of duty that will then confront me. I shall ask the Congress for the one remaining instrument to meet the crisis—broad Executive power to wage a war against the emergency, as great as the power that would be given to me if we were in fact invaded by a foreign foe.

For the trust reposed in me I will return the courage and the devotion that befit the time. I can do no less.

We face the arduous days that lie before us in the warm courage of national unity; with the clear consciousness of seeking old and precious moral values; with the clean satisfaction that comes from the stern performance of duty by old and young alike. We aim at the assurance of a rounded and permanent national life.

We do not distrust the future of essential democracy. The people of the United States have not failed. In their need they have registered a mandate that they want direct, vigorous action. They have asked for discipline and direction under leadership. They have made me the present instrument of their wishes. In the spirit of the gift I take it.

In this dedication of a Nation we humbly ask the blessing of God. May He protect each and every one of us. May He guide me in the days to come.

Fireside Chat on the
Accomplishments of the New Deal

FRANKLIN DELANO ROOSEVELT

(For *biographical sketch, see p. 146.*)

"But the simplest way for each of you to judge recovery lies
in the plain facts of your own individual situation. Are you
better off than you were last year?"

I *t has been several months* since I have talked with you
concerning the problems of Government. Since January,
those of us in whom you have vested responsibility have been engaged in the
fulfillment of plans and policies which had been widely discussed in previous
months. It seemed to us our duty not only to make the right path clear, but also
to tread that path.

As we review the achievements of this session of the Seventy-third Congress,
it is made increasingly clear that its task was essentially that of completing and
fortifying the work it had begun in March, 1933. That was no easy task, but
the Congress was equal to it.

It has been well said that while there were a few exceptions, this Congress
displayed a greater freedom from mere partisanship than any other peace-time
Congress since the administration of President Washington himself. The session
was distinguished by the extent and variety of legislation enacted and by the intelligence and good-will of debate upon these measures.

I mention only a few of the major enactments. It provided for the readjustment

Radio address, Washington, D.C., June 28, 1934. *The New York Times,* June 29, 1934, p.
2. Reprinted by permission of *The New York Times.*

of the debt burden through the Corporate and Municipal Bankruptcy Acts and the Farm Relief Act. It lent a hand to industry by encouraging loans to solvent industries unable to secure adequate help from banking institutions. It strengthened the integrity of finance through the regulation of securities exchanges.

It provided a rational method of increasing our volume of foreign trade through reciprocal trading agreements. It strengthened our naval forces to conform with the intentions and permission of existing treaty rights. It made further advances toward peace in industry through the Labor Adjustment Act. It supplemented our agricultural policy through measures widely demanded by farmers themselves and intended to avert price-destroying surpluses.

It strengthened the hand of the Federal Government in its attempts to suppress gangster crime. It took definite steps toward a national housing program through an act which I signed today designed to encourage private capital in the rebuilding of the homes of the Nation. It created a permanent Federal body for the just regulation of all forms of communication, including the telephone, the telegraph and the radio.

Finally, and I believe most important, it reorganized, simplified and made more fair and just our monetary system, setting up standards and policies adequate to meet the necessities of modern economic life, doing justice to both gold and silver as the metal bases behind the currency of the United States.

In the consistent development of our previous efforts toward the saving and safeguarding of our national life, I have continued to recognize three related steps. The first was relief, because the primary concern of any Government dominated by the humane ideals of democracy is the simple principle that in a land of vast resources no one should be permitted to starve. Relief was and continues to be our first consideration. It calls for large expenditures and will continue in modified form to do so for a long time to come. We may as well recognize that fact. It comes from the paralysis that arose as the after-effect of that unfortunate decade characterized by a mad chase for unearned riches, and an unwillingness of leaders in almost every walk of life to look beyond their own schemes and speculations.

In our administration of relief we follow two principles: first, that direct giving shall, wherever possible, be supplemented by provision for useful and remunerative work and, second, that where families in their existing surroundings will in all human probability never find an opportunity for full self-maintenance, happiness and enjoyment, we will try to give them a new chance in new surroundings.

The second step was recovery, and it is sufficient for me to ask each and every one of you to compare the situation in agriculture and in industry today with what it was fifteen months ago.

At the same time we have recognized the necessity of reform and reconstruction—reform because much of our trouble today and in the past few years has been due to a lack of understanding of the elementary principles of justice and fairness by those in whom leadership in business and finance and public affairs was placed—reconstruction because new conditions in our economic life as well as old but neglected conditions had to be corrected.

Substantial gains well known to all of you have justified our course. I could cite statistics to you as unanswerable measures of our national progress—statistics to show the gain in the average weekly pay envelope of workers in the great majority of industries—statistics to show hundreds of thousands reemployed in private industries, and other hundreds of thousands given new employment through the expansion of direct and indirect assistance of many kinds, although, of course, there are those exceptions in professional pursuits whose economic improvement, of necessity, will be delayed. I also could cite statistics to show the great rise in the value of farm products—statistics to prove the demand for consumers' goods, ranging all the way from food and clothing to automobiles, and of late to prove the rise in the demand for durable goods—statistics to cover the great increase in bank deposits, and to show the scores of thousands of homes and of farms which have been saved from foreclosure.

But the simplest way for each of you to judge recovery lies in the plain facts of your own individual situation. Are you better off than you were last year? Are your debts less burdensome? Is your bank account more secure? Are your working conditions better? Is your faith in your own individual future more firmly grounded?

Also, let me put to you another simple question: Have you as an individual paid too high a price for these gains? Plausible self-seekers and theoretical die-hards will tell you of the loss of individual liberty. Answer this question also out of the facts of your own life. Have you lost any of your rights or liberty or constitutional freedom of action and choice? Turn to the Bill of Rights of the Constitution, which I have solemnly sworn to maintain and under which your freedom rests secure. Read each provision of that Bill of Rights and ask yourself whether you personally have suffered the impairment of a single jot of these great assurances. I have no question in my mind as to what your answer will be. The record is written in the experiences of your own personal lives.

In other words, it is not the overwhelming majority of the farmers or manufacturers or workers who deny the substantial gains of the past year. The most vociferous of the Doubting Thomases may be divided roughly into two groups: First, those who seek special political privilege and, second, those who seek special financial privilege.

About a year ago I used as an illustration the ninety per cent of the cotton manufacturers of the United States who wanted to do the right thing by their employees and by the public, but were prevented from doing so by the ten per cent who undercut them by unfair practices and un-American standards. It is well for us to remember that humanity is a long way from being perfect and that a selfish minority in every walk of life—farming, business, finance and even Government service itself—will always continue to think of themselves first and their fellow beings second.

In the working out of a great national program which seeks the primary good of the greater number, it is true that the toes of some people are being stepped on and are going to be stepped on. But these toes belong to the comparative few who seek to retain or to gain position or riches or both by some short cut which is harmful to the greater good.

In the execution of the powers conferred on it by the Congress, the Administration needs and will tirelessly seek the best ability that the country affords. Public service offers better rewards in the opportunity for service than ever before in our history—not great salaries, but enough to live on. In the building of this service there are coming to us men and women with ability and courage from every part of the Union. The days of the seeking of mere party advantage through the misuse of public power are drawing to a close. We are increasingly demanding and getting devotion to the public service on the part of every member of the administration, high and low.

The program of the past year is definitely in operation, and that operation month by month is being made to fit into the web of old and new conditions. This process of evolution is well illustrated by the constant changes in detailed organization and method going on in the National Recovery Administration.

With every passing month we are making strides in the orderly handling of the relationship between employees and employers. Conditions differ, of course, in almost every part of the country and in almost every industry. Temporary methods of adjustment are being replaced by more permanent machinery and, I am glad to say, by a growing recognition on the part of employers and employees of the desirability of maintaining fair relationships all around.

So also, while almost everybody has recognized the tremendous strides in the elimination of child labor, in the payment of not less than fair minimum wages and in the shortening of hours, we are still feeling our way in solving problems which relate to self-government in industry, especially where such self-government tends to eliminate the fair operation of competition.

In this same process of evolution we are keeping before us the objectives of protecting, on the one hand, industry against chiselers within its own ranks, and, on the other hand, the consumer through the maintenance of reasonable competition for the prevention of the unfair sky-rocketing of retail prices.

But, in addition to this, our immediate task, we must still look to the larger future. I have pointed out to the Congress that we are seeking to find the way once more to well-known, long-established but to some degree forgotten ideals and values. We seek the security of the men, women and children of the nation.

That security involves added means of providing better homes for the people of the nation. That is the first principle of our future program.

The second is to plan the better use of land and water resources of this country to the end that the means of livelihood of our citizens may be more adequate to meet their daily needs.

And, finally, the third principle is to use the agencies of government to assist in the establishment of means to provide sound and adequate protection against the vicissitudes of modern life—in other words, social insurance.

Later in the year I hope to talk with you more fully about these plans.

A few timid people, who fear progress, will try to give you new and strange names for what we are doing. Sometimes they will call it "Fascism," sometimes "Communism," sometimes "Regimentation," sometimes "Socialism." But, in so doing, they are trying to make very complex and theoretical something that is really very simple and very practical.

I believe in practical explanations and practical policies. I believe that what we are doing today is a necessary fulfillment of what Americans have always been doing—a fulfillment of old and tested American ideals.

Let me give you a simple illustration:

While I am away from Washington this summer, a long-needed renovation of and addition to our White House office building is to be started. The architects have planned a few new rooms built into the present all-too-small one-story structure. We are going to include in this addition and in this renovation modern electric wiring and modern plumbing and modern means of keeping the offices cool in the hot Washington summers. But the structural lines of the old executive office building will remain. The artistic lines of the White House buildings were the creation of master builders when our Republic was young. The simplicity and the strength of the structure remain in the face of every modern test. But within this magnificent pattern, the necessities of modern government business require constant reorganization and rebuilding.

If I were to listen to the arguments of some prophets of calamity who are talking these days, I should hesitate to make these alterations. I should fear that while I am away for a few weeks the architects might build some strange new Gothic tower or a factory building or perhaps a replica of the Kremlin or of the Potsdam Palace. But I have no such fears. The architects and builders are men of common sense and of artistic American tastes. They know that the principles of harmony and of necessity itself require that the building of the new structure shall blend with the essential lines of the old. It is this combination of the old and the new that marks orderly, peaceful progress—not only in building buildings but in building government itself.

Our new structure is a part of and a fulfillment of the old.

All that we do seeks to fulfill the historic traditions of the American people. Other nations may sacrifice democracy for the transitory stimulation of old and discredited autocracies. We are restoring confidence and well-being under the rule of the people themselves. We remain, as John Marshall said a century ago, "emphatically and truly, a government of the people." Our Government "in form and in substance . . . emanates from them. Its powers are granted by them, and are to be exercised directly on them, and for their benefits."

Before I close, I want to tell you of the interest and pleasure with which I look forward to the trip on which I hope to start in a few days. It is a good thing for everyone who can possibly do so to get away at least once a year for a change of scene. I do not want to get into the position of not being able to see the forest because of the thickness of the trees.

I hope to visit our fellow-Americans in Puerto Rico, in the Virgin Islands, in the Canal Zone and in Hawaii. And, incidentally, it will give me an opportunity to exchange a friendly word of greeting with the Presidents of our sister Republics, Haiti and Colombia and Panama.

After four weeks on board ship, I plan to land at a port in our Pacific Northwest, and then will come the best part of the whole trip, for I am hoping to inspect a number of our new great national projects on the Columbia, Missouri and Mississippi Rivers, to see some of our national parks and, incidentally, to learn much of actual conditions during the trip across the continent back to Washington.

While I was in France during the War our boys used to call the United States "God's country." Let us make it and keep it "God's country."

Come Back to Your Father's House

ALFRED EMANUEL SMITH

*Born, New York City, December 30, 1873; died, New York
City, October 4, 1944. Elementary education at St. James
Parochial School on the Lower East Side. Worked his way
by stages through New York City politics. Member, New
York Assembly, 1903–1915. Sheriff of New York County,
1915–1917. Elected Governor of New York for four terms
during the 1920's. Democratic candidate for President, 1928.
One of the founders of the American Liberty League, he
repudiated Roosevelt and supported the Republican candidates for President in 1936 and 1940.*

"The young brain trusters caught the Socialists in swimming
and they ran away with their clothes."

*M*r. *Chairman, members and guests of the American
Liberty League, and my friends listening in, as I
have been told by the newspapers, from all parts of the United States:* At the
outset of my remarks let me make one thing perfectly clear. I am not a candidate
for any nomination by any party, at any time. What is more, I do not intend
even to lift my right hand to secure any nomination from any party at any time.

Further than that, I have no axe to grind. There is nothing personal in this
whole performance in so far as I am concerned. I have no feeling against any
man, woman or child in the United States. I am in possession of supreme happiness and comfort. I represent no group, no man, and I speak for no man or
no group, but I do speak for what I believe to be the best interests of the great
rank and file of the American people in which class I belong.

American Liberty League dinner, Washington, D.C., and national radio audience, January
25, 1936. Text based on a stenographic report, *The New York Times,* January 26, 1936, p. 36.
Reprinted by permission of *The New York Times.*

Now, I am here tonight also because I have a great love for the United States of America. I love it for what I know it has meant to mankind since the day of its institution. I love it because I feel that it has grown to be a great stabilizing force in world civilization. I love it, above everything else, for the opportunity that it offers to every man and every woman that desires to take advantage of it.

No man that I know of or that I probably ever read of has any more reason to love it than I have. They kept the gateway open for me. It is a matter of common knowledge throughout the country, and I do not state it boastfully, because it is well known, that, deprived by poverty in my early years of an education, that gateway showed me how it was possible to go from a newsboy on the sidewalks of New York to the Governorship of the greatest State in the Union.

Now listen. I have five children and I have ten grandchildren, and you take it from me I want that gate left open, not alone for mine—I am not selfish about it—not for mine, but for every boy and girl in the country. And in that respect I am no different from every father and mother in the United States.

Now, think it over for a minute, figure it out for yourself. It is possible for your children's success to be your success.

I remember distinctly my first inauguration as Governor of New York, and I am not sure that the young folks understood it thoroughly, but there were three people at that inauguration that did understand it: One was my mother, and the other was my sister, and the third was my wife, because they were with me in all of the early struggles.

I am here for another reason. I am here because I am a Democrat. I was born in the Democratic party and I expect to die in it. I was attached to it in my youth, because I was led to believe that no man owned it. Furthermore, that no group of men owned it, but, on the other hand, it belonged to all the plain people of the United States.

Now, I must make a confession. It is not easy for me to stand up here tonight and talk to the American people against a Democratic administration. It is not easy; it hurts me. But I can call upon innumerable witnesses to testify to the fact that during my whole public life I put patriotism above partisanship.

And when I see danger, I see danger. That is the stop, look and listen to the fundamental principles upon which this government of ours was organized. And it is difficult for me to refrain from speaking up. What are these dangers that I see? The first is the arraignment of class against class. It has been freely predicted that if we were ever to have civil strife again in this country it would come from the appeal to the passions and prejudices that come from the demagogues who would incite one class of our people against the other.

Of course in my time I met some good and bad industrialists. I met some good and bad financiers, but I also met some good and bad laborers. This I know—that permanent prosperity is dependent upon both capital and labor alike. I also know that there can be no permanent prosperity in this country until industry is able to employ labor, and there certainly can be no permanent recovery upon any governmental theory of soak the rich or soak the poor.

Even the children in our high schools, and let it be said to the glory of our educational institutions, that even the children in our high schools know that you can't soak capital without soaking labor at the same time.

The next thing that I view as being dangerous to our national liberty is government by bureaucracy instead of what we have been taught to look to: government by law. Just let me quote something from the President's message to Congress:

"In thirty-four months we have set up new instruments of public power in the hands of the people's government, which power is wholesome and appropriate, but in the hands of political puppets, of an economic autocracy, such power would provide shackles for the liberties of our people."

Now, I interpret that to mean that, if you are going to have an autocrat, take me.

But be very careful about the other fellow.

There is a complete answer to that, and it rises in the minds of the great rank and file, and that answer is just this—we will never, in this country, tolerate any law that provides shackles for our people.

We don't want any autocrats, either in or out of office. We wouldn't even take a good one.

The next thing that is apparent to me is the vast building up of new bureaus of government, draining the resources of our people, to pool and redistribute them, not by any process of law but by the whim of the bureaucratic autocracy.

Well, now, what am I here for? I am here not to find fault. Anybody can do that. I am here to make a suggestion. Now, what would I have my party do? I would have them re-establish and re-declare the principles that they put forth in that 1932 platform.

Even our Republican friends, and I know many of them—they talk to me freely, we have our little confidences among ourselves—they have all agreed that it is the most compact, the most direct and the most intelligent political platform that was ever put forth by any political party in this country.

The Republican platform was ten times as long as it. It was stuffy, it was unreadable, and in many points not understandable.

No administration in the history of the country came into power with a more simple, a more clear, or a more inescapable mandate than the party that was inaugurated on the 4th of March in 1933, and, listen, no candidate in the history of the country ever pledged himself more unequivocally to his party platform than did the President who was inaugurated on that day.

Well, here we are. Millions and millions of Democrats, just like myself, all over the country, still believe in that platform. What we want to know is, why wasn't it carried out?

And listen, there is only one man in the United States of America that can answer that question.

It won't do to pass it down to an Under-Secretary. I won't even recognize him when I hear his name. I won't know where he came from. I will be sure that he never lived down in my district.

Now, let us wander for a little while and let us take a look at that platform and let us see what happened to it. Here is the way it started out:

"We believe that a party platform is a covenant with the people to be faithfully kept by the party when entrusted with power and that the people are entitled to know in plain words the terms of the contract to which they are asked to subscribe.

"The Democratic party solemnly promises by appropriate action to put into effect the principles, policies and reforms herein advocated and to eradicate the political methods and practices herein condemned."

My friends, these were what we called "fighting words." At the time that that platform went through the air and over the wire, the people of the United States were in the lowest possible depths of despair, and the Democratic platform looked to them like a star of hope, it looked like the rising sun in the East to the mariner on the bridge of a ship after a terrible night, but what happened to it?

First plank: "We advocate an immediate drastic reduction of governmental expenditures by abolishing useless commissions and offices, consolidating departments and bureaus, and eliminating extravagance, to accomplish a saving of not less than twenty-five per cent in the cost of the Federal Government."

Well, now, what is the fact?

No bureaus were eliminated, but on the other hand the alphabet was exhausted in the creation of new departments and—this is sad news for the taxpayer—the cost, the ordinary cost, what we refer to as "housekeeping costs" over and above all emergencies, that ordinary housekeeping cost of government is greater today than it has ever been in any time in the history of the Republic.

Another plank: "We favor maintenance of the national credit by a Federal budget annually balanced on the basis of accurate executive estimates within revenue."

Why, how can you balance a budget if you insist upon spending more money than you take in? Even the increased revenue won't go to balance the budget, because it is "hocked" before you receive it.

It is much worse than that. We borrow. We owe something. We have borrowed so that we have reached a new high peak of Federal indebtedness for all time. Well, that wouldn't annoy me so very much ordinarily.

When I was Governor of New York, they said I borrowed a lot of money. That wouldn't worry me. If it solved our problems and we were out of trouble, I would say, "All right, let it go." But the sin of it is that we have the indebtedness, and at the end of three years we are just where we started.

Unemployment and the farm problem we still have with us. Now, here is something that I want to say to the rank and file: There are three classes of people in this country, there is the poor and the rich, and in between the two is what has often been referred to as the great backbone of America, that is the plain fellow, that is the fellow that makes from $100 a month up to the man that draws down five or six thousand dollars a year.

Now, there is that great big army. Forget the rich; they can't pay this debt; if you took everything they got away from them you could not pay it, there are not enough of them.

Furthermore, they ain't got enough. Now, there's no use of talking about the poor. They will never pay it, because they got nothing. This debt is going to be paid by that great big middle-class that we refer to as the backbone and the rank and file, and the sin of it is, they ain't going to know that they're paying it.

It is going to come to them in the form of indirect taxation. It will come in the cost of living, in the cost of clothing, in the cost of every activity they enter into, and because it isn't a direct tax, they won't think they are paying it, but take it from me, they are going to pay it.

Another point: "We advocate the extension of Federal credit to the States to provide for unemployment relief when the diminishing resources of the State render it impossible to provide for them."

That is pretty plain.

That was a recognition in the national convention of the rights of the States. But what happened? The Federal Government took over most of the relief problems, some of them useful and most of them useless. They started out to prime the pump for industry in order to absorb the ranks of the unemployed, and at the end of three years their affirmative policy is absolutely nothing but the negative policy of the administration that preceded it.

We favor unemployment and old age insurance under State laws. Now, let me make myself perfectly clear so that no demagogue or no crack pot in the next week or so will be able to say anything about my attitude on this kind of legislation. I am in favor of it, and I take my hat off to no man in the United States on the question of legislation beneficial to the poor, the weak, the sick or the afflicted, men, women and children.

Because when I started out a quarter of a century ago, when I had very few followers in my State, during that period I advocated, fought for and introduced, as a legislator, and finally as Governor, for eight long years, and signed more progressive legislation in the interest of men, women and children than any man in the State of New York. And the sin of this whole thing, and the part of it that worries me and gives me concern is, that this haphazard legislation is never going to accomplish the purpose for which it was designed. And bear this in mind—follow the platform—"under State law."

Here is another one: "We promise the enactment of every constitutional measure that will aid the farmers to receive for their basic farm commodities prices in excess of cost."

Well, what is the use of talking about that? "We promise every constitutional measure." The Supreme Court disposed of that within the last couple of weeks. And, according to the papers the other day, some brilliant individual has conceived the idea of how to get around the Constitution. We are going to have forty-eight AAA's, one for each State.

The day that the United States Supreme Court decided the case I left my office to attend a board of trustees meeting. I got in a taxicab to go downtown. The driver was reading the extra, "Supreme Court Declares AAA Unconstitutional."

We rode along for a few minutes and then we got caught at a red light. The taxi fellow turned around and said: "Governor, ain't there any lawyers in Congress any more?"

Just then the lights changed. I was afraid to answer him for fear I might disconcert him, but I was all ready to say: "Yes, son, but they don't function."

We got another plank! "We advocate strengthening and impartial enforcement of the anti-trust laws." What happened? The NRA just put a gas bag on the anti-trust laws and put them fast asleep.

And nobody said anything about it. I don't know whether they are good or whether they are bad, but I know that they didn't work.

Another one: "We promise the removal of government from all fields of private enterprise, except where necessary to develop public works and national resources in the common interest."

NRA! A vast octopus set up by government that wound its arms around all the business of the country, paralyzed big business and choked little business to death.

Did you read in the papers a short time ago where somebody said that business was going to get a breathing spell? What is the meaning of that? And where did that expression arise? I will tell you where it comes from.

It comes from the prize ring. When the aggressor is punching the head off the other fellow, he suddenly takes compassion on him and gives him a breathing spell before he delivers the knockout wallop.

Here is another one: "We condemn the open and covert resistance of administrative officials to every effort made by Congressional committees to curtail the extravagance and expenses of government and improvident subsidies rendered to private interests."

Now, just between ourselves, do you know any administrative officer that ever tried to stop Congress from appropriating money? Do you think there has been any desire on the part of Congress to curtail appropriations?

Why, not at all. The fact is, that Congress is throwing them left and right, don't even tell what they are for.

And the truth is that every administrative officer sought to get all he possibly could, to expand the activities of his own office, and throw the money of the people right and left.

As to the subsidy—never at any time in the history of this or any other country were there so many subsidies granted to private groups and on such a large scale. The fact of the matter is that most of the cases pending before the United States Supreme Court revolve around the point of whether or not it is proper for Congress to tax all the people to pay subsidies to a particular group.

Here is another one: "We condemn the extravagance of the Farm Board, its disastrous action which made the government a speculator in farm products, and the unsound policy of restricting agricultural products to the demands of domestic markets."

Listen, and I will let you in on something. This has not leaked out, so kind of keep it to yourself until you get the news.

On the first of February we are going to own 4,500,000 bales of cotton. The cost is $270,000,000.

And we have been such brilliant speculators that we are paying thirteen cents a pound for it when you add storage and carrying charges, and it can be bought in any one of the ten cotton markets of the South today for $11.50. Some speculators!

What about the restriction of our agricultural products and the demands of the domestic market? Why, the fact about that is that we shut out entirely the foreign market, and by plowing under corn and wheat and the destruction of foodstuffs, food from foreign countries has been pouring into our American markets, food that should have been purchased by us from our own farmers.

In other words, while some of the countries of the Old World were attempting to drive the wolf of hunger from the doormat, the United States of America flew in the face of God's bounty and destroyed its own foodstuffs. There can be no question about that.

Now, I could go on indefinitely with some of the other planks. They are unimportant, and the radio time will not permit it. But just let me sum up this way: regulation of the Stock Exchange and the repeal of the Eighteenth Amendment, plus one or two minor provisions of the platform that in no way touched the daily life of our people have been carried out, but the balance of the platform was thrown in the waste-basket. About that there can be no question.

And let us see how it was carried out. Make a test for yourself.

Just get the platform of the Democratic party and get the platform of the Socialist party and lay them down on your dining-room table, side by side, and get a heavy lead pencil and scratch out the word "Democratic" and scratch out the word "Socialist" and let the two platforms lay there, and then study the record of the present administration up to date.

After you have done that, make your mind up to pick up the platform that more nearly squares with the record, and you will have your hand on the Socialist platform; you would not dare touch the Democratic platform.

And incidentally, let me say that it is not the first time in recorded history that a group of men have stolen the livery of the church to do the work of the devil.

If you study this whole situation you will find that is at the bottom of all our troubles. This country was organized on the principles of a representative democracy, and you can't mix socialism or communism with that. They are like oil and water. They are just like oil and water, they refuse to mix.

Incidentally, let me say to you that is the reason why the United States Supreme Court is working overtime, throwing the alphabet out of the window, three letters at a time.

I am going to let you in on something else. How do you suppose all this happened? The young brain trusters caught the Socialists in swimming and they ran away with their clothes.

Now, it is all right with me, it is all right with me, if they want to disguise themselves as Karl Marx or Lenin or any of the rest of that bunch, but I won't stand for their allowing them to march under the banner of Jackson or Cleveland.

Now, what is worrying me is: Where does that leave us millions of Democrats? My mind is all fixed upon the convention in June in Philadelphia. The committee on resolutions is about to report. The preamble to the platform is:

"We, the representatives of the Democratic party, in convention assembled, heartily endorse the Democratic administration."

What happened to the recital of Jefferson and Jackson and Cleveland when that resolution was read out? Why, for us it is a washout. There is only one of two things we can do, we can either take on the mantle of hypocrisy or we can take a walk, and we will probably do the latter.

Now, leave the platform alone for a little while. What about this attack that has been made upon the fundamental institutions of this country, who threatens them, and did we have any warning of this threat? Why, you don't have to study party platforms, you don't have to read books, you don't have to listen to professors of economics. You will find the whole thing incorporated in the greatest declaration of political principle that ever came from the hand of man—the Declaration of Independence and the Constitution of the United States.

Always have in your mind that the Constitution and the first ten amendments were drafted by refugees and by sons of refugees, by men with bitter memories of European oppression and hardship, by men who brought to this country and handed down to their descendants an abiding fear of arbitrary, centralized government and autocracy and—listen, all the bitterness and all the hatred of the Old World was distilled, in our Constitution, into the purest democracy that the world has ever known.

There are just three principles and in the interest of brevity I will read them. I can read them quicker than I can talk them.

First, a Federal Government strictly limited in its powers, with all other powers except those expressly mentioned reserved to the States and to the people, so as to insure State's rights, guarantee home rule and preserve freedom of individual initiative and local control.

That is simple enough. The difference between the State Constitution and the Federal Constitution is that in the State you can do anything you want to do provided it is not prohibited by the Constitution, but in the Federal Government, according to that document, you can do only that which that Constitution tells you that you can do.

What is the trouble? Congress has overstepped its power, it has gone beyond that constitutional limitation, and it has enacted laws that not only violate that, but violate the home rule and the State's rights principle. And who says that?

Did I say it? Not at all. That was said by the United States Supreme Court in the last ten or twelve days.

Second, the government with three independent branches, Congress to make the laws, the Executives to execute them, the Supreme Court, and so forth, and you all know that.

In the name of heaven, where is the independence of Congress? Why, they just laid right down. They are flatter on the Congressional floor than the rug under this table here.

They centered all their powers in the Executives, and that is the reason why you read in the newspapers reference to Congress as the rubber-stamp Congress.

We all know that the most important bills were drafted by the brain trusters and sent over to Congress and passed by Congress without consideration, without debate, and, without meaning any offense at all to my Democratic brethren in Congress, I think I can safely say without 90 percent of them knowing what was in the bills, what was the meaning of the list that came over, and beside certain items was "must."

Speaking for the rank and file of the American people, we don't want any Executive to tell Congress what it must do. We don't want any Congress to tell the Executive what he must do.

We don't want Congress or the Executive, jointly or severally, to tell the United States Supreme Court what it must do.

On the other hand, we don't want the United States Supreme Court to tell either of them what they must do. What we want, and what we insist upon, and what we are going to have, is the absolute preservation of this balance of power which is the keystone upon which the whole theory of democratic government has got to rest, and when you rattle it you rattle the whole structure.

Of course, when our forefathers wrote the Constitution, it couldn't be possible that they had in their minds that that was going to be all right for all time to come, so they said, "No, we will provide a manner and method of amending," and that is set forth in the document itself. And during our national life we amended it many times.

We amended it once by mistake, and we corrected it.

And what did we do? We took the amendment out. Fine! That is the way we ought to do it. By recourse to the people.

But we don't want an administration that takes a shot at it in the dark and that ducks away from it and dodges away from it and tries to put something over in contradiction of it upon any theory that there is going to be a great public power in favor of it and it is possible that the United States Supreme Court may be intimidated into a friendly opinion with respect to it.

But I found all during my public life that Almighty God built this country and He did not give us that kind of a Supreme Court.

Now, this is pretty tough for me to have to go after my own party this way, but I submit that there is a limit to blind loyalty.

As a young man in the Democratic party I witnessed the rise and fall of Bryan and Bryanism, and in the memory of Bryan, what he did to our party, I know how long it took to build it after he got finished with it. But let me say this, for the everlasting memory of Bryan and the men that followed him, that they had the energy and the courage and the honesty to put into the platform just what their leaders told them.

They put the American people in the position of making an intelligent choice when they went to the polls. The fact of this whole thing is, I speak now not only of the executive but of the Legislature at the same time—that they promised one set of things. They repudiated that promise, and they launched off on a program of action totally different.

Well, in twenty-five years of experience I have known both parties to fail to carry out some of the planks of their platform, but this is the first time that I have known a party, upon such a huge scale, not only not to carry out the planks, but to do directly the opposite thing to what they promised.

Now, suggestions—and I make these as a Democrat, acting for the success of my party, and I make them in good faith. Here are my suggestions:

Number 1—I suggest for the members of my party on Capitol Hill here in Washington that they take their minds off the Tuesday that follows the first Monday in November.

Just take your mind off it to the end that you may do the right thing and not the expedient thing.

Yes, I suggest to them that they dig up the 1932 platform from the grave that they buried it in and read it over and study it, read life into it and follow it in legislative and executive action to the end that they make good their promises to the American people when they put forth that platform and the candidate that stood upon it 100 percent—in short, make good.

Third, I would suggest that they stop compromising with the fundamental principles laid down by Jackson and Jefferson and Cleveland.

Fourth, stop attacking all the forms of the structure of our government without recourse to the people themselves, as provided in their own Constitution which really belongs to the people, and it does not belong to any administration.

Next, I suggest that they read their oath of office to support the Constitution of the United States and I ask them to remember that they took that oath with their hands on the Holy Bible, thereby calling upon God Almighty himself to witness their solemn promise. It is bad enough to disappoint us.

Sixth, I suggest that from this moment on they resolve to make the Constitution again the Civil Bible of the United States and to pay it the same civil respect and reverence that they would religiously pay the Holy Scripture, and I ask them to read from the Holy Scripture the paragraph of the prodigal son, and to follow his example, "Stop, stop wasting your substance in a foreign land and come back to your father's house."

Now, in conclusion, let me give this solemn warning: There can be only one capital, Washington or Moscow.

There can be only one atmosphere of government, the clear, pure, fresh air of free America, or the foul breath of communistic Russia. There can be only one flag, the Stars and Stripes, or the flag of the godless Union of the Soviets.

There can be only one national anthem, "The Star-Spangled Banner" or the "Internationale."

There can be only one victor. If the Constitution wins, we win.

But if the Constitution—stop, stop there—the Constitution can't lose.

The fact is, it has already won, but the news has not reached certain ears.

Jacob's Voice but Esau's Hands

JOSEPH TAYLOR ROBINSON

Born near Lonoke, Arkansas, August 26, 1872; died, Washington, D.C., July 14, 1937. Attended the University of Arkansas for two years. Studied law in Lonoke; admitted to the bar, 1895. Member, United States House of Representatives, 1903–1913. Became Governor of Arkansas, 1913. Elected to United States Senate by Arkansas legislature, 1913, where he served continuously until his death. Democratic candidate for Vice-President, 1928, as Alfred E. Smith's running mate. Majority leader of the Senate, 1933–1937, he died while loyally urging Roosevelt's unpopular court-packing proposal. Known as a keen parliamentarian and vigorous debater.

"The policies of the Liberty League have become the platform of the unhappy warrior."

*L*adies *and Gentlemen of the Radio Audience:* I shall take for my text tonight Genesis, the Twenty-seventh Chapter, Verse 22: "The voice is Jacob's voice but the hands are the hands of Esau."

Alfred E. Smith sought the Presidency in 1928, when a man who raised his voice on behalf of the great causes of social justice and democratic principles was regarded by the stock-ticker patriots with smug toleration or as a potential enemy of his country.

Columbia Broadcasting System, Washington, D.C., January 28, 1936. *The New York Times,* January 29, 1936, p. 12. Reprinted by permission of *The New York Times.*

Governor Smith in 1928 waged a clean and honorable campaign in behalf of common men and women, but he was swept down to defeat by greed and privilege hiding behind a murky and malodorous smoke screen. Greed supplied the thirty pieces of silver and passion brought about the base betrayal of fundamental American principles.

Now we are on the threshold of another national campaign with the same two armies facing each other along the battle line. The preliminary skirmishing is under way, and what is our amazement to find Governor Smith enthroned in the camp of the enemy, warring like one of the Janizaries of old against his own people and against the men and women with whom he fought shoulder to shoulder in the past.

A few nights ago there was held in the city of Washington a banquet by the miscalled "American Liberty League," and the main attraction on that occasion was none other than our old friend, the "Happy Warrior," who won his spurs battling for the rights of the plain people.

Let me read to you a description of that occasion from a Washington newspaper:

"Jammed elbow to elbow, tailcoat to tailcoat, fluttery bouffant dress to sleek black velvet dress, the tables set so closely together in the main ballroom that the ushers in the Confederate gray mess coats and black pants scarcely could wiggle between the anti-New Dealers, Democrats and Republicans alike gathered to hear the magic, rasping voice of Alfred E. Smith belabor the present administration."

Another writer in the same paper described it as a billion dollar audience that glanced up with eyes of worship and love at the new champion who had come amongst them. It was the swellest party ever given by the du Ponts.

Yes, Governor Smith not only has changed sides in the great battle but his whole outlook seems to have undergone a transformation. He has forgotten apparently the issues upon which he ran for the Presidency. The brown derby has been discarded for the high hat; he has turned away from the East Side with those little shops and fish markets, and now his gaze rests fondly upon the gilded towers and palaces of Park Avenue.

In the old days, Governor Smith was one of the most constructive and penetrating critics in American public life.

But now what a change! His hour-long harangue before the miscalled Liberty League was barren and sterile, without a single constructive suggestion for meeting the great social and economic problems confronting this government. He laid down a six-point program in which he proposed somewhat childishly that the Democrats should forget about the election, resurrect the platform of 1932, cease compromising with fundamental principles, discontinue efforts to change the fundamental principles of government, remember oaths of office and regard the Constitution as a Bible.

Not a specific proposal in the whole batch. Just a rehash of confusing and meaningless generalities.

Why, the "Happy Warrior" even went further than that. He boldly asserted that our great offensive to overcome the depression and adjust the nation's economic life had accomplished nothing and brought us nowhere. Is that a serious declaration or does it come under the heading of oratorical license?

I challenge the accuracy of that assertion. Why, a table recently compiled shows that in the three years of the New Deal as compared to the last three years of the Old Deal unemployment has declined 30 percent, cotton, wheat and corn have increased 100 percent or more in value, industrial production has gone up 51 percent, listed stocks have increased 134 percent in value and listed bonds 22 percent.

The progress of our recovery is apparent to every man who looks about him, and the story of its onward rush fairly leaps at you every day from the pages of the daily press. Bear in mind that when the Roosevelt administration came into power hungry and abandoned men in the cities were searching the garbage pails for waste scraps and the American farmers were halting court foreclosures by physical force, which borders little short of revolution. And Governor Smith says there has been no progress!

President Roosevelt had not been in the White House twenty-four hours before bankers and other big business men now grouped in the Liberty League appealed to him to "do something," to "do anything," to relieve the paralysis of business and to save them.

The President and the Congress responded to their appeals, saved the banks, and in saving them also saved the insurance companies; saved the railroads, the farms and the homes. No sooner had these suppliants been made secure than they began to complain of the very processes by which their fortunes had been preserved against bankruptcy.

They did not, when they needed help, brand government aid to private enterprises as socialistic or communistic; nor did they complain of the government engaging in what is normally private enterprise. Now, being secure, they regard it as violative of sound principle to accord the same assistance to others which they themselves have enjoyed.

So much for what the Roosevelt administration has accomplished. Now let's look at Mr. Smith's other criticism of the present Democratic administration. You recall that before the Liberty Leaguers he started to read the Democratic platform of 1932, but for some strange reason he never finished it. I wonder why. Was there something further along, condemning stock market manipulations, that he didn't like to read before his wealthy friends?

In any event, he charged that the New Deal was fostering and promoting class hatred; second, that it enacted an unconstitutional farm program and an unconstitutional NRA; third, that public money was being wasted; fourth, that Congress had abdicated its powers to the Executive; and, fifth, in a flag-waving, soul-stirring crescendo he charged the New Deal with trying to undermine the Constitution and Supreme Court while it fastened a socialistic and communistic dictatorship upon this country.

Let's look at the record. Why, Governor Smith, from your own lips, with your own words, with your own matchless talent for illuminating the dark places of public discussion, I shall prove that you have advocated and championed every basic principle that has been written into law by the Roosevelt administration.

In his speech on Saturday night Mr. Smith made the ugly charge that the New Deal is fomenting class hatred. Let me read you what he said when he was addressing the Alumni Association of Harvard University on June 22, 1933:

> I remember when we first spoke about the Workmen's Compensation Act the Court of Appeals of our own State set aside the first enactment as being contrary to the Constitution. I remember when we enacted the Child Welfare Act it was referred to as paternalism and as socialism.
>
> Our whole democracy at that time seemed to be devoted to the part that constitutional law and statute law was intended only for the protection of property and of money, and the human element did not seem to enter into it.
>
> The same has to do with the factory code; the same has to do with the provision for modern, up-to-date housing for our small-income group; the same has to do with the development of State-owned water power and the ownership by the State of the power at the site. Twenty years ago those were regarded as socialistic. I was referred to many times by my political opponents as a Socialist. But, in the light of our present-day legislation, Mr. President, I claim I am one of the ultra-conservatives.
>
> We have nothing to fear in this country from a dictatorship. There can be nothing of that kind in this country. It cannot live here. We are not organized to carry it on. We have no desire for it. Great as may be the grant of temporary power in an emergency that Congress may by Congressional enactment put into the hands of a President, the thing we have to fear in this country, to my way of thinking, is the influence of the organized minorities, because somehow or other the great majority does not seem to organize.

Yes, those were Mr. Smith's own words. Somehow I think there must be two Al Smiths. One is the happy, carefree fellow behind whom we marched and shouted in 1928, proud of his principles and eager to place him in the White House. Now we have this other Al Smith, this grim-visaged fellow in the high hat and tails, who warns us that we are going straight to Moscow.

If I recall correctly, he came before the Senate Finance Committee in 1933 and urged us to recognize Soviet Russia and give it a five-year moratorium on debt payments.

Throughout his 1928 campaign Governor Smith hammered at the power trust, denounced greed and special privilege, and faithfully promised the people that if he were elected he would establish a new order of things and bring about what he called a "more equal distribution of prosperity." Now he talks about stirring up class hatred, but what he said then sounded a great deal more like "share the wealth" than it does like the comparatively mild statements of President Roosevelt.

I pass on to his next accusation. He charged the New Deal with fostering an unconstitutional farm-relief program. He forgets that in 1928 he advocated the principles of the McNary-Haugen bill, which in many respects was far more drastic in its use of the taxing power than the AAA ever was. That's just a case of second guessing. Let me quote you from his Jefferson Day speech on April 13, 1932. He said:

It is a perfectly easy thing to say we must restore the purchasing power of the farmer. Fine! Of course we must. But how are we going to do it? I would sooner have a short shake-hands with the fellow that knows how to do it than listen for a week to the fellow who knows how to tell you what the trouble is.

Well, Governor Smith, you should have stepped out of that Belshazzar feast and taken a walk to the White House to shake the hand of the man who raised the purchasing price of the farmers more than $2,000,000,000 in one year.

In his speech on Saturday night Mr. Smith denounced the NRA as a giant octopus that entangled itself around all business, big and small, and tried to smother it to death. Another second guess. He made a radio speech on August 22, 1933, in which he called attention to the fact that NRA was largely voluntary and he added:

The slightest reflection on these facts should dispose of the claim, from whatever source it came, that the National Industrial Recovery Act shakes the firm foundations of our Constitution, or marks revolution in our government and in the conduct of our everyday life.

Let us see whether, by shorter hours, higher wages and increased employment we can avoid the dole, called home relief, and the disguised dole popularly known as relief work, the evil consequences of which we all know. It is infinitely better to pay the bill by the methods proposed in the National Industrial Recovery Act than to pay it in the form of public or private charitable relief.

These words from Governor Smith constitute an endorsement of the act which he so bitterly condemned last Saturday night.

The next charge was that public money was being wasted and that the party had failed to fulfill its pledge of a 25 percent reduction in government expenditures. He neglected entirely to state that no President ever could have refused the call of suffering humanity that existed during the crisis of 1933. He knows very well that any Chief Executive too cowardly to use the national credit to save human life would have been consumed in the burning hatred of his own people.

I'll go further than that. Governor Smith himself was urging appropriations for public relief at the very time that platform plank about which he boasts so loudly was being drafted. He made speech after speech urging a public bond issue to provide employment. He appeared before a committee of Congress for that purpose. Here is what he said at the Jackson Day dinner in Washington on January 8, 1932:

> Now, if it is all right to put the credit of the government behind business, let the credit of the government be used to keep the wolf of hunger away from the doormat of millions of people.

In that same speech Mr. Smith declared that the conduct of the Hoover administration was "indefensible" because states, cities and private charities were out of funds and unable to cope with the relief situation. He forgot to mention that speech to his Liberty League friends at the Belshazzar feast last Saturday night. Once again he was second-guessing.

Let's pass on to his fourth charge that Congress has abdicated its legislative powers and, as he said, the country is now run by bureaucrats. Why, what Congress did is the very thing he advocated. In that Jackson Day speech from which I just quoted Smith said:

> I would therefore suggest that Congress empower the President of the United States to appoint a Federal Administrator of Public Works and put the President in such a position as he can clothe him with plenary power to cut, slash, dig into and run through all the red tape and through all the statutory restrictions that are placed upon the government in the progress of public works.
>
> In other words, invoke the tactics of war, instead of dotting all the i's and crossing the t's and going through all the cumbersome labor of the peacetime performance when it comes to public works construction.

Oh my dear Governor Smith, what a short memory you have! Your charge that the Roosevelt administration is fostering socialism and communism is so ridiculous it's actually funny. Honestly, Governor, I think you've been seeing things under the bed, you know, those Communist spies that our good friend Ham Fish[1] is always talking about. Where have I heard that charge of socialism and communism before? Oh, now I recall, that's the identical charge that Herbert Hoover made against you in 1928.

Remember, Governor, after you fearlessly advocated the public ownership, public control and public development of water-power sites. Poor Herbert whimpered that it was State Socialism because he lacked any adequate or statesmanlike reply to the position you took.

And how you nailed poor Herbert on that one. You reminded him that the same old cry had been raised against Theodore Roosevelt, Charles Evans Hughes, Woodrow Wilson and every other public servant who ever attempted to perform a public duty on behalf of the whole people. Very properly you said that silly charges of that kind did more to promote socialism in this country than any other cause. Let me quote just two short paragraphs from the Boston speech of yours on October 24, 1928. You said:

---

[1] Hamilton Fish, arch-conservative and isolationist member of the United States House of Representatives from New York.

The cry of socialism has been patented by the powerful interests that desire to put a damper on progressive legislation.

Failing to meet the arguments fairly and squarely, special interest falls back on the old stock argument of socialism. The people of New York State are tired of the stock argument, have discovered that it means nothing, that it is simply subterfuge and camouflage, and I am satisfied that the people of the nation in their wisdom will so appraise it.

Yes, Governor Smith, you very properly reminded Mr. Hoover that under his definition even Charles Evans Hughes, the present Chief Justice of the United States, was a Socialist.

Now, then, Governor Smith, I wish to comment on one more portion of your speech. You quoted from President Roosevelt's message to Congress and then by straining and distorting his meaning you charged the President with saying: "If you are going to have an autocrat, take me; be very careful about the other fellow."

Now the Chief Executive never said that and he never hinted at any such things. That looks just a little bit like a blow below the belt. Now suppose I read the record on you, not what some one else said, but what you yourself said. I am now going to read you verbatim a news dispatch which appeared in the usually reliable *New York Times,* in the issue of February 8, 1933, just before Mr. Roosevelt entered the White House. I quote:

Former Governor Alfred E. Smith told 400 guests at a dinner of the Catholic Conference on Industrial Problems at the Hotel Astor last night that the nation needs a director of public works with power to cut through red tape if appropriations of public funds are to count in the war against the depression.

The former Governor asserted that the economic crisis had caused more domestic damage than participation by the United States in the World War, and he declared it must be fought as a democracy traditionally fights, by arrogating to itself the powers of "a tyrant, a despot or a monarch."

"Let us look back a few years to 1917 and 1918," Mr. Smith proposed. "What did we do then? Why, we took the Constitution, wrapped it up and put it on the shelf and forgot it until it was over."

Just think of that! Alfred E. Smith proposed in 1933 that we wrap up the Constitution and put it on the shelf until the depression was defeated, and then coming down here in 1936 to lecture Democratic leaders on constitutional government!

Now let me say something about the Constitution. In the whole United States there is not a single individual who can honestly and truthfully charge Franklin D. Roosevelt with advocating the suppression of freedom of speech, freedom of the press, freedom of assemblage, freedom of worship, or any of those other basic rights guaranteed us in the immortal Bill of Rights.

The idea that Governor Smith wished to convey in 1933 is the idea we all had —namely, that in a time of stress and torment, when every moment demanded action, to preserve human life and prevent human suffering, it was imperative to cease wasteful quibbling. He meant the time had passed for legal hair-splitting and pompous phraseology.

Governor Smith meant he was tired of boresome, self-styled constitutional authorities like James M. Beck, the chief justice of the "Liberty League," who has appeared ten times before the Supreme Court on constitutional questions and been turned down eight times.

History will show, and the record now will show, that President Roosevelt has never advocated the adoption of a single measure designed to curb in any way the just liberties of any man.

Of course President Roosevelt was unable to say definitely and finally in the great emergency of 1933 just where State power ended and Federal power began. Of course Congress was unable to say flatly and finally that the measures adopted would come within the framework of the Constitution as interpreted by the Supreme Court. Who could say conclusively the AAA was constitutional or unconstitutional? Why, even the court itself differed on that issue and three of its keenest members gave their unqualified opinion that it was constitutional.

We anticipate unprincipled men, engaged only in promoting their own interests, to join the hypocritical and pharisaical chorus, to join the hue and cry of those who falsely accuse the President of the United States of trying to undermine the organic law of this country. But we don't expect it from high-minded individuals who know better, from men who themselves have advocated far more drastic policies and programs than Mr. Roosevelt has pursued. If you condemn the President, Governor Smith, you condemn yourself one hundredfold.

The list of directors and officers of the American Liberty League reads like a roll-call of the men who have despoiled the oil, coal and water-power resources of this country. With notable exceptions they were lined up against you in 1928, supplying the money with which Herbert Hoover went about the country denouncing you as a Communist and a Socialist.

It was strange to see you in such company, Governor Smith. Over here marches the same army with whom you fought for social justice for a quarter of a century —Senator Wagner, Franklin Roosevelt, Miss Perkins, Senator Norris, and those other comrades of your earlier and better days.

The glamour of your presence and the brilliance of your personality so completely dominated that gathering on last Saturday night that in the half-shadows were concealed the lurking figures of men who fought for twenty-five years against the principles of government you formerly advocated. Within a few feet of the table at which you sat were members of the power trust, some of whom you denounced by name in 1928.

I'm sure Mr. Hoover was with you in spirit, his cherubic face agleam and his chubby hands applauding ecstatically as you repeated against Mr. Roosevelt the very speech which he himself delivered against you in 1928.

Yes, Governor Smith, it was as difficult to conceive you at that Liberty League banquet as it would be to imagine George Washington waving a cheery good-bye to the ragged and bleeding band at Valley Forge while he rode forth to dine in sumptuous luxury with smug and sanctimonious Tories in near-by Philadelphia.

Perhaps in the heat of battle sometimes our commanding officer, President Roosevelt, has employed the wrong tactics. Perhaps there has been confusion and loss of energy. Those things always happen when human beings attempt mass operations in hurried formation under the pressure of adverse fate. But those things never yet have justified a change of allegiance in the face of the enemy.

It rests with no soldier who approaches the battlefield under the flag of his leader to retire while the war continues. Above all things, he must never go over to the enemy.

Yes, I agree with you, Governor Smith, that the Democratic party belongs to no individual and no group. It cannot be purchased by the American Liberty League. The financial angels of the League will discover they cannot buy a monopoly over the name of freedom in the same way they have purchased monopolies over oil, coal and waterpower.

Governor Smith, I've read you the record. You approved NRA, you approved farm relief, you urged Federal spending and public works, you urged Congress to cut red tape and confer power on the Executive, you urged autocratic power for the President and you exposed with merciless logic the false cry of communism and socialism. The New Deal was the platform of the "Happy Warrior."

The policies of the Liberty League have become the platform of the unhappy warrior.

Is the New Deal Socialism?

NORMAN MATTOON THOMAS

Born, Marion, Ohio, November 20, 1884. Graduated from Princeton, 1905, and Union Theological Seminary, 1911. Ordained Presbyterian clergyman, 1911. Associate minister, Brick Presbyterian Church, 1910–1911; pastor, East Harlem Church and chairman, American Parish, New York City, 1911–1918. Associated importantly with numerous organizations such as American Civil Liberties Union, Fellowship of Reconciliation, Postwar World Council. Socialist candidate for Governor of New York and twice candidate for Mayor of New York City. Six times Socialist candidate for President of the United States between 1928 and 1948. Newspaper columnist, author, and a foremost political speaker of the century.

"A nation which misunderstands socialism as completely as Al Smith misunderstands it is a nation which weakens its defense against the coming of war and fascism."

The air rings, the newspapers are filled with the politics of bedlam. There are still around 10,000,000 unemployed in the United States. Re-employment lags behind the increase of production, and the increase of money wages in industry lags behind both. The burden of debt piles higher and higher. The world, and America with it, drifts toward new war of inconceivable horror—war from which we shall not be delivered by

Nation-wide radio address, Columbia Broadcasting System, February 2, 1936. *The New York Times,* February 3, 1936, p. 6. Reprinted by permission of *The New York Times.*

spending out of our poverty more than a billion dollars a year on naval and military preparations without so much as squarely facing the issue: what are we protecting and how shall we protect it?

In this situation the leaders of our two major political parties have begun speaking, or rather shouting. And what do they say? First, President Roosevelt makes a fighting speech to Congress and the nation defending the record he has made, but proposing no new program. Scarcely has he finished his speech when the AAA decision of the Supreme Court and the enactment of the bonus legislation by Congress compel him to seek new laws and new taxes.

Then Mr. Roosevelt's one-time dearest political friend and sponsor, Alfred E. Smith, rushes to the fray. This erstwhile man of the people chooses a dinner of the Liberty League at which to proclaim the religion of Constitution worship, favorable incidental mention of the Holy Bible, Washington as the nation's capital and the Stars and Stripes forever.

It was attended, the newspapers tell us, by twelve du Ponts—twelve apostles, not of liberty but of big business and the profits of war and preparation for war. Indeed, the record of Mr. Smith's new friends shows that that organization is as much entitled to the name Liberty League as was the disease commonly known as German measles to be called liberty measles in the hysteria of war.

Mr. Smith was promptly answered in a speech read, if not written, by Senator Robinson, who is the close political and personal friend of the utility magnate, Harvey Crouch, and the protector of the plantation system which in his own State is now answering the demands of the exploited sharecroppers by wholesale evictions and organized terror. On this subject Senator Robinson and other defenders of the New Deal preserve a profound silence.

Then the Governor of Georgia[1] jumped into the fray along with an oil baron and Huey Long's share-the-wealth clergyman[2] to exploit race and sectional prejudice in the name of States' rights. These all are Democrats.

Meanwhile the Republicans who defeated Alfred E. Smith in 1928 rise to applaud him. Ex-President Hoover, rejuvenated by the skillful services of a new ghost writer, denounces Mr. Roosevelt's administration and proposes a plan of farm relief quite similar to Roosevelt's substitute for AAA.

Between him and the States' Rights Senator Borah,[3] who still believes that the country can be saved by the simple device of trying to smash monopoly, there is as deep a gulf fixed as there is in the Democratic party. Alf Landon floats somewhere in that gulf.[4]

---

[1] See text of Eugene Talmadge's speech repudiating the heresies of the New Deal and Roosevelt's political leadership before the Macon, Georgia, convention. *The New York Times,* January 30, 1936, p. 8.

[2] Gerald L. K. Smith, a well-known demagogue.

[3] See text of Senator William E. Borah's speech to Brooklyn Republicans. *The New York Times,* January 29, 1936, p. 13.

[4] See text of Governor Alfred M. Landon's nation-wide radio speech outlining his political philosophy. *The New York Times,* January 30, 1936, p. 6.

Yet basically beneath all the alarms and confusion these worthy warriors, happy and unhappy, are acting upon a common assumption—an assumption which is dangerously false. All of them are assuming the durability of the profit system, the security of a capitalist nationalist system in which our highest loyalties are to the principle of private profit and to the political power of an absolute jingoistic nationalist State. They assume that prosperity is coming back again to stay for a while.

Mr. Roosevelt and his followers assume that prosperity is coming back because of the New Deal. Al Smith and the rest of Roosevelt's assorted critics assume that it is in spite of the New Deal and perhaps because of the Supreme Court. Mr. Hoover plaintively protests that the catastrophic depression of January-February, 1933, was due merely to the shudders of the body politic anticipating the economic horrors of the New Deal.

All of these leaders or would-be leaders out of our wilderness, however they may abuse one another, however loosely they may fling around the charge of socialism or communism—the two are not the same—still accept the basic institutions and loyalties of the present system. A true Socialist is resolved to replace that system.

As a Socialist, I view the Smith-Roosevelt controversy with complete impartiality. I am little concerned to point out the inconsistencies in Al Smith's record, or to remind him that in 1924 and 1928, when I happened to be the Socialist candidate for high office against him, more than one of his close political friends came to me to urge me as a Socialist not to attack him too severely since he really stood for so many of the things that Socialists and other progressive workers wanted.

I am entirely willing to grant that Mr. Roosevelt did not carry out the Democratic platform of 1932. Could Mr. Smith have done it? As for myself, I much prefer the company in which Mr. Smith put me in his Liberty League speech to the company in which he put himself at that dinner.

But I am concerned to point out how false is the charge that Roosevelt and the New Deal represent socialism. What is at stake is not prestige or sentimental devotion to a particular name. What is at stake is a clear understanding of the issues on which the peace and prosperity of generations—perhaps of centuries—depend. A nation which misunderstands socialism as completely as Al Smith misunderstands it is a nation which weakens its defense against the coming of war and fascism.

But, some of you will say, isn't it true, as Alfred E. Smith and a host of others before him have charged, that Roosevelt carried out most of the demands of the Socialist platform?

This charge is by no means peculiar to Mr. Smith. I am told that a Republican speaker alleged that Norman Thomas rather than Franklin D. Roosevelt has been President of the United States. I deny the allegation and defy the allegator and I suspect I have Mr. Roosevelt's support in this denial. Matthew Woll, leader of the forces of reaction in the American Federation of Labor, is among the latest to make the same sort of charge.

Emphatically, Mr. Roosevelt did not carry out the Socialist platform, unless he carried it out on a stretcher. What is true is that when Mr. Roosevelt took office he had to act vigorously.

He looked at the Democratic platform and he found no line on which he could act. It was all very well to pledge support to sound money, but there wasn't any money. Mr. Roosevelt gave a hasty glance at the Republican platform, or perhaps he merely contented himself by noting its musty smell. Then, perhaps, he did look at the Socialist platform. He needed ideas and there was nowhere else to look.

We had demanded Federal relief for unemployment. Hence any attempts Mr. Roosevelt made at Federal relief could perhaps be called by his enemies an imitation of the Socialist platform. It was an extraordinarily poor imitation. We demanded Federal unemployment insurance. Hence any attempt to get Federal security legislation could be regarded as an imitation of the Socialist platform. It was an amazingly bad imitation.

If we were in swimming and if Mr. Roosevelt's brain trust stole our clothes, it's a pity they didn't steal more of them and put them on more carefully. It would have been a more decent performance.

As a matter of fact, the American people on March 4, 1933, weren't in swimming. They were all caught in a blizzard. Mr. Hoover had us sitting still waiting for death or divine deliverance from around the corner,[5] or a miraculous clearing of the storm. Mr. Roosevelt started us running. To be sure, we ran nowhere in particular, but we ran hard enough to keep the blood circulating and so did not perish from freezing. Under his program we accomplished the extraordinary feat of running in several directions at once. And that's not socialism.

Indeed, at various times Mr. Roosevelt has taken particular and rather unnecessary pains to explain that he was not a Socialist, that he was trying to support the profit system, which by the way, he defined incorrectly. In his last message to Congress his attack was not upon the profit system but on the sins of big business.

His slogan was not the Socialist cry: "Workers of the world, workers with hand and brain, in town and country, unite!" His cry was: "Workers and small stockholders unite, clean up Wall Street." That cry is at least as old as Andrew Jackson.

What Mr. Roosevelt and his brain trust and practical political advisers did to such of the Socialist immediate demands as he copied at all merely illustrates the principle that if you want a child brought up right you had better leave the child with his parents and not farm him out to strangers. Time fails me to illustrate this point by a detailed examination of the Roosevelt emergency legislation.

---

[5] A mocking play on Hoover's comment designed to inspire public confidence when he was President, "Prosperity is just around the corner."

Some of it was good reformism, but there is nothing Socialist about trying to regulate or reform Wall Street. Socialism wants to abolish the system of which Wall Street is an appropriate expression. There is nothing Socialist about trying to break up great holding companies. We Socialists would prefer to acquire holding companies in order to socialize the utilities now subject to them.

There was no socialism at all about taking over all the banks which fell in Uncle Sam's lap, putting them on their feet again, and turning them back to the bankers to see if they can bring them once more to ruin. There was no socialism at all about putting in a Coordinator to see if he could make the bankrupt railroad systems profitable so they would be more expensive for the government to acquire as sooner or later the government, even a Republican party government, under capitalism must.

Mr. Roosevelt torpedoed the London Economic Conference; he went blindly rushing in to a big army and navy program; he maintained, as he still maintains, an Ambassador in Cuba who, as the agent of American financial interests, supports the brutal reaction in Cuba. While professing friendship for China, he blithely supported a silver purchase policy of no meaning for America except the enrichment of silver mine owners which nearly ruined the Chinese Government in the face of Japanese imperialism. These things which Al Smith or Alf Landon might also have done are anything but Socialist.

Mr. Smith presumably feels that the President's Security Bill, so-called, was socialism. Let us see. We Socialists have long advocated unemployment insurance or unemployment indemnity by which honest men who cannot find work are indemnified by a society so brutal or so stupid that it denies them the opportunity to work. This insurance or indemnification should be on a prearranged basis which will take account of the size of the family. It should be Federal because only the national government can act uniformly, consistently and effectively.

What did Mr. Roosevelt give us? In the name of security, he gave us a bill where in order to get security the unemployed workers will first have to get a job, then lose a job. He will have to be sure that he gets the job and loses the job in a State which has an unemployment insurance law.

He will then have to be sure that the State which has the law will have the funds and the zeal to get the money to fulfill the terms of the law. This will largely depend upon whether it proves to be practical and constitutional for the Federal Government to collect a sufficient tax on payrolls so that 90 percent of it when rebated to employers to turn over to the State officers will be sufficient to give some kind of security to those who are unemployed!

The whole proceeding is so complicated, the danger of forty-eight competing State laws—competing, by the way, for minimum, not for maximum benefits— is so dangerous that the President's bill can justly be called an in-Security bill.

If Mr. Smith means that the program of public works either under PWA or WPA is Socialist, again he is mistaken. We do not tolerate the standards of pay set on much WPA work—$19 a month, for instance, in some States in the South.

We do insist not upon talk but upon action to re-house the third of America which lives in houses unfit for human habitation, which is possible given the present state of the mechanic arts in a nation of builders.

The administration, having spent billions of words, not dollars, on housing with little result, is now turning the job over to private mortgage companies. Would not Al Smith or Alf Landon do the same?

The one outstanding act of the administration that Socialists applaud is, of course, the Tennessee Valley Authority. That of itself is not socialism. No single measure of the sort can be socialism by itself. But it is Socialist to the extent that it substitutes production for use for production for profit. However, it is an impossible task to correlate satisfactorily this type of production with the economic activities of a region still governed by the profit system.

It is this that I had in mind when in an extemporaneous speech I made the statement, so often misquoted or misinterpreted, to the effect that TVA had many merits, but that there was danger that it would be like a beautiful flower planted in a garden of weeds with great corporations watering the weeds.

But even if Mr. Roosevelt and the New Deal had far more closely approximated Socialist immediate demands in their legislation, they would not have been Socialists, not unless Mr. Smith is willing to argue that every reform, every attempt to curb rampant and arrogant capitalism, every attempt to do for the farmers something like what the tariff has done for business interests, is socialism.

Not only is it not socialism, but in large degree this State capitalism, this use of bread and circuses to keep the people quiet, is so much a necessary development of a dying social order that neither Mr. Smith nor Mr. Hoover in office in 1937 could substantially change the present picture or bring back the days of Andrew Jackson, Grover Cleveland or Calvin Coolidge.

What Roosevelt has given us, and what the Republicans cannot and will not substantially change, is not the socialism of the co-operative commonwealth. It is a State capitalism which the Fascist demagogues of Europe have used when they came to power. The thing, Mr. Smith, that you ought to fear is not that the party of Jefferson and Jackson is marching in step with Socialists toward a Socialist goal; it is that, unwittingly, it may be marching in step with Fascists toward a Fascist goal.

It is not Moscow as a rival to Washington that you should fear, but Berlin.

I do not mean that Mr. Roosevelt himself is a Fascist or likely to become a Fascist. I credit him with as liberal intentions as capitalism and his Democratic colleagues of the South permit. I call attention to the solemn fact that in spite of his circumspect liberalism, repression, the denial of civil liberty, a Fascist kind of military law, stark terrorism have been increasing under Democratic Governors for the most part—in Indiana, Florida, Georgia, Alabama, Arkansas and, of course, in California, where Mr. Roosevelt did not even come to the aid of an ex-Socialist, Upton Sinclair, against the candidate of the reactionaries.

I repeat that what Mr. Roosevelt has given us is State capitalism; that is to say, a system under which the State steps in to regulate and in many cases to own, not for the purpose of establishing production for use but rather for the purpose of maintaining in so far as may be possible the profit system with its immense rewards of private ownership and its grossly unfair division of the national income.

Today Mr. Roosevelt does not want fascism; Mr. Hoover does not want fascism; not even Mr. Smith and his friends of the Liberty League want fascism. The last-named gentlemen want an impossible thing: the return to the unchecked private monopoly power of the Coolidge epoch.

All the gentlemen whom I have named want somehow to keep the profit system. Socialism means to abolish that system. Those who want to keep it will soon find that out of war or out of the fresh economic collapse inevitable when business prosperity is so spotty, so temporary, so insecure as it is today, will come the confusion to which capitalism's final answer must be the Fascist dictator.

In America that dictator will probably not call himself Fascist. He, like Mr. Roosevelt in his address to Congress, will thank God that we are not like other nations. But privately he will rejoice in the weakness of our opposition to tyranny. Under the forms of democracy we have not preserved liberty. It has not taken black shirts to make us docile.

Given the crisis of war or economic collapse we, unless we awake, will accept dictatorship by violence to perpetuate a while longer the class division of income. We shall acknowledge the religion of the totalitarian state and become hypnotized by the emotional appeal of a blind jingoistic nationalism. Against this Fascist peril and its Siamese twin, the menace of war, there is no protection in the New Deal, no protection in the Republican party, less than no protection in the Liberty League.

Who of them all is waging a real battle even for such civil liberties and such democratic rights as ostensibly are possible in a bourgeois democracy? When Al Smith appeals to the Constitution is he thinking of the liberties of the Bill of Rights or is he thinking of the protection the Constitution has given to property?

As a Socialist I was no lover of NRA or AAA. NRA, at least temporarily, did give the workers some encouragement to organize, but at bottom it was an elaborate scheme for the stabilization of capitalism under associations of industries which could regulate production in order to maintain profit. AAA was perhaps some relative help to many classes of farmers. It was no help at all to the most exploited agricultural workers and share-croppers, but rather the opposite. And it was, as indeed it had to be under capitalism, primarily a scheme for subsidizing scarcity.

The New Deal did not say, as socialism would have said: "Here are so many millions of American people who need to be well fed and well clothed. How much food and cotton do we require?" We should have required more, not less. What Mr. Roosevelt said was: "How much food and cotton can be produced for which the exploited masses must pay a higher price?"

This was not primarily the fault of AAA. It was the fault of the capitalist system which Roosevelt and Smith alike accept; that system which makes private profit its god, which uses planning, in so far as it uses planning at all, to stabilize and maintain the profits of private owners, not the well-being of the masses. In the last analysis the profit system inevitably depends upon relative scarcity. Without this relative scarcity there is no profit and there is no planning for abundance which accepts the kingship of private profit.

When the world went in for great machinery operated by power it went in for specialization and integration of work. It doomed the old order of the pioneers. The one chance of using machinery for life, not death, is that we should plan to use it for the common good. There is no planned production for use rather than for the private profit of an owning class which does not involve social ownership. This is the gospel of socialism.

We can have abundance. In 1929, according to the Brookings Institute—and that, remember, was our most prosperous year—a decent use of our capacity to produce would have enabled us to raise the income of the 16,400,000 families with less than $2,000 a year to that modest level without even cutting any at the top.

Instead, without any interference from workers, without any pressure from agitators, the capitalist system so dear to Al Smith and his Liberty League friends went into a nose-spin. The earned income dropped from $83,000,000,000 to something like $38,000,000,000 in 1932, and the temporary recovery, of which the New Deal administration boasts, has probably not yet raised that income to the $50,-000,000,000 level. It has, moreover, burdened us with an intolerable load of debt.

What we must have is a society where we can use our natural resources and machinery so that the children of the share-croppers who raise cotton will no longer lack the cotton necessary for underclothes. What we must have is a society which can use our resources and our mechanical skill so that the children of builders will not live in shacks and slums.

It is not that Socialists want less private property. We want more private property in the good things of life. We do not mean to take the carpenter's kit away from the carpenter or Fritz Kreisler's violin away from Fritz Kreisler, or the home or farm in which any man lives and works away from him.

We do intend to end private landlordism, and to take the great natural resources—oil, copper, coal, iron; the great public utilities, power, transportation; the banking system, the distributive agencies like the dairy trust, the basic monopolies and essential manufacturing enterprises out of the hands of private owners, most of them absentee owners, for whose profits workers with hand and brain are alike exploited. And we intend to put these things into the hands of society.

With all the handicaps of capitalist loyalties, society has done a pretty fair job with schools, roads, waterworks and the like. Consumers' cooperatives have succeeded even in America. Social ownership now has a better record than holding company collectivism has made.

We intend to make this change to social ownership in orderly fashion. In the meantime we can avert fresh economic collapse by the road of crazy inflation or cruel deflation only by an orderly process of taxing wealth in private hands, by a graduated tax, approaching expropriation of unearned millions, in order to wipe out debt and to help in the socialization of industry.

We do not mean to turn socialized industries over to political bureaucrats, to Socialist Jim Farleys,[6] so to speak. The adjective doesn't redeem the noun. For instance, we intend that a socialized steel industry shall be managed under a directorate representing the workers, including, of course, the technicians in that industry, and the consumers.

We intend to put over these socialized industries a national economic planning council, a kind of council of war in the holy war against poverty. This council will represent different branches of agricultural and industrial production. It will carry out the large policies for social well-being that the Congress may determine.

It can do it without conscription and without rationing our people. We ought not to pay the price Russia has paid because we are far more industrially advanced than was Russia and should learn from Russia's mistakes as well as her successes.

Many of the functions of this national planning board will have to become genuinely international or world-wide if we are to preserve peace. It is only in a family of nations where there is something like fair play in respect to the allocation of raw materials and in the establishment of industrial standards for workers that we can hope for lasting peace. It is this peace that we seek.

Our goal, Mr. Smith, is true democracy. It is we who lead in the fight for liberty and justice which you in recent years have sadly ignored. It is we who seek to make freedom and democracy constitutional by advocating a Workers Rights' Amendment in the interest of farmers, workers and consumers, giving to Congress power to adopt all needful social and economic legislation, but leaving to the courts their present power to help protect civil and religious liberty.

Our present judicial power of legislation is as undemocratic as it is in the long run dangerous to peace. Remember the Dred Scott decision! Congress rather than the States must act because these issues are national. The religion of the Constitution with the Supreme Court as the high priests and the Liberty League as its preacher will never satisfy human hunger for freedom, peace and plenty.

The Constitution was made for man and not man for the Constitution. We Socialists seek now its orderly amendment. We seek now genuine social security, real unemployment insurance. We seek now a policy which will make it a little harder for American business interests to involve us in war as a result of a mad chase after the profits of war.

These, gentlemen who quarrel over the way to save capitalism, are the things of our immediate desire. But deepest of all is our desire for a federation of co-operative Commonwealths. Some of you may like this far less than you like the New Deal, but will you not agree that it is not the New Deal?

[6] The reference is to James A. Farley, then Postmaster-General and Chairman of the Democratic Party's National Committee.

You said, Mr. Smith, in a peroration worthy of your old enemy, William Randolph Hearst, that there can be only one victory, of the Constitution.

And this is our reply: There is only one victory worth the seeking by the heirs of the American Revolution. It is the victory of a fellowship of free men, using government as their servant, to harness our marvelous machinery for abundance, not poverty; peace, not war; freedom, not exploitation.

This is the victory in which alone is practicable deliverance from the house of our bondage. This is the victory to which we dedicate ourselves.

A Holy Crusade for Liberty

HERBERT CLARK HOOVER

Born, West Branch, Iowa, August 10, 1874. Graduated from Stanford University, 1895, as a mining engineer. Engaged in mining operations the world over. During World War I era he served successively as chairman of the American Relief Committee, chairman of the Commission for Relief in Belgium, and United States Food Administrator. Served as Secretary of Commerce, 1921–1928. As Republican candidate, he was elected President of the United States, 1928. Renominated in 1932, he was defeated by Franklin D. Roosevelt. Chairman, Commission on Organization of the Executive Branch of the Government (Hoover Commission), 1947–1949.

"Either we shall have a society based upon ordered liberty and the initiative of the individual, or we shall have a planned society that means dictation no matter what you call it or who does it."

*I*n *this room rests* the greatest responsibility that has come to a body of Americans in three generations. In the lesser sense this is a convention of a great political party. But in the larger sense it is a convention of Americans to determine the fate of those ideals for which this nation was founded. That far transcends all partisanship.

There are elemental currents which make or break the fate of nations. There is a moral purpose in the universe. Those forces which affect the vitality and the

Republican National Convention, Cleveland, Ohio, June 10, 1936. *Vital Speeches of the Day*, II (June 15, 1936), pp. 570–573. Reprinted by permission of *Vital Speeches of the Day*.

soul of a people will control its destinies. The sum of years of public service in these currents is the overwhelming conviction of their transcendent importance over the more transitory, even though difficult, issues of national life.

I have given about four years to research into the New Deal, trying to determine what its ultimate objectives were, what sort of a system it is imposing on this country.

To some people it appears to be a strange interlude in American history in that it has no philosophy, that it is sheer opportunism, that it is a muddle of a spoils system, of emotional economics, of reckless adventure, of unctuous claims to a monopoly of human sympathy, of greed for power, of a desire for popular acclaim and an aspiration to make the front pages of the newspapers. That is the most charitable view.

To other people it appears to be a cold-blooded attempt by starry-eyed boys to infect the American people by a mixture of European ideas, flavored with our native predilection to get something for nothing.

You can choose either one you like best. But the first is the road of chaos which leads to the second. Both of these roads lead over the same grim precipice that is the crippling and possibly the destruction of the freedom of men.

Which of these interpretations is accurate is even disputed by alumni of the New Deal who have graduated for conscience's sake or have graduated by request.

In Central Europe the march of Socialist or Fascist dictatorships and their destruction of liberty did not set out with guns and armies. Dictators began their ascent to the seats of power through the elections provided by liberal institutions.

Their weapons were promise and hate. They offered the mirage of Utopia to those in distress. They flung out the poison of class hatred. They may not have maimed the bodies of men, but they maimed their souls.

The 1932 campaign was a pretty good imitation of this first stage of European tactics. You may recall the promises of the abundant life, the propaganda of hate.

Once seated in office the first demand of these European despotisms was for power and "action." Legislatures were told they "must" delegate their authorities. Their free debate was suppressed. The powers demanded are always the same pattern. They all adopted planned economy. They regimented industry and agriculture. They put the Government into business. They engaged in gigantic Government expenditures. They created vast organizations of spoils henchmen and subsidized dependents. They corrupted currency and credit. They drugged the thinking of the people with propaganda at the people's expense.

If there are any items in this stage in the march of European collectivism that the New Deal has not imitated it must have been an oversight.

But at this point this parallel with Europe halts—at least for the present. The American people should thank Almighty God for the Constitution and the Supreme Court. They should be grateful to a courageous press.

You might contemplate what would have happened if Mr. Roosevelt could

have appointed enough Supreme Court Justices in the first year of his administration. Suppose these New Deal acts had remained upon the statute books. We
would have been a regimented people. Have you any assurance that he will not
have the appointments if he is re-elected?

The succeeding stages of violence and outrage by which European despotisms
have crushed all liberalism and all freedom have filled our headlines for years.

But what comes next in the United States? Have the New Dealers dropped
their ideas of centralization of government? Have they abandoned the notion of
regimenting the people into a planned economy? Has that greed for power become cooled by the resistance of a people with a heritage of liberty? Will they
resume if they are re-elected?

When we examine the speeches of Tugwell, Wallace, Ickes and others, we see
little indications of repentance.

Let me say this: America is no monarchy where the chief of state is not responsible for his ministers. It has been traditional in our Government since the
beginning that the important officials appointed by the President speak in tune
with his mind. That is imperative if there is to be intellectual honesty in government. President Roosevelt finds no difficulty in disciplining his officials. Witness
the prompt dismissal of those who did not publicly agree with him. The President will not discharge these men on whom his New Deal is dependent. No
matter what the new platform of the New Deal party may say, the philosophy of
collectivism and that greed for power are in the blood of some part of these men.
Do you believe that if re-elected they intend to stand still among the wreckage of
their dreams? In the words of Mr. Hopkins, perhaps we are too profanely dumb
to understand.

So much for the evidence that the New Deal is a definite attempt to replace
the American system of freedom with some sort of European planned existence.
But let us assume that the explanation is simply hit-and-run opportunism, spoils
system, and muddle.

We can well take a moment to explore the prospects of American ideals of
liberty and self-government under that philosophy. We may take only seven
short examples:

The Supreme Court has reversed some ten or twelve of the New Deal major
enactments. Many of these acts were a violation of the rights of men and of
self-government. Despite the sworn duty of the Executive and Congress to defend
these rights, they have sought to take them into their own hands. That is an
attack on the foundations of freedom.

More than this, the independence of Congress, the Supreme Court, and the
Executive are pillars at the door of liberty. For three years the word "must" has
invaded the independence of Congress. And the Congress has abandoned its responsibility to check even the expenditures of money. They have turned open
appropriations into personal power. These are destructions of the very safeguards
of free people.

We have seen these gigantic expenditures and this torrent of waste pile up a national debt which two generations cannot repay. One time I told a Democratic Congress that "you cannot spend yourselves into prosperity." You recall that advice did not take then. It hasn't taken yet. Billions have been spent to prime the economic pump. It did employ a horde of paid officials upon the pump handle. We have seen the frantic attempts to find new taxes on the rich. Yet three-quarters of the bill will be sent to the average man and the poor. He and his wife and his grandchildren will be giving a quarter of all their working days to pay taxes. Freedom to work for himself is changed into a slavery of work for the follies of government.

We have seen an explosive inflation of bank credits by this government borrowing. We have seen varied steps toward currency inflation that have already enriched the speculator and deprived the poor. If this is to continue the end result is the tears and anguish of universal bankruptcy and distress. No democracy in history has survived its final stages.

We have seen the building up of a horde of political officials, we have seen the pressures upon the helpless and destitute to trade political support for relief. Both are a pollution of the very fountains of liberty.

We have seen the most elemental violation of economic law and experience. The New Deal forgets it is solely by production of more goods and more varieties of goods and services that we advance the living and security of men. If we constantly decrease costs and prices and keep up earnings the production of plenty will be more and more widely distributed. These laws may be re-stitched in new phrases but they are the very shoes of human progress. We had so triumphed in this long climb of mankind toward plenty that we had reached Mount Pisgah where we looked over the promised land of abolished poverty. Then men began to quarrel over the division of the goods. The depression produced by war destruction temporarily checked our march toward the promised land.

Then came the little prophets of the New Deal. They announce the striking solution that the way out is to produce less and to increase prices so the people can buy less. They have kept on providing some new restriction or burden or fright down to a week ago.

At least it has enabled the New Deal to take a few hundred thousand earnest party workers to the promised land. It takes the rest of us for a ride into the wilderness of unemployment.

Can democracy stand the strain of Mother Hubbard economics for long?

Any examination of the economic muddle of the past three years shows the constant threat of price fixing, restriction of production and drive against small business. That is the soul of monopoly. That has maintained from the N.R.A. to the last tax bill. These are old tricks in new disguise which put shackles upon the freedom of men.

In desperate jumping from one muddle to another we have seen repeated violation of morals and honor in government. Do I need recall the repudiation of obligations, the clipping of the coin, the violation of trust to guard the Constitution and the coercion of the voter? When the standards of honor and morals fail in government they fail in the people.

There are some moral laws written in a Great Book. Over all there is the gospel of brotherhood. For the first time in the history of America we have heard the gospel of class hatred preached from the White House. That is human poison far more deadly than fear. Every reader of the history of democracy knows that is the final rock upon which all democracies have been wrecked.

There is the suggestion in the Gospels that it is the meek who will inherit the earth. The New Deal will have little inheritance. There are recommendations as to righteousness for righteousness' sake only. I will not elaborate that.

If all this is the theory and practice of Muddle, where has it brought us even now? We have spent $15,000,000,000 more than the last Republican Administration. We have a debt ten billions greater than even the great war debt. After three years we still have the same number of unemployed that we had at the election of November, 1932. These actions are bringing injury to the well-being of people it purports to serve. It has produced gross reactionaryism in the guise of liberalism. And, above all, the New Deal has brought that which George Washington called "alterations which may impair the energy of the system and thus overthrow that which cannot be directly overthrown."

Republicans! After a hundred and fifty years, we have arrived at that hour.

Here where the tablets of human freedom were first handed down, their sacred word has been flouted. Today the stern task is before the Republican party to restore the ark of that covenant to the temple in Washington.

The New Deal may be a revolutionary design to replace the American system with despotism. It may be the dream stuff of a false liberalism. It may be the valor of muddle. Their relationship to each other, however, is exactly the sistership of the witches who brewed the cauldron of powerful trouble for Macbeth. Their product is the poisoning of Americanism.

The President has constantly reiterated that he will not retreat. For months, to be sure, there has been a strange quiet. Just as the last campaign was fought on promises that have been broken, so apparently this campaign is to be slipped through by evasion.

But the American people have the right to know *now,* while they still have power to act. What is going to be done after election with these measures which the Constitution forbids and the people by their votes have never authorized? What do the New Dealers propose to do with these unstable currencies, unbalanced budgets, debts and taxes? Fifty words would make it clear. Surely the propaganda agencies which emit half a million words a day could find room for these fifty. I noticed they recently spent three hundred words on how to choose a hat. It is slightly more important to know the fate of a nation.

You have the duty to determine the principles upon which the Republican party will stand. You make the laws of the party. Whether it is within the party or a government, our system is a government of laws and not of men. This party upholds its promises.

The immediate task is to set the country on the road of genuine recovery from the paths of instability. We have enough inventions and enough accumulated needs to start the physical rebuilding of America. The day the Republican party can assure right principles we can turn this nation from the demoralization of relief to the contentment of constructive jobs. Herein—and herein alone—is a guaranty of jobs for the 11,000,000 idle based upon realities and not on political claptrap. In the meantime the party which organized efficient relief of the unemployed three years before the New Deal was born will not turn from those in need. That support to distress comes from the conscience and sympathy of a people, not from the New Deal.

Four years ago I stated that the Republican party must undertake progressive reforms from evils exposed by the boom and depression. But I stated our first job was to restore men to work. The New Deal has attempted many reforms. They have delayed recovery. Parts of them are good. Some have failed. Some are tainted with collectivist ideas. That task must be undertaken anew by the Republican party.

A new danger is created to the republic in that the swing from the foolishness of radicalism will carry us to the selfishness of reaction.

The Republican party must achieve true social betterment. But we must produce measures that will not work confusion and disappointment. We must propose a real approach to social ills, not the prescription for them, by quacks, of poison in place of remedy.

We must achieve freedom in the economic field. We have grave problems in relation of government to agriculture and business. Monopoly is only one of them. The Republican party is against the greed for power of the wanton boys who waste the people's savings. But it must be equally adamant against the greed for power and exploitation in the seekers of special privilege. At one time I said: "We can no more have economic power without checks and balances than we can have political power without checks and balances. Either one leads to tyranny."

The Republican party must be a party that accepts the challenge of each new day. The last word in human accomplishment has not been spoken. The last step in human progress has not been made. We welcome change when it will produce a fairer, more just, and satisfying civilization. But changes which destroy the safeguards of free men and women are only apples of Sodom.

Great calamities have come to the whole world. These forces have reached into every calling and every cottage. They have brought tragedy and suffering to millions of firesides. I have great sympathy for those who honestly reach for short cuts to the immensity of our problems. While design of the structure of betterment for the common man must be inspired by the human heart, it can only be achieved by the intellect. It can only be builded by using the mould of justice, by laying brick upon brick from the materials of scientific research; by the pains-taking sifting of truth from the collection of fact and experience. Any other mould is distorted; any other bricks are without straw; any other foundations are sand. That great structure of human progress can be built only by free men and women.

The gravest task which confronts the party is to regenerate these freedoms.

There are principles which neither tricks of organization, nor the rigors of depression, nor the march of time, nor New Dealers, nor Socialists, nor Fascists can change. There are some principles which came into the universe along with the shooting stars of which worlds are made, and they have always been and ever will be true. Such are the laws of mathematics, the law of gravitation, the existence of God, and the ceaseless struggle of mankind to be free.

Throughout the centuries of history man's vigil and his quest has been to be free. For this the best and bravest on earth have fought and died. To embody human liberty in workable government, America was born. Shall we keep that faith? Must we condemn the unborn generations to fight again and to die for the right to be free?

There are some principles that cannot be compromised. Either we shall have a society based upon ordered liberty and the initiative of the individual, or we shall have a planned society that means dictation no matter what you call it or who does it. There is no half-way ground. They cannot be mixed. Government must either release the powers of the individual for honest achievement or the very forces it creates will drive it inexorably to lay its paralyzing hand more and more heavily upon individual effort.

Less than twenty years ago we accepted those ideas as the air we breathed. We fought a great war for their protection. We took upon ourselves obligations of billions. We buried our sons in foreign soil. But in this score of years we have seen the advance of collectivism and its inevitable tyranny in more than half the civilized world. In this thundering era of world crisis distracted America stands confused and uncertain.

The Whig party temporized, compromised upon the issue of slavery for the black man. That party disappeared. It deserved to disappear. Shall the Republican party deserve or receive any better fate if it compromises upon the issue of free-dom for all men, white as well as black?

You of this Convention must make the answer.

Let us not blink the difficulties. Throughout the land there are multitudes of people who have listened to the songs of sirens. Thousands of men, if put to the choice, would willingly exchange liberty for fancied security even under dictator-ship. Under their distress they doubt the value of their own rights and liberties. They do not see the Constitution as a fortress for their deliverance. They have been led to believe that it is an iron cage against which the wings of idealism beat in vain.

They do not realize that their only relief and their hope of economic security can come only from the enterprise and initiative of free men.

Let this convention declare, without shrinking, the source of economic prosperity is freedom. Man must be free to use his own powers in his own way. Free to think, to speak, to worship. Free to plan his own life. Free to use his own initiative. Free to dare in his own adventure. It is the essence of true liberalism that these freedoms are limited by the rights of others.

Freedom both requires and makes increased responsibilities. There is no freedom from exploitation of the weak or from the dead hand of bureaucracy.

There's something vastly bigger than payrolls, than economics, than materialism, at issue in this campaign. The free spirit of men is the source of self-respect, of sturdiness, of moral and spiritual progress. With the inspirations of freedom come fidelity to public trust, honor and morals in government. The social order does not rest upon orderly economic freedom alone. It rests even more upon the ideals and character of a people. Governments must express those ideas in frugality, in justice, in courage, in decency, and in regard for the less fortunate, and above all in honor. Nations die when these weaken, no matter what their material prosperity.

Fundamental American liberties are at stake. Is the Republican party ready for the issue? Are you willing to cast your all upon the issue, or would you falter and look back? Will you, for expediency's sake, also offer will-o'-the-wisps which beguile the people? Or have you determined to enter in a holy crusade for liberty which shall determine the future and the perpetuity for a nation of free men? That star shell fired today over the no man's land of world despair would illuminate the world with hope.

In another great crisis in American history, that great Republican, Abraham Lincoln, said: "Fellow citizens, we cannot escape history. We . . . will be remembered in spite of ourselves. No personal significance or insignificance can spare one or another of us. The fiery trial through which we pass will light us down in honor or dishonor to the latest generation . . . . We—even we here— hold the power and bear the responsibility. We shall nobly save or meanly lose the last, best hope of earth . . . . The way is plain . . . a way which, if followed, the world will forever applaud."

Republicans and fellow Americans! This is your call. Stop the retreat. In the chaos of doubt, confusion and fear, yours is the task to command. Stop the retreat, and turning the eyes of your fellow Americans to the sunlight of freedom, lead the attack to retake, recapture and retain the citadels of liberty. Thus only can America be preserved. Thus can the peace, plenty and security be reestablished and expanded. Thus can the opportunity, the inheritance and the spiritual future of your children be guaranteed. And thus you will win the gratitude of posterity, and the blessing of Almighty God.

HIGHER EDUCATION AND
SOCIAL CHANGE

It would have been strange if the polemics of the New Deal Era had not stirred educators to debate theories and practices of their field. Reassessment of traditional values and experimentation with new schemes so apparent in other aspects of American life were extended to the schools and colleges as well. And in education, as in politics and economics, there were those who resisted change, or who sought change in a return to the traditions of the past. Criticism of the educational system came from a variety of directions and increased in volume and intensity during the decade of the thirties. No one, it seemed, was completely satisfied with what the schools were doing. At the primary and secondary level, the excesses of "progressive" education brought charges of triviality and lack of mental effort, while in the colleges the elective system was blamed for an emphasis upon the purely practical to the detriment of the so-called "cultural" studies of the old prescribed curriculum.

Although criticisms of the existing system as well as plans for its reconstruction were many and various, two principal opposing groups were distinguishable, commonly designated for lack of more precise labels as conservatives or traditionalists, and progressives or experimentalists.[1] Both groups noted the confusion and lack of a unifying principle in education; both were dissatisfied with the results of the free elective system; both professed to regard education as an instrument for improving society. But the traditionalists tended to regard education as a

[1] See R. Freeman Butts, *The College Charts Its Course* (New York: McGraw-Hill Book Co., 1939), pp. 253–254. Representative of the conservative group were Robert M. Hutchins, Mortimer J. Adler, Stringfellow Barr, Abraham Flexner, and "New Humanists" Irving Babbitt and Paul Elmer More; among the progressives were John Dewey, Boyd H. Bode, Harry D. Gideonse, W. H. Cowley, William A. Neilson, and George S. Counts.

process of transmitting from one generation to another a "Great Tradition" of culture, and to emphasize strictly "intellectual" training, while the progressives stressed the investigative techniques of modern science as a means of discovering new truths, and advocated the education of the whole individual through integrating and unifying experiences. A clearer differentiation between these two groups can be made by examining the positions of their leading spokesmen on some of the principal issues which divided them.

Undoubtedly the most influential voice raised during the 1930s in favor of traditionalism was that of Robert M. Hutchins, youthful president of the University of Chicago. Upon assuming the presidency in 1929, Hutchins began expressing his opinions in a series of public addresses. The handsome young educator's forceful personality, his colorful, provocative style, and his ability to strike off memorable aphorisms soon established him as the most exciting figure in the educational world. The modern university, said Hutchins, is "a perfectly amazing institution. It does everything and will do it for anybody." In trying to do everything, in its preoccupation with vocationalism, athleticism, and specialization, it has forgotten what its real function is. "It sometimes seems to approximate a kindergarten at one end and a clutter of specialists at the other." Actually, the purpose of a university is to train the intellect. A university, he told the Parent-Teachers Association in a 1935 radio address, is a community of scholars. "It is not a kindergarten; it is not a club; it is not a reform school; it is not a political party; it is not an agency of propaganda. A university is a community of scholars."[2]

A volume containing twenty-four of Hutchins' speeches on various aspects of education was published in 1936.[3] A more systematic exposition of his views was presented in the Storrs Lectures at Yale University later in the same year.[4] The educational philosophy he set forth in these speeches and lectures became the focal point of a debate which continued for more than a decade. The two books were a target for scores of critical reviews, articles, books, and public speeches.

The chief characteristic of the higher learning, said Hutchins, is its confusion. This confusion has several causes. First is the love of money, which leads to a service-station conception of a university, a catering to the demands of every group in society, domination by alumni, and the attempt to amuse students through athletics and social activities. Second is a misconception of democracy

2 "What Is a University?" *Vital Speeches of the Day*, I (1935), p. 547.
3 *No Friendly Voice* (Chicago: University of Chicago Press, 1936).
4 *The Higher Learning in America* (New Haven: Yale University Press, 1936).

which maintains that everybody is entitled to the same amount and the same kind of education. Third is an erroneous notion of progress—a belief that everything is getting better and better, and a consequent tendency to break completely with the past. A fourth cause of confusion is an anti-intellectualism that emphasizes character-building instead of cultivation of the intellect. Hutchins concluded his indictment with a discussion of the conflict between two aims of the university: the pursuit of truth for its own sake, and the preparation of students for their life work. Noting an unmistakable trend toward vocationalism, he urged a return to the concept of a university as a haven where the search for truth may proceed unhampered by pressure for results.

To remedy the ills of higher education Hutchins proposed a four-year unit beginning with the third year of high school and extending through the sophomore year of college, devoted to a general education in the great books and in grammar, rhetoric, logic, and mathematics. Those who successfully completed this course would go on to three years of university study in three fields: metaphysics, natural science, and social science, the latter two being subordinate to the first. Research institutes for gathering information on subjects important to the public would be established adjacent to, but not within, the university. Professional schools as such would ultimately disappear.

The rationale for this plan was clearly and forcefully set forth. "Education implies teaching. Teaching implies knowledge. Knowledge is truth. The truth is everywhere the same. Hence education should be everywhere the same."[5] Education, rightly understood, is the cultivation of the intellect, and it is the same good for all men in all societies. The intellect is to be cultivated by exposure to the "permanent studies," the great books which contain the wisdom of the past and are contemporary in every age. Since the chief characteristic of the higher learning is disorder, some ordering principle must be found. Theology, the unifying principle of the medieval university, is out of the question since "we are a faithless generation and take no stock in revelation." We must turn then, as did the Greek world, to metaphysics, the study of first principles, for our principle of unity. "If we can revitalize metaphysics and restore it to its place in the higher learning, we may be able to establish rational order in the modern world as well as in the universities."[6]

Fearing that these personal convictions of President Hutchins were being con-

[5] *Ibid.*, p. 66.
[6] *Ibid.*, p. 105.

fused with the actual program in effect at the University of Chicago, Professor Harry D. Gideonse, a member of the Chicago faculty, published a reply to Hutchins' critique.[7] Gideonse quoted from a faculty resolution on educational objectives that eschewed isolated and exclusive cultivation of the intellect and stressed education of the whole person. He opposed Hutchins' proposal to separate the university from research and professional training, to divorce theory from practice, on the ground that liberal education should aim at both theory and practice—making theory available for practice, and fertilizing theory by practice. He objected strenuously to Hutchins' suggestion that order is to be restored by a return to metaphysics, particularly to the Platonic-Aristotelian-Thomistic tradition. This, he said, is the very tradition from which modern science has freed itself; instead of a set of absolute first principles not subject to modification, science stresses revision of every generalization when new data compel it. Gideonse insisted that in place of a metaphysical or theological orientation, the modern university must put its main emphasis on the method of science. The true scholar does not look to a superimposed authority to give meaning and unity to his efforts. "Truth to finite man is never single, complete, and static. It is rather multiple, fractional, and evolving. The true scholar finds his unifying principles in the humanistic spirit and in the methods of science."[8]

The Hutchins-Gideonse exchange was only one of many, yet from it emerged most of the basic issues which divided the disputants throughout the entire controversy: (1) concentration upon historical and theoretical studies *vs.* practical preparation for life; (2) reliance upon the authority of "great ideas" *vs.* scientific experimentation and democracy; (3) academic isolation *vs.* social participation and responsibility; (4) intellectual training *vs.* education of the whole man.

Practical vocational training received support from an unusual source when the eminent mathematician and philosopher Dr. Alfred North Whitehead defended the existing system as best serving the needs of the community. Writing in the *Atlantic Monthly* with reference to the tercentenary of Harvard University, Dr. Whitehead pointed out that in ancient Greece whatever occupied a free citizen was worth studying. In modern society, the student should have opportunities to apply knowledge. "In fact, the applications are part of the knowledge . . . unapplied knowledge is knowledge shorn of its meaning." Calling it "midsummer madness" for universities to withdraw from close contact with vocational prac-

[7] *The Higher Learning in a Democracy* (New York: Farrar and Rinehart, 1937).
[8] *Ibid.*, p. 32.

tices, he warned further: "The careful shielding of a university from the activities of the world around is the best way to chill interest and to defeat progress. Celibacy does not suit a university. It must mate itself with action."[9]

Replying to Whitehead in the same magazine, President Hutchins agreed that the goal of a university is intellectual leadership, but expressed doubt that Whitehead's means—vocational schools and association with practical affairs—would accomplish this desired end. "The danger of the American universities is not celibacy, but polygamy. They are mated to so many different kinds of action that nothing but a few divorces can save them from the consequences of their ardor."[10] The way out of the difficulty, Hutchins reasserted, was a return to the classics, the accumulated wisdom of the race.

It was inevitable that sooner or later the expression of such views should draw Hutchins into a controversy with John Dewey, the leader of the progressive group. Many of Hutchins' most trenchant criticisms were unmistakably directed at Dewey or at disciples who had distorted or gone beyond the teachings of their master. Dewey had for more than a generation been the most influential force in American education. For years he had opposed the very dualisms to which Hutchins was committed—the distinction between intellect and emotion, knowledge and action, theory and practice. For years his aim had been to bridge the gap between school and society, between what went on in the schoolroom and the actual experiences of life. For Dewey education was not simply the transmission of a Great Tradition of culture, but experience, the process of coming to grips with and solving real life problems. In 1897, as a young man in rebellion against the rigidity and formalism of education having little relevance to the child's world of experience, he had published a work entitled "My Pedagogic Creed," in which he asserted that "All education proceeds by the participation of the individual in the social consciousness of the race." Another item in this personal credo was that education is a process of living and not a preparation for future living.

The Dewey-Hutchins debate took place in the pages of The Social Frontier shortly after the publication of The Higher Learning in America.[11] After reviewing Hutchins' indictment of higher education and his remedy for the disorder

[9] "Harvard: The Future," Atlantic Monthly, CLVIII (September, 1936), p. 267.
[10] "A Reply to Professor Whitehead," Atlantic Monthly, CLVIII (November, 1936), p. 583.
[11] John Dewey, "Rationality in Education," The Social Frontier, III (December, 1936), pp. 71–73; John Dewey, "President Hutchins' Proposals to Remake Higher Education," III (January, 1937), pp. 103–104; Robert M. Hutchins, "Grammar, Rhetoric, and Mr. Dewey," III (February, 1937), pp. 137–139; John Dewey, "The Higher Learning in America," III (March, 1937), pp. 167–169.

he found there, Dewey proceeded to criticize Hutchins' proposals on the grounds of absolutism, authoritarianism, and withdrawal from the world of experience. The assumption that truth is absolute and unchanging, that it is embodied in the "permanent studies," and that "there is something in existence called the Intellect that is ready to apprehend it," Dewey refused to accept. One does not escape authoritarianism, he asserted, by calling one's hierarchy of principles "truths." Implicit in any assertion of eternal truths is the necessity for some *human* authority to decide just what these truths are, and in what order they are to be preferred. Particularly offensive to pragmatist Dewey was Hutchins' apparent contempt for science, his separation of intellect and experience, and his placing of the empirical studies at the bottom of his hierarchy of truths. "The cure for surrender of higher learning to immediate and transitory pressures is not monastic seclusion. Higher learning can become intellectually vital only by coming to that close grip with our contemporary science and contemporary social affairs which Plato, Aristotle, and St. Thomas exemplify in their respective ways." Hutchins' reply that he was not arguing for any specific metaphysical system and that he was not antiscientific did not, as Dewey pointed out in his final article, touch the main issue, namely, that there is a faculty of Intellect which is capable of grasping ultimate Truth which is the measure and criterion of all *inferior* forms of knowledge—those which deal with empirical matters.

To John Dewey the school was an instrument for the reconstruction of society. Speaking at the University of California at Los Angeles in 1930 he named education as "the most far-reaching and the most fundamental way of correcting social evils and meeting social issues." And in the speech reprinted in this book he pointed out that, although new social arrangements are brought about by legislation, changed minds, beliefs, and desires must first be produced by education. The needed "social arrangements," he made clear, were of the kind that would realize basic American democratic ideals. Hutchins also professed to believe in social improvement through education, but in quite a different way. He was contemptuous of courses in current events for, he said, events do not remain current. He did not believe that the prevention of soil erosion or juvenile delinquency was part of the task of a university. Society is improved by inquiry into the nature of the good society. The educational system cannot bring about social change, but it can facilitate social change by training the intellect. Train minds to think, he said in effect, by allowing them to feed on the permanent studies. Intellects so trained will then perceive the truth which is everywhere and at all times the same, and will make intelligent social changes. Dewey's dictum of learn-

ing through experience he repudiated on the ground that education cannot dupli-
cate the experiences a student will have later on, but can only hope to develop
correctness in thinking. General education may wisely "leave experience to life"
and train the intellect.

One of the chief points of conflict between traditionalists and progressives, one
from which many other disagreements sprang, was the question of whether the
colleges should train the intellect alone or the "whole man." To President Hutchins, Mortimer Adler, Stringfellow Barr, and other intellectualists, the phrase
"educating the whole man" was anathema. "Of all the meaningless phrases in
educational discussion," snorted Hutchins, "this is the prize." But to William H.
Cowley, President of Hamilton College, it was the concept of intellectualism
that was not only meaningless, but scientifically indefensible and socially dangerous. For it he proposed to substitute "holoism," which he defined as "that philosophy of education which asserts that the school and the college must be interested
in the emotional, moral, religious, social, aesthetic, and physical as well as in the
intellectual development of students. Holoism affirms, in brief, that educational
institutions must be concerned with the whole student in relationship to the
whole of society."[12]

According to Cowley, early American colleges had been holoistic in philosophy
and had remained so until the mid-nineteenth century, when colleges like Harvard, Yale, Princeton, and Columbia began to develop into great universities
modeled after the German pattern—impersonal, devoted to science and research,
concentrating on training superior minds. This was in Cowley's opinion a calamitous development. For, as he passionately affirmed in his inaugural address as
President of Hamilton, intelligence is not enough.

> Intelligence is not enough because thinking is only part of living;
> because students come to college not only for the training of their
> minds but also for the enrichment of their lives as people; because
> college students need the advice and direction of mature and experi-
> enced adults who understand their problems; . . . because not only
> the student's mind comes to college but also his body; because, as
> most alumni will testify, the lessons in human relations learned from
> one's fellow students complement the lessons learned from books and
> professors; because college is not only an intellectual enterprise but
> also a social and spiritual environment; because society expects from

[12] "Intelligence Is Not Enough," *Vital Speeches of the Day*, V (1938), p. 74.

college graduates not only intelligence but also civilized attitudes, matured emotions, and cultivated character.[13]

Earlier, Hutchins had engaged in a similar debate with another college president, William A. Neilson of Smith. President Neilson argued for physical, moral, spiritual, aesthetic, and social development through a variety of activities; Hutchins proposed that the college should exist primarily for the intellectual development of "book-minded" students, while those who were not book-minded should seek training elsewhere.[14] It must be noted that throughout this discussion both sides agreed that the intellect must be trained; on this point there was no dispute. But holoists maintained that production of whole men does not preclude training of intelligent men. More than this, they insisted that intelligent men who were not also whole men constituted a danger to society. While Hutchins found the term "the whole man" repugnant and called "character," "personality," and "facts" the three worst words in education, it would be unjust to imply that he had no interest in character. "A system of education that produced graduates with intellects splendidly trained and no characters," he once told a graduating class at the University of Chicago, "would be a menace to society." But to Hutchins character was a by-product, not to be developed directly by social activities and life-adjustment courses. Character was developed indirectly by hard mental effort. In short, he maintained that the way to develop character is to train the intellect, and the less said about character in the process the better.

In the fall of 1940, a year after the beginning of World War II, President Cowley in a speech at the University of Rochester renewed his attack on intellectualism. France had fallen and Britain was fighting for her life. Cowley predicted that the United States would sink into insignificance, perhaps into slavery, unless this crippling doctrine was abandoned. Hitler, he argued, had succeeded in capturing the enthusiasm and devotion of German youth because, "fed up with the bloodless objectivity of German professors," they had "swung from the extreme of intellectual objectivity to the opposite extreme of emotional drunkenness." America, rendered apathetic, cynical, spiritually neutral, by an educational system which feeds the mind but not the spirit, faced a similar fate. Intelligence is not enough, Cowley reiterated. "Colleges and universities must rededicate themselves to nurture the fire of the spirit else we shall not be equal to the tremendous responsibilities which a world situation has catapulted upon us."

Ironically, only a month before, Professor Mortimer J. Adler, intellectualist

[13] *Ibid.,* p. 77.
[14] "What Is the Job of Our Colleges?" *The New York Times Magazine,* March 7, 1937, p. 2.

par excellence, had placed the blame for America's precarious position upon the failure of her educators to accept the doctrines of President Hutchins—particularly his advocacy of metaphysics as an organon for the derivation of authoritative first principles.[15] The professors, he said, have dismissed philosophy as opinion and religion as superstition and have exalted science. But to deny that philosophy is knowledge is to deny the self-evidence of moral principles. Hence professors can be for democracy only because they happen to like it, not because they *know* through moral demonstration that it is right. "Science contributes nothing whatever to the understanding of Democracy. Without the truths of philosophy and religion, Democracy has no rational foundation." Adler went so far as to say that mankind had more to fear from the professors than from Hitler. Whether Hitler wins or not, he predicted, the culture formed by an educational system based on positivism and naturalism cannot support even such democracy as we have against internal decay.

The discussion of the nature and function of higher education in a democracy continues to this day, and is likely to continue indefinitely. But of the lively debate carried on during the 1930s it is probably not inaccurate to conclude that it was resolved for the time in favor of the progressives. The "Hutchins Plan" did not catch on in American colleges; only at St. Johns College at Annapolis was it permanently established. In 1940 Mortimer Adler announced bitterly to a Conference on Science, Philosophy, and Religion that Hutchins had heroically failed.[16] In 1947, President Truman's Commission on Higher Education, a group of distinguished educators from all parts of the nation appointed to formulate long-range objectives, issued its report.[17] The first sentence of the first volume was a repudiation of Hutchins' doctrine that education is everywhere the same: "Education is an institution of every civilized society, but the purposes of education are not the same in all societies." Educational programs and policies, the report continued, should be relevant to the needs of contemporary society. "Effective democratic education will deal directly with current problems." The Commission acknowledged the importance of tradition, but warned against getting lost in the past.

> No one would deny that a study of man's history can contribute immeasurably to understanding and managing the present. But to

---

[15] "God and the Professors," *Vital Speeches of the Day,* VII (1940), pp. 98–103.
[16] *Ibid.,* p. 99.
[17] *Higher Education for American Democracy: A Report of the President's Commission on Higher Education.* 6 vols. (Washington, D.C., 1947).

assume that all we need do is apply to present and future problems
"eternal" truths revealed in earlier ages is likely to stifle creative
imagination and intellectual daring. Such an assumption may blind
us to new problems and the possible need for new solutions. It is
wisdom in education to use the past selectively and critically, in order
to illumine the pressing problems of the present.[18]

With such a statement John Dewey, W. H. Cowley, and most critics of traditionalism would doubtless find themselves in complete agreement.

[18] *Ibid.*, I, p. 6.

Education and New Social Ideals

JOHN DEWEY

Born, Burlington, Vermont, October 20, 1859; died, New York City, June 1, 1952. Graduated from University of Vermont, 1879; Ph.D. degree, Johns Hopkins, 1884. Taught at University of Minnesota, 1888–1889; University of Michigan, 1889–1894; University of Chicago, 1894–1904; Columbia University, 1904–1930. Founder of a school of philosophy called instrumentalism, closely related to pragmatism of C. S. Peirce and William James, based on experience as the ultimate authority in knowledge and conduct. Author of a prodigious number of books, articles, and lectures. Among his books are School and Society *(1899),* How We Think *(1910),* Democracy and Education *(1916),* Freedom and Culture *(1939). Although unskilled as a public speaker, he spoke with authority and influence on social philosophy and education.*

"The alternative to advance through sheer force is advance through education taking effect in shaping the ideas and desires that lie back of action."

In opening the course for 1936 upon Education and New Social Ideals, I wish to direct attention especially to the question of what the new social ideals are and why they are necessary.

Radio address, Station WEVD, New York City, January 14, 1936. *Vital Speeches of the Day,* II (February 24, 1936), pp. 327–328. Reprinted by permission of *Vital Speeches of the Day.*

The point I want most to emphasize is that fundamentally and inherently the social ideals that demand a change in education are *not* new. They are a new version of the very same ideals that inspired the Declaration of Independence one hundred and sixty years ago. A new version is needed because of the enormous social changes that have taken place in this period of time. But the ideals themselves are those of the democracy, of the liberty and equality, that animated our forefathers in establishing upon pioneer soil a kind of government and a kind of political institution they recognized to be new and revolutionary in the history of governments upon this earth.

No; the ideals that we assert to be necessary for the conduct of our educational system are not new in themselves; they are new only in relation to the method and means demanded in order that the ideals may be realized. One has only to hear a speech by any reactionary or read an editorial in any reactionary newspaper about what are called "American traditions" to see how dim and how distorted the sense of the genuine American tradition has grown in the minds of many who still claim the title of American.

In the true and original tradition, the ideal of liberty applied to all individuals and applied to them in every walk of life. The reactionary interpretation put forth with such subsidized energy today by the so-called Liberty League and all those interests it stands for, confines the realization of the ideal of liberty to the privileged few, the few privileged in economic position. It confines the manifestation of liberty to just one channel of expression: Ability to make money in a society where control of economic forces is concentrated in the hands of the few.

There is a similar prostitution and degradation of the ideal of equality. The original and genuine American tradition was based on the idea of securing equality of opportunity for all; establishing the basic conditions through which and because of which every human being might become all that he was capable of becoming. This high conception has been distorted into the notion that because laws are nominally the same for all, therefore equality already exists; although the slightest exercise of common sense discloses that actual equality of opportunity is impossible when vast economic inequality is the established rule.

The demand for a *new social order* is in fact a demand for the existence of economic and political conditions that will allow the realization of the *old democratic ideas* of liberty for all and of equality of opportunity to all for personal development.

The reasons why new social arrangements are needed in order that old American social ideals may be actualities and not mere words, bandied about in behalf of the interests of a small but dominant class, are written large on the face of present society.

In 1776 there were a few million persons scattered along the Atlantic seaboard. There are now over a hundred and a quarter million of persons stretched across the continent. One hundred and fifty years ago there was an immense amount of land awaiting settlement and inviting possession and use, with all that this fact meant in the way of unappropriated natural resources. Today these avenues are closed. This fact alone is enough to show that new social and political means must be set up to give the ideal of equality of opportunity any reality. We must either admit that the ideal was a dream that had meaning only as long as there was free land, or else we must take measures to provide an effective substitute for the opportunities that free land held out.

Again, the population was found in scattered localities that communicated with one another only by stage-coach and where commerce between different sections was sparse and slow. We now live in a nation where the most distant portions are held together by telegraph and telephone and radio and airplane, and where steam and electricity have broken down natural barriers to transportation and commerce. Yet the ideas of states' rights and local autonomy that were appropriate to the period of isolation are now used to prevent action being taken by the national agencies that can alone provide, under existing conditions, for the common and general public good. We find the courts engaged in setting aside federal legislation on the ground that the matter legislated about is the concern of the several states—while they well know that it is impossible for the states to take effective action, and while also they set aside state legislation on the ground that it infringes on federal power. Thus they create a legal no-man's territory in which predatory interests hostile to freedom and equality have all but full sway.

Finally, the ideals of liberty and equality were set forth in an agrarian society. James Watt made his application of steam to machinery less than ten years before the Declaration of Independence was written. It was about sixty years after that event before there was a railway in the country and it was almost seventy years before there was a telegraph line even the short distance between Washington and Baltimore. Mechanical inventions and applications have been more numerous in the last half-century and have produced more social changes than occurred in all the thousands of years of man's life on earth before that time. The problems of organized labor, of distribution of income, of private control of the conditions of labor, of unemployment and insecurity on a vast scale, have either originated or grown to vast size because of the rapid change of an agrarian into an industrial society. We have passed from an age of scarcity and want into one of potential plenty, and yet the transition is attended with intensification of all human problems and with increase of needless suffering.

In the long run, those who are fighting against the attempt to use new industrial and political means of a collective sort to realize the original American ideals are fighting against vast and impersonal forces which in the end are sure to bring the efforts to nought. But their efforts may postpone the institution of that political and industrial order that will give reality to our old American social ideals. During the period of postponement they will create confusion, prolong and multiply unnecessary human suffering, waste life, and make a mockery of the democratic ideals of liberty and equality.

It is at this point that the connection between the changes in the existing social order that are necessary to realize our traditional American ideals and the work of education becomes evident. Legislation and administration are the direct and overt means by which social arrangements are changed. But change in the minds of great numbers of people, change in their habits of thought, in their beliefs, their desires and purposes, their hopes and fears, are prerequisites of change effected by political means. These necessary preliminary changes are brought about by education.

Unless the schools are free to produce these changes in belief and purposes; unless those who conduct the schools, administrators and teachers, have a full grasp of the reality of true American ideals; unless they can detect the sham forms in which these ideals masquerade; unless they perceive the economic and political obstacles that now prevent the realization of original ideals of democratic freedom and equality, the changes that are bound to come about sometime will come attended with a maximum of violence and probable bloodshed. The alternative to advance through sheer force is advance through education taking effect in shaping the ideas and desires that lie back of action. Everything that obstructs the latter puts a premium on the former. It is an old story that it is reactionaries rather than revolutionaries who evoke violent revolutions. It remains to be proved whether men can learn collectively from the collective experience of the past as they learn individually from past individual experience. The Bourbonism that neither forgets, remembers, nor learns is much in evidence at the present time. Yet no matter what the personal belief of any one about what is desirable industrially and politically, any one who is interested in peaceful evolution instead of violent and bloody revolution will realize the central position held by a genuinely free educational system in the peaceful development of society and will bend every energy to defeat the enemies, now so numerous and so active, of schools that are free in inquiry, in teaching and learning; that are intellectually and morally free, the only genuine kind of free school, which are our boast.

Education and Social Improvement

ROBERT MAYNARD HUTCHINS

Born, Brooklyn, New York, January 17, 1899. Graduated from Yale, 1921; honorary A.M., 1922; LL.B., 1925. Lecturer, Yale Law School, 1925–1927; Professor and Acting Dean, 1927–1928; Dean, 1928–1929. President, University of Chicago, 1929–1945; Chancellor, 1945–1951; author of "Chicago Plan"—four-year junior college and liberal arts university separate from professional schools. Associate Director, Ford Foundation, 1951–1954; President, Fund For the Republic since 1954. Author, No Friendly Voice *(1936)*; The Higher Learning in America *(1936)*; Education For Freedom *(1943)*; St. Thomas and the World State *(1949)*; Morals, Religion, and Higher Education *(1950)*.

"The task of education is to make rational animals more perfectly rational."

I should like this afternoon to try to make one simple point. I should like to show the relation between education and the improvement of society. We all want to improve society, and we want college graduates because of their education to want to improve society and to know how to do it. Differences appear when we come to the method by which these educational objects may be attained. I shall not attempt to deal with the problem of how a university may through its scientific investigations best prevent or cure soil erosion, juvenile delinquency, or the current depression. I shall discuss

Annual Meeting of the American Council on Education, Washington, D.C., May 7, 1938. *Vital Speeches of the Day*, IV (June 1, 1938), pp. 498–501. Reprinted by permission of *Vital Speeches of the Day*.

only the method by which an institution may through its educational efforts develop in its students a social consciousness and a social conscience.

At first glance it would seem that we should all agree that in order to talk about society or its improvement we should have to inquire into the nature of society, into the common and abiding characteristics of society, and of those unusual animals who compose it, namely, men. We should want to consider the history of societies, their rise, development, and decay. We should wish to examine their object, the various ways of achieving it, and the degree to which each succeeded or failed. In order to talk about success or failure we should have to have some notions about what a good society was. Without such notions we could not appraise the societies that came under our eye or the one in which we lived. We should need to have some conception of a good society in order to decide what improvement was; for we all know that we have welcomed many measures as beneficent which when adopted have seemed to leave us in as unsatisfactory condition as we were before. In short, if we approached the great task of improving society without prejudice, we should think at once of trying to understand the nature, the purpose, and the history of the institutions which man has created. The quest for social improvement is a perpetual quest. Ever since societies existed men have been trying to make them better. The ideas and the experience of mankind should, one would think, be placed in the hands of the rising generation as it goes forward on the perpetual quest.

This would mean that if we wanted to give a student a sense of social responsibility and the desire to live up to his obligations we should have to give him for this purpose whatever we gave him for other purposes, an education in history and philosophy, together with the disciplines needed to understand those fields. For the purpose of making him an improver of society we should hope to make him master of the political wisdom of the race. Without it he could not understand a social problem. He could not criticize a social institution. He would be without the weapons needed to attack or to defend one. He could not tell a good one from a bad one. He could not think intelligently about one. Even politicians seem to have gained an inkling of this truth; for Governor La Follette[1] said ten days ago that the country has failed to meet the problems of the depression because "we have not done better thinking. Before we can act straight," he said, "we must first think straight."

It is hardly necessary for me to add that nobody can think straight about a practical problem like the problem of improving society unless he knows the facts. He cannot comment usefully on the situation in Germany unless he knows what the situation is. Neither can he do so unless he has some standard of criticism and of action. This standard cannot, of course, be a mathematical formula or some miraculous automatic intellectual gadget which when applied to the facts will immediately and infallibly produce the right answer. The practical

[1] Philip La Follette, Governor of Wisconsin and son of Robert M. La Follette, a nationally known Progressive of the first quarter of this century.

world is a world of contingent singular things and not a mathematical system. No one has emphasized this point more forcibly than Aristotle. But this did not restrain him from attempting in the Ethics and Politics to work out the general principles of the good life and the good state, or from trying to show the utility of such principles, with due allowance for changes in circumstances, in his society, and, as I think, in any other.

If, then, we are to have standards of social criticism and social action, and if they are to be anything but emotional standards, they must result from philosophical and historical study and from the habit of straight thinking therein. It would be a wonderful thing if we were all so conditioned that our reflexes worked unanimously in the right direction when confronted by political and economic injustice, if we could be trained in infancy to recognize and fight it. But even if we could arrive at adolescence in this happy state I am afraid that our excellent habits might fall away under pressure. Something is needed to preserve them, and this is understanding. This is another way of saying that the intellect commands the will. Our parents should make every effort in our childhood to moderate our passions and to habituate us to justice and prudence. But the role of higher education in this connection must be to supply the firm and enduring groundwork to sustain these habits when the tumult of adult life beats upon them.

It seems obvious to me, therefore, that the kind of education that I have been urging is the kind that helps to develop a social consciousness and a social conscience. Why isn't it obvious to everybody else? The first reason, I think, is the popularity of the cult of skepticism. I have been saying that I want to give the student knowledge about society. But we have got ourselves into such a state of mind that if anybody outside of natural science says he knows anything, he is a dogmatist, an authoritarian, a reactionary, and a fascist. Anybody who says, "I don't know because nobody can;" or, "Everything is a matter of opinion;" or, "I will take no position because I am tolerant and open-minded" is a liberal, progressive, democratic fellow to whom the fate of the world may safely be entrusted. All philosophical knowledge of society is superstition. All superstitions hinder progress. Therefore all philosophical knowledge of society hinders the progress of society.

I regret that I am forced to remind you that the two most eminent skeptics of modern times were among its most stalwart reactionaries. Hume was a Tory of the deepest dye, and Montaigne was, too. This was a perfectly natural consequence of their philosophical position. Montaigne held, in effect, that

. . . there was nothing more dangerous than to touch a political order once it had been established. For who knows whether the next will be better? The world is living by custom and tradition; we should not disturb it on the strength of private opinions which express little more than our own moods and humors, or, at the utmost the local prejudices of our own country.

The decision to which the skepticism of Hume and Montaigne led them was the decision to let the world alone. There is another decision to which they could have come and at which others of their faith have actually arrived. If we can know nothing about society, if we can have only opinion about it, and if one man's opinion is as good as another's, then we may decide to get what we irrationally want by the use of irrational means, namely, force. The appeal to reason is vain in a skeptical world. That appeal can only be successful if those appealed to have some rational views of the society of which they are a part.

A second reason why some people doubt the social utility of the education I favor is that they belong to the cult of immediacy, or of what may be called presentism. In this view the way to comprehend the world is to grapple with the reality you find about you. You tour the stockyards and the steel plants and understand the industrial system. There is no past. Any reference to antiquity or the Middle Ages shows that you are not interested in social progress. Philosophy is merely a function of its time and place. We live in a different time and usually a different place. Hence philosophers who lived yesterday have nothing to say to us today.

But we cannot understand the environment by looking at it. It presents itself to us as a mass of incomprehensible items. Simply collecting these items does not enlighten us. It may lead only to that worship of information which, according to John Dewey, still curses the social studies, and understanding escapes us still. We attack old problems not knowing they are old and make the same mistakes because we do not know they were made. So today Stuart Chase and Thurman Arnold, those great discoverers, are renewing the mediaeval controversy between the nominalists and the realists without realizing that the subject was ever discussed before and without the knowledge or training to conduct the discussion to any intelligible end.

The method of disposing of philosophy by placing it in a certain time and then saying that time is gone has been adequately dealt with by a contemporary historian. He says,

It ascribes the birth of Aristotelianism to the fact that Aristotle was a Greek and a pagan, living in a society based on slavery, four centuries before Christ; it also explains the revival of Aristotelianism in the thirteenth century by the fact that St. Thomas Aquinas was an Italian, a Christian, and even a monk, living in a feudal society, whose political and economic structure was widely different from that of fourth-century Greece; and it accounts equally well for the Aristotelianism of J. Maritain, who is French, a layman, and living in the "bourgeois" society of a nineteenth-century republic. Conversely, since they were living in the same times and the same places, just as Aristotle should have held the same philosophy as Plato, so Abelard and St. Bernard, St. Bonaventura and St. Thomas Aquinas, Descartes and Gassendi, all these men, who flatly contradicted one another, should have said more or less the same things.

You will see at once that skepticism and presentism are related to a third ism that distorts our view of the method of education for social improvement. This is the cult of scientism, a cult to which, curiously enough, very few natural scientists belong. It is a cult composed of those who misconceive the nature or the role of science. They say that science is modern; science is tentative; science is progressive. Everything which is not science is antiquated, reactionary, or at best irrelevant. A writer in so respectable and learned a publication as the *International Journal of Ethics* has called upon us to follow science in our quest for the good life, and the fact that he is a philosopher suggests that the cult of scientism has found members in the most unlikely places. For it must be clear that though we can and should use science to achieve social improvement, we cannot follow it to this destination. The reason is that science does not tell us where to go. Men may employ it for good or evil purposes; but it is the men that have the purposes, and they do not learn them from their scientific studies.

Scientism is a disservice to science. The rise of science is the most important fact of modern life. No student should be permitted to complete his education without understanding it. Universities should and must support and encourage scientific research. From a scientific education we may expect an understanding of science. From scientific investigation we may expect scientific knowledge. We are confusing the issue and demanding what we have no right to ask if we seek to learn from science the goals of human life and of organized society.

Finally, we have the cult of anti-intellectualism, which has some oddly assorted members. They range from Hitler, who thinks with his red corpuscles, through the members of the three other cults, to men of good will, who, since they are men of good will, are at the opposite pole to Hitler, but who can give no rational justification for being there. They hold that philosophy of the heart which Auguste Comte first celebrated. Comte belonged to the cult of scientism. Therefore he could know nothing but what science told him. But he wanted social improvement. Hence he tried to make a philosophy and finally a religion out of science, and succeeded only in producing something which was no one of the three and which was, in fact, little more than sentimentalism.

Sentimentalism is an irrational desire to be helpful to one's fellow-men. It sometimes appears as an ingratiating and even a redeeming quality in those who cannot or will not think. But the sentimentalist is really a dangerous character. He distrusts the intellect, because it might show him he was wrong. He believes in the primacy of the will, and this is what makes him dangerous. You don't know what you ought to want; you don't know why you want what you want. But you do know that you want it. This easily develops into the notion that since you want it, you ought to have it. You are a man of good will, and your opponents by definition are not. Since you ought to have what you want, you should get it if you have the power; and here the journey from the man of good will to Hitler is complete.

This is indeed the position in which the members of all four cults—skepticism, presentism, scientism, and anti-intellectualism—find themselves on questions of social improvement. Since they cannot know, they must feel. We can only hope that they will feel good. But we cannot be very hopeful. Where does the good will come from? The campaign before the Austrian plebiscite brought us the news that Hitler is now guided by a special revelation. Most other men of good will do not claim intimate contact with the Deity. But they are uniformly mysterious about the source of their inspiration. If it is not knowledge, and hence in this case philosophy, it must be habit and habit of the most irrational kind. A university can have nothing to do with irrational habits, except to try to moderate the bad ones and support the good ones. But if by hypothesis we cannot do this by rational means, we are forced to the conclusion that a university must be a large nursery school, tenderly preserving good habits from shock, in the hope that if they can be nursed long enough they will last through life, though without any rational foundation. In this view the boarding-school in the country would be the only proper training ground for American youth, and the University of Chicago could take no part in social improvement. In fact, it would be a subversive institution.

It hardly helps us here to say, as many anti-intellectuals do, that education must educate "the whole man." Of all the meaningless phrases in educational discussion this is the prize. Does it mean that education must do the whole job of translating the whole infant into the whole adult? Must it do what the church, the family, the state, the Y.M.C.A., and the Boy Scouts allege they are trying to do? If so, what is the place of these important or interesting organizations, and what becomes of that intellectual training which educational institutions might be able to give if they could get around to it? Are we compelled to assume that our students can learn nothing from life or that they have led no life before coming to us and lead none after they come? Moreover, what we are seeking is a guide to the emphasis that higher education must receive. Talk of the whole man seems to imply that there should be no emphasis at all. All "parts" of the man are of equal importance: his dress, his food, his health, his family, his business. Is education to emphasize them all? That would be like saying, if we were going to study the financial situation, that in studying it we should emphasize the financial situation. A flat equality among subjects, interests, and powers will hardly lead to the satisfactory development of any. Is it too much to say that if we can teach our students to lead the life of reason we shall do all that can be expected of us and do at the same time the best thing that can be done for the whole man? The task of education is to make rational animals more perfectly rational.

We see, then, that the quest for social improvement is a perpetual one. Men have always wanted not a different society, but a better one. What a better society is and how to get it has been one of the persistent problems of philosophy and one of the fundamental issues in the tradition of the Western World. Only those who recognize the important place that philosophy and the wisdom of the race must hold in education for citizenship can hope to educate men and women who can contribute to the improvement of society and who will want to do so. The cults of skepticism, presentism, scientism, and anti-intellectualism can lead us only to despair, not merely of education, but of society.

Fire Always Makes Room for Itself

WILLIAM H. COWLEY

Born, Petersburg, Virginia, May 28, 1899. Graduated from Dartmouth College, 1924; Ph.D., University of Chicago, 1930. With Bell Telephone Company Laboratories, New York, 1924–1925. Administrative staff, University of Chicago, 1927–1929. Research Associate and Assistant Professor of Psychology, Bureau of Educational Research, Ohio State University, 1929–1934; Associate Professor, 1934–1935; Professor, 1935–1938. President, Hamilton College, 1938–1944. Professor of Higher Education, Stanford University, 1945–1954; David Jacks Professor of Higher Education since 1954.

"We must recognize that intelligence is not enough, that men are not mere thinking machines, and that to train the minds of students and to neglect their spirit is to give them stones for the bread they seek."

I take for the text of this convocation address an old Japanese proverb which reads: "Fire always makes room for itself." We are today witnessing a calamitous demonstration of the truth of that proverb. London is in danger of being destroyed, not because of the battering of demolition bombs but rather because of the fires caused by incendiary bombs. Since fire always makes room for itself, the London fire-fighters must control the huge blazes being lit every night by raiding airplanes or London is doomed.

Fall Convocation, University of Rochester, October 23, 1940. *Vital Speeches of the Day,* VII (November 15, 1940), pp. 87–90. Reprinted by permission of *Vital Speeches of the Day.*

I cite the danger of fire in London to illustrate the soundness of the Japanese proverb and to apply it to the relationship of education to the crisis we face in America and throughout the world. My thesis is that colleges and universities must rededicate themselves to nurture the fire of the spirit else we shall not be equal to the tremendous responsibilities which the world situation has catapulted upon us. Fire always makes room for itself be it a physical or an emotional fire. In democratic countries we are staring into catastrophe because our emotional fire has been but a flicker compared with the huge flame of sulphuric energy which has been bursting forth from the totalitarians. Unless we become aroused as they have been aroused, we shall most certainly be enslaved by them, and we shall see the Anglo-Saxon tradition of freedom chained if not slaughtered outright.

The problem of emotional fire in the crisis we face has numerous facets, and it is possible this evening to discuss but one of them. I devote myself, therefore, to the relationship of educational philosophy to our national welfare. I begin by making what may seem to many of you to be a brash statement. It is this: a large share of the spiritual and emotional poverty which has characterized American life in recent decades is the direct result of misconceived and destructive educational doctrines. In colleges and universities we have been following false gods, and because of our adherence to them we have almost smothered the fire that should give education its heat and power, its light and its leading.

One doctrine has in particular been crippling us: the doctrine of intellectualism. In my judgment we must cut our colleges and universities free of this false educational concept or as a nation we shall sink into insignificance if not into slavery.

Intellectualism is the concept which asserts that education is concerned only with the intellectual development of students, and that social, physical, emotional, and spiritual education should be left to other institutions—to the boy scouts, the Sunday School, the church, and the junior league. This doctrine is widely held by college professors, and the president of one of our great universities has achieved national prominence in recent years by espousing it with all the power of his potent pen and with all the force of his platform skill.

May I begin an analysis of intellectualism with some history? Until the time of the Civil War American colleges followed the British educational tradition and sought to educate the whole student. Educators were interested in the student's mind, of course, but also in his morals, in his manners, in his religion, and in his sense of values—indeed in everything that contributed to a complete or a whole education. During the middle of the last century this concept of education began to be abandoned. America had been changing from an agricultural and maritime to an industrial society. It needed trained engineers, agriculturalists, architects, chemists and dozens of other varieties of professional and business men for whom the old-time college provided no training. Obviously, a new type of higher education had to be provided; and since England offered no models, educators turned to Germany which had developed broader curriculums and a new variety of university, a university devoted to intensive specialization in all the modern arts and sciences.

The adoption of German methods by such leading educators as President Eliot of Harvard, President White of Cornell, and President Gilman of Johns Hopkins, produced a growth and development in higher education of tremendous importance. The reorganized universities and the newly-established technical and professional schools, which these leaders of 19th century education and their associates headed, trained the men and women to build the nation's railroads, exploit its mines, ferret out the basic physical and chemical facts upon which modern industry is built. They also trained more and better trained lawyers, physicians, engineers, and professional and business men of all kinds. Because they looked to Germany and followed its educational example, America met the opportunities of the 19th century and grew in wealth and strength beyond the wildest dreams of former generations.

But this material development is not the whole story. The ten thousand Americans who between 1850 and 1940 returned from Europe with German Ph.D.'s brought back with them something else besides preeminent skill as specialists. They brought intellectualism, and they saddled it upon the American college. German universities, after the crushing defeat that Napoleon administered to their fatherland early in the century, threw overboard all interest in students as individuals. They sought to raise a race of intellectual supermen, and they consciously concentrated all their energies upon the minds of students. What a student did between the time he matriculated and the time he took his examinations, no one in German universities knew or cared. Where he lived, the condition of his health, his social life, his physical and spiritual growth—these were of no interest to the German academic authorities. They considered their job to be the training of superior minds, and they conducted their universities as if nothing else counted.

This is the doctrine that German-trained professors brought back to the United States, that they foisted upon the American college, that they promoted until we tossed into the discard the tradition of wholeness and completeness that Anglo-Saxon educators had cherished for centuries. Germany has made a huge contribution to the intellectual education of America, but for this help we have paid a staggering price. Impelled by German examples we have stressed the training of the minds of students, and we have fallen into the calamitous error of assuming that the intellect dominates life, that the intellect is our chief personal and social instrument, that the intellect is the only concern of education.

Merely to state the doctrine of intellectualism constitutes a refutation of it, but I should like to discuss three of the major arguments against it. So strong is the hold which intellectualism has upon us that its fallacies cannot too often be exposed nor too frequently ridiculed.

The first argument comes from biology. After a century of amazingly illuminating research biologists have arrived at a new and far-reaching generalization, a new orientation. Historically biologists concentrated their attention upon discernible differences in the *parts* of organisms and the functioning of these *parts*. Recently, however, a growing number of biologists have asserted that *parts* must be seen in relationship to *the whole organism*. Thus they hold that it is impossible to understand the functioning of, say the lungs, except in relationship to the sympathetic nervous system, and indeed, to every other part of the organism. This point of view is called organismic or holistic biology. John Scott Haldane, eminent British biologist, describes it in these words:

> The organism maintains itself as a whole. It is not a mere federation of individual cells acting mechanically like a machine, but is, on the contrary, a closely unified organization whose nature is such that each part or even each cell partakes of and contributes to the life of the whole. The behaviour of an individual cell is unintelligible apart from its being also an expression of the life of the higher organism as a whole. The individual cells as such express in their genesis, behaviour, and deaths, the life of the whole organism.

The bearing of this observation upon intellectualism is obvious: the mind cannot—except in the laboratory—be abstracted from the rest of an organism. Educators cannot wisely, therefore, devote all their energies to the minds of students and neglect their bodies, their social development, their systems of values, their spirits. Such a concept of education is biologically ridiculous. American higher education, largely controlled during the past seventy years by intellectualists, has remarkably multiplied our intellectual and our material resources; but because it has frowned upon and neglected all objectives except the development of the intellect, we have become impoverished in all other directions—particularly in emotion and spirit.

This statement sets up the second count against intellectualism: the time-honored philosophical and psychological postulate that the intellect is never the master of the spirit but always its servant—in brief that the mind takes its direction and its energy not from within itself, but from the purposes and systems of values of the entity which we call the Self. Thirty years ago in a powerful address Woodrow Wilson dramatically expressed this judgment in these words:

> We speak of this as an age in which mind is monarch, but I take it for granted that, if that is true, mind is one of those modern monarchs who reigns but do not govern. As a matter of fact, the world is governed in every generation by a great House of Commons made up of the passions; and we can only be careful to see that the handsome passions are in the majority.

Woodrow Wilson's epigram that "the world is governed by the passions" checks with everyone's commonsense interpretation of his own experience. Attitudes, sentiments, values, purposes—these are the controlling factors in the behaviour of us all. The fact is admitted by everyone except the professors and administrators who have been blinded by intellectualism. We shall equate education with reality only when we take President Wilson's advice and rededicate education to the task of seeing that "the handsome passions are in the majority." That is the supreme task of education, not the training of students' minds.

May I make it entirely clear that I am not being critical of intellectual development. Indeed, colleges and universities must be the place *par excellence* in our society for the highest intellectual achievement. I give way to no one in my insistence that the college has failed if it does not effectively train the minds of the students. I insist, however, that we must go a great deal further, that we must recognize that intelligence is not enough, that men are not mere thinking machines, and that to train the minds of students and to neglect their spirit is to give them stones for the bread they seek.

The distinction which the intellectualists make between the intellect and the emotions throws into relief the third of the three arguments against their doctrine of which I would speak. The first argument stems from biology, the second from philosophy and psychology, and this third comes from logic. The intellectualists have fallen into error which logicians call the disjunctive fallacy and which laymen call the either-or fallacy. Thus intellectualists assert that education must be one thing or the other—intellectual or anti-intellectual. This is a splendid example of the crooked thinking produced by the disjunctive fallacy. It's like asserting that all men are either tall or short, fat or thin, black or white, good or bad, brilliant or stupid, charming or gauche, egotistic or modest, etc., etc.

It would seem to be impossible for any intelligent individual to fall into the clutches of this fallacy, but the fact is that the intellectualists have done exactly that. They say in effect that colleges must devote their energies entirely to the intellectual development of students and that it is impossible—or at least undesirable—to give time and thought to student social life, to athletics, to the persistent problem of personal purposes and values which every college student faces. In a word, they assert that the college must concentrate all of its attention upon intellectual training or else become a mere country club. They insist that the college must be either tall or short: tall and intellectual or short and country clubbish. They admit no possibility of a middle ground where the whole student is educated—socially as well as intellectually, in spirit as well as in a professional specialty.

It would be interesting to explore the implications of this disjunction as it affects fraternities, athletic teams, and student life in general. I prefer, however, to discuss a much larger question: the bearing of intellectualism upon the spirit, upon the spirit of faculty members and therefore upon the spirit of students.

In his brilliant address given before the American Philosophical Society last spring one of our outstanding American poets, Archibald MacLeish, deplores the disappearance of fire, of passion, and of broad social purpose from among college professors, scholars, and writers. He entitled his address "The Irresponsibles" and described and criticized them in this passage:

The irresponsibility of the scholar is the irresponsibility of the scientist upon whose laboratory insulation he has patterned all his work. The scholar in letters has made himself as indifferent to values, as careless of significance, as bored with meanings as the chemist. He is a refugee from consequences, an exile from the responsibilities of moral choice. His words of praise are the laboratory words—objectivity, detachment, dispassion. His pride is to be scientific, neuter, skeptical, detached—superior to final judgment or absolute belief. . . .

It is not for nothing that the modern scholar invented the Ph.D. thesis as his principal contribution to literary form. The Ph.D. thesis is the perfect image of his world. It is work done for the sake of doing work—perfectly conscientious, perfectly laborious, perfectly irresponsible. The modern scholar at his best and worst is both these things— perfectly conscientious, laborious, and competent: perfectly irresponsible for the saving of his world. . . . He has his work to do. He has his book to finish. He hopes the war will not destroy the manuscripts he works with. He is the pure, the perfect type of irresponsibility—the man who acts as though fire could not burn him because he has no business with the fire. He knows, because he cannot help but know, reading his papers, talking to his friends—he knows this fire has consumed the books, the spirit, everything he lives by, flesh itself, in other countries. He knows this but he will not know. It's not his business. Whose business is it then? He will not answer even that. He has his work to do. He has his book to finish.

This is as pointed an indictment of intellectualism as anyone has written since Tennyson in 1830 deplored the spiritual and emotional poverty that had come to dominate Cambridge, his Alma Mater. The verse Tennyson wrote is perhaps an even more stinging rebuke. Here it is:

> Therefore, your halls, your ancient colleges,
> Your portals statued with old kings and queens,
> Your gardens, myriad-volumed libraries,
> Waxed-lighted chapels, and rich carven screens,
> Your doctors, and your proctors, and your deans,
> Shall not avail you, when the day-beam sports
> New-risen o'er awakened Albion—No!
> Nor yet your solemn organ pipes that blow
> Melodious thunders thro' your vacant courts
> At noon and eve: because your manner sorts
> Not of this age, wherefrom ye stand apart,
> Because the lips of little children preach
> Against you, you that do profess to teach
> And teach us nothing, feeding not the heart.

Because the great majority of men and women who teach in our colleges and universities are consciously or subconsciously giving their allegiance to intellectualism, we have fallen into the bog of irresponsibility which MacLeish deplores. In Tennyson's words we are not feeding the hearts of our students. We are feeding their minds, but we ignore their spirits, their passions, their latent fire.

Thus intellectualism has crippled us not only educationally but also in our national life. For decades we have been graduating young men and women who have been taught to look at everything intellectually, to be objective, to weigh all the evidence, to see both sides of every question, to be supercritical, to hold judgments in abeyance. This is all very well in the abstractions of science, but where the values of our civilization are at stake, it is criminally destructive. It has made of us a sceptical if not a cynical people. It has lulled us into a false impartiality. It has made us apathetic about our heritages of democracy, of freedom of speech and of the press. It has driven us individually and collectively into a selfish hunt for security. In brief, it has deprived us of emotion, of enthusiasm, of national spirit and passion.

It would obviously be an over-simplification to lay our current spiritual poverty entirely at the door of intellectualism, but that intellectualism has played a large part there can be no question. It has made of us spiritual neutrals in a world where everything we cherish is being viciously attacked. If we continue in this frame of mind we'll soon be ripe either for subjection by passionate Nazism or by some native leader who will make capital of our spiritual starvation and lead us to God-knows-what extremes of uncontrolled emotional debauch. That is exactly what has happened in Germany. Hitler succeeded in enlisting the enthusiasm and the devotion of German university students to his hooked-cross banner because they were fed up with the bloodless objectivity of German professors, and in a few short years Germany swung from the extreme of intellectual objectivity to the opposite extreme of emotional drunkenness. The same fate awaits us unless we achieve a balance between intelligence and spirit. Neither can be neglected. We must have both. We must denounce and renounce the coldness of reason alone and the hotness of passion alone. Unless in our colleges and our universities and in our national life we reaffirm and reestablish the place of spirit, we shall sink to a shadow of our powers. We must temper spirit with reason, of course, but we must disavow the intellectualistic doctrine that reason is sufficient. Instead we must give the place of honor to the driving force of spirit without which intelligence drugs us into torpor and emotional impotence.

Because of the inroads that intellectualism has made, the world situation which threatens our national life comes in the nick of time to save us from spiritual atrophy. Once again we have national cohesion, a consuming enthusiasm, a great passion to unite us. It will purge us of our impurities and reinfuse spirit into our cold, intellectualistic hearts. We shall pay a large price in wealth and perhaps in lives. If such sacrifices will reestablish our national spirit and kill off intellectualism, the price will not be too great.

The future of the country will soon be in the hands of you young men and women who are students in our colleges during these present years. We are a great and wealthy people in things material. Whether or not it is great and wealthy in things spiritual depends upon you. Thomas Huxley expressed the situation clearly when he came to this country in 1876 to speak at the founding of Johns Hopkins University. This is what he said:

I cannot say that I am in the slightest degree impressed by your bigness, or your material resources as such. Size is not grandeur, and territory does not make a nation. The great issue, about which hangs a true sublimity and the terror of an overhanging fate is what you are going to do with all these things.

"What are you going to do with all these things?" This is the question which faces the nation and every college man and woman. It cannot be answered in intellectual terms alone. It must be answered in terms of spirit. It must be answered by our response to the challenge that totalitarianism has thrown at us. Fire always makes room for itself. We shall be equal to the challenge only if we fight the fire of the dictators with a greater and more powerful fire burning in each of us—a fire consecrated to the protection of the Anglo-Saxon tradition both in government and in education.

ISOLATIONISM VS. ONE WORLD

As WAS still the custom in 1920, a committee called on Senator Warren G. Harding to notify him formally that he had been nominated for the Presidency by the Republican party. The committee's spokesman, Henry Cabot Lodge, knew Harding's habits of equivocation and therefore left nothing to chance in extracting from him a public repudiation of Wilson's League of Nations. "In that work," said Lodge, pointedly referring to the Senate's rejection of the League in 1919, "you, sir, took a conspicuous part, and we know that you were in full accord with the belief of your Republican colleagues that the League of Nations as proposed by Mr. Wilson and upon which he and his party still insist, ought never to be accepted by the American people."

Harding responded with a cloud of words, proclaiming friendship for other nations and promising them the full benefit of our moral influence. Then, as if reciting lines supplied in advance by Lodge, he ventured that "The resumption of the Senate's authority saved to this Republic its independent nationality, when autocracy [Lodge's favorite characterization of Wilson's presidency] misinterpreted the dream of a world experiment to be the vision of a world ideal." To Lodge's satisfaction, Harding declared that "Our Party means to hold the heritage of American nationality unimpaired and unsurrendered."[1]

In the 1920 campaign, the Democratic Presidential and Vice-Presidential candidates, James M. Cox and Franklin D. Roosevelt, tried to resuscitate public interest in the League of Nations with small success. Buffeted by both the internationalist and isolationist wings of his party, Harding artfully sought to harmonize them by hinting at some vague compromise he called a world Association of Nations. But after his thumping victory at the polls, he dismissed the League as "now deceased," in favor of a rapid return to "normalcy"—a nostalgic euphoria

---

[1] See full texts of speeches by Lodge and Harding in *Official Report of the Proceedings of the Seventeenth Republican National Convention* (New York: The Tenny Press, 1920), pp. 254–272.

compounded of McKinley's domestic policies and the traditional isolationism enjoined by Jefferson.

If Harding mistook his huge plurality as a mandate for isolationism, as many people still insist, his disregard for "the public will" provoked no screams from the bleachers. Most Americans soured quickly on European postwar struggles, acknowledging ruefully they had overreacted to Wilson's plea to save the world for democracy. Old convictions about national self-sufficiency based on bounteous nature and a blessed Atlantic moat were revived; America turned its back on Europe and gave its attention to consumers' goods and the building of private fortunes. Automobiles and radios rolled off conveyor belts; standards of living soared; and millions of people lived high, wide, if unhandsomely on their swollen prosperity behind sturdy protective tariff walls. Domestic prosperity fostered the spirit of nationalism: America was constructive, Europe destructive. Nationalism attained xenophobic proportions in the harangues of William Hale Thompson, Chicago's lowbrow mayor, who, in his mayoralty campaign of 1927, cried huskily: "I wanta make the King of England keep his snoot out of America. That's what I want. I don't want the League of Nations! I don't want the world court! America first and last, and always! That's the issue of this campaign. That's what Big Bill Thompson wants!"[2] Thompson was ridiculous, of course, but the demagogic stuff he peddled was dredged up from a substratum of popular thought.

Admittedly there were the faithful few who pursued the grail of internationalism amidst the Bacchanalia of the twenties—some teachers, philanthropists, cosmopolitan businessmen, and clergymen of modernist persuasion. But their number and influence reached a vanishing point by the election year of 1928. Hungry for power, the Democratic party pledged itself to outlaw war while remaining free from entangling alliances. The League issue was buried without obsequies.

Prosperity in the twenties stimulated isolationism, but so did the economic depression of the thirties. In the United States, as elsewhere, the searing and widespread impact of the depression encouraged national programs of relief and recovery with small regard for consequences beyond the water's edge. Despite the opposition of a thousand professional economists, in 1930 President Hoover signed the Hawley-Smoot Tariff Act that hiked tariff rates, depressed foreign trade, stimulated retaliatory tariffs abroad, and provoked European nations to default on their war debts—debts that they ultimately repudiated. Americans became thoroughly roiled over these European defalcations. And only a few months

---

[2] Quoted in Lloyd Wendt and Herman Kogan, *Big Bill of Chicago* (Indianapolis: The Bobbs-Merrill Company, 1953), p. 248.

after he took office President Roosevelt scuttled the World Economic Conference that met in London to cope with problems of foreign debt and international currency stabilization. Roosevelt wanted a free hand to manipulate the nation's currency so as to raise commodity prices at home.

Widespread preoccupation among nations with their economic crises created conditions for international anarchy. In September, 1931, Japan seized the moment to invade the Chinese province of Manchuria, affording the spectacle of one member of the League of Nations callously violating the territorial integrity of another. The League's failure to enforce sanctions against Japan was an open invitation to lawlessness that Mussolini, the Fascist dictator of Italy, accepted in his good time.

In the twenties Americans had divided in their estimates of Mussolini and Italian Fascism. Those who were sensitive to civil liberties had fumed over Mussolini's suppression of democratic rights (Hadn't Wilson said something about making the world safe for democracy?); those more disturbed by international Communism had gone along with the British Chancellor of the Exchequer, Winston S. Churchill, when he praised Italians for their "victorious struggle against the bestial appetites and passions of Leninism," adding that "Your movement has rendered a service to the whole world." But as for most Americans, they shrugged off Mussolini as a swaggering, chest-beating Italian who ruled over an infantile and turbulent people that had let democracy run amuck. He had put down debilitating labor strikes and put the trains on schedule. Even President Harding's Ambassador to Italy, Richard Washburn Child, in a speech in Rome, publicly applauded the way Mussolini went about shoring up Italy's national interests. Child derided "theorizing nations of whining peoples" and extolled those "who develop a national spirit so finely tempered that they offer to the world an example of organization, discipline and fair play. . . ."[3]

A decade later Mussolini exhibited his spirit of fair play in a naked assault upon helpless Ethiopia. As he gathered his legions, the League of Nations threatened economic sanctions if he took the plunge. In turn Mussolini sought to intimidate the Council of the League through an international radio broadcast on October 2, 1935. Italy had been gulled at the Versailles Peace Conference, he shouted, and "only the crumbs of a rich colonial booty were left for us to pick up." Italy would not now be denied her expansionist designs on "a barbarian country, unworthy of ranking among civilized nations." If the League imposes

[3] For full text of Child's speech of June 28, 1923, and Mussolini's reply, see Bernardo di San Severino, ed., *Mussolini as Revealed in His Political Speeches* (London and Toronto: J. M. Dent & Sons, Ltd., 1923), pp. 335–342.

sanctions, he warned, we shall answer with military measures. "To acts of war, we shall answer with acts of war."[4] Mussolini shattered whatever vestiges of world confidence remained in the League of Nations.

The Italo-Ethiopian crisis spurred the United States Congress between 1935 and 1937 to pass Neutrality Acts, calculated to keep the nation free from European power struggles. Other events intensified this determination. After two years of sensational hearings, a committee of the United States Senate headed by Gerald P. Nye issued a report in 1936 that indicted munition makers as "merchants of death" and charged that the nation had been sucked into the World War by nefarious war profiteers. That same year, 1936, Hitler put out his feelers and marched his Nazi soldiers into the demilitarized Rhineland, defying the "Dictat of Versailles." Made confident by success, Mussolini and Hitler gave substantial support to Franco's Fascist forces in the Spanish civil war then raging, while Russia came to the aid of the beleaguered Republican government. Franco's victory extended Fascism and afforded his allies invaluable lessons in modern warfare.

The year 1937 foretold directions history was to follow. In July fighting broke out between Chinese and Japanese forces near Peiping, and Japanese troops poured into North China. In September Mussolini and Hitler exhibited a triumphal display of concord and strength in ceremonial confirmation of the Rome-Berlin Axis of the previous year. Mussolini came to Germany for a show of unexcelled pageantry: a sea of banners bearing swastika and Fascist symbols; torchbearing battalions; goosestepping fife and drum corps executing complicated maneuvers; bands playing "Deutschland Uber Alles" and the Horst Wessel song. The climax came in Berlin on the night of September 28, when both dictators spoke to densely packed acres of people before them (Hitler said there were one million persons) and to listeners in twenty countries of Europe and the Americas through a gigantic international radio hookup arranged by Hitler's minister of propaganda, Joseph Goebbels. While the world gaped, Hitler proclaimed:

> The common trend of ideas expressed in the Fascist and National Socialist Revolutions . . . will have a salutary influence on the world, in which destruction and deformation are trying to win the upper hand. Fascist Italy has been transformed into a new Imperial Romanum by the ingenious activities of a compelling personality.
>
> You, Benito Mussolini, will have realized that in these days, due

[4] "Italy's Solemn Hour," NBC Radio, October 2, 1935. *Vital Speeches of the Day,* II (1935), pp. 2–3.

to the National Socialist state, Germany has become a great power, thanks to her racial attitude and her military strength. The inherent strength of the two countries is the best guarantee for the preservation of Europe, which is inspired by a sense of responsibility in the discharge of its cultural mission. It is not willing to allow destructive elements to cause its decline and dissolution.[5]

Disillusioned by Mussolini's policies of external aggrandizement, and aroused by the gravity of the German menace, Winston Churchill, almost alone among British political figures, had been speaking out since 1932, first against disarmament, then for rearmament and a return to balance of power schemes. Now in 1937 President Roosevelt decided to challenge Japanese belligerency and the hostile gestures of European dictators. On October 5, he traveled to Chicago, often considered the heartland of isolationism, to dedicate the Outer Drive bridge. Facing the Chicago *Tribune* tower, Roosevelt declared bluntly that "an epidemic of world lawlessness is spreading." Pursuing his analogy, he added: "When an epidemic of physical disease starts to spread, the community approves and joins in a quarantine of patients in order to protect the health of the community against the spread of the disease." But the President threaded his way cautiously, for as late as April, the public had been polled on the question "Do you think it was a mistake for the United States to enter the World War?" and 71 percent said "yes."[6] Roosevelt's final words therefore identified him unmistakably with the common sentiment: "America hates war. America hopes for peace. Therefore America actively engages in the search for peace." Newspaper reaction to the speech reflected mounting moral indignation at the aggressors, although a segment of the isolationist press had some worried afterthoughts. Ambiguous as was the President's proposed quarantine, historians today tend to regard the "Quarantine" speech as a turning point in official quarters from isolationism.[7]

The saber rattlers abroad were undeterred by speeches or appeals of any kind. In March, 1938, Hitler annexed Austria. At Munich in September he persuaded Prime Minister Chamberlain of England and Premier Daladier of France that the Reich was entitled to the German-populated Sudetenland of Czechoslovakia, that once this claim was honored he would seek no more territory. With their

[5] For a detailed account of the Berlin event and texts of speeches, see *The New York Times,* September 29, 1937, pp. 1, 12.

[6] Walter Johnson, *The Battle Against Isolation* (Chicago: University of Chicago Press, 1944), p. 19.

[7] For a detailed study of the speech, see Dorothy Borg, "Notes on Roosevelt's 'Quarantine' Speech," *Political Science Quarterly,* LXXII (1957), pp. 405–433.

approval, Hitler dismembered Czechoslovakia and then, to their utter dismay, devoured the whole of it. On August 23, 1939, Hitler signed a nonaggression pact with Russia, which opened the way for his invasion of Poland on September 1. On September 3, Britain and France honored their treaty obligations to Poland and World War II began.

Bombs fell on Warsaw that day of September 3, 1939, when President Roosevelt spoke in measured tones to his anxious countrymen:

> This nation will remain a neutral nation, but I cannot ask that every American remain neutral in thought as well. Even a neutral has a right to take account of facts. Even a neutral cannot be asked to close his mind or his conscience.
>
> I have said not once, but many times, that I have seen war and that I hate war. I say that again and again.
>
> I hope the United States will keep out of this war. I believe that it will. And I give you assurance and reassurance that every effort of your government will be directed toward that end.
>
> As long as it remains within my power to prevent, there will be no black-out of peace in the United States.

Above all, Americans wanted to stay out of the war, but they also shared the President's outrage at international banditry; hence, unlike Wilson in 1914, Roosevelt did not ask for an impossible neutrality in thought. On September 21, the President called Congress into extraordinary session to modify existing neutrality laws. Among other things, he requested (1) repeal of the arms embargo so that arms as well as other nonmilitary items might be sold to France and England; (2) authority to keep American ships out of danger zones where they might provoke incidents. Here were overtures to both interventionists and isolationists. The maneuver succeeded, but the turbulence of the congressional debating forecast the storms ahead.

There was stillness in Europe in the winter of 1939–1940, and with a trace of bravado, people spoke of the "phony war." Then in April, Hitler swept through Denmark and Norway, and the blitzkrieg replaced the "sitzkrieg." Holland, Belgium, and Luxembourg were next. Without further delay, Parliament made Winston Churchill Prime Minister of Great Britain on May 10, and three days later, in a speech to Parliament, he said: "I would say to the House, as I said to those who have joined this Government: I have nothing to offer but blood, toil, tears and sweat." His grim prophecy was soon fulfilled when, late in May, a trapped British Expeditionary Force had to be rescued from Dunkirk under enemy gunfire and aerial bombing by every description of craft capable of plying the English Channel. With France reeling under German blows, Mussolini— "that crafty, cold-blooded, black-hearted Italian," Churchill now called him— came in for the kill. And in a speech at the University of Virginia, Roosevelt threw away diplomatic discretion and let "the old red blood" have its way: "On this tenth day of June, 1940, the hand that held the dagger has struck it into the back of its neighbor." On June 22 France fell.

Four days before France's surrender, Churchill spoke over the British Broadcasting System as he had spoken earlier to the House of Commons. He predicted that "the Battle of Britain is about to begin" and warned that if Britain were to fall, the whole world—including the United States—"will sink into the abyss of a new Dark Age. . . ." Then, with monumental eloquence he cried: "Let us therefore brace ourselves to our duties, and so bear ourselves that, if the British Empire and its Commonwealth last for a thousand years, men will still say, 'This was their finest hour.' "

As prelude to invasion, Hitler now turned his bombers westward in a massive attempt to reduce England to rubble. Britain's finest hour stretched out into months of unrelieved horror and bleakness. Vicariously, Americans absorbed the sights and sounds of London under the blitz through the daily broadcasts of Edward R. Murrow, who always opened with his distinctive salutation, "This— is London." Through Murrow Americans became party to Churchill's growling eloquence in Parliament and to his sorties among the ruins of ancient buildings. Murrow was at his graphic best in vignettes of the poorly circumstanced but unbroken Britisher whom he described through episodes such as this, taken from his account of a shopping expedition: "I went on to another shop to buy flashlight batteries. I bought three. The clerk said: 'You needn't buy so many. We'll have enough for the whole winter.' But I said: 'What if you aren't here?' There were buildings down in that street, and he replied, 'Of course we'll be here. We've been in business here for a hundred and fifty years.' "[8] Murrow, said Eric Sevareid, "made the British and their behavior human and thus compelling to his countrymen at home. . . . There is no doubt of his immense aid to the President in awakening the American people to the issue before them."[9] What is more, his broadcasts, and those of other correspondents from far points of the

[8] *This Is London* (New York: Simon and Schuster, 1941), pp. 171–174.
[9] *Not So Wild a Dream* (New York: Alfred A. Knopf, 1946), p. 178.

globe, undermined isolationism by shrinking the planet men had heretofore carried in their heads.

Americans empathized with the British but pursued life pretty much as usual. Back home after witnessing the fall of France, Eric Sevareid spent a day in Congress and was filled with revulsion by "tobacco-chewing, gravy-stained, overstuffed gila monsters who, nestled in their bed of chins, would doze through other speeches, then haul up their torpid bodies and mouth the same old, evil shibboleths about King George III, the war debts, and 'Uncle Sap,' and 'decadent France.' "[10]

To combat American torpidity, the Committee to Defend America by Aiding the Allies was founded in June, 1940, under the leadership of William Allen White, the Republican editor of the Emporia *Gazette*. Working closely with Roosevelt, the committee sought to build public support for all-out aid to Britain short of a shooting war. It encouraged or sponsored prominent leaders to speak out for aid to Britain. In a rare radio appearance, General John J. Pershing of World War I fame urged the Government to turn over at once to Britain its reserves of overage destroyers.[11] James Bryant Conant, President of Harvard University, went further in a radio talk: "I shall mince no words. *I believe the United States should take every action possible to insure the defeat of Hitler.* And let us face honestly the possible implications of such a policy. The actions we propose might eventuate in war."[12] With the blessing of Roosevelt, the United States Ambassador to the France that was no more, William Bullitt, declared hemispheric defense to be a chimera, charged that the United States was being softened for invasion by conspirators at home, and passionately demanded that the country mobilize for war at once if we chose not to see "Hitler in Independence Hall making fun of the Liberty Bell."[13] It was an inflammatory speech, and when the Committee to Defend America by Aiding the Allies distributed printed copies of it, Senator D. Worth Clark described it as "very little short of treason," and Congressman John Schafer thought the speaker should be "locked up."[14]

Pressure to shift from neutralism to intervention, even at the risk of war,

[10] *Ibid.*, p. 197.

[11] "Keep War from the Americas," August 4, 1940. *Vital Speeches of the Day*, VI (1940), p. 646.

[12] "Immediate Aid to the Allies," CBS Radio, May 29, 1940, *Speaking as a Private Citizen* (Cambridge: Harvard University Press, 1941), pp. 11–15.

[13] *Report to the American People* (Boston: Houghton Mifflin Company, 1940), 29 pp.

[14] Johnson, *op. cit.*, p. 105.

rallied the isolationists in September, 1940, under the banner of the America First Committee with General Robert E. Wood, of Sears, Roebuck and Company, as national chairman, and R. Douglas Stuart, Jr., as national director. America First harbored strange bedfellows—pacifists and nonpacifists, New Dealers and anti-New Dealers, Socialists and reactionaries—held together in uneasy tension by convictions that the United States must not enter the war and that Roosevelt's Machiavellian policies were a threat. America First had its galaxy of orators too, and high in that firmament was Charles A. Lindbergh.

Lindbergh was a household name, the idolized youth of the twenties who had flown the Atlantic Ocean nonstop in a primitive monoplane. More recently he had inspected the war machines of Europe. Like his father, a pre-World War I congressman from Minnesota, Lindbergh felt strongly that America must stand aloof from the blood baths of Europe, and since 1939 he had waged a lone-eagle type campaign against intervention. The America First Committee welcomed Lindbergh, and he proved to be its best drawing card at mass meetings. He was the personification of American innocence, and audiences shook the rafters with their approval of this slender, intense, tousled hero who pled with them to regard the war from a "purely American standpoint." "If we enter the quarrels of Europe during the war," he cautioned, "we must stay with them in time of peace as well. . . . We must either keep out of European wars or stay in European affairs permanently." And whereas Bullitt made hair rise on necks with his allegations of fifth columnists within the gates, Lindbergh insisted that the only threat to American security came from "powerful elements" among us who manipulate much of the machinery of propaganda to involve us in war.[15]

The same month in which America First was founded, Roosevelt transferred fifty overage destroyers to Britain by executive decree in order to avoid interminable debate in Congress. Churchill wrote later that "this act brought the United States definitely nearer to us and to war, and it was the first of a long succession of increasingly unneutral acts in the Atlantic which were of utmost service to us." It was a risky move for Roosevelt in a Presidential election year. His opponent, Wendell Willkie, an avowed short-of-war interventionist, favored giving Britain

---

[15] Lindbergh's usefulness was ultimately destroyed by one of his own speeches when on September 11, 1941, he specified the "powerful elements" to be the British, the Roosevelt Administration, and the Jews. He deplored Nazi treatment of the Jews, but warned they were likely to reap a harvest of intolerance at home if they persisted in seeking to involve the nation in war. The speech opened a Pandora's box and charges of anti-Semitism filled the air. There is small doubt but that the speech seriously damaged the America First Committee in the few months that still remained to them. Wayne S. Cole, *America First* (Madison: The University of Wisconsin Press, 1953), pp. 141–154.

the destroyers but railed against Roosevelt's circumvention of Congress as but one more manifestation of dictatorial tendency that marked his administrations. Goaded by Willkie and egged on by his advisors, Roosevelt finally entered the campaign in October. In Boston, on October 30, after linking isolationists with obstructionists to his domestic policies, the President offered a guarantee that was to mock him: "And while I am talking to you mothers and fathers, I give you one more assurance. I have said this before, but I shall say it again and again and again: Your boys are not going to be sent into any foreign wars."

Roosevelt won handily and almost immediately asked the Congress and country to venture further toward active intervention. Great Britain was close to being broke, and to meet this emergency, the President asked for sweeping power to lend, lease, sell or barter arms, ammunition, food, or any "defense article" to any country whose security was vital to the United States. In a press conference on December 17, 1940, the President prepared the way for his lend-lease invention: "Suppose my neighbor's house catches fire, and I have a length of garden hose four or five hundred feet away. If he can take my garden hose and connect it up with his hydrant, I may help him to put out his fire. Now, what do I do? I don't say to him before that operation, 'Neighbor, my garden hose cost me $15; you have to pay me $15 for it.' What is the transaction that goes on? I don't want $15—I want my garden hose back after the fire is over." Robert Sherwood, then one of the President's speech writers, thought this "neighborly analogy" won the fight for lend-lease then and there. Perhaps so, but the President proceeded with elaborate preparations to base his case on national self-interest and to take it to the people. Alerted to the forthcoming address, persons from all over the nation wrote or wired suggestions to Roosevelt. When the President spoke over the radio on the night of December 29, the world was his audience, and Hitler staged an all-out blitz of London in the vain hope of capturing the morning headlines. Roosevelt himself regarded "the arsenal of democracy" speech, as it came to be called, as his most important since the banking crisis of 1933, and the mail response was the largest since his first inaugural.[16]

The next night, Senator Burton K. Wheeler replied to the President in a nationwide radio talk that is reproduced in this volume. A New Dealer, Wheeler had been at odds with the Administration since 1937, when he helped to frustrate Roosevelt's court-packing plan. By early summer, 1940, Wheeler was the acknowl-

---

[16] For fascinating accounts of the evolution and circumstances of Roosevelt's speech see Samuel I. Rosenman, *Working with Roosevelt* (New York: Harper & Brothers, 1952), chap. XV; Robert Sherwood, *Roosevelt and Hopkins* (New York: Harper & Brothers), chap. X.

edged leader of the isolationist bloc in the Senate. He had fought unsuccessfully against military conscription and the transfer of destroyers; hence the battle against lend-lease loomed as crucial. His strategy, then, on December 30 was to stir up public opposition while Roosevelt's speech was fresh in everyone's mind. Again on January 12, 1941, Wheeler took to the air to attack lend-lease legislation as outlined by the President in his State of the Union Address. Wheeler described it as "another New Deal Triple-A foreign policy; it will plow under every fourth American boy." Roosevelt resentfully called this remark "the most untruthful, the most dastardly, unpatriotic thing that has been said in public life in my generation." Thus launched, lend-lease was bitterly contested in the Senate until March 8, when it passed by a two-to-one vote.

In April, Wheeler began to stump the country, often talking under the auspices of America First. Everywhere crowds jammed auditoriums to hear this lean, hard-hitting Montanan with voice of metallic cutting edge. Wheeler begged them to reject all "isms" but Americanism, and after Hitler turned on Russia in June, audiences screamed approval as he shouted, "I'm opposed to Nazism, to Fascism and to Communism, and I hope they'll beat each other's brains out on the plains of Russia."[17]

Back in the summer of 1940, Wheeler once said: "You can't put your shirttail into a clothes wringer, and then pull it out suddenly while the wringer keeps turning."[18] The remark was prophetic. By stages the United States was pulled from neutrality to active intervention. Lend-lease required convoys and the arming of merchant vessels, which inevitably provoked incidents on the high seas, which called forth Roosevelt's "shoot on sight" order. And although isolationist orators continued to speak feverishly throughout the summer and fall of 1941, almost everyone felt in his bones it was now only a matter of time. Time ran out on December 7, when Japan struck at Pearl Harbor.

The Administration now had to mobilize resources of nations united for war and for the peace that must one day return. To these ends, the President sent his 1940 rival, Wendell Willkie, on a globe-girdling tour. Upon his return, Willkie caught the public's imagination with his pamphlet entitled *One World,* and through it and his public speeches he helped mightily to shift popular thinking from a national to a global scale. In 1944 steps were taken at Dumbarton Oakes and Bretton Woods to form a permanent international organization. Clearly a

[17] Buffalo *Evening News,* July 5, 1951, quoted in Donald J. Cameron, "Burton K. Wheeler as a Public Campaigner," unpublished doctoral dissertation, Northwestern University, 1960, p. 277.
[18] Washington *Post,* June 8, 1940, *ibid.,* p. 249.

new mood was on the land, and in the elections of 1944 many prominent isolationists were ousted from Congress. Against this backdrop, Arthur Vandenberg spoke to the Senate on January 10, 1945. Vandenberg was highly respected, a powerful orator, and the most influential Republican on the Senate's Foreign Relations Committee. Now disengaging himself from his lifelong record of isolationism, he proclaimed: "I am prepared by effective international cooperation to do our full part in charting happier and safer tomorrows." Vandenberg's declaration enabled the President to assert with some validity in his Fourth Inaugural Address, "We have learned to be citizens of the world, members of the human community."

At home Vandenberg strengthened the President's hand as the latter negotiated with Churchill and Stalin at Yalta for an international conference to establish a permanent organization among nations of the world. Upon his return from Yalta, Roosevelt spoke to a joint session of Congress, advising them of the forthcoming conference scheduled for April 25: "The Senate and the House of Representatives will both be represented at the San Francisco Conference. The Congressional delegates will consist of an equal number of Republican and Democratic members. The American delegation is—in every sense—bipartisan. World peace is not a party question (I think that Republicans want peace just as much as Democrats), any more than is military victory."

Two weeks before the San Francisco meeting, the voice of Franklin Roosevelt was stilled forever, but his spirit of bipartisanship prevailed. Arthur Vandenberg and other Republicans joined Democrats in drafting a United Nations Charter, and when that Charter came before the Senate's Foreign Relations Committee, the sole dissenting voice was that of the old and ailing isolationist, Hiram Johnson of California. And whereas the Covenant of the League of Nations had been debated for eight months before the Senate rejected it, the Senate debated the Charter of the United Nations for six days and then accepted it by a vote of 89 to 2. Even Burton K. Wheeler went along.

Isolationism was a casualty of World War II. When the war ended, many sanguine Americans looked for peace and brotherhood to rise phoenix-like from the ashes. It proved a forlorn hope, for the peace had somehow still to be won, perhaps through the medley of voices that now debated the destiny of the world in the starkly modern headquarters of the United Nations.

The Arsenal of Democracy

FRANKLIN DELANO ROOSEVELT

(For biographical sketch, see p. 146.)

"Never before since Jamestown and Plymouth Rock has our American civilization been in such danger as now."

My friends: This is not a fireside chat on war. It is a talk on national security; because the nub of the whole purpose of your President is to keep you now, and your children later, and your grandchildren much later, out of a last-ditch war for the preservation of American independence and all of the things that American independence means to you and to me and to ours.

Tonight, in the presence of a world crisis, my mind goes back eight years to a night in the midst of a domestic crisis. It was a time when the wheels of American industry were grinding to a full stop, when the whole banking system of our country had ceased to function.

I well remember that while I sat in my study in the White House, preparing to talk with the people of the United States, I had before my eyes the picture of all those Americans with whom I was talking. I saw the workmen in the mills, the mines, the factories; the girl behind the counter; the small shopkeeper; the farmer doing his Spring plowing; the widows and the old men wondering about their life's savings.

I tried to convey to the great mass of American people what the banking crisis meant to them in their daily lives.

Tonight I want to do the same thing, with the same people, in this new crisis which faces America.

Radio address, Washington, D.C., December 29, 1940. *The New York Times,* December 30, 1940, p. 6. Reprinted by permission of *The New York Times.*

We met the issue of 1933 with courage and realism. We face this new crisis—this new threat to the security of our nation—with the same courage and realism.

Never before since Jamestown and Plymouth Rock has our American civilization been in such danger as now.

For on September 27, 1940—this year—by an agreement signed in Berlin, three powerful nations, two in Europe and one in Asia, joined themselves together in the threat that if the United States of America interfered with or blocked the expansion program of these three nations—a program aimed at world control—they would unite in ultimate action against the United States.

The Nazi masters of Germany have made it clear that they intend not only to dominate all life and thought in their own country, but also to enslave the whole of Europe, and then to use the resources of Europe to dominate the rest of the world.

It was only three weeks ago that their leader stated this: "There are two worlds that stand opposed to each other." And then in defiant reply to his opponents he said this: "Others are correct when they say: 'With this world we cannot ever reconcile ourselves.' . . . I can beat any other power in the world." So said the leader of the Nazis.

In other words, the Axis not merely admits but the Axis proclaims that there can be no ultimate peace between their philosophy—their philosophy of government—and our philosophy of government.

In view of the nature of this undeniable threat, it can be asserted, properly and categorically, that the United States has no right or reason to encourage talk of peace until the day shall come when there is a clear intention on the part of the aggressor nations to abandon all thought of dominating or conquering the world.

At this moment the forces of the States that are leagued against all peoples who live in freedom are being held away from our shores. The Germans and the Italians are being blocked on the other side of the Atlantic by the British and by the Greeks, and by thousands of soldiers and sailors who were able to escape from subjugated countries. In Asia the Japanese are being engaged by the Chinese nation in another great defense.

In the Pacific Ocean is our fleet.

Some of our people like to believe that wars in Europe and in Asia are of no concern to us. But it is a matter of most vital concern to us that European and Asiatic war-makers should not gain control of the oceans which lead to this hemisphere.

One hundred and seventeen years ago the Monroe Doctrine was conceived by our government as a measure of defense in the face of a threat against this hemisphere by an alliance in Continental Europe. Thereafter, we stood guard in the Atlantic, with the British as neighbors. There was no treaty. There was no "unwritten agreement."

And yet there was the feeling, proven correct by history, that we as neighbors could settle any disputes in peaceful fashion. And the fact is that during the whole of this time the Western Hemisphere has remained free from aggression from Europe or from Asia.

Does any one seriously believe that we need to fear attack anywhere in the Americas while a free Britain remains our most powerful naval neighbor in the Atlantic? And does any one seriously believe, on the other hand, that we could rest easy if the Axis powers were our neighbors there?

If Great Britain goes down, the Axis powers will control the Continents of Europe, Asia, Africa, Australasia, and the high seas—and they will be in a position to bring enormous military and naval resources against this hemisphere. It is no exaggeration to say that all of us in all the Americas would be living at the point of a gun—a gun loaded with explosive bullets, economic as well as military.

We should enter upon a new and terrible era in which the whole world, our hemisphere included, would be run by threats of brute force. And to survive in such a world, we would have to convert ourselves permanently into a militaristic power on the basis of war economy.

Some of us like to believe that even if Britain falls, we are still safe, because of the broad expanse of the Atlantic and of the Pacific.

But the width of those oceans is not what it was in the days of clipper ships. At one point between Africa and Brazil the distance is less than it is from Washington to Denver, Colorado, five hours for the latest type of bomber. And at the north end of the Pacific Ocean, America and Asia almost touch each other.

Why, even today we have planes that could fly from the British Isles to New England and back again without refueling. And remember that the range of the modern bomber is ever being increased.

During the past week many people in all parts of the nation have told me what they wanted me to say tonight. Almost all of them expressed a courageous desire to hear the plain truth about the gravity of the situation. One telegram, however, expressed the attitude of the small minority who want to see no evil and hear no evil, even though they know in their hearts that evil exists. That telegram begged me not to tell again of the ease with which our American cities could be bombed by any hostile power which had gained bases in this Western Hemisphere. The gist of that telegram was: "Please, Mr. President, don't frighten us by telling us the facts."

Frankly and definitely there is danger ahead—danger against which we must prepare. But we well know that we cannot escape danger, or the fear of danger, by crawling into bed and pulling the covers over our heads.

Some nations of Europe were bound by solemn nonintervention pacts with Germany. Other nations were assured by Germany that they need never fear invasion. Nonintervention pact or not, the fact remains that they were attacked, overrun, thrown into modern slavery at an hour's notice or even without any notice at all.

As an exiled leader of one of these nations said to me the other day, "the notice was a minus quantity. It was given to my government two hours after

German troops had poured into my country in a hundred places." The fate of these nations tells us what it means to live at the point of a Nazi gun.

The Nazis have justified such actions by various pious frauds. One of these frauds is the claim that they are occupying a nation for the purpose of "restoring order." Another is that they are occupying or controlling a nation on the excuse that they are "protecting it" against the aggression of somebody else.

For example, Germany has said that she was occupying Belgium to save the Belgians from the British. Would she then hesitate to say to any South American country: "We are occupying you to protect you from aggression by the United States"?

Belgium today is being used as an invasion base against Britain, now fighting for its life. And any South American country, in Nazi hands, would always constitute a jumping off place for German attack on any one of the other republics of this hemisphere.

Analyze for yourselves the future of two other places even nearer to Germany if the Nazis won. Could Ireland hold out? Would Irish freedom be permitted as an amazing pet exception in an unfree world? Or the islands of the Azores, which still fly the flag of Portugal after five centuries? You and I think of Hawaii as an outpost of defense in the Pacific. And yet the Azores are closer to our shores in the Atlantic than Hawaii is on the other side.

There are those who say that the Axis powers would never have any desire to attack the Western Hemisphere. That is the same dangerous form of wishful thinking which has destroyed the powers of resistance of so many conquered peoples. The plain facts are that the Nazis have proclaimed, time and again, that all other races are their inferiors and therefore subject to their orders. And most important of all, the vast resources and wealth of this American hemisphere constitute the most tempting loot in all of the round world.

Let us no longer blind ourselves to the undeniable fact that the evil forces which have crushed and undermined and corrupted so many others are already within our own gates. Your government knows much about them and every day is ferreting them out.

Their secret emissaries are active in our own and in neighboring countries. They seek to stir up suspicion and dissension, to cause internal strife. They try to turn capital against labor, and vice versa. They try to reawaken long slumbering racial and religious enmities which should have no place in this country. They are active in every group that promotes intolerance. They exploit for their own ends our own natural abhorrence of war.

These trouble-breeders have but one purpose. It is to divide our people, to divide them into hostile groups and to destroy our unity and shatter our will to defend ourselves.

There are also American citizens, many of them in high places, who, unwittingly in most cases, are aiding and abetting the work of these agents. I do not charge these American citizens with being foreign agents. But I do charge them with doing exactly the kind of work that the dictators want done in the United States.

These people not only believe that we can save our own skins by shutting our eyes to the fate of other nations. Some of them go much further than that. They say that we can and should become the friends and even the partners of the Axis powers. Some of them even suggest that we should imitate the methods of the dictatorships. But Americans never can and never will do that.

The experience of the past two years has proven beyond doubt that no nation can appease the Nazis. No man can tame a tiger into a kitten by stroking it. There can be no appeasement with ruthlessness. There can be no reasoning with an incendiary bomb. We know now that a nation can have peace with the Nazis only at the price of total surrender.

Even the people of Italy have been forced to become accomplices of the Nazis; but at this moment they do not know how soon they will be embraced to death by their allies.

The American appeasers ignore the warning to be found in the fate of Austria, Czechoslovakia, Poland, Norway, Belgium, the Netherlands, Denmark and France. They tell you that the Axis powers are going to win anyway; that all of this bloodshed in the world could be saved, that the United States might just as well throw its influence into the scale of a dictated peace and get the best out of it that we can.

They call it a "negotiated peace." Nonsense! Is it a negotiated peace if a gang of outlaws surrounds your community and on threat of extermination makes you pay tribute to save your own skins?

Such a dictated peace would be no peace at all. It would be only another armistice, leading to the most gigantic armament race and the most devastating trade wars in all history. And in these contests the Americas would offer the only real resistance to the Axis powers. With all their vaunted efficiency, with all their parade of pious purpose in this war, there are still in their background the concentration camp and the servants of God in chains.

The history of recent years proves that the shootings and the chains and the concentration camps are not simply the transient tools but the very altars of modern dictatorships. They may talk of a "new order" in the world, but what they have in mind is only a revival of the oldest and worst tyranny. In that there is no liberty, no religion, no hope.

The proposed "new order" is the very opposite of a United States of Europe or a United States of Asia. It is not a government based upon the consent of the governed. It is not a union of ordinary, self-respecting men and women to protect themselves and their freedom and their dignity from oppression. It is an unholy alliance of power and pelf to dominate and to enslave the human race.

The British people and their allies today are conducting an active war against this unholy alliance. Our own future security is greatly dependent on the outcome of that fight. Our ability to "keep out of war" is going to be affected by that outcome.

Thinking in terms of today and tomorrow, I make the direct statement to the American people that there is far less chance of the United States getting into war if we do all we can now to support the nations defending themselves against attack by the Axis than if we acquiesce in their defeat, submit tamely to an Axis victory, and wait our turn to be the object of attack in another war later on.

If we are to be completely honest with ourselves, we must admit that there is risk in any course we may take. But I deeply believe that the great majority of our people agree that the course that I advocate involves the least risk now and the greatest hope for world peace in the future.

The people of Europe who are defending themselves do not ask us to do their fighting. They ask us for the implements of war, the planes, the tanks, the guns, the freighters which will enable them to fight for their liberty and for our security. Emphatically we must get these weapons to them, get them to them in sufficient volume and quickly enough so that we and our children will be saved the agony and suffering of war which others have had to endure.

Let not the defeatists tell us that it is too late. It will never be earlier. Tomorrow will be later than today.

Certain facts are self-evident.

In a military sense Great Britain and the British Empire are today the spearhead of resistance to world conquest. And they are putting up a fight which will live forever in the story of human gallantry.

There is no demand for sending an American expeditionary force outside our own borders. There is no intention by any member of your government to send such a force. You can therefore, nail, nail any talk about sending armies to Europe as deliberate untruth.

Our national policy is not directed toward war. Its sole purpose is to keep war away from our country and away from our people.

Democracy's fight against world conquest is being greatly aided, and must be more greatly aided, by the rearmament of the United States and by sending every ounce and every ton of munitions and supplies that we can possibly spare to help the defenders who are in the front lines. And it is no more unneutral for us to do that than it is for Sweden, Russia and other nations near Germany to send steel and ore and oil and other war materials into Germany every day in the week.

We are planning our own defense with the utmost urgency, and in its vast scale we must integrate the war needs of Britain and the other free nations which are resisting aggression.

This is not a matter of sentiment or of controversial personal opinion. It is a matter of realistic, practical military policy, based on the advice of our military experts who are in close touch with existing warfare. These military and naval experts and the members of the Congress and the Administration have a single-minded purpose—the defense of the United States.

This nation is making a great effort to produce everything that is necessary in this emergency—and with all possible speed. And this great effort requires great sacrifice.

I would ask no one to defend a democracy which in turn would not defend every one in the nation against want and privation. The strength of this nation shall not be diluted by the failure of the government to protect the economic well-being of its citizens.

If our capacity to produce is limited by machines, it must ever be remembered that these machines are operated by the skill and the stamina of the workers. As the government is determined to protect the rights of the workers, so the nation has a right to expect that the men who man the machines will discharge their full responsibilities to the urgent needs of defense.

The worker possesses the same human dignity and is entitled to the same security of position as the engineer or the manager or the owner. For the workers provide the human power that turns out the destroyers, and the planes and the tanks.

The nation expects our defense industries to continue operation without interruption by strikes or lockouts. It expects and insists that management and workers will reconcile their differences by voluntary or legal means, to continue to produce the supplies that are so sorely needed.

And on the economic side of our great defense program, we are, as you know, bending every effort to maintain stability of prices and with that the stability of the cost of living.

Nine days ago I announced the setting up of a more effective organization to direct our gigantic efforts to increase the production of munitions. The appropriation of vast sums of money and a well-coordinated executive direction of our defense efforts are not in themselves enough. Guns, planes, ships and many other things have to be built in the factories and the arsenals of America. They have to be produced by workers and managers and engineers with the aid of machines which in turn have to be built by hundreds of thousands of workers throughout the land.

In this great work there has been splendid cooperation between the government and industry and labor. And I am very thankful.

American industrial genius, unmatched throughout all the world in the solution of production problems, has been called upon to bring its resources and its talents into action. Manufacturers of watches, of farm implements, of linotypes and cash registers and automobiles, and sewing machines and lawn mowers and locomotives, are now making fuses and bomb packing crates and telescope mounts and shells and pistols and tanks.

But all of our present efforts are not enough. We must have more ships, more guns, more planes—more of everything. And this can be accomplished only if we discard the notion of "business as usual." This job cannot be done merely by superimposing on the existing productive facilities the added requirements of the nation for defense.

Our defense efforts must not be blocked by those who fear the future consequences of surplus plant capacity. The possible consequences of failure of our defense efforts now are much more to be feared.

And after the present needs of our defense are past, a proper handling of the country's peacetime needs will require all of the new productive capacity, if not still more.

No pessimistic policy about the future of America shall delay the immediate expansion of those industries essential to defense. We need them.

I want to make it clear that it is the purpose of the nation to build now with all possible speed every machine, every arsenal, every factory that we need to manufacture our defense material. We have the men—the skill—the wealth—and above all, the will.

I am confident that if and when production of consumer or luxury goods in certain industries requires the use of machines and raw materials that are essential for defense purposes, then such production must yield, and will gladly yield, to our primary and compelling purpose.

So I appeal to the owners of plants—to the managers—to the workers—to our own government employes—to put every ounce of effort into producing these munitions swiftly and without stint. With this appeal I give you the pledge that all of us who are officers of your government will devote ourselves to the same whole-hearted extent to the great task that lies ahead.

As planes and ships and guns and shells are produced, your government, with its defense experts, can then determine how best to use them to defend this hemisphere. The decision as to how much shall be sent abroad and how much shall remain at home must be made on the basis of our overall military necessities.

We must be the great arsenal of democracy. For us this is an emergency as serious as war itself. We must apply ourselves to our task with the same resolution, the same sense of urgency, the same spirit of patriotism and sacrifice as we would show were we at war.

We have furnished the British great material support and we will furnish far more in the future.

There will be no "bottlenecks" in our determination to aid Great Britain. No dictator, no combination of dictators, will weaken that determination by threats of how they will construe that determination.

The British have received invaluable military support from the heroic Greek Army and from the forces of all the governments in exile. Their strength is growing. It is the strength of men and women who value their freedom more highly than they value their lives.

I believe that the Axis powers are not going to win this war. I base that belief on the latest and best of information.

We have no excuse for defeatism. We have every good reason for hope—hope for peace, yes, and hope for the defense of our civilization and for the building of a better civilization in the future.

I have the profound conviction that the American people are now determined to put forth a mightier effort than they have ever yet made to increase our production of all the implements of defense, to meet the threat to our democratic faith.

As President of the United States, I call for that national effort. I call for it in the name of this nation which we love and honor and which we are privileged and proud to serve. I call upon our people with absolute confidence that our common cause will greatly succeed.

America's Present Emergency

BURTON KENDALL WHEELER

Born, Hudson, Massachusetts, February 27, 1882. Graduated from University of Michigan Law School, 1905. Admitted to Montana bar, 1906, and practiced law in Butte, Montana. Member, Montana House of Representatives, 1911–1913. United States District Attorney, 1913–1918. Democratic member of the United States Senate from Montana for four terms, 1923–1947. Candidate for Vice-President of the United States on the Progressive party ticket, 1924, as Robert M. La Follette's running mate. Engaged in legal practice since 1947.

"I, for one, believe the policy advocated by the interventionists is insane because it will lead to total war, and war is insanity."

The views I express to you tonight are not the views of the *Star,* which has generously afforded me an opportunity to speak to you. They are not the views of any international banker, nor are they dictated by interventionists or warmongers. The thoughts I am about to express are not based upon any fear of wild boasts of American conquest by Stalin, Hitler, or Mussolini. I know that neither they nor their ideologies will capture the people of the United States or our imagination to the point that we would adopt fascism, communism, or nazi-ism as American doctrine.

You and I are Americans—and as Americans, of course, we are interested in

Radio address, Washington, D.C., December 30, 1940. *Congressional Record,* 76th Cong., 3rd Sess., vol. 86, pt. 18, pp. A7030–A7032. (Reprinted from the Washington *Evening Star,* December 31, 1940.)

the well-being of the people of all the world. Coming as we do from the four corners of the earth, we know that our business, our race, and our religion color our reaction to any European war. We know that today wars in Europe or Asia affect us economically, politically, and emotionally.

We sympathize with the oppressed and persecuted everywhere.

We also realize that we have great problems at home—that one-third of our population is ill-fed, ill-housed, and ill-clad—and we have been told repeatedly, upon the highest authority, that unless and until this situation is corrected, our democracy is in danger. I fully subscribe to this view.

Believing as I do in this thesis, I cannot help but feel that we should settle our own problems before we undertake to settle the problems of Asia, Africa, Australasia, South America, and Europe.

As Americans, interested first in America, what is our present stake? Our stakes are our independence, our democracy, and our trade and commerce. Every red-blooded American would fight to preserve them.

What is the best way to preserve them? There are two schools of thought. One group feels—as they felt before the last World War—that England is our first line of defense and that we must go to England's aid every time she declares war, and that some European dictator is after rich loot in the United States, perhaps our gold buried in the hills of Kentucky. This group wants to repeal our Neutrality Act and the Johnson Act. They want to loan our ships, our guns, and our planes—even though it may involve us in the European conflict. They profess to believe it is necessary for the preservation of our country, our religion, and civilization.

We were told the same things in almost the same terms before the last war.

The other group feels that we should build our defenses to meet any emergency that may arise. But we do not believe that the preservation of the American people or our democracy depends upon any foreign nation. It is hard for us to visualize a nation of 130,000,000 people so weak that we cannot defend ourselves when our forefathers in the Thirteen Original Colonies—poor, divided, and weak— were not only able to conquer an army already in our midst but to build the greatest democracy the world has ever known.

Just as I love the United States so do I dislike Hitler and all that he symbolizes. My sympathy for the British is both deep and genuine, and is exceeded only by the depth and sincerity of my Americanism. No anti-British feeling dictates my opposition to the evasion or repeal of the Johnson and Neutrality Acts. I am opposed to American convoy of British ships. I oppose all these because they lead us down that road with only one ending—total, complete, and futile war. And William Allen White, chairman of the Committee to Defend America by Aiding the Allies, agrees that the convoying of British ships by American vessels and the repeal of the Neutrality and Johnson Acts would mean war for us.

Remember, if we lease war materials today, we will lend or lease American boys tomorrow. Last night we heard the President promise that there would be no American expeditionary force, but we received no promise that our ships and sailors and our planes and pilots might not at some time within the near future be cast into the cauldron of blood and hate that is Europe today.

Our independence can only be lost or compromised if Germany invades the Western Hemisphere north of the equator. This would be fantastic, as it would require the transportation of at least 2,000,000 men, with planes, tanks, and equipment in one convoy across the Atlantic. This would require two or three thousand transports plus a fleet larger than our Navy, plus thousands of fighter-escorted bombers. Such a fleet cannot possibly be available. Certainly it cannot be trained efficiently before our 2-ocean Navy is ready. It is not possible for the German Navy to prepare an effective plan for such an invasion which our Navy and Army, with our air force, cannot defeat. Remember, Hitler has already been 7 months in vainly trying to cross 20 miles. If Hitler's army can't cross the narrow English Channel in 7 months, his bombers won't fly across the Rockies to bomb Denver tomorrow.

The only threat to our independence would be to join in some "union of free nations," so-called, in which we would be but a unit and outnumbered and outgeneraled by our good neighbors across the sea.

Democracy! We cannot hold our democracy except by prosperity and improvement in the mechanics of democracy. This will not be aided by joining the war.

The cost of this war will come out of the millions of poor people—the common folk of the world who will toil for generations to pay the cost of the destruction.

War inevitably means back-breaking debt, blighted lives, bedeviled futures. War means the end of civil liberties—the end of free speech, free press, free enterprise. It means dictatorship and slavery—all the things we abhor in nazi-ism, communism, and fascism. It means Stalin or Hitler will have achieved their boasts for a totalitarian world without conquering America.

The President in his speech last night ridiculed the idea of a peace in Europe. Conceding all that he so eloquently said about "outlaws," the "concentration camps," and the "servants of God in chains"—what about Russia and Joseph Stalin's communism? And have we not recognized Hitler and Franco? Did we not at least acquiesce in Mussolini and all his works?

If we follow the logic of Mr. Roosevelt, then we ought immediately to break off diplomatic relations with Russia, Italy, Germany, Japan, and other nations whose domestic and foreign policies we abhor.

And where do we go from there?

Regardless of when or who is proclaimed victor in the present war—it cannot last forever. Peace, fleeting though it may be, will eventually come to Europe. At some time in the future representatives of England and Germany will sit around a table—sometime they will agree upon peace—and until that day, the world suffers. Each of us, from the President of the United States to the most humble citizen, should exert his every effort for peace, now.

Removal of Hitler, even the defeat of the German armies, will not destroy that which Hitler symbolizes. Hitlerism can be destroyed and banished from Europe only by destroying that which caused or maintains nazi-ism.

Ask yourselves who and what were responsible for the real birth and growth of Hitlerism.

Lord Lothian, until his recent death wartime Ambassador from Great Britain to the United States, said of nazi-ism—I quote him: "In great measure it was rebellion against the discriminations of the treaty of Versailles. . . ." That wasn't some Nazi sympathizer; that was your friend, Lord Lothian, speaking.

I firmly believe the German people want peace just as any people prefer peace to war—and the offer of a just, reasonable, and generous peace will more quickly and effectively crumble Hitlerism and break the morale of the German people than all the bombers that could be dispatched over Berlin.

A just peace is difficult, if not impossible, to abstractly define while war rages. It is too completely dependent on the attitude of the belligerents.

A working basis for a just peace might involve among other factors the following:

1. Restoration of Germany's 1914 boundaries with an autonomous Poland and Czechoslovakia.
2. Restoration of independent France, Holland, Norway, Belgium, and Denmark.
3. Restoration of Alsace-Lorraine to France.
4. Restoration of German colonies.
5. Protection of all racial and religious minorities in all countries.
6. Internationalization of the Suez Canal.
7. No indemnities or reparations.
8. Arms limitation.

The United States is no longer trudging along the road to war. We are running. Some feel that we have gone so fast and so far that there can be no stopping—no return to complete peace except via war. But we are at peace and we can remain at peace if either one of two lines of action is pursued. First, Americans in greater number must firmly resolve and express themselves, that we will fight no offensive war. And, secondly, we can remain at peace if the horrible European debacle of death and destruction ends in the near future.

Though today we stand as close to the brink of war as we stood in January of 1917, some people still oppose a European peace. Warmongers, sordid romanticists, reckless adventurers, and some whose sympathies and sentiments are stronger than their reasoning powers would plunge this Nation into war; plunge us into a war from which we could gain nothing; plunge us into a war that would destroy democracy—that would bring deep, harrowing anguish to millions of hearts. And how would they bring this to pass? They would take us in today as they did in 1917.

The right Honorable Sir Gilbert Parker, writing for *Harper's Magazine* of March 1918, said of American entry into the last war:

> Practically since the day war broke out between England and the Central Powers, I became responsible for American publicity. . . . We established connection with the man in the street through cinema pictures of the Army and Navy, as well as through interview, articles, pamphlets, etc. . . . We had reports from important Americans constantly, and established association, by personal correspondence, with influential and eminent people of every profession in the United States, beginning with university and college presidents, professors, and scientific men, and running through all the ranges of the population.
>
> We had our documents and literature sent to great numbers of public libraries, Y. M. C. A. societies, universities, colleges, historical societies, clubs, and newspapers. It is hardly necessary to say that the work was one of extreme difficulty and delicacy.

Do Sir Gilbert's words in any way explain the warmongering telegram to the President urging greater aid to Britain? Has British propaganda again reached the college and university professors? Twenty-nine educators signed the highly publicized wire that urged steps that would take the United States into war on the side of Britain.

And have you and I, "the man in the street," felt the insidious force of war propaganda through the movies?

Is there another Sir Gilbert Parker in the United States? Perhaps not, but there are a lot of foreign slackers—European royalty, princes and potentates, and their idolaters—who, instead of being wined and dined in high places in Washington and urging us to go to war, ought to be home fighting the battles for liberty and Christianity they so glibly tell us about. Poor things! As usual, they were forced to leave their country while their subjects had to remain to do the fighting.

My friends, it is this satanically clever propaganda that appeals to the Christianity, the idealism, the humanity, and the loyalty of the American people that takes us to war. It is this that we must resist. It is this that we must cast aside if we truly love our country and democracy. We must remain at peace and dedicate ourselves to effecting peace for a war-torn world.

We have reached a strange situation in America when those who advocate peace—who do not follow the party line—are branded appeasers or unwitting tools of the dictators. This still is a democracy, and American citizens whose beliefs vary from those of the Government ought not to be howled down or intimidated by threats of the F.B.I. Free speech still belongs to all the people, not to just a few at the top.

I do not believe that the great majority of our people are eager to be embraced by war—and I call upon them not to be afraid to say so. I, for one, believe the policy advocated by the interventionists is insane because it will lead to total war, and war is insanity.

I say so now and I intend to continue to say so, even if at the end I stand alone. Americans! Do not let yourselves be swayed by mass hysteria. Do not travel again the road that you took in 1917. You hanged Bob La Follette in effigy because he opposed war, and lived to repent your action and put him in the Hall of Fame. Fifteen years after that war, when the secret treaties were exposed, you realized that you had been duped. Has history suddenly changed?

Are the facts of yesterday no longer facts? Has this war a sweeter odor than the last? Don't let yourselves be misled by the so-called notables. Numerically they are few—a few hundred—even though they command the newspaper headlines. But they do not speak for the mass of Americans. They do not represent labor, the farmer, the youth, the mothers or the fathers of America. The great mass of our people are inarticulate, but it is time you were heard. You must not be driven like sheep to the slaughtering pens.

There is a war that I call upon you to enter—a noble war which the royalty of Europe and our Tory friends at home are unwilling to face—a war to end economic inequality and poverty and disease in this, the richest land in the world.

America's war ought to be a war against industrial unemployment and low farm prices.

Whether the stroke of 12 will usher in a really happy new year tomorrow night depends upon you—and upon your sincere loyalty to Christian ideals. "Peace on earth to men of good will" is a sacred cause for which we should pray and work. Let your Representatives in Washington know that you have not surrendered the independence of America to warmongers and interventionists—and God will bless America.

Fourth Inaugural Address

FRANKLIN DELANO ROOSEVELT

(For biographical sketch, see p. 146.)

"We have learned to be citizens of the world, members of the human community."

*M*r. *Chief Justice, Mr. Vice President, my friends,* you will understand and, I believe, agree with my wish that the form of this inauguration be simple and its words brief.

We Americans of today, together with our allies, are passing through a period of supreme test. It is a test of our courage—of our resolve—of our wisdom—of our essential democracy.

If we meet that test—successfully and honorably—we shall perform a service of historic importance which men and women and children will honor throughout all time.

As I stand here today, having taken the solemn oath of office in the presence of my fellow countrymen—in the presence of our God—I know that it is America's purpose that we shall not fail.

In the days and in the years that are to come we shall work for a just and honorable peace, a durable peace, as today we work and fight for total victory in war.

We can and we will achieve such a peace.

We shall strive for perfection. We shall not achieve it immediately—but we still shall strive. We may make mistakes—but they must never be mistakes which result from faintness of heart or abandonment of moral principle.

Delivered from the portico of the White House, January 20, 1945. *Inaugural Addresses of the Presidents of the United States,* House Document No. 540 (Washington: Government Printing Office, 1952), pp. 237–238.

I remember that my old schoolmaster, Dr. Peabody, said, in days that seemed to us then to be secure and untroubled: "Things in life will not always run smoothly. Sometimes we will be rising toward the heights—then all will seem to reverse itself and start downward. The great fact to remember is that the trend of civilization itself is forever upward; that a line drawn through the middle of the peaks and the valleys of the centuries always has an upward trend."

Our Constitution of 1787 was not a perfect instrument; it is not perfect yet. But it provided a firm base upon which all manner of men, of all races and colors and creeds, could build our solid structure of democracy.

And so today, in this year of war, 1945, we have learned lessons—at a fearful cost—and we shall profit by them.

We have learned that we cannot live alone, at peace; that our own well-being is dependent on the well-being of other nations far away. We have learned that we must live as men, not as ostriches, nor as dogs in the manger.

We have learned to be citizens of the world, members of the human community.

We have learned the simple truth, as Emerson said, that "The only way to have a friend is to be one."

We can gain no lasting peace if we approach it with suspicion and mistrust or with fear. We can gain it only if we proceed with the understanding, the confidence, and the courage which flow from conviction.

The Almighty God has blessed our land in many ways. He has given our people stout hearts and strong arms with which to strike mighty blows for freedom and truth. He has given to our country a faith which has become the hope of all peoples in an anguished world.

So we pray to Him now for the vision to see our way clearly—to see the way that leads to a better life for ourselves and for all our fellow men—to the achievement of His will, to peace on earth.

PART THREE

Grave New World

THE COLD WAR ERA

WITH HIS EYE on the clock, the President waited silently behind his desk in the Oval Room of the White House in the early evening of August 14, 1945. Promptly at seven o'clock, as arranged with London and Moscow, Harry Truman began to read: "I have just received this afternoon a message from the Japanese Government in reply to the message forwarded to that Government by the Secretary of State on August eleventh. I deem this reply a full acceptance of the Potsdam Declaration which specifies unconditional surrender of Japan. In the reply there is no qualification." White House correspondents dived for telephones; almost instantaneously the streets of downtown America were jampacked with joyously screaming, gyrating humanity. The more sedentary sampled the bedlam from coast to coast through their radio sets.

The uncomplicated emotions released on August 14 were quickly spent and then replaced by gnawing concern over the probable shape of the postwar world. War production had thrown the national economy into high gear, but what would happen to jobs and income once the reconversion to peacetime began? Told they would have to face up to the embarrassment of adjusting to a living standard fifty percent higher than they had ever known, most adults, still haunted by memory of depression years, found the prophecy more facile than convincing. Labor unrest was in the air, and in this shrinking world employers had cause to be disquieted by the unexpected outcome of the British general elections in July, 1945. Immediately after the defeat of Germany, British voters had turned out of office their greatest wartime hero, Winston Churchill, and his Conservative party, in favor of Clement Attlee, the Labor party, and their Socialist program. The very foundations of the prewar world seemed to be cracking up.

More disturbing still, how could the human race secure itself against future holocausts, perhaps its final one? Surely the grisly wastelands of Europe and Asia were proof enough that civilization could not withstand national madness backed by laboratories in the service of annihilation. But this wisp of rationality had already been contaminated by a trail of radioactivity from the billowing mushroom clouds over the ruins of Hiroshima and Nagasaki. Part of the fallout was a new age of anxiety. To be sure, the United States was the only nation to own the bomb; it was also the only nation to have used it. If what one nation has another must have, then the race would soon be on again. Behind this bone-deep anxiety lurked a very tangible and threatening source—the postwar ascendancy of the Soviet Union, a country Winston Churchill once called a "riddle wrapped in a mystery inside an enigma."

Russia had been a stout if demanding ally during the war, winning admiration from Americans, however grudging, for the punishment it absorbed and delivered. But even before V-J Day, Moscow exhibited disquieting disregard for agreements entered into at Yalta and Potsdam. At these conferences Russia had insisted upon friendly provisional governments on its borders as part of the postwar settlement, to which the United States and England acquiesced. Almost at once Russia began to rivet Communism on these countries and to deny them the privilege of choosing their own form of government through free elections. These untoward developments provoked Truman's first important policy speech on October 27, 1945, at a Navy Day celebration in New York City. Standing before a huge audience in Central Park, the President, without mentioning Russia, outlined twelve fundamentals of foreign policy that emphasized freedom and self-determination for all nations.

Russia continued to give trouble. "I'm tired of babying the Soviets," Truman exploded in a letter to the Secretary of State in January, 1946. His exasperation mounted as problems accumulated: Russia continued to convert liberated countries into satellites, to raid Manchuria of industrial equipment without Allied authorization, to retain troops in Iran in violation of agreements, and to evade negotiation on outstanding problems such as the control of atomic energy. Out of these provocations came a tougher line toward Russia.

Three speeches given on successive days between February 27 and March 1, 1946, furnished the tip-off to sterner attitudes. All of the speakers had just returned from the first meeting of the United Nations Assembly in London. While voicing confidence in the future of the United Nations, each momentarily slipped off the velvet glove. In the Senate, Arthur Vandenberg warned: "There is a line beyond which compromise cannot go—even if we once crossed that line under the pressure of the exigencies of war." Secretary of State Byrnes, speaking to the Overseas Press Club of New York, affirmed our intention to live up to the covenant of the United Nations and to see that other countries live up to it also: "We must make it clear in advance that we do intend to prevent aggression. . . ." John Foster Dulles, a delegate to the United Nations, told the Foreign Policy Association of Philadelphia that Russia's obstructionism in the UN must be halted.[1] Favorable press reactions to the three speeches suggested public agreement with an accent on firmness without bellicosity.

On March 5, Winston Churchill, in a speech at Westminster College in Fulton, Missouri, gave off threatening sounds. The event had been engineered by the President of Westminster and General Harry Vaughan, an alumnus of the college who was now Truman's aide. Truman added his name to the invitation, and Churchill accepted. The President and the former Prime Minister traveled to Fulton together. Truman introduced Churchill to the 2600 people squeezed into the college gymnasium and to millions listening to the radio broadcast. "The President has told you that it is his wish, as I am sure it is yours," said Churchill, "that I should have full liberty to give my true and faithful counsel in these anxious and baffling times." A new threat to the peace of the world, he warned, is contained in the proselytizing and expansionist tendencies of the Soviet Union. "From Stettin in the Baltic to Trieste in the Adriatic, an iron curtain has descended across the continent. Behind that line lie all the capitals of the ancient states of Central and Eastern Europe. Warsaw, Berlin, Prague, Vienna, Budapest, Belgrade, Bucharest, and Sofia, all these famous cities and the populations around them lie in the Soviet sphere and all are subject in one form or another, not only to Soviet influence but to a very high and increasing measure of control from Moscow."[2] Because Russian expansionism carried a temptation to trial by strength, Churchill urged the creation of a United Nations police force, retention of atomic secrets, and a fraternal alliance with military ties among the English-speaking peoples.

Reactions were vigorous but varied. Some Americans felt Churchill had dusted off his old prewar hostility toward Communism; some regarded the speech as special pleading to shore up a shaky British Empire; some deplored it as a virtual declaration of an ideological war that threatened to aggravate delicate international relations and scuttle the United Nations. Americans favorable to the speech agreed that concessions to the Kremlin not only failed to yield agreements but actually increased world tensions, and that Churchill had only made explicit inescapable

[1] *The New York Times* contains the texts of speeches by Vandenberg, Byrnes, and Dulles, respectively, in issues from February 28 to March 2, 1946.
[2] For the text of Churchill's address, see A. Craig Baird, ed., *Representative American Speeches: 1945–1946* (New York: The H. W. Wilson Company, 1946), pp. 20–32.

truths: the United States must accept leadership of the free world in fact as well as name; the destinies of Britain and the United States were inexorably linked.

Truman was cagey. He passed off his part in the Fulton event as a gesture of respect and good will toward Churchill and a chance to help put Harry Vaughan's college on the map. But it was clear that the general intent of Churchill's address conformed to the stiffening attitudes recently exhibited by Vandenberg, Byrnes, and Dulles. Within the Cabinet, the sole dissenter from the get-tougher line was the Secretary of Commerce, Henry A. Wallace, widely regarded by liberals as the legitimate heir of Roosevelt's mantle.

In August, 1946, Wallace began shaping his dissenting views into a speech for a political rally sponsored by the National Citizens Political Action Committee and the Independent Citizens of the Arts, Sciences and Professions to be held in Madison Square Garden on September 12, 1946. In advance of the event, Wallace showed the speech to the President, who flipped through the text and commented approvingly on Wallace's statement that, "I am neither anti-British nor pro-British, neither anti-Russian nor pro-Russian." In substance Wallace opposed support for British "balance-of-power manipulations" and expressed willingness to accept a Russian sphere of influence in Eastern Europe comparable to that of the United States in the Western Hemisphere under the Monroe Doctrine.[3] Unmistakably, the speech was a reply to Churchill, and its doctrine ran counter to the President's developing foreign policy. Having scanned their advance copies, newsmen hurried to ask the President if he had seen the text. He had, he said; he endorsed it!

Both Wallace and Truman were now trapped in a bewildering crossfire. Although highly esteemed by his Madison Square Garden audience with its strong leftist leanings, Wallace's occasional slaps at Russia elicited hisses, boos, and catcalls. Upset by the heckling, he deleted some of his most severe strictures on Russia from his prepared text. Press reaction to the speech was generally unfavorable, and Secretary of State Byrnes, then attending a Paris meeting of foreign ministers, was outraged by this obvious contravention of American foreign policy. Senator Robert A. Taft, eager to rub salt into political wounds, jeered that "the Democratic party is so divided between Communism and Americanism that its foreign policy can only be futile and contradictory and make the United States the laughing stock of the world." After two days of chaos, Truman called a press conference. It was all a misunderstanding, he said lamely; he had only approved

[3] For the text of Wallace's speech, see A. Craig Baird, ed., *Representative American Speeches: 1946–1947* (New York: The H. W. Wilson Company, 1947), pp. 33–42.

Wallace's right to make the speech, not its content; therefore his nod to the Secretary had not signified a reversal in foreign policy. In the confusion of the week, a letter Wallace had sent to Truman on July 23 was made public. In it the Secretary had outlined his views on foreign policy several weeks before the Madison Square Garden speech. Once again cablegrams started coming and headlines screamed. Truman had had enough. Without ado he peremptorily dismissed his Secretary, observing that "Mr. Wallace will be happier in the exercise of his right to present his views as a private citizen." The incredibly muddled affair was symptomatic of still unsettled views on foreign policy, further complicated by domestic political alignments. But events soon resolved the uncertainties.

Early in 1947, the British Government informed the United States that it faced a financial crisis, forcing it to withdraw its support from the Greek Government then being harassed by Communist guerrillas. If Greece fell to the Communists, Russia was sure next to reduce Turkey to a satrapy and establish bases on the Dardanelles. With both Greece and Turkey as satellites, Moscow would have an open field in the Middle East. The Kremlin's design was clear. Washington must either acquiesce or intervene. Which?

On March 12, 1947, Arthur Vandenberg, then presiding over the Senate, asked Senator Holland to suspend his remarks "in order that we may keep our date with destiny. . . ." Vandenberg's choice of words offered a cue to the high importance of the forthcoming Presidential speech before a joint session of Congress and to its bipartisan auspices. Speaking at an uncommonly slow pace, the President outlined a policy "to support free peoples who are resisting attempted subjugation by armed minorities or by outside pressures." To this end, Truman asked the Congress for $400,000,000 to provide Greece and Turkey with military and economic aid; but it was clear enough that the policy looked beyond these countries and pointed to a long-range program for containing Communism. Said Representative Bender, after the President had left the chamber: "Every member of the House must feel, as I do, most apprehensive as to what the future has in store for us. The program that is recommended here is a departure from our traditional foreign policy."

Vandenberg warned the Senate: "In such a critical moment the President's hands must be upheld." The acknowledged leader of right-wing Republicans, Robert Taft, chafed but went along with Vandenberg. A few members of Congress railed bitterly that the Truman doctrine was an eleventh-hour reversal of administrative softness toward the Kremlin that reached back to our diplomatic recognition of Russia in 1933 and had found expression most recently in concessions at Yalta. "The Greek tragedy," cried Congressman Alvin O'Konski, "is merely the result of our chickens coming home to roost. To stop Communism in Greece we must first stop breeding and producing Communist chickens." At the very moment the President asked for aid to block Communists in Greece, exclaimed O'Konski, the State Department was offering handouts to Communists elsewhere. He was sure that the State Department itself harbored subversives.[4]

From another angle of criticism, Henry Wallace fired his salvos at the Truman proposal. Early in April, speaking at a leftist rally in London's Central Hall, Wallace charged that the containment doctrine bore no relationship to the real needs of people, from which stem Communist-inspired revolutions. In England and on the Continent, Wallace called the Truman policy a "one-way road to war." Once again he proved his ability to stir up the animals. In the patois that was becoming the language of baiters, voices from Capitol Hill angrily condemned Wallace's speeches for sounding "as if they were written in the Kremlin."

The developing acrimony had a constrictive influence on free discussion while yielding a new crop of words and phrases for public consumption. The phrase "iron curtain," a graphic description of the impenetrable barriers being drawn between Communist and non-Communist countries, was used by Vandenberg in a speech to the Senate late in 1945, but it was popularized by Churchill at Fulton in 1946.[5] The single word "containment" went to the heart of the Truman doctrine.[6] In 1946, when Herbert Bayard Swope, the journalist, suggested that Bernard Baruch use the phrase "cold war" in a speech, Baruch rejected it as too harsh. A year later on April 16, 1947, Baruch used it in an address to the South Carolina legislature, admonishing: "Let us not be deceived—we are in the midst of a cold war. Our enemies are to be found abroad and at home."[7] The metaphor caught the eye of Walter Lippmann, who gave it national prominence through a series of articles he published in the New York *Herald Tribune* in 1947. Not only were problems of incredible complexity compressed in a word or two, but

[4] O'Konski is worth reading as a forerunner of McCarthyism in his outlook and speaking tactics. See, for example, his speech on aid to Greece and Turkey, *Congressional Record,* 80th Cong., 1st Sess., vol. 93, pt. 2, pp. 2045–2047.

[5] Vandenberg used the phrase several times in his November 15, 1945 speech, as for example: "When the iron curtain of secrecy falls around an area suspicion is unavoidable. . . ." *Congressional Record,* 79th Cong., 1st Sess., vol. 91, pt. 8, pp. 10696–10699.

[6] George Kennan, then chairman of the State Department's Policy Planning Staff and a foremost architect of the Truman Doctrine and the Marshall Plan, gave currency to the word "containment" in an article entitled "The Sources of Soviet Conduct" by "X" in the July, 1947, issue of *Foreign Affairs.*

[7] Bernard M. Baruch, *Baruch: The Public Years* (New York: Holt, Rinehart and Winston, 1960), p. 388.

their popular impact and currency molded public sentiment in support of further measures.

Congresswoman Frances P. Bolton, a Republican, called Truman's stand on Greece and Turkey an historic speech, and added: "Just as we must be careful in our use of words so must we guard against carelessness in our actions. Let us also bear in mind that totalitarian aggression, while it is expressed in many ways, achieves its maximum results through poverty and hunger. To combat it we must put at least some food into empty stomachs and make it possible for these countries to reach out towards economic stability. . . ."[8] The war-torn economies of Europe, she warned, were susceptible to Communism, and throwing up sea walls was not enough. The Administration was of the same mind. On May 8, 1947, Truman dispatched his Under Secretary of State, Dean Acheson, to the Delta Council in Cleveland, Mississippi, where he sent up a trial balloon for a comprehensive program of foreign aid to Europe. Though the speech drew little attention, it was in effect a preliminary statement of the Marshall Plan.

Europe was plunging toward disaster. Time was so desperately critical that George Marshall, Secretary of State, asked Harvard University to reissue its earlier invitation to him to accept an honorary degree and appear on its commencement program. At Harvard on June 5, 1947, the Secretary announced what is popularly called the Marshall Plan and which, with the full support of Senator Vandenberg, became law in less than a year under the official caption of the European Recovery Program. In the interest of peace and freedom, Marshall declared, the United States is prepared to do "whatever it is able to do to assist in the return of normal economic health in the world. . . . Our policy is directed not against any country or doctrine but against hunger, poverty, desperation, and chaos." Other inventions followed, such as the North Atlantic Treaty Organization, the Rio pact, defense pacts with countries of the Far Pacific, aid to underdeveloped countries, known as the Point Four Program because it was first proposed as the fourth point in Truman's 1949 Inaugural Address. Within three years, from 1947 to 1950, the United States had accepted long-range, global commitments unthinkable before World War II. Moscow reacted to the new developments by engineering a coup d'état in Czechoslovakia, establishing the Cominform, and throwing up the Berlin blockade. The cold war warmed perceptibly. When Russia exploded its first atomic bomb in 1949 a "balance of terror" had been struck.

Even so, the Truman program began to show good results in Europe. But now

[8] *Congressional Record,* 80th Cong., 1st Sess., vol. 93, pt. 2, p. 1986.

Asia turned into a caldron. Since V-J Day the United States had pumped over three billion dollars of credits, grants, and war matériel into Chiang Kai-shek's National Government. Official reports to the State Department of corruption and inefficiency within the Nationalist regime discouraged further outlays. Late in 1948, Mao Tse-tung's Communist armies had Chiang's forces on the run, and in May, 1949, the Nationalist Government fled to Formosa. Now two Communist countries, Russia and China, dominated a quarter of the earth's surface and more than a quarter of its peoples. Angry voices in the United States wanted to know just who had sold China down the river. A dark cloud of suspicion hovered over the State Department. The incumbent Secretary, Dean G. Acheson, had been a leading proponent since 1946 of every measure to check Soviet expansionism, but ironically he was singled out as the architect of ruin by Congressmen who, in their frustration, were convinced that the country was in the grip of a great conspiracy. The fall of China and the rising tide of accusations sent Acheson out on the road to "sell" Truman's foreign policy in a series of public lectures. His most important, given at the University of California in Berkeley on March 16, 1950, laid bare the sources of difficulties between Moscow and Washington and specified stern conditions under which peaceful coexistence was possible in a troubled world.[9] Within three months after Acheson's speech, however, the prospects of coexistence seemed even dimmer.

In June, 1950, the Communist army of North Korea, with ill-disguised Soviet support, invaded South Korea. At the behest of Truman, the United Nations moved promptly to repel the invaders, and containment was put to its severest test. Late in November the Chinese Communist military might came to the support of the North Koreans. The gravity of the situation prompted the President to make a radio speech and to announce a declaration of national emergency.

At the outset Congress and the public wholeheartedly applauded the President's swift, decisive leadership for what he called "police action" in Korea, but as the war dragged on inconclusively in the hills of that remote country and as casualty lists lengthened, bitter criticism replaced initial approval. Late in 1950 and extending into 1951, a running debate on foreign policy and military strategy took place on Capitol Hill and over the air waves. In a series of radio talks, Herbert Hoover emerged as a foremost critic of the Truman policies, warning that the nation risked disaster through dispersal of its manpower and resources all over the world. We must withdraw to the Western Hemisphere as "the Gibraltar of Western Civilization," while maintaining one "frontier" in Great Britain

[9] For text of Acheson's speech, see *The Department of State Bulletin*, XXII (March 27, 1950), pp. 473–478.

and another in Japan, Formosa, and the Philippines.[10] Speaking at Northwestern University on January 28, 1951, the Governor of Illinois, Adlai E. Stevenson, deplored the revival of isolationist thinking manifested in the Gibraltar theory. "Haven't they [the isolationists] heard about Pearl Harbor or the atom bomb?" he asked. "Was the last war in vain? Haven't they heard that we are not self-sufficient?"

Criticism of "Truman's war" turned to fury when in April, 1951, the President relieved General Douglas MacArthur of his command of the United Nations troops. The General had publicly chafed under restraints of a limited war for limited objectives, prompting Truman to remove him for insubordination. Here and there flags were lowered to half-mast, and some Congressmen talked darkly about impeaching both Truman and Acheson. MacArthur returned to a hero's welcome, spoke stirringly to a joint session of Congress in behalf of his views on the war, toured the country speaking at rallies, and then faded away, another casualty of the cold war.

In season and out, Senator Robert A. Taft was in the vanguard of critics. Taft, an old-fashioned conservative and a pre–Pearl Harbor isolationist, had watched with jaundiced eye the erosion of his world by Roosevelt's New Deal and Truman's Fair Deal. After the war he protested the stigma of isolationism, but he retained a decidedly circumscribed view of America's foreign policy requirements, castigating Truman's program as a global WPA. Basically he regarded the Truman Doctrine as the international counterpart of the welfare state at home; both were foreign importations and therefore alien to American principles and tradition. By 1950 Taft's frustrations were so intense that he declared flatly that "the State Department with 'its pro-Communist allies'—allies he did not name or otherwise identify—had deliberately turned China over to the Communists."[11] A perennial Presidential hopeful, Taft's long campaign for the 1952 Republican nomination was expressive of right-wing indictments of the Truman policies, and his speech of June 9, 1951, to some 6,000 Republicans at Milwaukee, Wisconsin— McCarthy territory—was illustrative of his hard-hitting attacks on Truman's misguided foreign policy.

Taft did not specialize in low blows, but he happily egged on his colleague, Senator Joe McCarthy of Wisconsin, who relished bare-knuckle jobs. A tempestuous political adventurer, McCarthy skyrocketed into national prominence with a Lincoln Day speech first delivered in Wheeling, West Virginia, on February 9, 1950. In it he alleged that the State Department harbored 205 Communists, de-

[10] See, for example, Hoover's radio speech of December 15, 1950. *Vital Speeches of the Day*, XVII (1951), pp. 162–165.
[11] William S. White, *The Taft Story* (New York: Harper & Brothers, 1954), p. 89.

spite the President's Loyalty Order that prescribed a check on all employees in the executive branch. In the quietest of times the allegation would have been a shocker; in the traumatic context of 1950, featuring thermonuclear weapons, Communist successes abroad, espionage disclosures in Canada and the United States, and the disturbing trial of Alger Hiss for passing State secrets to the Soviets, it was enough to cut people loose from their moorings.[12]

Having hit pay dirt, McCarthy, with wild abandon, went on to broadcast seeds of distrust, inspiring a nation-wide witch hunt that brought under suspicion not only high-placed foreign policy makers but educators, clergymen, labor leaders, entertainers, and even the Girl Scouts. Whether to express opprobrium or approval, the term "McCarthyism" gained international currency. By 1952, McCarthy's grip on the right wing of his party guaranteed him a spot on the program of the Republican National Convention. Although his speech was heralded as the most important yet in his meteoric career, and succeeded mightily in whipping up delegates, actually it turned out to be more typical than remarkable in its allegations that America had been betrayed by enemies within its gates.

The new President, Dwight D. Eisenhower, acquiesced in McCarthy's roughhouse tactics for the time being in order to preserve party unity. Without restraining influence, the Senator plunged ahead with his unproductive, headline-making investigations to flush out Communists, flattening the morale of entire departments of the Government. In the off-year election campaign of 1954 McCarthy concocted another sensational Lincoln Day speech for delivery here and there, charging that the political tenure of the Democrats since Franklin Roosevelt's days was a record of twenty years of treason. He "documented" his preposterous charges with twenty alleged deeds of betrayal "chosen at random." McCarthy's career had reached a point where he had become a severe liability to his party and to the serious business of government. His crisis was at hand. Eisenhower slipped public rebukes into his speeches, and McCarthy's running feud with the Secretary of the Army over "Communist coddling" culminated in extended televised subcommittee hearings that stamped the Senator as a ruffian in the eyes of millions of viewers. Public antipathy toward McCarthy strengthened the case of Senator Ralph Flanders, who alone among Republicans kept prodding his colleagues to censure the Wisconsin Senator. Actually Flanders found "much to praise" as well as "much to deplore" in McCarthy. Although satisfied that McCarthy had found "dirt under the rug," Flanders was utterly convinced that his

---

[12] For an account of McCarthy's speaking tactics, see Barnet Baskerville, "Joe McCarthy, Brief Case Demagogue," *Today's Speech*, II (September, 1954), pp. 8–15.

methods menaced freedom's health and that his daily cops and robbers acts diverted national attention from the truly serious business of fighting Communism. Flanders' campaign ultimately persuaded the Senate late in 1954 to condemn McCarthy for contumelious behavior, thus bringing the latter's career to an abrupt and ignominious end.

It was against this backdrop that first Truman and then Eisenhower had to bring the nation to accept world leadership with all of its burdensome and frustrating consequences. Following Roosevelt, Truman's first years seemed inauspicious, but he ended his second administration in 1953 with a televised valedictory that bespoke personal confidence in his record as President and regard for his place in history. Above all, the speech was Truman himself, conveying in human, everyday language the awesome responsibility that had devolved upon the President of the United States in the cold war era.

"The clearest-cut and most important consequence of the Republican National Convention," wrote Ernest Lindley in 1952, "is that the main lines of American foreign policy have been confirmed." The defeat of Taft and the nomination of Eisenhower were in effect a guarantee to the world that whoever was elected, Eisenhower the Republican or Stevenson the Democrat, the United States would not retreat into "fortress America," to use Herbert Hoover's rallying cry.

During the early years of the Eisenhower Administration, various factors helped to relax international tensions, particularly the end of the Korean War, the economic revival of Western Europe, the death of Stalin, and the denunciation of Stalinism by Nikita Khrushchev. A national hero, Eisenhower was able to dissipate much of the hostility accumulated by the Truman Administration during its difficult years of basic policy formulation—policies which provided the guidelines for the new administration. Hence it was possible for Eisenhower to experiment in personal diplomacy and Summitry in an attempt to penetrate the iron curtain and establish a tolerable *modus vivendi* with the new leadershsip in the Kremlin. At the first Summit meeting in Geneva in 1955, Eisenhower acknowledged that deep-rooted problems divided the world, but spoke hopefully of a new spirit that would provide the conditions for a viable peace. The "spirit of Geneva" was short-lived, and mutual denunciations were resumed. But the quest for peace with honor, the President affirmed, must be pursued relentlessly on a global scale. In his second inaugural address, with Herbert Hoover on the platform, Eisenhower rejected "fortress America" in favor of our "deep involvement in the destiny of men everywhere." "For one truth must rule all we think and all we do. No people can live to itself alone. The unity of all who dwell in freedom is their only sure defense. The economic need of all nations—in mutual dependence—makes isolation an impossibility; not even America's prosperity could long survive if other nations did not prosper. No nation can longer be a fortress, lone and strong and safe. And any people, seeking such shelter for themselves, can now build only their own prison." The President went on: "We honor, no less in this divided time, the people of Russia. We do not dread, rather we do welcome, their progress in education and industry." Within months of this magnanimous nod, Americans were stunned by the Soviet's successful launching of Sputnik, man's first space satellite. At once the cry went up, "Are we losing the cold war?" Russian technical successes touched off a panic of self-examination and accusatory debates over the quality of American education.

The cold war was now carried on artificial satellites and missiles through the stratosphere and into outer space. With each spectacular blast-off arose the anxious question: Whose achievements and model—that of the U.S.A. or the U.S.S.R.—will capture the imagination of emergent nations struggling to emancipate themselves from poverty, colonialism, and feudalism? Despite professions of concern for peoples seeking to shake off their chains, throughout both the Truman and Eisenhower administrations, the weight of American dollars and influence was used to maintain equilibrium in a world where revolution was tipping the scales.

In this setting, John F. Kennedy, age forty-three, took the Presidential oath. American prestige, he had insisted in his campaign, had slipped badly under Republican management and our rate of economic growth was not commensurate with our responsibilities. He promised an administration that would energize the nation and regain our prestige abroad. In his Inaugural Address, devoted exclusively to America vis-à-vis the world, Kennedy challenged "those nations who would make themselves our adversary" to renew "the quest for peace, before the dark powers of destruction unleashed by science engulf all humanity in planned or accidental self-destruction." We may not succeed in establishing a new world of law in our lifetime, Kennedy acknowledged, "But let us begin."

"Now the trumpet summons us again—not as a call to bear arms, though arms we need—not as a call to battle, though embattled we are—but a call to bear the burden of a long twilight struggle, year in and year out, 'rejoicing in hope, patient in tribulation'—a struggle against common enemies of man: Tyranny, poverty, disease, and war itself." With overtones of Churchill, Kennedy's address enunciated a grave yet evocative credo for the "long twilight struggle" of the cold war that stretched ahead into an uncertain future.

There Are No Gibraltars

ADLAI EWING STEVENSON

Born, Los Angeles, California, February 5, 1900. Graduated from Princeton, 1922; attended Harvard Law School; graduated from Northwestern's School of Law, 1926. Admitted to Illinois bar, 1926. Practiced law in Chicago, 1927–1941, with intermittent government service. Served the United States Government in a succession of important offices and missions at home and abroad, 1941–1947. Elected Democratic Governor of Illinois, 1948. Drafted as candidate for President of the United States by the Democratic National Convention, 1952, he was defeated by Dwight D. Eisenhower. Again nominated in 1956, he was again defeated by Eisenhower. Ambassador to the United Nations, 1961.

"Have we discovered that there are no Gibraltars, no fortresses impregnable to death or ideas, any more?"

S *ome five years ago* this University, for reasons best known to its trustees, conferred an honorary degree on me. Having thus honored me I suppose the least the Governor of Illinois could do in appreciation would have been to decline President Miller's and Mr. Burgess' invitation to speak at this hundredth anniversary convocation. Instead I accepted, after the manner of insensitive and egotistical politicians. I apologize.

Northwestern University's Founders' Day Convocation honoring the University's 100th anniversary, Evanston, Illinois, January 28, 1951. *Vital Speeches of the Day*, XVII (February 15, 1951), pp. 284–288. Reprinted by permission of *Vital Speeches of the Day*. This text has been checked against a recording made of the speech by Station WNUR, Northwestern University, and minor corrections have been made.

Because there are others who can speak with authority about the founding of Northwestern University, I am, with, I am sure, your enthusiastic approval, going to resist the temptation to tell you of the faith and convictions of the founders who stood here 100 years ago and dreamed of "a university of the highest order of excellence." All that we see about us testifies that they founded well and that their successors have wrought well upon those foundations. In the 100 years the dream by the Lake here in Dr. Evans' town has become one of the world's large and honored communities of scholars.

Early Illinois was notoriously inhospitable to higher education and I recall the remark of a lusty legislator of those early days who, speaking in opposition to a bill to charter the first three higher educational institutions in this state, said that he was "born in a briar thicket, rocked in a hog trough and never had his genius cramped by the pestilential air of a college."

Northwestern, too, was born upon a scene on which the light of higher education shone but fitfully. But now in our time one never sees a considered catalogue of the assets of Illinois that does not always proudly list its universities at the top.

And personally I doubt if there's any significance whatever to the fact that the number of college graduates each year in the United States now equals almost exactly the number of people that are admitted to our mental institutions. I once heard it said, Dr. Miller, that Massachusetts Institute of Technology "humanized the scientist" while Harvard "simonized the humanist." Just what Northwestern does I don't know; perhaps both. But at all events its contributions to the sciences and the humanities and also to the wholesome goodness and gaiety we associate with American student life have brought to this campus imperishable distinction and affection.

Thanks to Northwestern, to its neighbor, the University of Chicago, and to the great State University, and the many distinguished lesser institutions, Illinois, and particularly this section of the state, is now one of the treasure houses, one of the major repositories, of the Western world's culture.

It is proper, therefore, that we pause to note the 100th birthday of this proud university; that we pause a moment in our feverish preparations for defense to recall what we are defending. Certainly one of the things we are defending is the future security and health of privately supported universities such as Northwestern. In turn we confidently expect the universities to defend for generations to come the spirit of free inquiry and fearless scholarship which is a basic condition of free men. For that protection and for the contribution of the universities to "a large resolute breed of men" which Walt Whitman called the only bar against tyranny, we will have to trust to the future; we will have to trust that the guardians here and elsewhere of the riches of our learning will never forget what the treasure they guard is, what it is composed of. We will have to trust that the guardians of Western thought will never permit its vitality and beauty to be smothered by strong, arrogant men who burn books and bend thought to their liking, nor obscured by timid men trembling in the darkness of anxiety.

The continuity of our heritage of scholarship, which is the peculiar and price-less possession of the university, must, then, be entrusted to the future. But what of the present, which has such a bearing on the health and the strength and the continuity of the custodians of our culture?

Are the universities to be stripped of students in order to defend our cultural heritage? The young of college age are the seed corn of a society and a nation. To survive must we eat our seed corn? And if we do, can we survive? We must and we will, I think, find at least a partial answer to this disturbing question. And we will find it in calm deliberation, and not in frantic fright.

Then, like you, after some experience, I have made the disturbing observation that absence of thought in wartime seems to be mandatory. And, of course, total abstinence from thought is very agreeable for most of us, and a uniformly pop-ular condition among adolescents. But is it necessary in mobilization, in half war, if you please? Perhaps we have something to think about here as we enter the new and unexplored era of the garrison state.

. . . .

Northwestern was born here in a quiet village on Lake Michigan by a bur-geoning city just one hundred years ago. That too was a time of revolution abroad and of transition here. In 1851 Illinois was filling up with immigrants from the south and the east. A steel plough to cut the tough prairie sod had at last been invented. The reaper had come to our prairies. On plank roads Illinois was rising out of the mud. A railroad was pushing westward. The Irish and the Germans were coming in search of something better and more hopeful for the average man. With not 30,000 souls Chicago was struggling out of the swamps. Illinois was passing from the log cabin frontier era and shouldering its way into the new industrial day that was dawning upon the Union.

A hundred years have passed; a hundred years which have seen the culmination of a great historic expansive movement of peoples from Europe to the West, and the conquest, development and integration into the world community of the two great American continents, severed by revolutions but tied by cultural inheritance to their western European roots.

At the same time that this was going on there came another great expansion—from West to East. The Slavic peoples and culture passed through the Ural Moun-tains, across the vastness of Siberia to the Pacific and on across the Bering Sea to Alaska and our own West Coast. The Russian tide collided at last with the Jap-anese, just emerging from the hermits' hut with vaulting ambitions too. And there it stopped—for a time—but the land mass over which the Russian expansion surged has for the most part remained firmly in Russian hands, while the Euro-pean overseas expansion created a new and independent center of power here on our continent.

Twice in 25 years our new center of power, stretching from the tropics to the Arctic and facing both the Pacific and the Atlantic, has been compelled to intervene to redress the balance of power in the world. And now with Britain and France enfeebled by these wars, with the German and the Japanese power crushed, the United States and Russia, which have risen from the mists of these short hundred years, even as this university, stand face to face, with the other nations polarized around them, drawn by the gravitational pulls of proximity, coercion, self-interest and kinship.

Believing as we do in a community of free nations and free peoples acting peacefully and responsibly through governments freely chosen, we conclude at last that we cannot live in comfortable security with a great imperial power—Czar or Commissar, it makes no difference—which has seen the barriers to its expansion collapse and is on the move again, taking here, probing there, and pressing relentlessly against the uncommitted, discontented millions of the earth. Capitalizing the ancient racial xenophobia and the messianic zeal to missionize the world of the Russian people, the leaders of the new Russia, armed with force and the old weapon of fomented revolution, use the seductive new weapon of communism to soften their victims. But whatever the trappings, the methods, the weapons, the objective is domination—imperialism. And I often think that it would be both more accurate and more effective if we talked less of communism with all its appeal for ignorant, miserable peoples and more of imperialism which threatens the freedom and the independence of everyone and has no appeal. Communism can be a fighting faith, but imperialism is subtle slavery.

So, as Northwestern enters its second century, America, rich, peaceful and undisciplined, finds itself face to face across both the seas with an inscrutable, ruthless conqueror, strong, cunning and armed with an egalitarian idea that has great appeal for the miserable masses of humanity. No longer is there anyone to protect us. No longer can we sow when and where we are certain to reap. There is no safe investment, no certain harvest any longer. We cannot even measure the price of saving ourselves. Indeed, we seem to be in some doubt as to whether we should save ourselves at all; whether we are worth the cost!

The quiet past in which this great university grew to manhood is no more. The bright land is troubled and sorely tried. Things are badly out of balance when we spend $235 million for one aircraft carrier, almost four times the endowment of this university. Its future is in doubt. Our future is in doubt. Some say fight now. Some say despotism is the wave of the future. Some say abandon Asia. Some say abandon Europe. And worst of all, everybody says something—including me!

In our time peace has become as abnormal as war used to be because this is the revolution. And revolution is extremely irritating, vexatious and bewildering to a prosperous, peaceful, contented people that want nothing except to be left alone.

How have we reacted to this condition of perpetual danger? It seems to me that for five years we have suffered from the confusion and distraction of alternate moments of illusion and despair. Hoping always for a cheap and painless escape from the realities of a distasteful destiny, aided and abetted by politicians who will say anything to be popular and by editors either myopic or worse, public opinion has moved in violent pendular swings between optimism and pessimism, between the mountains of complacency and the marshes of despair.

In fatuous haste to be shut of war, worry and expense, we obliterate our power and leave it to the United Nations to keep a peace that never existed. When things go right we gush paeans of praise for the U.N.; when they go wrong we damn it and even propose to forsake the good because it is not the perfect. In fear we overestimate the danger; imperil our liberties, exaggerate the foe's cunning and strength; even demand a showdown as though the certainty of doom were preferable to the uncertainty. Again, perpetual danger invites the complacency of status and we underestimate the peril by overconfidence in our virtue and our power, as though that were enough in a moral contest. But the self-hypnosis of loud and repeated talk about our righteousness and freedom will rally no allies nor blow down the Kremlin walls.

And now as things get tough and we can't buy, threaten or preach our way to peace, we are menaced again by a myriad of amateur military and political strategists. Even the isolationists have reappeared, flexing their muscles, or rather their tongues, and proclaiming "Let the whole world go. We should worry. We can defend ourselves with a strong navy and air force." Haven't they heard about Pearl Harbor or the atom bomb? Was the last war all in vain? Haven't they heard that we are not self-sufficient? Inevitably won't a garrison state become a police state? And do they forget that nothing succeeds like success? If they do, conquerors don't. I suppose any moment even America First will emerge full blown again, except that I hope this time it is more properly entitled America Last—last on the Kremlin's list.

The reemergence of the straight isolationist doctrine—the same people saying the same things we heard a decade ago before the whirlwind—is to me the great regurgitation. They remind me of Charles Lamb's remark: "I cannot make present things present to me."

But fortunately for us the great debate about foreign policy, which was mostly a debate about military strategy and not foreign policy, appears to be about over. And, none too soon, it appears that we have about made up our mind to stop fighting each other, gather all the like-minded allies we can find and settle down seriously to the very serious business of getting stronger than the brigands that are preying on the world.

Perhaps an occasional national debate like this one is a healthy thing. It clears the air, releases tensions, focuses torpid attention on great issues, and melts divisionist controversy into a mould of common conviction.

Maybe we have about reached a common conviction that peace through power is our salvation. Maybe we have decided that only by once again redressing the balance of power in the world and confronting Russia with a preponderance of force can we thwart an imperialism more sinister than the world has ever seen.

But we should profit from an experience like this, because it won't be the last time we get rattled; it won't be the last time we doubt our beliefs and believe our doubts.

I suppose, for example, we will have to assume that the isolationist argument will have at least nine lives, for the very human reason that it pleases the average man because it spares him any immediate inconvenience or sacrifice, and it flatters his sense of power to feel that America can live alone and like it.

And have we learned that while the whole nation may debate the broad policy of whether to defend or not to defend, whether to defend alone or with allies, the details of the where, when and how we will defend are sometimes questions of military, political and diplomatic strategy which cannot be settled safely or wisely by public debate? Nor can they be wisely settled in all cases by men who behave, to borrow a line from King Lear, "as if they were God's spies," but who are neither military strategists nor geopoliticians.

Have we learned that what 160 million Americans know about our plans the enemy knows too? Have we learned that hunting scapegoats is not a foreign policy?

Have we learned that our mission is the prevention, not just the survival of a major war? Have we discovered that there are no Gibraltars any more, no fortresses impregnable to death or ideas, any more?

While the debate talks incessantly in terms of our crisis and our survival, it is not just our crisis, it is the crisis of the whole free world. Have we learned that making domestic political capital out of world crisis is not the way to win friends and influence people? Do we realize that the Russians have already gained a portion of their objective by using our indecision and moral confusion to weaken our leadership in the free world? The Russians know the value of even reluctant allies in this final struggle for power. Do we? Or are we going to risk the slow strangulation that comes from whittling away the friendly world?

If we have not yet learned that having the most to lose we have the most to save, then, I say, let us pray.

But if we have, if the immensity of the responsibility and the stakes has dawned upon us, then the great debate has been a great blessing and we are on the way to thwart this latest greatest threat to all that this university symbolizes.

And why should we be poor in spirit? The task is great, the price is high, but the prize is better than life. With Europe and its great industrial concentration and forward bases shored up and steadfast, with access to the tin and rubber of south Asia, middle eastern oil, African manganese and uranium, the scales are still weighted to the west, and the waves of the future are still free. Aggression must be called aggression in the United Nations. But in insisting on no equivocation about the legal and moral position, we dare not forget that the allegiance of India, uncommitted to East or West, is the ultimate objective of both East and West in the orient. And we dare not fall into the trap, the oubliette, Russia has prepared for us in China. War there will drain our resources and at the same time make China completely dependent militarily on Russia. With every Russian jet at least six Russians go along. A weakened China means a stronger Russia pressing from behind against Hong Kong, Indo-China, South Asia, Japan, and finally—India. Hounded by people of small vision and great emotion it will not be easy to withstand the pressure to help Russia solve her problems with China. And with us mired in the morass of the China mainland the Soviet could turn next summer to some unfinished business with Tito in Jugoslavia.

Pray heaven we can remember amid the discord and chagrin of defeat that military force alone cannot win the day for us in Asia. Our moral authority there is low because we are white and Asia is colored. Desperately poor, struggling to shake off the shackles of white colonialism, Asia is just now passing through the era of revolution, independence and self-determination that swept the western world long ago. It will take great patience, great insight, great restraint for us who tend to see the whole world in our own image and likeness to win confidence and faith in the great uncommitted areas of Asia. It can't be done with the white man's sword. But it can be done; they can be convinced that communist imperialism is not liberation but a more deadly enemy of normal aspirations for freedom and social justice than colonialism.

And are we, I wonder, moving as a nation from our Greek period to our Roman period; from a period in which the validity of our ideas was the important consideration to one in which the effectiveness of our ideas is crucial? Good intentions and reliance on the rightness of our cause will avail us little against an enemy that cares nothing about validity and is concerned only with effectiveness. The Greeks were right, but the Greeks died.

A danger greater, it seems to me, than Germany or Japan in the last war, or communist imperialism now is moral fatigue, disintegration, half loyalty, timid faith—the "weakening of the central convictions to which Western man had hitherto pledged allegiance."

When freedom didn't exist it too was a fighting faith that men would die for. But now that it is old, it looks a little pale and gentle and lacks the appeal to the militant irrational sentiments once mobilized by conquering religions and now by imperial communism.

But communism resolves no anxieties. It multiplies them. It organizes terror. It is without spiritual content or comfort. It provides no basic security. In the long run it cannot cure the disease of this anxious age. But its short term methods are grimly effective. We can't sit still and wait for the fever to run its course. Without combative faith in our spiritual heritage, we won't long hold out against the subtleties of selfishness and fear. If Western civilization is to save its body, it must save its soul too. It must awake again the emotionalism, the confidence, the defiant faith of a resolute breed of men to whom liberty and justice mean something positive every day—not just when war has reduced us to the stark issue of self preservation.

It's easy to care mightily then; it's hard now. It's easier to fight for principles than it is to live up to them. But now is the time that a passionate belief counts if we are to avoid another war, and if we are to avoid the greater menace of cowardly surrender to our own doubts and fears.

Don't the universities have a large, indeed the leading, role to play in articulating the purpose and the combative faith of a great people in this era of convulsive transition and this hour of discord and doubt? Don't they know best what we stand to lose?

We have proclaimed our military weakness, our vacillation, our hesitation, our fear. Enough of that! The test of a nation is in defeat. The time has come to proclaim our faith in all its might and majesty. History will go on and "The Forfeiture of Freedom" would be a sorry title to this chapter; rather the historian must write that in arousing America to re-define and defend its ideals the ugliest despotism dug its grave in the twentieth century.

It was in 1776 that Tom Paine wrote: "The heart that feels not now is dead; the blood of his children will curse his cowardice, who shrinks back at a time when little might have saved the whole."

Our Misguided Foreign Policy

ROBERT ALPHONSO TAFT

Born, Cincinnati, Ohio, September 8, 1889, the son of William Howard Taft, 27th President of the United States; died, New York City, July 31, 1953. Graduated from Yale, 1910, and from Harvard Law School, 1913. Practiced law in Cincinnati. Member of Ohio House of Representatives, 1921–1926; member of Ohio Senate, 1931–1932. As a Republican, elected to the United States Senate, 1938; re-elected, 1944 and 1950. A Presidential hopeful from 1940 on, he made an all-out though unsuccessful campaign to secure the Republican nomination in 1952. He was spoken of as "Mr. Republican" by devoted followers.

"This Russian threat exists because of the weak and wrongheaded policies of this and the preceding administration at Teheran, Yalta, Potsdam, and in China."

*I*t is an honor and a privilege to be invited to address this great Republican assembly, interested in providing the material support for the Republican Party of Wisconsin, and looking to an overwhelming Republican victory in 1952. It is quite right that you begin this campaign today. One of the difficulties with recent Republican campaigns is that they haven't started soon enough. A successful campaign requires carefully prepared publicity, in the newspapers, on the radio and television, in magazines, and in pamphlets. It takes time to prepare good, effective publicity, and to be effective

Republican fund-raising dinner, Milwaukee, Wisconsin, June 9, 1951. *Congressional Record*, 82nd Cong., 1st Sess., vol. 97, pt. 13, pp. A3462–A3464.

it must be distributed long before election day. Organization, both among political groups and nonpolitical groups, also takes time, in these days when 50 percent of the people apparently take little natural interest in politics and are even likely to stay at home on election day. In 1952 our organization must be complete enough to reach and interest millions of potential voters. And so I compliment the Republican Party of Wisconsin on its foresighted action, and I am delighted to be a part of its effort.

It is too early to define all the issues of the 1952 campaign. Broadly speaking, the issue, as I see it, is the restoration of honest principle to government. The Republican Party offers a return to honesty and frankness in the day-to-day conduct of the vast, sprawling Federal Government. It offers a return to the principles of liberty which are threatened by a creeping socialism masquerading as welfare and planning and social insurance. It offers a return to a foreign policy based on definite principles and aimed at protecting the security and the peace of the people of the United States.

[Taft particularizes charges of scandal in the Truman administration.]

. . . .

Only a Republican administration can protect the principles of liberty, justice, and equality against the creeping forces of socialism. Under New Deal administrations there has been a steady growth of Government until Harry Truman spent twice as much in 1 year as Herbert Hoover spent in 4 years. This country was conceived in liberty and owes its tremendous development and progress to that liberty—liberty of the individual to live his own life and think his own thoughts, liberty to teach whatever doctrine is worth teaching, liberty of the local community to run its own affairs and determine how its children shall be educated, liberty of men to choose their own occupations and run their own business as they see fit as long as they don't interfere with the rights of others to do the same. It is this liberty which has built this country up to a point where we have achieved the greatest production and the highest standard of living the world has ever seen.

But the Truman administration adopted the theories of British socialism while denying that they were doing so. The President demanded power for the Government to go into any business. He demanded the right to fix wages, prices, and rents in time of peace. He proposed the Brannan plan to give the Government complete control over the detailed operations of agriculture. He proposed to socialize medicine and make every doctor an employee of the Government. He departed from the American concept of welfare service, health service, and other assistance to those with low incomes, furnished by local communities, administered by local authorities with Federal assistance only when necessary. He proposed vast social-insurance ideas along the line of the English Beveridge plan to provide hand-outs from the National Treasury to millions well able to support themselves. This whole program, like British socialism, masqueraded in the guise of a slight extension of welfare service, when, in fact, it threatened a complete change in the whole function of Government leading inevitably to a destruction of liberty as we have known it in America.

Furthermore, the President followed the philosophy of those who believed that the people were too dumb to understand, and that the millennium could only be brought about by long-haired economic planners directing the daily lives of the people and the operations of every business.

The Republican Party offers a government based on the same principles of liberty for which this Nation was established. It promises progress and an increased standard of living within those principles of liberty, justice, and equality. The basis for still higher standards of living is sound consistent fiscal policy, and the encouragement of all that industrial and natural resource development which have made liberty a material as well as an intellectual benefit. When it comes to plans for the expansion of government, it proposes to analyze every plan by weighing its advantages against the increased Federal payroll and the limitation of the people's liberty. It is opposed to throwing away an American system at the height of its success in favor of half-baked programs which have failed in all the countries where they have been tried.

In the field of foreign policy the Republican Party promises an American foreign policy based on sound and consistent principles made known to our own people and to the world, administered by men with common sense and good judgment. The main principle of that foreign policy must be the liberty and the security of the people of the United States. The second principle must be the maintenance of peace unless war becomes absolutely necessary to protect American liberty itself. As a good neighbor we desire to help the rest of the world in every reasonable way, but certainly that cannot be a prime object of foreign policy, or an excuse for the terrible tragedy of war.

I have always favored an international organization, hoping that it might be able to protect the peace of the world. At the present moment the United Nations itself has become impotent because of its faulty Charter and the aggressive attitude of Russia. We are forced to establish a much greater American armed force because, for the first time in our history, another nation may actually threaten our security. Soviet Russia is a threat because of the great extension of air power, because of its possession of the atomic bomb, because of its vast manpower, and because of the aggressive, fanatical spirit of communism. We are forced into a long-term military program which it will strain our capacity to support, and may temporarily postpone many of the internal programs and improvements in which we are also interested.

This Russian threat exists because of the weak and wrong-headed policies of this and the preceding administration at Teheran, Yalta, Potsdam, and in China. Even during the war the policies adopted by the Government completely ignored the danger of Soviet expansion after the war though many of us pointed it out. The policy of unconditional surrender and increased resistance has left a vacuum in Germany into which Russia has ever since threatened to move. Our Government was inspired by the stupid fear that Russia might make a separate peace with Germany, and the equally stupid assumption that we had to invite Russia into the Japanese War when, in fact, we had already won that war.

We acted as if it were a favor to us for Russia to accept our lend-lease assistance. I pointed out after the Teheran conference that the whole Roosevelt policy was based on the delightful theory that Joe Stalin in the end would turn out to have an angelic nature if we gave him everything he asked.

At Yalta this attitude was supplemented by something more sinister in the indirect influence of communism and Communists on American statesmen. Hopkins and Harriman, who seemed to have had most to do with the Far Eastern agreement, apparently accepted completely the idea that Russia was a peace-loving nation. William C. Bullitt, former ambassador to France, says that the President and Hopkins developed the theory that the Soviet Union was a peace-loving democracy. Henry Wallace thought that Russian democracy was in some ways better than American democracy. The Communist Party had made a deliberate drive to place people in positions where they could affect public opinion or public policy or influence others who could do the same. They planted spies in the Government. We know of Hiss and Marzani and Coplon and Wadleigh. We know that the Englishman, Fuchs, a Communist, was admitted to all the secrets of the Atomic Energy Commission, and delivered all the plans for the atom bomb to Russia. Communists successfully planted among many American leaders the philosophy which was adopted at Yalta—that communism was, in fact, a form of government more or less consistent with American ideals. I could never understand how any man who even went through an American high school, and understood what America is about, could reach such a conclusion.

The result was that at Yalta our Government accepted all Stalin's promises, although he had never kept a promise which he had made. They accepted them without any means of enforcing them. They set Russia up in Berlin and Prague and Vienna where they could dominate Central Europe. We agreed to give Russia a position in Manchuria which Japan had occupied—in effect, military control of Manchuria—contrary to every principle of American foreign policy since the days of John Hay and the open door in China. We gave Russia Sakhalin and the Kurile Islands without strings of any kind. This whole agreement was made without even letting Chiang Kai-shek know for four months that we had bargained away his most important industrial province. In short, we put Russia in a position in Manchuria where they could back the Chinese Communists, which, of course, they promptly did. General Marshall was sent to China to insist that Chiang Kai-shek take Communists into his cabinet and when he refused, cut off further military aid to Nationalist China for 9 months at the most crucial period of the conflict.

Throughout this whole period there was a strong pro-Communist influence in the Far Eastern Division of the State Department, which supported the Communist propaganda that the Chinese Communists were just agrarian reformers and that Chiang Kai-shek was some kind of a reactionary Fascist. Even after we turned definitely against communism in Europe, the whole attitude of the administration toward communism in Asia has been soft and often friendly.

Again, the administration has been less than frank. They are obsessed with the idea that they must never admit a mistake. When Senators MUNDT and NIXON brought out the treachery of Hiss, the President referred to all such investigations as red herrings. Secretary Acheson refused to turn his back on Hiss, even after he had been convicted. When Joe McCarthy performed a public service by demanding an investigation of conditions in the State Department, the administration appointed a hatchet committee headed by Senator Tydings to apply a complete whitewash to the whole smelly situation in the State Department. Efforts to investigate the Atomic Energy Commission were suppressed by smear and propaganda.

There has been no consistent principle in the administration policy dealing with communism in the world and at home, except the principle of covering up their past mistakes.

The history of the Korean War shows that the administration has no foreign policy, has no consistency, and no principle. Secretary Acheson testified last week that our Formosa policy is and always has been based on the principle that Formosa has strategic importance and that we must keep Formosa out of the hands of a power which would be hostile to the United States, but without the use of American troops. Yet, after I suggested in December 1949, that Formosa should be defended because it was a simple operation requiring only the presence of the Seventh Fleet, I was violently attacked by the President and Mr. Acheson, who said that the United States would not provide military aid, or even advice, to Chinese forces in Formosa.

On December 23, 1949, Secretary Acheson put out the famous Policy Information Paper to all State Department officers, in which it was clearly stated as a matter of fact that Formosa had no special military significance—although the Joint Chiefs said it had—that it was a mistaken popular conception that it had strategic importance, that civil and military conditions there had deteriorated under the Nationalists, that American assistance would accomplish no good for China or its Nationalist regime, and that it was about to be taken over by the Communists. The Secretary of State dares to take the position today that all these statements, completely at variance with the Formosa policy he now espouses, were false and promulgated for the purpose of saving our face if Formosa should fall. It is clear that we were either lying then or we are lying now. Personally it is clear to me that the Seventh Fleet could always have defended Formosa without the slightest difficulty, that the State Department wanted Formosa to fall into the hands of the Communists, that the Policy Information Paper was promulgated to assist that result, and that we never did adopt the Formosa policy which the Secretary of State now pretends was our policy. Even today the Secretary really wants to deliver Formosa to the tender mercies of the United Nations, which would probably turn it over to Communist China.

The full consequence of a weak and wavering policy is exhibited by the Korean War. The administration invited that war. We withdrew our troops from Korea without arming the South Koreans. In September 1947 General Wedemeyer had pointed out the danger of this course. He said then that the Soviet-equipped and trained North Korean Communist Army of 125,000 men was vastly superior to the United States-organized constabulary of 16,000 Koreans equipped with Japanese small arms. He pointed out that if the Russians withdrew and we withdrew, the North Koreans would be able to carry out an invasion without actual presence of Soviet troops. He recommended a South Korean force of sufficient strength to cope with the threat from the North.

But we withdrew our troops without following Wedemeyer's advice. The State Department obtained money to arm Korea, but it developed that none of the money was spent. We gave the South Koreans neither tanks nor heavy artillery nor airplanes and, of course, the North Koreans knew that the South was helpless.

Then in January 1950, Secretary Acheson made a public statement to the effect that the American line of defense in the Pacific was Japan, Okinawa, and the Philippines. In order to assert vigorously the State Department's left-wing prejudice against Chiang Kai-shek and the policy of defending Formosa, Acheson asserted emphatically the policy that the United States would not assure either Korea or Formosa against attack. With such a reaffirmation of our Far Eastern policy, with the fact before them that we had not helped the Nationalist Government against Chinese Communists, is it any wonder that Soviet Russia and the Korean Communists took the Secretary of State at his word? To Soviet Russia, Korea was a soft spot into which they could move their Communist satellites without cost. If we had kept our troops there, or if we had really armed the South Koreans, or if we had given notice that we intended to return as we did, it is doubtful if the war would ever have occurred.

Then, when the Koreans attacked, the President reversed his entire policy and sent American troops into Korea. He sent them without consulting Congress and without waiting for the United Nations, and then persuaded the United Nations to back him up, with words, but with few troops. While there was some logical argument for the United States, by action of President and Congress, to reverse our announced policy and punish outright military aggression, the President completely usurped authority in sending troops into a foreign country to defend it against attack by another country. This Korean War is a Truman war. The United Nations Charter provided for special agreements for the providing of troops to a United Nations Army, which agreements had to be ratified by Congress, and never were. Secretary Acheson, before the committee this last week, practically asserted the right of the President to make war in any emergency without the approval of Congress. This is an assertion of power which no President has ever made before. It threatens the whole constitutional basis of the United States and only exhibits again the complete disregard of this administration for principle, for law, and for the Constitution itself.

And yet now the President is trying to pose as the advocate of peace, and trying to blame the Republicans for advocating a policy which might produce a third world war. It must be recognized in the first place that the policy of containing communism throughout the world—a policy adopted by the administration and supported by both parties—is always risking a third world war if the Russians want to start it. We risked the third world war when we went into Greece; when we armed Turkey; when we proposed a European army or a German army; when we operated the air lift.

The President risked a third world war when he started the Korean War. General Bradley clearly implied that in his October 1950 article when he said:

"And if the defense of South Korea was risking allout war, the choice was not ours, for the Communists have thrown down the gauntlet."

Another strange inconsistency was exhibited by the President in his radio speech on April 11. He said that he had prevented World War III by moving into Korea on the theory that failure to punish aggression would have encouraged Russia to make war. But in the second half of his speech he says that he is preventing World War III by not punishing aggression when the aggressor is Communist China and waging only a soft war. If the success of aggression encourages war, then the present American policy is encouraging war. Under our policy of a cease-fire at the thirty-eighth parallel, the aggressor apparently has everything to gain and nothing to lose. The Chinese Communists have captured half of Korea and their aggression is peculiarly flagrant because it is against the United Nations itself. Yet they are perfectly safe. They can lose nothing. No bombs can be dropped on their land; no blockade can be enforced against them. The Nationalist Chinese Army is prevented from making any attempt to invade South China or build up a popular front in South China against communism. True, there is a loss of Chinese manpower, but, as the President pointed out in his speech, "Behind the North Koreans and Chinese Communists in the front lines stand additional millions of Chinese soldiers." Manpower is cheap in China.

Apparently the President is willing to get out of the present war as best he can. The State Department apparently is still willing to discuss the surrender of Formosa and the admission of Chinese Communists to the United Nations. It is willing to consider the retirement of American troops from Korea if the Chinese will withdraw. That would restore us to exactly the position we were in when we withdrew our troops in 1949 and set the stage for a repetition of the whole Korean tragedy. It would undoubtedly bring about the same ultimate result of a Communist Korea.

The administration has been moved to be somewhat more emphatic against the Chinese because of the protest against MacArthur's dismissal, but they still look longingly to such a peace. If such a peace is made, we have wasted 140,000 casualties and billions of dollars.

The Russians must indeed be laughing up their sleeves. They have involved the Americans in an interminable and costly war in which we refuse to strike any effective blow at the enemy. The whole theory of punishing aggression has become a joke. Hereafter, no aggressor is ever to be punished for his aggression, and only the luckless nation which has been attacked is to be ruined by those who undertake to defend him.

Of course, it is beyond our capacity to punish a big aggressor like Communist China. No one advocates the invasion of China by American troops. But that only shows that we cannot carry through the theory of punishing aggression through the United Nations, at least in the Far East, and that World War III can only be prevented by building up our own Armed Forces and using them wisely within our own national capacity.

The MacArthur dismissal has outraged the American people, but it is interesting indeed to note again the strange inconsistency in the President's position. He says that for a year he has been considering the dismissal of General MacArthur; yet, at the Wake Island conference he pinned upon the general a Distinguished Service decoration and publicly praised MacArthur's leadership. As late as January 13, 1951, he sent him a private message saying that "The entire Nation is grateful for your leadership." How can a nation have confidence in double dealing of this kind?

Assistant Secretary Rusk[1] on May 17 suddenly made a major policy speech in which he says we now believe the National Government of Chiang Kai-shek authentically represents the views of the great body of the people of China, and will continue to receive important aid and assistance from the United States. He suddenly announces that we do not recognize the authorities in Peiping for what they pretend to be; that the Peiping regime is not even Chinese. No one who has followed the course of the State Department can reconcile that position with the attitude of Secretary Acheson and the President in January 1950, when they disowned the Nationalist Government and refused even advice. *The New York Times* and the *Washington Post* construed the Rusk speech as a complete reversal of policy. Yet Secretary Acheson can see no difference and goes on asserting that white is black and black is white. So now no one knows what is our policy in China. How can foreign policy be conducted on such a basis?

There can be many disputes as to whether our foreign policy has been right or wrong, but there can be no dispute about the fact that it has lacked frankness, it has lacked consistency, it has been based on pure opportunism and an utter lack of principle.

---

[1] Dean Rusk, who was appointed Secretary of State a decade later by President Kennedy.

In domestic and foreign affairs alike, the American people demand an honest administration, an administration that has some common sense and judgment, an administration that believes in the principles of America and sticks to those principles. The Nation is heartsick that for 19 months more it cannot rid itself of those whose administration is endangering the safety and the liberty of the people.

The Great Betrayal

JOSEPH RAYMOND McCARTHY

Born, Grand Chute, Wisconsin, November 14, 1909; died, Bethesda, Maryland, May 2, 1957. LL.B., Marquette University, Wisconsin, 1935. Admitted to Wisconsin bar, 1935; elected Circuit Court judge, 1939. Served with United States Marine Corps, 1942–1945. Elected to United States Senate, 1946; re-elected, 1952. Established reputation as militant anti-Communist beginning with speech in Wheeling, West Virginia, in February, 1950; his activities added a new word, "McCarthyism," to the language. Chairman, Committee on Government Operations and its Permanent Investigations Sub-Committee, 1953. Censured by Senate, December, 1954, for conduct reflecting on the dignity and integrity of the Senate; his political power declined sharply thereafter.

"Our job is to dislodge the traitors from every place where they have been sent to do their traitorous work."

*T*hank you, *Walter Hallanan* [*the temporary chairman*], *and thank you, fellow Americans,* for the privilege of discussing with you the great overshadowing evil which is the issue of 1952. That issue—or that question—is: Shall America continue to squander her blood, waste her resources and sacrifice her position of world leadership? This is not a Republican issue. This is not a Democrat issue. This, my good friends, is an American issue.

Republican National Convention, Chicago, Illinois, July 9, 1952. *Official Report of the Proceedings of the Twenty-fifth Republican Convention* (Washington: Judd & Detweiler, Inc., 1952), pp. 141–147.

As we approach the all-important November elections, all Americans must keep in mind the facts as they are, not as we wish them to be—even though those facts are raw, harsh and disturbing.

Fact No. 1.   We are at war today, we are at war in Korea, but the Korean war is merely a small phase of the great world war with atheistic Communism.

Fact No. 2.   For the past seven years we have been losing that world war at the rate of nearly one hundred million people a year, not one hundred thousand, but one hundred million people a year to International Communism.

Fact No. 3.   Today on July 9, 1952, the same men who delivered nearly half of the world to Communist Russia are still in control in Washington and in Moscow. There has been no change. The same men are doing your planning, the same planners who have been in control since before 1945—1945, when we were the most powerful nation on earth. Then all we needed with our unlimited military and economic power was enough brains, enough honesty, and enough loyalty to restore a decent and peaceful world. Instead, we allowed Communism to spread its dark shadow over half of Europe and almost all of Asia, and, for the first time there are appearing on the pages of American history such words as stalemate, retreat, compromise.

Now Truman says that the Democrat Party must run on its record. To that I say, Amen, so they must. Let's briefly look at that record. On foreign policy the Democrat Party has produced two planks and two alone. Those planks are: Number 1, fear, and Number 2, war.

At war's end, our foreign policy, if we can call it that, was to tear down America's might and build up Russia. We put torches to our planes. We destroyed in Europe equipment for 60 divisions. We dumped into the Atlantic and Indian Oceans hundreds of thousands of tons of military equipment. Nothing secret about this. It is all part of the cold documented record before Congressional committees. We dissipated our strength despite the warnings of our great veterans' organizations. We decimated our army in a matter of months.

Why, ladies and gentlemen, has this Administration deliberately built up Russia while tearing down the strength of America? I have been proving that it was because of a combination of abysmal stupidity and treason. If I am wrong, if no treason is involved, if the last traitor left with Alger Hiss, then the only answer for our loss and Russia's gain is that those in power are guilty of stumbling, fumbling incompetence. But in either event, whether it is because of treason or stupidity—if America and her sons are to live—then, that Yalta-Teheran-Potsdam crowd must go. I have enough faith in America to feel sure that they will go— on November 4, 1952.

Now why is it so hard to uncover those who would betray America? Why must we have a Republican President and Congress to get rid of those who are found at every time and place where success comes to Communist Russia and disaster comes to America? Here perhaps is the best answer, in the testimony before the McCarran Committee, the testimony of General Willoughby, for years the head of the intelligence staff of one of the greatest Americans ever born, General Douglas MacArthur.

Listen to what General Willoughby said when asked to give a Senate Committee the record of some of the State Department's architects for disaster—records which were carefully documented in Army Intelligence files. Let me read it to you. On pages 387 and 388 of the hearings of August 9, 1951. He was asked about some of those unusual individuals in the State Department. This is his answer. He said: "Mr. Chairman, as a citizen I am most anxious to assist this important committee. However, as a Federal officer I am expected to obey Army orders and the President's directives."

"Question. Read the President's directive."

Listen to this, if you will. Here is the order to the head of the intelligence section:

"You shall give no information of any sort relating to any Federal employee's loyalty or his Communistic proclivities to any Congressional Committee."

Then he was asked to read the Army directive:

"Any individual who appears as a witness before a Congressional Committee will respectfully decline to testify concerning the loyalty of any person and will refer the answer to such question to the Inspector General of the Army."

Ladies and gentlemen, is there anyone in this hall, anyone in this audience who will tell you why the Secretary of Defense says it is a crime not to betray this nation but a crime to expose those who are betraying this nation?

This task of taking down from the watchtowers of this nation those who have been so bad for America should not be a fight between America's two great political parties. Certainly the millions of Americans who have long voted the Democrat ticket are no less loyal to America than the Republicans. Certainly they love America as much as the average Republican. Certainly, their hatred for Communism is just as great as that of Republicans. But unfortunately the loyal Democrats of this nation no longer have a party. I do not ask those loyal Democrats to desert their party. I merely ask them to look at the cold record and find out that their party has deserted them.

I call upon those Democrats today to scrub and flush and wash clean this Government by voting the Republican ticket this fall.

In this fight, some of my good friends have accused me of being too rough. To them I say there is a common-sense limit to gentleness and delicacy. That limit is where disloyalty and treason begin, where organized deceit and godlessness begin. If we are to win this fight, my friends, we must use all the intelligence, all the courage, all the skill, every effort of mind and body, if as is obviously the case, a rough fight is the only fight Communists can understand, take my word for it, the Republican Party will give them a rough fight. Even though it might be less unpleasant to do it another way, we cannot fight Communists or Communism in the Acheson-Lattimore[1] fashion of hitting them with

[1] Among McCarthy's favorite targets were Secretary of State Acheson, Owen Lattimore, a

a perfumed silk handkerchief at the front door while they batter our friends with brass knuckles and blackjacks at the back door.

My good friends, I say one Communist in a defense plant is one Communist too many.

One Communist on the faculty of one university is one Communist too many.

One Communist among the American advisers at Yalta was one Communist too many.

And even if there were only one Communist in the State Department, that would still be one Communist too many.

Our job is to dislodge the traitors from every place where they have been sent to do their traitorous work.

You, the American people, 155 million American people, have given the administration Democrats the task of manning the watchtowers of this nation for the past 20 years. You have given them every cent of money they asked and more. You, the American people, have given them power surpassed only by an absolute dictatorship. During that 20 years America has fought one World War and in the Korean War—which, according to Truman, is not a war—they have squandered the blood of 110,631 sons of American mothers. They have increased the debt of this nation from 23 billion dollars to 257 billion dollars. They have made dishonesty, graft, corruption, and immorality the rule and not the exception.

On November 4, if this nation is to live, the American people must say: We are through with the Trumans, the Achesons, the Lattimores, and the Jessups. America must say to them at long last: "Make an accounting of thy stewardship for thou canst be steward no longer." Make an accounting of Korea.

The Acheson-Truman-Lattimore party says, "Oh, but it is a limited war in Korea." Yes, limited, my friends, to the area to which the Communists want it limited, limited as to honor, but unlimited as to dishonor, unlimited as to the amount of blood and agony and tears that they have squandered and will squander, unlimited as to the number of American mothers and wives who shall go so deep into the valley of darkness and despair.

Today on July 9, 1952, let me cite to you the most incredibly fantastic order ever issued in war or peace time. Nothing secret about it. The order is in existence at this very moment. It is an order to our 7th Fleet—an order to kill, to shoot down the planes and sink the ships of any anti-Communist Chinese who attempt to interfere with the slaughter of American boys by Communists. Impossible, yes! Unbelievable, yes! But it is all a matter of cold record.

Let me quote, if I may, the effect of that treasonable order. Let me quote Ambassador Bill Bullitt testifying on April 8, 1952. Listen to this, if you will. It is transcript page No. 7578. Ambassador Bullitt was being asked about the effect of this order. He was asked if the Chinese could destroy the Communist ships.

Johns Hopkins professor and occasional State Department consultant, and Philip Jessup, professor of International Law at Columbia and United States Ambassador-at-large. He used them as symbols of striped-pants dilettantism in the State Department.

Ambassador Bullitt was testifying before the McCarran Committee and Senator Watkins had just asked him about the Navy of the anti-Communist Chinese. Here is Bullitt's answer:

"Oh, yes, they (the anti-Communist Chinese) have a Navy. As a matter of fact, it has been quite an efficient force, although it is forbidden to act in any way by order of our Government, which has given orders to our fleet to prevent it from stopping the Communist supply ships going up to Korea. They sail right by Formosa, equipped with Soviet munitions put in the Polish Communist ships in Gdynia. They come all the way around and go right by Formosa and sail past there taking those weapons up to be used to kill American soldiers in Korea, and by order of our Government, the Chinese Navy is flatly forbidden to stop them on their way up there."

Why does our State Department insist that the sons of American mothers must protect and guard the weapons being shipped to kill the sons of other American mothers?

Now you, 155 million Americans, can decide whether you want more of this. If you do, just go ahead and vote Democrat this fall. If, as I am sure, you are sick way down deep inside at the dishonesty, the corruption, the sellout of America in every corner of the world, then give us, the Republicans, a chance to do the job which the Democrats have so miserably failed to do over the past 20 years.

I would like to make one solemn promise to the millions of Americans in our radio and television audience. That promise is this: Put the Republicans in power this fall and I promise that you won't be in any wars that we are afraid to win.

The job of every Republican in this dark year of 1952 is to take the facts to the American people. We need not try to argue or persuade. Our task is merely to give the American people unvarnished truth. Then don't worry. If the American people have the facts on November 4, it will be one of the greatest days for America and for the world in many decades.

Robert Vogeler returned to this country a short time ago after 18 months in a Communist prison cell—18 months of being tortured because he dared to be a loyal American.[2] He has been carrying on an apparently hopeless battle to induce this nation to do something about the other 5,000 Americans who, as of tonight, July 9th, 1952, are rotting in Communist prison cells throughout Russia and her satellite nations.

Bob Vogeler is here in this hall this afternoon. He is here and not being tortured in a Communist prison cell, thanks to a courageous wife who has refused to let the State Department forget him. If you want to get more of the story ask Bob Vogeler.

Bob Vogeler, will you stand up?

[Mr. and Mrs. Robert Vogeler, in the balcony, arise and receive an ovation.]

Thank you, Bob Vogeler, and Mrs. Vogeler.

[2] Vogeler had been imprisoned by the Hungarian Government on spy charges.

But Mr. Truman says there is nothing wrong in the State Department, he says everything is just fine, he has actually said that if anyone hears of anything wrong, just call him collect and he personally will take care of things.

Mr. Truman, your telephone is ringing tonight. Five thousand Americans are calling, calling from prison cells deep inside Russia and her satellite nations. They are homesick, Mr. Truman. They are lonely and maybe a little afraid. Answer your telephone, Mr. Truman. It will be interesting to hear what you have to say. Some of them haven't heard an American speak for years. But, Mr. Truman, they are getting a busy signal on your line. They will call Washington again; they will call again when the American people are through with you, Mr. Truman, and through with the Achesons, the Jessups, and the Lattimores.

And I say to Bob Vogeler and his courageous wife and to those five thousand Americans that when we, the Republican Party, take over we promise that the telephone line won't be busy to five thousand people any longer.

Why must we, the American people, be forced to cringe in the face of Communism? What has happened to our courage, our determination, and our intelligence?

That is not what America wants. The American people are not soft, nor are we afraid. What we need in Washington is someone to express the resolute determination of the people of the United States to back down no further, to fight back with the weight of skill, intelligence, courage, and the truth that is ours. We can as a country no longer stand idle as the mimics of the Moscow party line sell us short. The days of dilettante diplomacy are running out. Sugared phrases are fine for Washington teas. But this is not a tea party. Put some men with grass-roots common sense in charge of the Government, and then watch America go. It is peace we want and peace we can have. Peace with courage, and with honor.

That is what the Republican Party promises the American people.

There was a time when the United States could sit with honor in the council of nations. Today she must cast down her eyes in shame for the sons she has betrayed—the allies she has betrayed—Poland, Czechoslovakia, Yugoslavia, the Baltic States, Korea, China.

Fellow Americans, if our civilization is to live, this groveling and indecision on the part of this great nation must stop. And it will stop when we elect a Republican President and Congress on November 4th of this year.

For the past five years I have witnessed the complete moral decay of the leadership of what should be the greatest nation on earth. I would like to tell you a story that was told me by a good friend from Wisconsin. I would like to repeat it to you here today, if I may.

In the South Pacific there had been a dive bombing attack on our boys. I guess Truman would call it a police action. As our soldiers were struggling through the Pacific Islands, they finally got bases at Bougainville. I recall the morning before our first strike, when we were all gathered together, after the briefing had been completed, after the sections and squads were told where they had to go and what they were to do. My commanding officer said to the Chaplain, "We know a lot of these young men are going to die today. I thought you might have a few words to say to them."

The Chaplain got up and said, "Yes, Major, I have a few words to say to them." And I might say in passing that that chaplain was killed a few minutes later. But that morning he rose up and here is what he said, "You young men, regardless of whether you are killed in the next six hours or whether you live for sixty years, if you will remember two fundamental truths taught by every religious group, by every religious sect, since the beginning of time, if you will recall, No. 1, that there is a God ever eternal, and, second, that you have a soul which is immortal, then you need have no fear for yourself or for your country, regardless of whether it is six hours or sixty years."

Ladies and gentlemen, I have often thought over the past five years, as I witnessed our steady, deliberate retreat from the victory those young men achieved with their blood, that if only those Democrats and Republicans alike had only kept in mind the words of that chaplain, who was about to die, to those young men who were about to die, then the 155 million American people can hope, even at this time, even though the sands in the hour-glass of time are running out. If the American people can get together, America's two great parties, and both join in this fight, do the job which can still be done in the creation of a decent people's republic, then the rights of all men can be saved.

Colossal Innocence in the United States Senate

RALPH E. FLANDERS

Born, Barnet, Vermont, September 28, 1880. Graduated, high school, Central Falls, Rhode Island, 1896. Apprenticed to Brown and Sharpe Manufacturing Company, Providence, Rhode Island, to learn machinist trade. At age of 22, began study of engineering by mail from International Correspondence Schools. Remained in machine tool industry as draftsman, designer, editor, engineer, and executive for nearly fifty years. President, Federal Reserve Bank of Boston, 1944–1946. Resigned as Chairman of the Board of Jones and Lamson Machine Company to accept appointment to United States Senate to fill unexpired term of Senator Warren Austin, 1946. Elected to Senate, 1946; re-elected, 1952, retiring at the end of his second full term.

"Were the junior Senator from Wisconsin in the pay of the Communists, he could not have done a better job for them."

*M*r. *President,* I propose for a few minutes to address this body on the subject of the colossal innocence of the junior Senator from Wisconsin [Mr. McCarthy].

I am not using the word "innocence" in the meaning of freedom from guilt for no question of guilt is involved. Rather the meaning is that of the blithe heed-

United States Senate, June 1, 1954. *Congressional Record*, 83rd Cong., 2nd Sess., vol. 100, pt. 6, pp. 7389–7390.

lessness of the young, who blunder innocently into the most appalling situations, as they ramble through the world of adults. Perhaps the best illustration of this kind of innocence is to be found in a popular cartoon series published daily under the title "Dennis the Menace."

Our busy Senator does get us adults into all kinds of trouble. His constructive activities consist largely in pulling personalities out of the FBI files and displaying them under the television lights. This is certainly a labor-saving operation, but it is not his only activity. Besides this, and while doing this, he spreads division and confusion wherever he goes. Note, for instance, the foreboding he inspires in our fellow citizens of Jewish blood and faith. Among them this is well-nigh universal, in spite of the fact that some of his closest associates are Hebrews. In seeking the origin of this foreboding, I have been led to remember the part the Senator played in the investigation of the Malmedy massacres, and the strange tenderness he displayed for the Nazi ruffians involved.

Perhaps this would not have been enough to perpetuate foreboding, but his anticommunism so completely parallels that of Adolf Hitler as to strike fear into the heart of any defenseless minority. We should always remember, by the way, that communism, nazism, and other dictatorships resemble each other far more closely than any of them resembles the free world into which we were born, and in which we hope that our children and grandchildren will live.

It was not the Jews alone who had reason to be troubled. The former chief of staff of the Senator's committee, without a word of rebuke from his superior, charged the Protestant ministry with being, in effect, the center of Communist influence in this country. Here the attack was on a vigorous, indignant majority, and the chief of staff had to go.

But the ghost of religious intolerance was not laid. Clearer and clearer evidence came to light of the danger of setting church against church, Catholic against Protestant. At a recent communion breakfast of the New York police force, the Senator made a characteristic speech, blaming the Pentagon for not compelling the release of the remaining prisoners of the Chinese Communists. He did not say how this could be done short of renewing the war. Then he referred to his own proudest achievement—the detection of the pink dentist.[1] Loud cheers from most of the audience—others silent.

Then Monsignor McCaffrey went into a eulogistic oration on the public service of our Senator. More cheers and silences.

Cardinal Spellman entered during the Monsignor's introduction and shook hands with our Senator. He arrived late and left early, but he did shake hands. Did this mean that the imprimatur of "nihil obstat" had been set by the church on these debonair campaigns to divide Americans from each other on religious lines? It looked like a pretty serious business.

[1] Seeking to prove that the Pentagon was soft toward Communism, McCarthy blew up the case of Irving Peress, an army dentist with allegedly left-wing sympathies, who had been promoted automatically to Major under the Doctors Draft Law.

But soon, thank God, from Chicago another voice was heard. It was that of a high and respected member of the Catholic Church, Bishop Sheil. He said that our Senator is doing more harm than good, and is dividing the United States instead of uniting it in a cause that of itself is supported by every good citizen. Continuing, the bishop said:

An America which has lost faith in the integrity of the Government, the Army, the schools, the churches, the labor unions, and most of all an America whose citizens have lost faith in each other—such an America would not need to bother about being anti-Communist; it would have nothing to lose.

Such an America—

He added—

would have nothing to recommend it to freedom-loving men—nothing at all, not even the shining image of its victorious junior Senator from Wisconsin.

Thus it became evident that Dennis the Menace had driven his blundering ax deep into the heart of his own church.

His success in dividing his country and his church is paralleled by his un-paralleled success in dividing his own party. While only a minority leader, his following is faithful and loud. This again raises uncomfortable comparisons with dictators elsewhere in the world. Not so long ago our Senator made one—just one —Republican speech. It was extreme, but it contained some painful truths. There were hopes that he might rejoin the party. But he soon dissipated these hopes, and instead resumed his ax-happy efforts to split it.

He has achieved the incredible success of persuading Republican Senators into a detailed and relentless search for some significant evidence of subversions in the Republican administration—and this in an election year. The search has no limits in minuteness or altitude. It reaches into the White House itself.

The cooperating group in the Senate is not large. It is not completely hypno-tized. It is led on by the pitiful hope that some magic means may be found whereby Dennis the Menace will be transformed into a Republican asset.

Meanwhile, the investigation goes on and on. There are new synthetic and irrelevant mysteries served up each day, like the baker's breakfast buns, delivered to the door hot out of the oven. But the committee has not yet dug into the real heart of the mystery. That mystery concerns the personal relationships of the Army private, the staff assistant, and the Senator.[2]

This hubbub centers on the Army private. What is it really all about? His usefulness as an investigator is continually asserted, but never documented. Let

---

[2] Flanders refers here to the Army-McCarthy hearings then in progress. A subcommittee of the United States Senate was investigating charges by Robert Stevens, Secretary of the Army, that McCarthy at the behest of Roy Cohen, his staff assistant, sought preferential treatment for Private D. David Schine, another McCarthy staff member. McCarthy countered Stevens' allega-tions by charging that the Army was using Private Schine as a hostage to halt further in-vestigations of "Communist coddling" in the Army.

him also be investigated. When he is released for committee work, what does he do hour by hour? Whom does he see? What material does he analyze? What does he report? These questions are important and unanswered.

Then, there is the relationship of the staff assistant to the Army private. It is natural that he should wish to retain the services of an able collaborator, but he seems to have an almost passionate anxiety to retain him. Why?

And, then, there is the Senator himself. At times he seems anxious to rid himself of the whole mess, and then again, at least in the presence of his assistant, he strongly supports the latter's efforts to keep the Army private's services available. Does the assistant have some hold on the Senator? Can it be that our Dennis, so effective in making trouble for his elders, has at last gotten into trouble himself? Does the committee plan to investigate the real issues at stake?

Let us now leave these interesting domestic details and look at the worldwide strategy of communism. Let us begin by remembering that a while ago the Senator from Maine [Mrs. Smith] was denounced by the Moscow press as an enemy of the people—that is, of communism. I have myself been honored by the same accolade. If the junior Senator from Wisconsin has ever been attacked by *Pravda,* it has not come to my attention.

In every country in which communism has taken over, the beginning has been a successful campaign of division and confusion. Race is set against race, party against party, religion against religion, neighbor against neighbor, and child against parent. Until lately we have been free of that. We are so no longer.

We have marveled at the way in which the Soviet Government has won its military successes in Asia without risking its own resources or its own men. It has been willing to continue the conflict until the last Chinese Communist is killed.

What we are now seeing is another example of economy of effort and expansion of success in the conquest of this country for communism. The preliminary campaign is successfully under way. One of the characteristic elements of Communist and Fascist tyranny is at hand, as citizens are set to spy upon each other. Established and responsible government is besmirched. Religion is set against religion, race against race. Churches and parties are split asunder. All is division and confusion.

Were the junior Senator from Wisconsin in the pay of the Communists, he could not have done a better job for them.

This is colossal innocence, indeed.

Valedictory

HARRY S TRUMAN

Born, Lamar, Missouri, May 8, 1884. Educated in the local public schools. Operated family farm, 1906–1917. Served in Field Artillery during World War I. Studied nights at Kansas City School of Law, 1923–1925. Judge of Jackson County Court, 1922–1924, and Presiding Judge, 1926–1934. As a Democrat, he was elected to the United States Senate from Missouri, 1934, and re-elected, 1940. Achieved prominence during World War II as chairman of the Senate Committee to Investigate the National Defense Program. Nominated and elected Vice-President of the United States, 1944. Succeeded to the Presidency upon the death of Roosevelt, April 12, 1945. Won a second term in 1948 with a surprising defeat of Thomas Dewey, the Republican candidate, as well as candidates of the Progressive party and the Dixiecrats. His second administration was primarily occupied with cold war policies.

"But when history says that my term of office saw the beginning of the 'cold war,' it will also say that in those eight years we have set the course that can win it."

I am happy to have this opportunity to talk to you once more before I leave the White House.

Next Tuesday, General Eisenhower will be inaugurated as President of the United States. A short time after the new President takes his oath of office, I will once again be a plain, private citizen of this Republic.

Delivered to the nation over radio and television, Washington, D.C., January 15, 1953. *The New York Times,* January 16, 1953, p. 10. Reprinted by permission of *The New York Times.*

That is as it should be. Inauguration Day will be a great demonstration of our democratic process. I am glad to be a part of it—glad to wish General Eisenhower all possible success, as he begins his term—glad the whole world will have a chance to see how simply and how peacefully our American system transfers the vast power of the Presidency from my hands to his. It is a good object lesson in democracy. I am proud of it. I know you are, too.

During the last two months, I have done my best to make this transfer an orderly one. I have talked with my successor on the affairs of the country, both foreign and domestic, and my cabinet officers have talked with their successors. I want to say that General Eisenhower and his associates have cooperated fully in this effort. Such an orderly transfer from one party to another has never taken place before in our history. I think a real precedent has been set.

In speaking to you tonight, I have no new revelations to make—no political statements—no policy announcements. There are simply a few things in my heart I want to say to you. I want to say "good-bye" and "thanks for your help." And I want to talk with you a little about what has happened since I became your President.

I am speaking to you from the room where I have worked since April, 1945. This is the President's office in the west wing of the White House. And this is the desk where I have signed most of the papers that embodied the decisions I have made as President. It has been the desk for many Presidents, and will be the desk of many more.

Since I became President, I have been to Europe, Mexico, Canada, Brazil, Puerto Rico and the Virgin Islands—Wake Island and Hawaii. I have visited almost every state in the Union. I have traveled 135,000 miles by air, 77,000 by rail and 17,000 by ship. But the mail always followed me, and wherever I happened to be, that's where the office of the President was.

The greatest part of the President's job is to make decisions—big ones and small ones, dozens of them almost every day. The papers may circulate around the Government for a while but they finally reach this desk. And then, there's no place else for them to go. The President—whoever he is—has to decide. He can't pass the buck to anybody. No one else can do the deciding for him. That's his job.

That's what I've been doing here in this room, for almost eight years now. And over in the main part of the White House, there's a study on the second floor— a room much like this one—where I have worked at night and early in the morning on the papers I couldn't get to at the office.

Of course, for more than three years, Mrs. Truman and I were not living in the White House. We were across the street in the Blair House. That was when the White House almost fell down on us and had to be rebuilt. I had a study over at the Blair House, too, but living in the Blair House was not as convenient as living in the White House.

The Secret Service wouldn't let me walk across the street, so I had to get in a car every morning to cross the street to the White House office, again at noon to go to the Blair House for lunch, again to go back to the office after lunch, and finally take an automobile at night to return to the Blair House. Fantastic, isn't it? But necessary, so my guard thought—and they are the bosses on such matters as that.

Now, of course, we're back in the White House. It is in very good condition, and General Eisenhower will be able to take up his residence in the house and work right here. That will be much more convenient for him, and I'm very glad the renovation job was all completed before his term began.

Your new President is taking office in quite different circumstances than when I became President eight years ago. On April 12, 1945, I had been presiding over the Senate in my capacity as Vice President. When the Senate recessed about 5 o'clock in the afternoon, I walked over to the office of the Speaker of the House, Mr. Rayburn, to discuss pending legislation.

As soon as I arrived I was told that Mr. Early, one of President Roosevelt's secretaries, wanted me to call. I reached Mr. Early, and he told me to come to the White House as quickly as possible, to enter by way of the Pennsylvania Avenue entrance, and come to Mrs. Roosevelt's study.

When I arrived, Mrs. Roosevelt told me the tragic news, and I felt the shock that all of you felt a little later—when the word came over the radio and appeared in the newspapers. President Roosevelt had died. I offered to do anything I could for Mrs. Roosevelt, and then I asked the Secretary of State to call the Cabinet together.

At 7:09 P.M., I was sworn in as President by Chief Justice Stone in the Cabinet room.

Things were happening fast in those days. The San Francisco conference to organize the United Nations had been called for April 25. I was asked if that meeting would go forward. I announced that it would.

After attending President Roosevelt's funeral I went to the hall of the House of Representatives and told a joint session of the Congress that I would carry on President Roosevelt's policies.

On May 7, Germany surrendered. The announcement was made on May 8, my sixty-first birthday.

Mr. Churchill called me shortly after that and wanted a meeting with me and Prime Minister Stalin of Russia. Later on, a meeting was agreed upon and Churchill, Stalin and I met at Potsdam, in Germany.

Meanwhile, the first atomic explosion took place out in the New Mexico desert.

The war against Japan was still going on. I made the decision that the atomic bomb had to be used to end it. I made that decision in the conviction it would save hundreds of thousands of lives—Japanese as well as American. Japan surrendered, and we were faced with the huge problems of bringing the troops home and reconverting the economy from war to peace.

All these things happened within just a little over four months—from April to August, 1945. I tell you this to illustrate the tremendous scope of the work your President has to do.

All these emergencies and all the developments to meet them have required the President to put in long hours—usually seventeen hours a day, with no payment for overtime. I sign my name on the average 600 times a day, see and talk to hundreds of people every month, shake hands with thousands every year, and still carry on the business of the largest going concern in the world.

There is no job like it on the face of the earth—in the power which is concentrated here at this desk, and in the responsibility and difficulty of the decisions.

I want all of you to realize how big a job, how hard a job, it is—not for my sake, because I am stepping out of it—but for the sake of my successor. He needs the understanding and the help of every citizen. It is not enough for you to come out once every four years and vote for a candidate, and then go back home and say, "Well, I've done my part, now let the new President do the worrying." He can't do the job alone.

Regardless of your politics, whether you are Republican or Democrat, your fate is tied up with what is done here in this room. The President is President of the whole country. We must all give him our support as citizens of the United States. He will have mine, and I want you to give him yours.

I suppose that history will remember my term in office as the years when the "cold war" began to overshadow our lives. I have had hardly a day in office that has not been dominated by this all-embracing struggle—this conflict between those who love freedom and those who would lead the world back into slavery and darkness. And always in the background there has been the atomic bomb.

But when history says that my term of office saw the beginning of the "cold war," it will also say that in those eight years we have set the course that can win it. We have succeeded in carving out a new set of policies to attain peace—positive policies, policies of world leadership, policies that express faith in other free people. We have averted World War III up to now, and we may already have succeeded in establishing conditions which can keep that war from happening as far ahead as man can see.

These are great and historic achievements that we can all be proud of. Think of the difference between our course now and our course thirty years ago. After the first World War we withdrew from world affairs—we failed to act in concert with other peoples against aggression—we helped to kill the League of Nations—and we built up tariff barriers which strangled world trade.

This time, we avoided those mistakes. We helped to found and to sustain the United Nations. We have welded alliances that include the greater part of the free world. And we have gone ahead with other free countries to help build their economies and link us all together in a healthy world trade.

Think back for a moment to the Nineteen Thirties and you will see the difference. The Japanese moved into Manchuria, and free men did not act. The Fascists moved into Ethiopia, and we did not act. The Nazis marched into the Rhine-land, into Austria, into Czechoslovakia, and free men were paralyzed for lack of strength and unity of will.

Think about those years of weakness and indecision, and World War II which was their evil result. Then think about the speed and courage and decisiveness with which we have moved against the Communist threat since World War II.

The first crisis came in 1945 and 1946, when the Soviet Union refused to honor its agreement to remove its troops from Iran. Members of my Cabinet came to me and asked if we were ready to take the risk that a firm stand involved. I re-plied that we were. So we took our stand—we made it clear to the Soviet Union that we expected them to honor their agreement—and the Soviet troops were withdrawn.

And then, in early 1947, the Soviet Union threatened Greece and Turkey. The British sent me a message saying they could no longer keep their forces in that area. Something had to be done at once, or the Eastern Mediterranean would be taken over by the Communists.

On March 12, I went before the Congress and stated our determination to help the people of Greece and Turkey maintain their independence. Today, Greece is still free and independent; and Turkey is a bulwark of strength at a strategic corner of the world.

Then came the Marshall Plan which saved Europe, the heroic Berlin Airlift, and our military aid programs.

We inaugurated the North Atlantic Pact, the Rio Pact binding the Western Hemisphere together, and the defense pacts with countries of the Far Pacific.

Most important of all, we acted in Korea.

I was in Independence, Missouri, in June, 1950, when Secretary Acheson tel-ephoned me and gave me the news about the invasion of Korea. I told the Secre-tary to lay the matter at once before the United Nations, and I came on back to Washington.

Flying back over the flatlands of the Middle West and over the Appalachians that summer afternoon I had a lot of time to think. I turned the problem over in my mind in many ways, but my thoughts kept coming back to the Nineteen Thirties—to Manchuria—Ethiopia—the Rhineland—Austria—and finally to Munich.

Here was history repeating itself. Here was another probing action, another testing action. If we let the Republic of Korea go under, some other country would be next, and then another. And all the time, the courage and confidence of the free world would be ebbing away, just as it did in the Nineteen Thirties. And the United Nations would go the way of the League of Nations.

When I reached Washington I met immediately with the Secretary of State, the Secretary of Defense and General Bradley, and the other civilian and military officials who had information and advice to help me decide what to do. We talked about the problems long and hard.

It was not easy to make the decision that sent American boys again into battle. I was a soldier in the first World War and I know what a soldier goes through. I knew well the anguish that mothers and fathers and families go through. So I knew what was ahead if we acted in Korea.

But after all this was said, we realized that the issue was whether there would be fighting in a limited area now or on a much larger scale later on—whether there would be some casualties now or many more casualties later.

So a decision was reached—the decision I believe was the most important in my time as President.

In the days that followed, the most heartening fact was that the American people clearly agreed with the decision.

And in Korea, our men are fighting as valiantly as Americans have ever fought—because they know they are fighting in the same cause of freedom in which Americans have stood ever since the beginning of the Republic.

Where free men had failed the test before, this time we met the test.

We met it firmly. We met it successfully. The aggression has been repelled. The Communists have seen their hopes of easy conquest go down the drain. The determination of free people to defend themselves has been made clear to the Kremlin.

As I have thought about our world-wide struggle with the Communists these past eight years—day in and day out—I have never once doubted that you, the people of our country, have the will to do what is necessary to win this terrible fight against communism. I know the people of this country have that will and determination and I have always depended upon it.

Because I have been sure of that, I have been able to make necessary decisions even though they called for sacrifices by all of us. And I have not been wrong in my judgment of the American people.

That same assurance of our people's determination will be General Eisenhower's greatest source of strength in carrying on this struggle.

Now, once in a while, I get a letter from some impatient person asking, why don't we get it over with? Why don't we issue an ultimatum, make all-out war, drop the atomic bomb?

For most Americans, the answer is quite simple: We are not made that way. We are a moral people. Peace is our goal, with justice and freedom. We cannot, of our own free will violate the very principles that we are striving to defend. The whole purpose of what we are doing is to prevent World War III. Starting a war is no way to make peace.

But if anyone still thinks that, just this once, bad means can bring good ends, then let me remind you of this: We are living in the eighth year of the atomic age. We are not the only nation that is learning to unleash the power of the atom. A third World War might dig the grave not only of our Communist opponents but also of our own society, our world as well as theirs.

Starting atomic war is totally unthinkable for rational men.

Then, some of you may ask, when and how will the "cold war" ever end? I think I can answer that simply. The Communist world has great resources, and it looks strong. But there is a fatal flaw in their society. Theirs is a godless system, a system of slavery; there is no freedom in it, no consent. The Iron Curtain, the secret police, the constant purges, all these are symptoms of a great basic weakness —the rulers' fear of their own people.

In the long run, the strength of our free society, and our ideals will prevail over a system that has respect for neither God nor man.

Last week, in my State of the Union message to the Congress—and I hope you will all take the time to read it—I explained how I think we will finally win through.

As the free world grows stronger, more united, more attractive to men on both sides of the Iron Curtain—and as the Soviet hopes for easy expansion are blocked —then there will have to come a time of change in the Soviet world. Nobody can say for sure when that is going to be, or exactly how it will come about, whether by revolution, or trouble in the satellite states, or by a change inside the Kremlin.

Whether the Communist rulers shift their policies of their own free will—or whether the change comes about some other way I have not a doubt in the world that the change will occur.

I have a deep and abiding faith in the destiny of free men. With patience and courage, we shall some day move on into a new era—a wonderful golden age— an age when we can use the peaceful tools that science has forged for us to do away with poverty and human misery everywhere on earth.

Think what can be done, once our capital, our skills, our science—most of all atomic energy—can be released from the tasks of defense and turned wholly to peaceful purposes all around the world.

There is no end to what can be done.

I can't help but dream out loud a little here.

The Tigris and Euphrates Valley can be made to bloom as it did in the times of Babylon and Nineveh. Israel can be made the country of milk and honey as it was in the time of Joshua.

There is a plateau in Ethiopia some six to eight thousand feet high, that has sixty-five thousand square miles of land just exactly like the corn belt of northern Illinois. Enough food can be raised there to feed a hundred million people.

There are places in South America—places in Colombia and Venezuela and Brazil—just like that plateau in Ethiopia—places where food could be raised for millions of people.

These things can be done, and they are self-liquidating projects. If we can get peace and safety in the world under the United Nations, the developments will come so fast we will not recognize the world in which we now live.

This is our dream of the future—our picture of the world we hope to have when the Communist threat is overcome.

I've talked a lot tonight about the menace of communism—and our fight against it—because that is the overriding issue of our time. But there are some other things we've done that history will record. One of them is that we in America have learned how to attain real prosperity for our people.

We have 62,500,000 people at work. Business men, farmers, laborers, white collar people, all have better incomes and more of the good things of life than ever before in the history of the world.

There hasn't been a failure of an insured bank in nearly nine years. No depositor has lost a cent in that period.

And the income of our people has been fairly distributed, perhaps more so than at any time in recent history.

We have made progress in spreading the blessings of American life to all of our people. There has been a tremendous awakening of the American conscience on the great issues of civil rights—equal economic opportunities, equal rights of citizenship and equal educational opportunities for all our people, whatever their race or religion or status of birth.

So, as I empty the drawers of this desk, and as Mrs. Truman and I leave the White House, we have no regret. We feel we have done our best in the public service. I hope and believe we have contributed to the welfare of this nation and to the peace of the world.

When Franklin Roosevelt died I felt there must be a million men better qualified than I to take up the Presidential task. But the work was mine to do, and I had to do it. I have tried to give it everything that was in me.

Through all of it, through all the years that I have worked here in this room, I have been well aware I did not really work alone—that you were working with me.

No President could ever hope to lead our country, or to sustain the burdens of this office, save as the people helped with their support. I have had that help— you have given me that support—on all our great essential undertakings to build the free world's strength and keep the peace.

Those are the big things. Those are the things we have done together.

For that I shall be grateful, always.

And now the time has come for me to say good night and—God bless you all.

The Price of Peace

DWIGHT DAVID EISENHOWER

Born, Denison, Texas, October 14, 1890. Graduated from West Point Military Academy, 1915; commissioned Second Lieutenant, Infantry, U.S. Army; advanced through grades to General of the Army, December, 1944. Allied Commander-in-Chief, North Africa, November 8, 1942; Commanding General, Allied Powers, E.T.O., December 31, 1943; Commander, United States Occupational Forces in Germany, 1945; Chief of Staff, United States Army, 1945–1948. President, Columbia University, 1948–1952; granted indefinite leave of absence to serve as Commander of NATO forces in Europe, 1950. Resigned from the Army, July, 1952. Elected President of the United States, 1952; reelected, 1956.

"We recognize and accept our own deep involvement in the destiny of men everywhere."

*M*r. *Chairman, Mr. Vice President, Mr. Chief Justice, Mr. Speaker, members of my family and friends, my countrymen, and the friends of my country, wherever they may be,* we meet again, as upon a like moment four years ago, and again you have witnessed my solemn oath of service to you.

I, too, am a witness, today testifying in your name to the principles and purposes to which we, as a people, are pledged.

Before all else, we seek, upon our common labor as a nation, the blessings of

Second Inauguration as President of the United States, Washington, D.C., January 21, 1957. *Congressional Record*, 85th Cong., 1st Sess., vol. 103, pt. 1, pp. 805–806.

Almighty God. And the hopes in our hearts fashion the deepest prayers of our whole people.

May we pursue the right without self-righteousness.

May we know unity without conformity.

May we grow in strength without pride in self.

May we, in our dealings with all peoples of the earth, ever speak truth and serve justice.

And so shall America—in the sight of all men of good will—prove true to the honorable purposes that bind and rule us as a people in all this time of trial through which we pass.

We live in a land of plenty, but rarely has this earth known such peril as today.

In our Nation work and wealth abound. Our population grows. Commerce crowds our rivers and rails, our skies, harbors, and highways. Our soil is fertile, our agriculture productive. The air rings with the song of our industry—rolling mills and blast furnaces, dynamos, dams, and assembly lines—the chorus of America the bountiful.

This is our home—yet this is not the whole of our world. For our world is where our full destiny lies—with men, of all peoples, and all nations, who are or would be free. And for them—and so for us—this is no time of ease or of rest.

In too much of the earth there is want, discord, danger. New forces and new nations stir and strive across the earth, with power to bring, by their fate, great good or great evil to the free world's future. From the deserts of North Africa to the islands of the South Pacific one-third of all mankind has entered upon a historic struggle for a new freedom; freedom from grinding poverty. Across all continents, nearly a billion people seek, sometimes almost in desperation, for the skills and knowledge and assistance by which they may satisfy from their own resources, the material wants common to all mankind.

No nation, however old or great, escapes this tempest of change and turmoil. Some, impoverished by the recent World War, seek to restore their means of livelihood. In the heart of Europe, Germany still stands tragically divided. So is the whole Continent divided. And so, too, is all the world.

The divisive force is international communism and the power that it controls.

The designs of that power, dark in purpose, are clear in practice. It strives to seal forever the fate of those it has enslaved. It strives to break the ties that unite the free. And it strives to capture—to exploit for its own greater power—all forces of change in the world, especially the needs of the hungry and the hopes of the oppressed.

Yet the world of international communism has itself been shaken by a fierce and mighty force: the readiness of men who love freedom to pledge their lives to that love. Through the night of their bondage, the unconquerable will of heroes has struck with the swift, sharp thrust of lightning. Budapest is no longer merely the name of a city; henceforth it is a new and shining symbol of man's yearning to be free.

Thus across all the globe there harshly blow the winds of change. And, we—though fortunate be our lot—know that we can never turn our back to them.

We look upon this shaken earth, and we declare our firm and fixed purpose—the building of a peace with justice in a world where moral law prevails.

The building of such a peace is a bold and solemn purpose. To proclaim it is easy. To serve it will be hard. And to attain it, we must be aware of its full meaning—and ready to pay its full price.

We know clearly what we seek, and why.

We seek peace, knowing that peace is the climate of freedom. And now, as in no other age, we seek it because we have been warned, by the power of modern weapons, that peace may be the only climate possible for human life itself.

Yet this peace we seek cannot be born of fear alone: it must be rooted in the lives of nations. There must be justice, sensed and shared by all peoples, for without justice the world can know only a tense and unstable truce. There must be law, steadily invoked and respected by all nations, for without law, the world promises only such meager justice as the pity of the strong upon the weak. But the law of which we speak, comprehending the values of freedom, affirms the equality of all nations, great and small.

Splendid as can be the blessings of such a peace, high will be its cost, in toil patiently sustained, in help honorably given, in sacrifice calmly borne.

We are called to meet the price of this peace.

To counter the threat of those who seek to rule by force, we must pay the costs of our own needed military strength, and help to build the security of others.

We must use our skills and knowledge and, at times, our substance, to help others rise from misery, however far the scene of suffering may be from our shores. For wherever in the world a people knows desperate want, there must appear at least the spark of hope, the hope of progress—or there will surely rise at last the flames of conflict.

We recognize and accept our own deep involvement in the destiny of men everywhere. We are accordingly pledged to honor, and to strive to fortify, the authority of the United Nations. For in that body rests the best hope of our age for the assertion of that law by which all nations may live in dignity.

And beyond this general resolve, we are called to act a responsible role in the world's great concerns or conflicts—whether they touch upon the affairs of a vast region, the fate of an island in the Pacific, or the use of a canal in the Middle East. Only in respecting the hopes and cultures of others will we practice the equality of all nations. Only as we show willingness and wisdom in giving counsel, in receiving counsel, and in sharing burdens, will we wisely perform the work of peace.

For one truth must rule all we think and all we do. No people can live to itself alone. The unity of all who dwell in freedom is their only sure defense. The economic need of all nations—in mutual dependence—makes isolation an impossibility; not even America's prosperity could long survive if other nations did not prosper. No nation can longer be a fortress, lone and strong and safe. And any people, seeking such shelter for themselves, can now build only their own prison.

Our pledge to these principles is constant, because we believe in their rightness.

We do not fear this world of change. America is no stranger to much of its spirit. Everywhere we see the seeds of the same growth that America itself has known. The American experiment has, for generations, fired the passion and the courage of millions elsewhere seeking freedom, equality, and opportunity. And the American story of material progress has helped excite the longing of all needy peoples for some satisfaction of their human wants. These hopes that we have helped to inspire, we can help to fulfill.

In this confidence, we speak plainly to all peoples.

We cherish our friendship with all nations that are or would be free. We respect, no less, their independence. And when, in time of want or peril, they ask our help, they may honorably receive it; for we no more seek to buy their sovereignty than we would sell our own. Sovereignty is never bartered among freemen.

We honor the aspirations of those nations which, now captive, long for freedom. We seek neither their military alliance nor any artificial imitation of our society. And they can know the warmth of the welcome that awaits them when, as must be, they join again the ranks of freedom.

We honor, no less in this divided world than in a less tormented time, the people of Russia. We do not dread, rather do we welcome, their progress in education and industry. We wish them success in their demands for more intellectual freedom, greater security before their own laws, fuller enjoyment of the rewards of their own toil. For as such things come to pass, the more certain will be the coming of that day when our peoples may freely meet in friendship.

So we voice our hope and our belief that we can help to heal this divided world. Thus may the nations cease to live in trembling before the menace of force. Thus may the weight of fear and the weight of arms be taken from the burdened shoulders of mankind.

This, nothing less, is the labor to which we are called and our strength dedicated.

And so the prayer of our people carries far beyond our own frontiers, to the wide world of our duty and our destiny.

May the light of freedom, coming to all darkened lands, flame brightly—until at last the darkness is no more.

May the turbulence of our age yield to a true time of peace, when men and nations shall share a life that honors the dignity of each, the brotherhood of all.

Inaugural Address

JOHN FITZGERALD KENNEDY

Born, Brookline, Massachusetts, May 29, 1917. Graduated from Harvard, cum laude, 1940. Served in the United States Navy, 1941–1945. A Democrat, he was elected to the United States House of Representatives from Massachusetts, 1946; re-elected, 1948 and 1950. Elected to the United States Senate, 1952; re-elected, 1958. Unsuccessful candidate for Democratic Vice-Presidential nomination, 1956. Elected President of the United States, 1960, in a hotly contested campaign featuring four TV debates with his rival, Richard M. Nixon. Author, Why England Slept *(1940) and* Profiles in Courage *(1956), a Pulitzer prize-winning biography.*

"My fellow citizens of the world: Ask not what America will do for you, but what together we can do for the freedom of man."

V *ice President Johnson, Mr. Speaker, Mr. Chief Justice, President Eisenhower, Vice President Nixon, President Truman, Reverend Clergy, Fellow Citizens:* We observe today not a victory of party but a celebration of freedom—symbolizing an end as well as a beginning—signifying renewal as well as change. For I have sworn before you and Almighty God the same solemn oath our forebears prescribed nearly a century and three quarters ago.

Washington, D.C., January 20, 1961. *Congressional Record,* 87th Cong., 1st Sess., vol. 107, pt. I, pp. 970–971. This text has been checked against a tape recording of the speech and minor corrections made. The speech is presented here exactly as delivered.

The world is very different now. For man holds in his mortal hands the power to abolish all forms of human poverty and all forms of human life. And yet the same revolutionary beliefs for which our forebears fought are still at issue around the globe—the belief that the rights of man come not from the generosity of the state but from the hand of God.

We dare not forget today that we are the heirs of that first revolution. Let the word go forth from this time and place, to friend and foe alike, that the torch has been passed to a new generation of Americans—born in this century, tempered by war, disciplined by a hard and bitter peace, proud of our ancient heritage —and unwilling to witness or permit the slow undoing of those human rights to which this nation has always been committed, and to which we are committed today, at home and around the world.

Let every nation know, whether it wishes us well or ill, that we shall pay any price, bear any burden, meet any hardship, support any friend or oppose any foe to assure the survival and the success of liberty.

This much we pledge—and more.

To those old allies whose cultural and spiritual origins we share, we pledge the loyalty of faithful friends. United, there is little we cannot do in a host of cooperative ventures. Divided, there is little we can do—for we dare not meet a powerful challenge at odds and split asunder.

To those new states whom we welcome to the ranks of the free, we pledge our word that one form of colonial control shall not have passed away merely to be replaced by a far more iron tyranny. We shall not always expect to find them supporting our view.

But we shall always hope to find them strongly supporting their own freedom —and to remember that, in the past, those who foolishly sought power by riding the back of the tiger ended up inside.

To those people in the huts and villages of half the globe struggling to break the bonds of mass misery, we pledge our best efforts to help them help themselves, for whatever period is required—not because the Communists may be doing it, not because we seek their votes, but because it is right. If a free society cannot help the many who are poor, it cannot save the few who are rich.

To our sister republics south of our border, we offer a special pledge—to convert our good words into good deeds—in a new alliance for progress—to assist free men and free governments in casting off the chains of poverty. But this peaceful revolution of hope cannot become the prey of hostile powers. Let all our neighbors know that we shall join with them to oppose aggression or subversion anywhere in the Americas. And let every other power know that this hemisphere intends to remain the master of its own house.

To that world assembly of sovereign states, the United Nations, our last best hope in an age where the instruments of war have far outpaced the instruments of peace, we renew our pledge of support—to prevent it from becoming merely a forum for invective—to strengthen its shield of the new and the weak—and to enlarge the area in which its writ may run.

Finally, to those nations who would make themselves our adversary, we offer not a pledge but a request: That both sides begin anew the quest for peace, before the dark powers of destruction unleashed by science engulf all humanity in planned or accidental self-destruction.

We dare not tempt them with weakness. For only when our arms are sufficient beyond doubt can we be certain beyond doubt that they will never be employed.

But neither can two great and powerful groups of nations take comfort from our present course—both sides overburdened by the cost of modern weapons, both rightly alarmed by the steady spread of the deadly atom, yet both racing to alter that uncertain balance of terror that stays the hand of mankind's final war.

So let us begin anew—remembering on both sides that civility is not a sign of weakness, and sincerity is always subject to proof. Let us never negotiate out of fear. But let us never fear to negotiate.

Let both sides explore what problems unite us instead of belaboring those problems which divide us.

Let both sides, for the first time, formulate serious and precise proposals for the inspection and control of arms—and bring the absolute power to destroy other nations under the absolute control of all nations.

Let both sides seek to invoke the wonders of science instead of its terrors. Together let us explore the stars, conquer the deserts, eradicate disease, tap the ocean depths and encourage the arts and commerce.

Let both sides unite to heed in all corners of the earth the command of Isaiah —to "undo the heavy burdens . . . (and) let the oppressed go free."

And if a beachhead of cooperation may push back the jungle of suspicion, let both sides join in creating a new endeavor: not a new balance of power, but a new world of law, where the strong are just and the weak secure and the peace preserved.

All this will not be finished in the first one hundred days. Nor will it be finished in the first one thousand days, nor in the life of this administration, nor even perhaps in our lifetime on this planet. But let us begin.

In your hands, my fellow citizens, more than mine, will rest the final success or failure of our course. Since this country was founded, each generation of Americans has been summoned to give testimony to its national loyalty. The graves of young Americans who answered the call to service surround the globe.

Now the trumpet summons us again—not as a call to bear arms, though arms we need—not as a call to battle, though embattled we are—but a call to bear the burden of a long twilight struggle, year in and year out, "rejoicing in hope, patient in tribulation"—a struggle against the common enemies of man: Tyranny, poverty, disease and war itself.

Can we forge against these enemies a grand and global alliance, North and

South, East and West, that can assure a more fruitful life for all mankind? Will you join in that historic effort?

In the long history of the world, only a few generations have been granted the role of defending freedom in its hour of maximum danger.

I do not shrink from this responsibility—I welcome it. I do not believe that any of us would exchange places with any other people or any other generation. The energy, the faith, the devotion which we bring to this endeavor will light our country and all who serve it—and the glow from that fire can truly light the world.

And so, my fellow Americans: Ask not what your country can do for you— ask what you can do for your country.

My fellow citizens of the world: Ask not what America will do for you, but what together we can do for the freedom of man.

Finally, whether you are citizens of America or citizens of the world, ask of us here the same high standards of strength and sacrifice which we ask of you. With a good conscience our only sure reward, with history the final judge of our deeds, let us go forth to lead the land we love, asking His blessing and His help, but knowing that here on earth God's work must truly be our own.

TO SECURE THESE RIGHTS

"THIS IS NOT a 'White Man's Government,'" Thaddeus Stevens thundered at his opponents in the debate over Reconstruction measures after the Civil War. "To say so is political blasphemy, for it violates the fundamental principles of our gospel of liberty. This is man's Government; the Government of all men alike; not that all men will have equal power and sway within it. . . . But equal rights to all the privileges of the Government is innate in every immortal being, no matter what the shape or color of the tabernacle which it inhabits."[1]

During the Reconstruction period Thaddeus Stevens, Charles Sumner, and their followers in the Congress—partly from humanitarian, partly from political motivations—sought to establish for the American Negro equal rights to all the privileges of the Government. The Thirteenth and Fourteenth Amendments to the Constitution abolished the institution of slavery and made citizens of the former bondsmen. The Fifteenth Amendment made it illegal to deny a citizen the right to vote because of his race or color. For a time it looked as if America might be on the way to giving substance to her Fourth of July slogans of equality for all men under the law.

But the final quarter of the nineteenth century brought a violent reaction against Reconstruction in the South. Negroes were terrorized by the Ku Klux Klan and the threat of lynching by hate-crazed mobs (there were 3000 lynchings from 1876 to 1905). These years saw also wholesale disenfranchisement of the Southern Negro through a variety of devices such as poll taxes, grandfather clauses, and inequitably administered educational and property qualifications. The Negro was effectively consigned to his "place" in society—a separate and inferior place—by means of Jim Crow laws that segregated him from the whites in transportation, recreation, education, and housing. By the 1880s the white Southerners, having swept away or circumvented legal safeguards established during Reconstruction, had regained ascendancy and absolute control.

[1] Speech in the United States Houses of Representatives, December 18, 1865. See Wrage and Baskerville, *American Forum*, pp. 204–212.

Thrown on his own resources, without even such security and protection as the slavery system had afforded, the Negro was without means for acquiring the education upon which advancement depended. Of course, he had received no education before the war either, but then (as his white master was fond of saying) he had no need for education.[2] One of the few successful postwar experiments in Negro education was Tuskegee Institute in Alabama. Established in 1881, Tuskegee sought to provide for its students a high school education and knowledge of a trade, thus making them self-supporting and an asset to the economy of the South, and ultimately of the nation. The articulate young principal of this school, Booker T. Washington, was to become the outstanding spokesman for the Negro race in America for two decades.

Invited to address the Cotton States and International Exposition at Atlanta, Georgia, September 18, 1895, Washington delivered a speech which brought him national recognition as a leader of the Negro people. Booker T. Washington's purpose at Atlanta was "to say something that would cement the friendship of the races." The need of the hour as he saw it was to provide a basis for peaceful coexistence and mutual coöperation between the races, rather than to agitate for the Negroes' "rights." To this end, he urged members of his race to "Cast down your bucket where you are"—in agriculture, mechanics, commerce, domestic service, in the professions, and in making friends with the people of all races. He reminded his people that they must begin at the bottom of life, not at the top; that they would have to advance by the work of their hands; and that they must learn the dignity of common labor. To the whites he made a similar appeal: "Cast down your bucket where you are"—among the loyal people who have tilled your fields, cleared your forests, built your railroads and cities. Calming their fears with the assurance that the wisest Negroes regarded the agitation of questions of social equality as "the extremest folly," he expressed the opinion that the enjoyment of privileges would come ultimately as a result of constant effort toward self-improvement, rather than through "artificial forcing." In his famous metaphor of the hand he accepted social segregation as a fact to be lived with: "In all things that are purely social we can be as separate as the fingers, yet one as the hand in all things essential to mutual progress."

The *modus vivendi* implicit in Washington's proposals was embraced by most whites, North and South, and, perforce, by most Negroes. But some Negro intellectuals regarded Washington's Atlanta doctrine as servile acquiescence in an

---

[2] Georgia's Robert Toombs, for example, stated in 1853, "their station in society makes education neither necessary nor useful." "Slavery in the United States," in Wrage and Baskerville, *American Forum*, pp. 158–168.

unjust system. They ridiculed as "Uncle Tomism" his conciliatory spirit and his advocacy of vocational training for the Negro. The leader of this group was William E. B. DuBois, a scholar of considerable competence, who received his Ph.D. from Harvard in the same year as Washington's Atlanta Address. Where Washington preached that the Negro's advancement would come slowly but inevitably through developing manual skills, making himself economically useful, and acquiring wealth and property, DuBois advocated full manhood suffrage and the advanced education of a "Talented Tenth" who would guide the colored race to a higher civilization and culture.

The DuBois philosophy was given concrete expression in a meeting at Niagara Falls in 1905. The "Niagara Movement" held its first conference the following year at Harpers Ferry, West Virginia, and adopted this militant resolution: "We claim for ourselves every right that belongs to a freeborn American, civil and social, and until we get these rights we shall never cease to protest, and assail the ears of America with the stories of its shameful deeds toward us. We want our manhood suffrage and we want it now." The resolution continued with demands for free association, an end to discrimination in public accommodations, equal enforcement of the laws, and education for Negro children. The Niagara Movement never came to much, coming into conflict as it did with the power and prestige of Booker T. Washington and what DuBois called "The Tuskegee Machine." But it served to dramatize two antithetic points of view among Negro people—the Washington strategy of accommodation, conciliation, and gradualism, and the DuBois strategy of vigorous and continuous protest against a caste system.

Despite the short life of the Niagara Movement, the spirit of protest which it embodied did not die but was perpetuated through another more successful organization, the National Association for the Advancement of Colored People. On September 3, 1908, after a series of violent race riots in Springfield, Illinois, the preceding summer, an article by William E. Walling entitled "Race War in the North" appeared in *The Independent*. Walling urged a revival of the spirit of Lincoln and Lovejoy, and called for a body of citizens to come to the aid of the Negro to prevent an extension of the race war to the North. The article came to the attention of Mary White Ovington, who immediately wrote a letter to its author. In a subsequent meeting between Walling, Miss Ovington, and Dr. Henry Moskowitz, plans were laid for a conference to be held later in New York. On February 12, 1909, the centenary of Lincoln's birth, a call drafted by Oswald Garrison Villard, editor of the New York *Evening Post,* was issued "to all believers in democracy to join in a national conference for the discussion of present evils, the voicing of protests, and the renewal of the struggle for civil and political liberty." Among the fifty-three signers of *The Call* were prominent members of both races, including the Reverend John Haynes Holmes, Rabbi Stephen S. Wise, Professor John Dewey, William Dean Howells, William DuBois, Lincoln Steffens, and Harriett Stanton Blatch. The conference was held in May, and the following year, in May, 1910, the organization was incorporated as the National Association for the Advancement of Colored People, with Moorfield Storey of Boston as its first president. DuBois, the only Negro among the original officers, was named Director of Publications and Research and became the first editor of *The Crisis,* official journal of the NAACP. He was a dominant influence in the new organization from its inception, and at the death of Booker T. Washington in 1915, this advocate of immediate social action against segregation and discrimination succeeded the moderate Tuskegee educator as leading spokesman for his race in America. The NAACP swiftly became, and remains today, the central organization of Negro protest and the outstanding biracial champion of Negro rights.

During its first twenty-five years of existence, the NAACP was able to secure little advancement for colored people.[3] There were slight gains during World War I, but they proved to be temporary. Writing on "The Negro Crisis" in 1907, Washington Gladden—a noted minister of the Social Gospel—quoted a prediction by Carl Schurz that there would be a movement either toward reducing the Negro to permanent serfdom "alongside of the mule," or toward accepting him as a citizen in the full sense of the term. One or the other must prevail. The evidence pointed toward serfdom, but Gladden kept alive a hope that real citizenship would finally be achieved.[4] Governor Coleman Blease of South Carolina, however, expressed a more prevalent attitude toward the colored man in 1913: "God Almighty never intended he should be educated, and the man who attempts to do what God Almighty never intended should be done will be a failure. God made that man to be your servant. The Negro was made to be a hewer of wood and a drawer of water. If he intended him to be your equal, he would have made him white like you and put a bone in his nose."[5]

Repeated humiliation and injustice brought about a disintegration of the faith which since emancipation had sustained the Negro people. In the summer of 1922 Mordecai Johnson, later the distinguished president of Howard University,

[3] Harry S. Ashmore describes the years between 1900 and the New Deal as "the long twilight period," a period when the Negro was no longer a slave, but not yet a citizen. *The Negro and the Schools* (Chapel Hill: University of North Carolina Press, 1954), p. 15.

[4] *The American Magazine,* LXIII (January, 1907), pp. 296–301.

[5] Quoted in Robert L. Jack, *History of the National Association for the Advancement of Colored People* (Boston: Meador Publishing Co., 1943), p. 67.

delivered an address at the Harvard University Commencement which was perhaps the most notable speech given by a Negro since Booker T. Washington's Atlanta Exposition Address.[6] Johnson reported widespread disillusionment among Negroes:

> They see themselves surrounded on every hand by a sentiment of antagonism which does not intend to be fair. They see themselves partly reduced to peonage, shut out from labor unions, forced to an inferior status before the courts, made subjects of public contempt, lynched and mobbed with impunity, and deprived of the ballot, their only means of social defense. They see this antagonistic sentiment consolidated in the places of power in the former slave States and growing by leaps and bounds in the North and West. They know that it is gradually reducing them to an economic, political, and social caste. And they are now no longer able to believe with Dr. Booker T. Washington, or with any other man, that their own efforts after intelligence, wealth, and self-respect can in any wise avail to deliver them from these conditions unless they have the protection of a just and beneficent public policy in keeping with American ideals.

In behalf of his people, Johnson entered a plea for protection of life and property, for freedom from peonage, for justice in the courts, for public education, for the boon of the ballot—in short, "for public equality under the protection of the Federal Government."

Johnson's plea went largely unheeded, and during the great depression Negroes were among those hardest hit, since so many were among the ranks of the unskilled workers at the bottom of the economic ladder. With the advent of the New Deal, however, Negro leaders shared the buoyant spirit abroad in the land. Mary McLeod Bethune, director of an Office of Minority Affairs in the National Youth Administration, expressed the opinion that "Never before in the history of America has Negro youth been offered such opportunities."[7] Government solicitude for the Negro may have been motivated by a cynical bid for votes as much as by warm humanitarianism, for the northward migration of Negroes and their concentration in industrial cities like Chicago, New York, and Detroit had begun to attract the attention of northern politicians.

World War II brought a few more halting steps toward "public equality under

---

[6] "The Faith of the American Negro." Text in the *Nation*, CXV (July 19, 1922), pp. 64–65.

[7] Quoted in Arthur M. Schlesinger, Jr., *The Politics of Upheaval* (Boston: Houghton Mifflin Co., 1960), p. 436.

the protection of the Federal Government." In 1941, President Roosevelt issued an executive order establishing the Committee on Fair Employment Practice to formulate and execute policies for prevention of racial discrimination in employment in governmental agencies and in work done under government contract.[8] In 1942 the first Negro officers in the Air Force were commissioned, the first Negro Marine Corps units were activated, the Navy relaxed limited quotas for Negro personnel; and in 1944 the Navy commissioned its first Negro officers. In 1946 the Supreme Court ruled against racial segregation of passengers in interstate bus travel, and both the CIO and AFL conducted drives to organize labor without racial restrictions.

A dramatic step forward came in December, 1946, when President Truman appointed a fifteen-member Committee on Civil Rights headed by industrialist Charles E. Wilson, "to inquire into and to determine whether and in what respect current law-enforcement measures and the authority and means possessed by federal, state, and local governments may be strengthened and improved to safeguard the civil rights of the people."[9] The Committee's report, issued in 1947, presented an extensive catalogue of impairments of civil rights, particularly through racial discrimination. The Committee strongly urged "the elimination of segregation, based on race, color, creed, or national origin, from American life."

Some, though by no means all, of the Committee's specific recommendations brought subsequent action at the state or national level. In 1948 the Supreme Court of the United States outlawed restrictive covenants prohibiting the sale or lease of real property to people of certain racial or religious groups. Fair employment practice laws were enacted in some states. In 1954, the Supreme Court, in a unanimous decision, declared unconstitutional the segregation of Negro and white students in public schools, and by implication condemned the practice of racial segregation wherever found. In 1957, Congress passed the first civil rights legislation since the Reconstruction era. In its final form, it dealt almost exclusively with the right to vote, and not very effectively with that—but it was a start. Another civil rights law was enacted in 1960, after a Southern filibuster lasting eighty-two hours. It provided for appointment of federal referees to pass

---

[8] A new committee was established in 1943 with increased funds and powers. The end of the war diminished its influence and on May 3, 1946, the committee was suspended for lack of funds. Its final report to President Truman noted a postwar rise in racial discrimination and recommended legal action. A bill to establish a permanent FEPC failed of passage in January, 1946.

[9] *To Secure These Rights:* The Report of the President's Committee on Civil Rights (New York: Simon and Schuster, 1947).

on voting qualifications in areas where a pattern of racial discrimination could be discerned. Clumsy and overinvolved in its mechanics, it aroused no enthusiasm among champions of civil rights. In the 1960 Presidential election both major parties, with an eye on the Negro vote, included strong civil rights planks in their platforms. The year also marked the beginning of the "sit-in," a form of passive resistance for breaking the barriers of segregation. Despite reprisals, the passive "sit-ins" spread throughout the South, and, as they were accompanied by boycotts of nonsegregated departments of the stores affected, they exerted strong economic leverage upon merchants dependent upon Negro trade.

The Negro was beginning to exert important political and economic influence; he could take pride in his remarkable progress since the 1930s; but in 1960 he was still far from enjoying the full rights of American citizenship.

In recent years, largely as a result of the 1954 Supreme Court decision, the Negro's battle for equal rights has been focused on the field of education. The basic pattern of relations between Negroes and whites, in education as elsewhere, was set in 1896 (the year following Booker T. Washington's Atlanta address) when the Supreme Court in the *Plessy v. Ferguson* case announced its famous "separate-but-equal" doctrine. For more than half a century the South has professed allegiance to this doctrine. Nevertheless, separate-but-equal has never been taken literally; the emphasis has always been upon separateness rather than equality. Unquestionably Negro education has advanced since the days of Booker T. Washington, but by and large it still falls far short of that afforded to whites. In the South, where the majority of the nation's Negro children go to school, and where per capita income is lower, the burdens of maintaining a dual educational system have resulted in gross inequities. School buildings are usually inferior; the school term is often shorter; teachers' salaries are lower.[10]

Because of palpable inequality under the guise of separate-but-equal, there were some attempts on the part of the courts to insure a more literal application of the Plessy doctrine. But as time went on Negro leadership showed less interest in achieving equality between separate systems, and more concern with abolishing segregation itself. In 1952 five cases were brought before the United States Supreme Court in which the Plessy doctrine was challenged. Since all involved the same basic issue—the constitutionality of segregation in the public schools—the Court agreed to a joint consideration of the five cases. On May 17, 1954, Chief Justice Warren read the historic decision: "We conclude that in the field of public

[10] In his study of biracial education in the United States financed by the Fund for the Advancement of Education, Harry S. Ashmore illustrates the striking contrast between Negro and white education. *The Negro and the Schools,* pp. 25–30; 153–160.

education the doctrine of 'separate but equal' has no place. Separate educational facilities are inherently unequal. Therefore, we hold that the plaintiffs and others similarly situated for whom the actions have been brought are by reason of the segregation complained of, deprived of the equal protection of the laws guaranteed by the Fifteenth Amendment." One year later, on May 31, 1955, after permitting reargument on the mechanics of enforcement and the desirability of setting exact time limits for compliance, the Supreme Court sent the cases back to the federal district courts, requiring "a prompt and reasonable start toward full compliance," and directing the courts to order school desegregation "with all deliberate speed." The Plessy doctrine was legally dead, but it would take a long time to lay it to rest in the educational system of the South.

Though the Court had not demanded immediate action, steps toward compliance were taken promptly in some areas. Secretary of Defense Charles E. Wilson ordered all military post schools of the Army, Navy, and Air Force to end the practice of segregation not later than September 1, 1955. Desegregation of schools in Washington, D.C., and in certain border states began at once, though such compliance was in some cases on a "token" basis only. But in the Deep South, where Negroes constituted a large proportion of the population, opposition hardened. Personal attacks were launched against members of the Supreme Court. Mississippi, Georgia, and South Carolina threatened to abolish their public school systems rather than seat Negro and white children in the same classroom. Governor Herman Talmadge of Georgia and Senators John Stennis and James Eastland of Mississippi publicly asserted their defiance. Senator Sam J. Ervin, Jr., of North Carolina issued a "Declaration of Constitutional Principles," accusing the Supreme Court of abusing judicial power by "undertaking to legislate, in derogation of the authority of Congress," and of encroaching upon individual and states' rights. This document was signed by seventeen Senators and seventy-seven Representatives and presented in both houses March 12, 1956. Numerous devices were proposed to evade or set aside the decision of the Court, among them a memorial to Congress to declare the Fourteenth and Fifteenth Amendments null and void, an amendment to the Constitution explicitly reserving to the states the power "to provide for good order, education, and harmonious race relations therein," and an amendment vesting the United States Senate with appellate court functions to review decisions of the Supreme Court.[11]

One tangible manifestation of Deep South opposition to integration was the

[11] These documents, together with the Ervin "Declaration," have been conveniently assembled in *Desegregation and the Supreme Court,* Benjamin M. Ziegler, ed. (Boston: D. C. Heath and Co., 1958), pp. 103–113.

organization of White Citizens' Councils. The first of these Councils was formed by a group of business and professional men in Indianola, Mississippi, July 11, 1954, just two months after the Court decision; its declared purpose was to fight integration and "mongrelization." After a slow start, the Council idea caught fire rapidly, and on April 7, 1956, at a secret meeting in New Orleans, delegates from eleven states founded the Citizens' Councils of America.[12] A year later their total membership was estimated at 300,000.

Members of the Citizens' Councils, though stout advocates of states' rights, do not couch their objections to integration in legalistic terms as do many more gentlemanly but less candid Southerners. They believe in the basic inferiority of the Negro, and say so without hesitation. They picture the Supreme Court decision as part of a monstrous Communist plot to establish Negro ascendancy, destroy the white Southerner's "way of life," and ultimately to communize America. A leading spokesman for the Councils is Judge Thomas P. Brady of Brookhaven, Mississippi. Shortly after the 1954 decision, Judge Brady delivered a speech entitled "Black Monday" (the reference is to the day of the Court decision) to the Sons of the American Revolution at Greenwood, Mississippi. The speech was later issued as a pamphlet, and subsequently expanded into a book. This document, which imputes racial inferiority to the Negro, attacks the Supreme Court and its decision, and warns against various "Communistic" attempts to subvert the American political, economic, and social system, has been called by a student of the movement "the most comprehensive exposition of Council thought."[13]

In 1957, Brady was invited to address the famous Commonwealth Club of California at San Francisco. His speech, delivered on October 4, was a hard-hitting, uncompromising statement of the extreme Southern position. Brady asserted the intellectual, moral, and social inferiority of the Negro and provided an elaborate documentation of his claims. In contrast to those who pleaded for more time for the South to work out her problems gradually and without outside interference, he flatly dismissed the possibility of even an eventual acceptance of integration: "As long as we live, so long shall we be segregated, and after death, God willing, thus it will still be!"

This speech proved so controversial that Roy Wilkins, Executive Secretary of

---

[12] See John B. Martin, *The Deep South Says "Never"* (New York: Ballantine Books, 1957), pp. 3–4; 137–138. Martin believes that the year of delay between the 1954 decision and the 1955 order to proceed "with all deliberate speed" gave the Councils time to solidify opposition in a South, which in May, 1954, was "divided, perplexed, and resigned."

[13] *Ibid.,* p. 16.

the NAACP, was summoned from New York to present "the other side." On November 1, speaking from the same platform, he addressed the members of the Commonwealth Club on the subject "Deep South Crisis." Wilkins, a popular and persuasive speaker, whose life has been devoted to the cause of full equality for Negroes, had been an NAACP official since 1931, when he became Assistant Secretary. Long an opponent of Communist sympathizers within the organization, he took vigorous exception to Brady's charge that it had been Communist-founded and controlled. Then, without further reference to the Mississippi judge, he replied to segregationist arguments, closing with a strong appeal for internal unity to meet the challenges of the cold war.

Judge Brady and the White Citizens' Councils, though professing to defend the "Southern way of life," did not speak for the South as a whole. Many white Southerners (how many no one knew) were deeply troubled by the inconsistency between the democratic ideal and a system of forced segregation. Others, though instinctively opposed to racial integration, as law-abiding citizens were disturbed by the threat of mob violence. Though discretion dictated a policy of silence, a few voices of moderation were raised. One was the voice of Congressman Brooks Hays of Arkansas. A prominent Christian layman, twice elected president of the Southern Baptist Convention, Hays had for years worked for improved relations between the races. In September, 1957, in an attempt to alleviate the school integration crisis in Little Rock, Congressman Hays arranged a meeting between President Eisenhower and Governor Orval E. Faubus of Arkansas, who had been largely responsible for precipitating the crisis. These efforts failed, however, for mob action ultimately made it necessary for the President to dispatch federal troops to Little Rock to enforce integration at Central High School. Addressing the Little Rock Lions Club the day following the arrival of the troops, Hays spoke with feeling and candor. The issue, he emphasized, is not integration or federal authority in school matters, but how to deal with lawlessness. He was hopeful that on that issue segregationists and integrationists, Republicans and Democrats, could unite.[14]

Another spokesman for moderation was Governor LeRoy Collins of Florida. His address on September 22, 1958, to the Southern Governors' Conference of which he was chairman, attracted national attention. Acknowledging the unpopularity of the 1954 Supreme Court decision, Collins pointed out the impossibility of allowing citizens to choose which decisions of the Court they will obey and

[14] Brooks Hays, *This World: A Christian's Workshop* (Nashville: Broadman Press, 1958), pp. 92–100.

which they will disregard. He stressed the need for equitable implementation and safeguarding procedures through legislation enacted by Congress. Such legislation, he thought, should facilitate desegregation in communities where and when it is feasible, and should provide protection against forced desegregation where and when it is not feasible.[15]

In March, 1960, when the Greensboro sit-ins had spread to Florida, and Tallahassee was in a state of high tension, Governor Collins spoke to the people of Florida over radio and television. He expressed personal sympathy with the sit-ins and asserted that the legal rights of all citizens in the state would be protected. He would not, he said, allow the issue to be decided by mobs, whether white or black. Calling attention to the presence of extremists on both sides, and addressing himself to the moderates, he asked, "Where are the people in the middle? Why aren't they talking? Why aren't they working? They must start working. They must start efforts that are going to bring about solutions if we are going to get over these problems and these troubles. . . ."[16]

Of concern to both Southern moderates and Northern liberals was the impact of racial strife in America upon our prestige abroad. Brooks Hays spoke at Little Rock of the international implications of the problem. "The world is in a crisis and our enemy is powerful. He will exploit our failures, and we cannot afford to give him any advantage." To the Governors' Conference and later to the people of Florida, LeRoy Collins spoke in similar terms. Roy Wilkins emphasized the point in his address to the Commonwealth Club. And Chester Bowles, former Ambassador to India, returning from abroad early in 1954, noted that colored peoples of Africa and Asia "simply cannot think about the United States without considering bitterly the limitations under which our 15,000,000 Americans with colored skins are living." Bowles warned that: "If we do not soon end the last vestiges of second-class citizenship in America, I have grave doubts about our ability to achieve understanding with the colored peoples of those powerful, rising continents, who represent two-thirds of all mankind and on whom the future peace of the world may depend."[17] But the series of events following the Supreme Court decision—the riots at Little Rock, similar scenes in New Orleans, the unsuccessful attempt of Miss Autherine Lucy to break the race barrier at the University of Alabama, the sit-ins, the Freedom Riders—all widely publicized abroad

[15] Remarks by Governor LeRoy Collins of Florida, Chairman, Southern Governors' Conference, Lexington, Kentucky. Press release, September 22, 1958.

[16] Transcript of statewide TV-radio talk to the people of Florida on race relations, by Governor LeRoy Collins. Delivered over statewide TV-radio network, Sunday, March 20, 1960.

[17] "The Negro—Progress and Challenge," The New York Times Magazine, February 7, 1954, p. 50.

in picture and story, served to exacerbate rather than allay the fears and suspicions reported by Chester Bowles.

In October, 1960, nearly six years after the Supreme Court had written an epitaph for the Plessy doctrine and ordered an end to school segregation, the Southern Educational Reporting Service announced that of 2,838 biracial districts in seventeen southern states and the District of Columbia, only 766 were desegregated. The number of Negro students actually in the same schools with whites was only 183,104, or about six percent of the total. Public institutions of higher learning in Alabama, Georgia, Mississippi, and South Carolina were still completely segregated, as were all public elementary and secondary schools in Alabama, Georgia, Louisiana, Mississippi, and South Carolina. Clearly, the Negro's battle to secure the rights guaranteed him by the Constitution, and reaffirmed in numerous court decisions, was still far from won.

Segregation and the South

THOMAS PICKENS BRADY

Born, New Orleans, Louisiana, August 6, 1903. Graduated from Yale, 1927; LL.B., University of Mississippi, 1930. Instructor of Sociology, University of Mississippi, 1929–1930. Admitted to Mississippi bar, 1930; attorney in Brookhaven, Mississippi since 1930. Judge, Circuit Court, Fourteenth Judicial Circuit, Mississippi, since 1950. National Chairman, speakers' bureau of States Rights party, 1948. Vice-President, Mississippi State Bar, 1954–1955. Distinguished Service citation from Mississippi Legislature, 1956. National Democratic Committeeman from Mississippi, 1960. Author, The South at Bay *(1948),* Black Monday *(1954).*

"Segregation in the South is a way of life. It is a precious and sacred custom. It is one of our dearest and most treasured possessions."

*I*t is indeed an honor to be invited to address the distinguished membership and the guests of the renowned Commonwealth Club of California.

I have been asked to speak on Segregation and the South, and I have been requested to do in twenty-seven minutes that which cannot be adequately done in several hours. I will do my best to present the case for the South. I know you will give me a fair hearing. I shall try to be objective, but if I fail in this regard, I assure you that I can and will be truthful. I earnestly hope that no one will be offended, but let me assure you, I will not sacrifice truth on the altar of courtesy.

The Commonwealth Club of California, San Francisco, October 4, 1957. Transcript provided by the Commonwealth Club. Printed by permission of Judge Brady.

Segregation is defined by Webster: "To separate or set apart from the others or from the rest; to isolate."

It is essential that you realize that in the twelve Southern States, segregation means something quite different than what it means in the other States. In the South, segregation is something more than a definition in the dictionary. It is something more than a political program. It supersedes a philosophical conception. It is more than a sociological platitude. Segregation in the South is a way of life. It is a precious and sacred custom. It is one of our dearest and most treasured possessions. It is the means whereby we live in social peace, order and security. It is the guarantee whereby our wives and children are afforded the common decency and protection which is essential if any harmonious relationship is to exist between two different races. Segregation exists not simply because we prefer it, but because we must maintain it. For over a hundred and fifty years, we have been maintaining and protecting this sacred custom. Self-preservation, the first law of life, has required that we do so. It is the first commandment and not the last. It is our shield and buckler. Segregation, moreover, is preferred by both the white and the Negro races in the South. Ninety-eight percent of both races desire it. It does not work any hardship upon the Negro, nor does it deprive him of any of his constitutional rights. It should be admitted that a white man and a white woman have the same equal right to associate with whom they please as does the Negro man and the Negro woman.

Historically, our problem today dates back to the passage of the 14th Amendment. In 1866, after one of the world's bloodiest wars was ended, the South lay prostrate at the feet of a Northern victor, devoid of mercy and gallantry. Full of hatred and determination to forever crush the South, Congress submitted to the States the 13th, 14th and 15th Amendments, hoping upon the passage of said Amendments to enact legislation which would forever weaken the Southern States so that the Federal Government could dominate the South through Negro Carpetbag rule. The 13th and 15th Amendments, which prohibited slavery and provided that the power to vote should not be denied on account of race or color, were promptly ratified by a three-fourths majority of the States. The Southern States, with an all-white electorate and all-white legislatures, voted for these amendments which were promptly passed. The 14th Amendment, however, loaded with the dynamite of social integration, was completely rejected. The 14th Amendment was lawfully submitted and lawfully rejected under the constitutional procedure. That should have ended the matter, but Congress became infuriated and from thenceforth adopted high-handed measures. It proclaimed military rule in the South and took over the Southern States by military occupation. The white people were disfranchised, the ballot was put into the hands of the illiterate Negro, coached by carpetbaggers.

In 1868, the 14th Amendment was re-submitted and, of course, ratified almost unanimously by the Southern States, the white people being denied the right to vote. The United States Army attended to the details. This last ratification was unlawful and in violation of the Constitution. Now hear this. In so far as the Negro is concerned, the 14th Amendment, the creature of unending hate against the South, has never been of any moral force in the South. This may sound fantastic but it is true, as every white child in the South fully knows. The ultimate results of this Amendment of hate and corruption, I prophesy, in the future will not only operate against the South but will ultimately be one of the principal means whereby the rights of all the sovereign states will be usurped or destroyed by a totalitarian inclined government, if the government continues on its present course.

My grandfather was a Captain in the Mississippi Rifles. He fought for four years in the War Between the States. He buried his brother who was killed by his side at Vicksburg. From my grandfather's lips, as millions of other Southerners heard from their grandfather's lips, I obtained a vivid description of the first Reconstruction Era. The homes, cotton and corn fields which had escaped the scourge of war were destroyed under the Negro Carpetbag military rule which lasted 3½ years in Mississippi. Drunken, marauding bands of crazed Negroes shot and broke into homes, raping and killing the women and children whom they dragged screaming from their flaming homes. The crackle of the flames and the groans and screams of the helpless victims, though not loud, are still audible in the minds of Southerners. The Negro gangs now operating in South Chicago, Harlem, Pennsylvania and Washington are mildly reminiscent of that First Reconstruction. We know what unbridled Negro rule can produce, and the South is never going to relinquish into the hands of the ignorant, the unqualified, the unscrupulous, the primitive and uncontrolled the rein of our Government. To do so is simple suicide.

I want it distinctly understood that the South does not hate the Negro. You know little, if anything, about the true Southern Negro. As a matter of fact, there is a great deal of genuine affection and understanding between the races. We have lived harmoniously together, with a minimum of violence and bloodshed. We have nurtured the Negro, taught him, provided for him, educated him and endeavored to make of him a worthwhile citizen. He has made great strides. Though he pays about only 12 percent of the taxes, we have in the last 20 years given him equally of the benefits to be afforded from taxation. I realize that this statement may provoke disagreement, but the fact nevertheless remains that in Mississippi, and in other Southern States, Negroes, who desired to do so, have become well educated and wealthy. Millionaires are included in this group. This group has within its numbers, doctors, lawyers, teachers, business men and plantation owners. There is no field of economic endeavor which has been barred to the Negro. It is only in the social sphere that the barrier is raised.

There are many reasons why the Southerner flatly refuses to permit integration with the Negro in the social sphere of our life. Time will not permit an analysis of all of them but the basic ones can be enumerated. First, the high percentage of Negroes in the South is of grave importance. The national average which the Negro bears to the white man in America is 10 percent. In Mississippi, however, it is 45.3 percent. In Georgia, it is 38.8 percent. In South Carolina, it is 38.8 percent. In Louisiana, it is 32.9 percent. In Alabama, it is 32 percent. In Arkansas, it is 22.3 percent, and in Florida, it is 21.7 percent. The great State of California has but 4.4 percent. The State of New York, that yearns so for the welfare of the Negro in Mississippi, has but 6.2 percent. New Jersey has 6.6 percent, and Pennsylvania has 6.1 percent. Ohio has 6.5 percent, Oregon has but eight-tenths of one percent. Montana and Nevada have but two-tenths of one percent. South Dakota has .01 of one percent. If the State of New York, where so much turmoil has arisen over the desegregation in the public schools, or in Pennsylvania and Illinois, where similar mass demonstrations of violence have taken place, had 45.3 percent of their population Negro, I shudder to think what would have taken place between the Negroes and whites. If, in this county, as in many counties in Mississippi, and other Southern States, the Negroes outnumbered the whites five and six to one, I wonder whether or not you would be willing to have or consent to complete educational and social integration?

There is, as every sociologist knows, a distinct correlation between the degree of segregation of the races and the numerical strength of the Negro. The reason for this, I will later conclusively show. If in the South the Negro was permitted, as he is in some Northern States, to obtain the ballot by simply reaching 21 years of age, it would mean that no white man in many counties would ever hold public office. It would also mean that in the Halls of Congress, as is earnestly desired by the Communists of America, the seats now occupied by our representatives would be held by incompetent, illiterate and ignorant Negroes.

While I regret that I must do so, I must nevertheless comment upon the intellectual and moral aspects of the reason why the South must remain segregated socially. The average vocabulary of the Negro in the South consists of approximately 650 words. The reason for this is that the average Negro boy quits school around the age of 13 or 14 years. The average Negro girl generally goes through high school, and has a larger vocabulary. I hesitate to estimate the I.Q. of the average Negro of the South since I could not obtain from the Federal Government the results of the intelligence tests given in World War Two and in the Korean conflict. The NAACP objects, but I can safely say that based upon the tests which were available from World War One, there is a great gulf of difference between the I.Q. of the Negro of the South, as well as in America, and the average white man. Northern left-wing educators and sociologists explain this deficiency by saying that it is caused by an inefficient and inferior educational system for Negroes. This is wholly false. It is because of a deficiency in mental ability; it is due to indifference and indolence on the part of the Negroes. That fact cannot be disputed, and that is that of all the races that have ever been on this earth, assuming that they all started out at approximately the same time in God's calendar, the Negro race is the only race that lacked the imagination and mental ability to put its hopes, dreams and thoughts in writing. The Negro race was the only race that was unable to invent even picture writing.

Exhaustive study of the program of integration in the schools of Washington, D.C., which the NAACP and other groups fostering integration said would be an example for the rest of the United States to follow, clearly indicates that the average white student who was integrated in the classes with the Negroes has been retarded two to three years in his educational progress. This, in itself, should convince the most dubious that it is not to the best interest of America that the white children in certain congested sections be retarded two years, or more, in their educational advancement. Remember that the left-wing socialistic groups of this country are always grading down, never grading up the intelligence, the industry and the genius of this country.

While there is undoubtedly fear of ultimate intermarriage between a small segment of the whites and Negroes if complete social integration should take place, still, this is not yet a major concern. The late Walter White, Secretary of the NAACP for many years, when questioned as to whether integration in the schools would lead to intermarriage, was forced to admit that association leads to friendship and friendship leads to love and marriage. He said, however, without any explanation, that he doubted if this would happen. There is certainly less than one percent of the white people of the South who would agree to marry a Negro. Miscegenation has largely taken place, I am glad to say, North of the Mason and Dixon line, and whatever laxity has existed in Southern mores permitting clandestine relationships between Negroes and whites has almost entirely disappeared. The rule is now hard and adamant. Such is taboo in the South.

The main objection to social integration of the races by Southerners is for moral reasons. As revealed by Representative John Bell Williams, of Mississippi, in his remarkable treatise, WHERE IS THE REIGN OF TERROR, it is shown that the white boys and girls were subjected to untold vulgarity, immorality and filth because of the integration which has taken place in Washington. The truth is often brutal, but I must speak it. As revealed in the treatise of Representative Williams, the white children of Washington, D.C., were retarded two to three years in their educational advancement. The obscenity, the vulgarity and brutality which existed required the constant maintenance of policemen in the halls and corridors of many of the schools. Obscene notes and pictures were placed on the desks of white girls by Negroes. The radiators, stairs and halls were utilized as urinals and toilets by the Negroes. The carrying of concealed weapons and aggravated assaults and the rape and attempted rape of white girls and even teachers are some of the results found in the model example of what integration in our high schools can do. Make no mistake about this, the Southern fathers and mothers are not going to permit their daughters to be insulted by Negroes, or anyone else! They are not going to permit their daughters to have to resist the advances of Negro boys. They are not going to permit their sons and daughters to be subjected to the vulgarity of Negro boys and girls who are urged to take every possible advantage of the white children that can be taken. Possibly I cannot speak for the South, but I can speak for Mississippi, and I can tell you this, we have already, by constitutional amendment, authorized our Legislature to abolish the public school system in Mississippi if the Negro and white children are integrated therein. Make no mistake about it, we will abolish our public school system and establish private schools for children. We will have private academies for the white children only, and we will still see that the Negro is educated separately. It will cost dearly, but we will do it!

There have been but few isolated cases in either the white or Negro schools in Mississippi where assaults with deadly weapons have taken place. Such assaults are numerous in Washington and other placees where the Negroes and white children have been integrated. The Negro, in so far as sex is concerned, is not immoral, he is simply non-moral. He merely obeys his natural instincts. The pregnancies and illegitimate births which have occurred among the Negro girls in the schools of Washington is not abnormal, merely astounding. In the South there is a double standard in so far as sex morals are concerned. The white man has his standard and the Negro has his standard. Perhaps we are responsible, because we have not and do not punish the Negro except in rare instances for desertion, illegitimacy or bigamy. The white race laid aside cannibalism thousands of years before the Negro race was forced to do so. The white race is on the verge of forever abolishing incest. The Negro race is far behind. We punish the Negro for incest and there is now on my docket, as is frequently the case, indictments for incest by Negroes. Negro men who beget children by their daughters are tried.

We cannot count for naught the natural indolence and indifference of the Negro's nature. We cannot disregard his utter disregard for the laws relating to theft. We cannot overlook his proclivity for drunkenness and dope addictions. We cannot overlook his natural tendencies to immorality and violence and subject our children to the terrible consequences resulting from such traits, notwithstanding the socialist mouthings by socialist preachers.

In California, the Negro constitutes 4.4 percent of your total population, yet 19 percent of all crimes committed in California were committed by Negroes. In the State of New York, the Negro constitutes 6.2 percent of the total population, and yet 40.1 percent of the prison population of New York is Negro. In Mississippi, the Negro constitutes 45.3 percent of the population and commits 73.4 percent of the crimes. In the District of Columbia, the Negro's mecca of America, according to the 1950 census, the Negro constituted 35 percent of the total population, and the Negro prison population is 70 percent, or twice the ratio of Negro population to that of white population. This is a national disgrace. The District of Columbia has more Negro convicts than either Louisiana, Mississippi, Arkansas, Alabama, Florida, Texas, Kentucky or Maryland. The pattern seems to be the larger the concentration of Negro population, the higher the incidence of crime. This conclusion is further established in the Northern and Eastern States where the crime rate percentages have taken another advance. In this group, California fits very well also. The exception to the pattern is in the Southern States where we have the largest concentration of Negro population, but in spite of the great concentration, the incidence of crime among the Negroes is considerably less than in the Northern and Midwestern States.

. . . .

The passage of the Civil Rights bill of August 29, 1957, marks the beginning of another Reconstruction Era in the South. It is as dark a day as was May 17, 1954, the date of the illegal, unconstitutional and Communistic Black Monday decision. The Black Monday decision was a total usurpation of the rights of Congress. The Supreme Court, by edict, has sought to pass a law which only Congress had the authority to do.

The South is the citadel of conservatism. It is a fortress for constitutional government. Throughout Mississippi and the other Southern States, a feeling of concern over the socialist trend of our Federal Government has been constantly growing. Beginning with the administration of F.D.R., the South viewed with alarm the birth of the welfare state, and the growth of the 130 Communist-front organizations which nourish it. It was greatly concerned over the prodigal give-away program to the socialist countries abroad. It resented the competing by the Federal Government with private industry. It deplored the tolerance shown the Communist and left-wing groups in America. None of these stimuli were sufficient to precipitate a wholesale grass roots movement, though Mississippi, South Carolina and Louisiana did cry protest in 1948 when these States walked out of the National Democratic Convention in Philadelphia, organized the States Rights Party, nominated and voted for Strom Thurmond of South Carolina and Fielding L. Wright of Mississippi as its Presidential and Vice-Presidential nominees. The people of the United States had an opportunity then to vote for two men who were opposed to the gradual socialization of America and the destruction of the sovereign rights and powers of the 48 States by a totalitarian-inclined Federal Government. Our protest provoked only ridicule and abuse.

It was only when the Supreme Court of the United States, on May 17, 1954, handed down its Black Monday decision that the people of the South realized that the "Rubicon had been crossed," and that they had no alternative except to organize completely and resist this infamous sociological, unconstitutional decision. Thus it was that the Citizens' Councils were born. Membership therein, however, is restricted. The Citizens' Council is a good cross-section of that city or county it represents. Lawyers, doctors, ministers, industrialists, merchants, employees, farmers, plantation owners and laborers compose the Councils. Jews, Catholics, and Protestants alike become members when they subscribe to an oath of non-violence and pledge themselves to support in every legal way possible the maintenance of segregation and the preservation of the sovereign rights of the States of this Union. We have no Ku Klux Klans in Mississippi, and we want none. The Klan is negligible in the South.

There are in Mississippi 360 Councils with approximately 85,000 members, and throughout the South, though some States utilize different names such as The

Defenders of State Sovereignty in Virginia, there are more than 300,000 members. Each Council is completely autonomous and has a State Charter. In each State, however, there is a State Board of Directors which represents every Council in that State, and there is a South-wide coordinating agency in which eleven of the twelve Southern States are represented. This organization is known as the Citizens' Councils of America.

These organizations are financed solely by individual contributions and by membership dues of $5.00 per year. One, two or three dollars is sent to the State Headquarters. One dollar is sent to subscribe to the Citizens' Council paper, if the Council so decides, and the remainder is left in the local Council to defray expenses of publicity and local management. The Citizens' Council paper has a circulation of 65,000, and is sent into every State of the Union and is placed on the desk of every State Legislator and important public official. Every high school library receives it. Every member of Congress and many Federal Agencies likewise receive this paper. This was accomplished without any aid whatsoever from the Fund of [sic] the Republic, Carnegie Foundation, PAC or CIO.

Primarily, the Councils are dedicated to the preservation of segregation and the sovereign rights of the States of this Union. The Councils are unalterably opposed to the socialization of our basic industries, including transportation, banking, agriculture, electric power, medicine and education. They are opposed to the communizing and socializing of our labor organizations, schools and churches. The Citizens' Councils are determined to do everything possible to prevent the broadening of the powers of the executive branch of our Government and the usurpation by the judiciary of powers which are under our Constitution vested solely in the Congress. The Citizens' Councils are determined to resist the enormous and unwarranted pressure which is brought to bear on all branches of our Government by the aforesaid left-wing minority groups. Last, but not least, the Councils are opposed to the proposed welfare state and all of its destruction of the responsibilities and liberties of the citizens of this country, and above all, the Citizens' Councils are dedicated to non-violence. The Councils firmly believe that within the Constitution of the respective States, an orderly, peaceful and legal means exist whereby these objectives can be secured and maintained.

In conclusion, we in the South realize and firmly believe that the resurgence of demand and effort for the advancement of the Negro politically and socially in the last thirty years was conceived and promoted by world-wide communism. Though there are many facets to the movement to completely integrate the Negro in the South, the basic cause we know is of Communist origin and Socialist plan. We know also that the drive for integration of the races in the South is but a small segment in the overall checkerboard plan to first socialize and then communize America. The proof of this can be found in the Workers (Communist) Party National Platform adopted on May 25, 1928, which included every demand for Negroes which is found in *Target for 1963*, a pamphlet published by the NAACP in 1956. As a matter of fact, the World Communists at one time actually and fantastically contemplated having the Negroes in the South violently over-throw the Southern States. Russia proposed to recognize the Negro Republic. It must be said to the lasting credit of the Negro that his loyalty to the white Southerner and to his country made this ridiculous plan impossible. Subsequently, the Communists then decided that every Negro in the South must be franchised so that the Negroes would hold political offices in the State Legislatures and would occupy the Southern seats in Congress.

Much of what has been done to advance and strengthen the fight against the South in recent months is directly in line with suggestions made in a statement on Negro Rights issued by the National Committee of the Communist Party of October 5, 1955, which concluded with this advice, "Most important is the fur-ther strengthening of a great united movement based on the maximum mobility of the Negro people and organization with the united support of the labor move-ment. Simultaneously, the Communists will play their part in helping to guaran-tee the participation and the militant initiative of the Left. Pass Civil Rights Legislation! End Segregation! Full equality for the Negro people—now!"

The February number of the Red Magazine, *Party Voice,* said: "Victory would mean desegregation, majority rule and Negro representation. Victory would mean the replacement of the Dixiecrat delegations to State and National Legislatures by spokesmen for the Negro people, labor and the poor farmers."

I cannot help but wonder what would happen to this country if the 24 South-ern Senators were replaced by ignorant Negro or Communist labor leaders. I cannot help but wonder how the rights of Californians and the people of all the States would fare if the seats of the United States Senate which have been filled by men such as Cordell Hull, Walter George, Harry Byrd, James F. Byrnes, Strom Thurmond, Ellender, Lyndon Johnson, Jim Eastland were usurped by communis-tic Negroes or labor leaders. What would happen if one hundred-odd Southern members of the House of Representatives in Congress were replaced by Angelo Herndons?[1] It cannot be disputed that the Communist Party has infiltrated and dominates many of our great labor parties. It is a fact that Communist sympa-thizers and Communist-front organizers founded the NAACP and largely control it.[2] It cannot be disputed that the left-wing groups have infiltrated our colleges and our churches. A war is on to capture the American mind. The South above all other sections of the country has stubbornly resisted and opposed these groups which would communize our Government. The NAACP knows this, labor knows this, and the Communists know this, and we are, therefore, the target of their resentment and unending hate. We have grown accustomed to the vicious mis-representations, the vituperation and abuse that is daily heaped upon us by

[1] Herndon, Negro labor organizer, subject of a celebrated civil liberties case (1932–1937). A Communist, Herndon led a demonstration in Atlanta (1932) protesting the dropping of 23,000 families from state relief rolls. He was arrested and sentenced to eighteen years in prison. In 1937, the United States Supreme Court ruled that the evidence did not warrant his conviction.

[2] Cf. reply by Roy Wilkins, p. 345 below.

means of the northern left-wing newspaper, radio and television. We have taken it and we can still take it. We are waiting for that day, and believe that it is not far distant, when conservative Americans in all the States will unite, when all constitutional Americans in this country will rise up in our defense and join hands with us in waging our lonely fight to protect and preserve America from Godless Communism!

We sometimes weary in fighting the four great lies which are being deliberately fostered [sic] upon an unsuspecting public by the Communists, the NAACP and the Marxian Christians of this country. Just as Goebbels, Minister of Propaganda in Germany, the greatest exponent of mass psychology the world has ever known, perpetuated his great lie of Germanic superiority on an unsuspecting public, so are the people of America being subjected to the merciless barrage of the four great lies calculated to produce integration of the races in America. They are: 1. No racial differences save that of our skin, hair and eyes, which are unimportant. 2. That laws create second-class citizenship. 3. That segregation is un-Christian. 4. That all men are created equal. Four greater lies cannot be imagined.

[Judge Brady next discusses Communist influence upon labor unions. He returns to the Supreme Court decision of 1954 and the 1957 Civil Rights Bill, which he says, have accomplished "two of the Communist aims calculated to destroy the conservative South."]

. . . .

In an address in the United States House of Representatives, Congressman William Colmer of Mississippi stated:

The Civil Rights Bill recently enacted by Congress, which inaugurates a Second Reconstruction in the South, will, however, affect not only the South. The sovereign rights of every State in this Union have been violated. August 29, 1957, is a day of infamy. This iniquitous act, like a loaded pistol, is aimed at the South which has contributed so much to the foundation and perpetuation of our Republic. It is not the South, the Democratic Party or the Republican Party which will suffer most. The real victim in the tragedy which was concluded will be the Republic itself, for once the trigger is pulled, the freedom and real rights of the citizens of all sections of this country will be further curtailed. The powerful arm of an already powerful Federal Government will be further stretched out into every metropolitan center as well as every hamlet of this great country, North, South, East and West, for the further regimentation of our citizens. The existing election machinery of the Southern States which they were granted under the 10th amendment, the right to create and utilize will be henceforth conducted under the scrutiny and intimidation of armed marshals of the Central Government in Washington. This could well be the final step next to achieve the goal of the true proponents of this legislation: The complete destruction of the sovereignty of the States and the centralization of all power of the people in one strong centralized government under the dome in the Capitol in Washington. . . .

R. Carter Pittman of Georgia has written in his splendid booklet "The Broken

Constitution": "As we in the South once more pass into our garden of Gethsemane, thence to bear our social judicial cross, we plead to our brothers to the North and to the West not to let their sympathy and understanding be limited by longitude and latitude." We are going to fight the good fight. We are going to run the straight race. We will not resort to violence. We condemn and deplore the sporadic acts of violence which have occurred in the South. We will fight within the confines of our respective State Constitutions and the Constitution of the United States.

To quote again from Carter Pittman:

If this country is to be saved from Communism, it must be saved by the white people of the South. We did not ask for this burden, but we will bear it. Our Yankee friends to the North may not want to be saved, but let's save them too, and the white race and the Negro race. Let it be known, however, that we in the South do not intend to obey men, however exalted their seats or black their robes or hearts. We do intend to obey the laws of God and to obey the laws of this country which are made in accordance with our Constitution. We will live as free men, or die as becomes the descendants of those who died that we might live in the freedom to be different with the liberty to be left alone.

Finally, so that there may be no vestige of doubt in your minds, I now fervently say, "Dum vivamus tum segrebimur et post mortem—deo volente, etiam nunc sic erit," which literally translated means, As long as we live, so long shall we be segregated, and after death, God willing, thus it will still be! Though you may not agree with what I have said, it is indeed a great honor and sacred right for you to have permitted me to say it.

Deep South Crisis

ROY WILKINS

Born, St. Louis, August 30, 1901. Graduated University of Minnesota, 1923. Managing Editor, Kansas City Call, *a Negro weekly, 1923–1931. Assistant Secretary of National Association for the Advancement of Colored People, 1931–1949; Acting Secretary, 1949–1950; Administrator, 1950–1955; Executive Secretary since 1955. Succeeded W. E. B. DuBois as editor of* Crisis, *official N.A.A.C.P. journal, 1934; served in dual capacity, 1934–1949. Consultant to War Department on training and use of Negro soldiers, 1941. Consultant, United Nations Conference on International Organization, San Francisco, 1945. Frequent speaker before clubs, forums, college groups, on various aspects of race relations.*

"The Negro citizens of our common country . . . are determined that the verdict at Appomattox will not be renounced, that the clock will not be turned back, that they shall enjoy what is justly theirs."

I am deeply grateful for the honor and privilege of addressing the Commonwealth Club of California, whose members have provided over the years a forum for the discussion of hundreds of perplexing issues which have faced the nation and the world.

It is no exaggeration, I think, to state that the situation presented by the resist-

The Commonwealth Club of California, San Francisco, November 1, 1957. Issued as a pamphlet by the National Association for the Advancement of Colored People, New York, 1957. Reprinted by permission.

ance to the 1954 decision of the United States Supreme Court in the public school segregation cases is fully as grave as any which have come under the scrutiny and study of the Commonwealth Club.

And I say advisedly "by the resistance," because it is this resistance, not the decision itself, which is the source of the crisis. The leaders of the resistance and their echoing and uninformed followers have challenged the authority of the nation's highest court and have not hesitated to impugn its integrity and that of its individual members. They have stooped to unconscionable and palpably false slander, too spitefully incredible to repeat here. They have gone beyond resistance or disagreement and actually have counselled defiance.

Not content with challenging the authority of the Court, they have attacked the constitutional basis for its finding, namely, the Fourteenth Amendment, and have come forward boldly with the contention that the Amendment is illegal and of no force and effect.

They also have denounced those who disagree with them as "left-wingers" or "Communists." These include the NAACP, as a matter of course; the National Council of Churches of Christ in the U.S.A.; most non-Southern magazines, and newspapers; the radio and television networks; the organized trade union movement; the Attorney General of the United States; the organized student movement; the Supreme Court; and even the President of the United States!

In this connection, I would like to comment on only one statement in a speech given before this body last month by a spokesman for the most extreme wing of the segregationists. It was, and I quote: "It is a fact that Communist sympathizers and Communist-front organizers founded the NAACP and largely control it."

This is a completely false statement. The NAACP was founded in 1909, eight years before the Communist revolution in Russia in October, 1917, and ten years before there was a Communist Party in America. The 1909 gathering which formed the NAACP was called together by the late Oswald Garrison Villard, member of the famed Abolitionist Garrison family, and owner of the old New York *Evening Post,* then the voice of conservative, aristocratic Republicanism. Some fifty eminent Americans of both races signed the call including bishops, ministers, rabbis, college professors, social workers, editors and publicists.

As for control, the Communists and their sympathizers have been busy for almost thirty years, trying either to supplant the NAACP by "front" organizations and thus drive it out of business, or to infiltrate it and take it over. It is a tribute to the loyalty of Negro Americans and to the good sense of their leaders that the Communists have not succeeded in either effort—and they will not succeed.

The NAACP has clung firmly to the democratic promise of America—to its Constitution, its Bill of Rights, its Declaration of Independence, its courts and its laws. It has been steadfast in its faith in the democratic process, in representative government, in equality of opportunity, in reward according to merit, in fair play—in short, in all the things which constitute the American ideal.

The NAACP and Negro Americans have kept this faith despite decades of physical persecution and heart-breaking discrimination. The depth of their devotion can be measured by their willingness to rely entirely upon the slow processes of the law and of orderly government to achieve their goals.

The last thing the Communists desire in America is the functioning of law and order so as to eliminate racial discrimination and segregation. They want frustration, defeat and bitterness to engulf American Negroes. They want anger, recrimination, suspicion, hatred and conflict to ensue. They want the Negro convinced that there is no hope for him under the American system.

And the segregationists seem to have the same objectives—in this area—as the Communists. They say to Negroes over and over again that the system will *never* be changed, no matter what the Supreme Court may say, or what the President may do, or what the rest of the country may think. They invoke cruel and senseless economic reprisals against Negro domestic servants, sharecroppers and little merchants who dare to believe in the Supreme Court and to press for their rights as citizens.

They persecute the NAACP. In Alabama we have been fined $100,000. In Virginia we have been hamstrung by five special laws. Yesterday the Little Rock City Council ordered the arrest there of our NAACP officers.

They mobilize enormous political, social and economic pressures against Southern white people who dare to disagree. And they have the colossal effrontery to try to wrap themselves in the Constitution and attempt to persuade the white residents of the North and West that they, too, would be well advised to join in the degradation of all nonwhite Americans. This tender concern for the Constitution is a recent phenomenon on the part of Southerners and their anguished cries against central government have arisen only because the government has interfered with their "handling" of "their" Negroes.

This is madness, of course, but a madness at one with Communism, which seeks to destroy unity, mutual respect and hope in America. The segregationists, whether suave like your October speaker, or oily like the Governor of Arkansas, or raucous like the members of the Klan, are serving the ends of the Kremlin.

Little Rock brought the desegregation crisis sharply to the attention of the American people and the world. Here at home, it awakened many citizens for the first time to the ugly realities of a challenge to the very unity of our nation. Abroad, it dealt a stab in the back to American prestige as the leader of the free world and presented our totalitarian enemies with made-to-order propaganda for use among the very nations and peoples we need and must have on the side of democracy.

It has become the fashion of the Southern provincial opposition to sneer at this danger and to inquire, in the manner of 1914, why America must base its actions on the opinion of foreign nations.

Well, this is not 1914. England does not rule the far corners of the globe and thus give us security. France is weak and Germany is divided. A once manageable

China has become strong, stubborn and conscious of her strength. India has become a free nation in the British Commonwealth. Africa is stirring and looking for independence. The Dutch are out of Southeast Asia. The English are out of Egypt, and France is having her troubles in Algeria. And instead of the weak Czars, we now have the tough and single-minded gangsters of the Soviet Union.

No, indeed, this is not the same world, and unless we wish to be isolated by the Soviets, we have got to win allies among those peoples, largely nonwhite, who have not yet been beguiled or captured by the Communists.

Shall the Soviets, not we or Europe, get the oil of the Middle East? Shall the Soviets, not we, have access to the vast resources of Africa? Shall our steel mills be denied the manganese of the Far East? We could go on and on, for the list is a long one. Who will buy the goods of our huge industrial plants and the produce of our mechanized farms?

Who will keep our workers employed—and what will become of the newly industrialized South should the Kremlin call the world's economic tune?

The world cannot understand nor long respect a nation in which a governor calls out troops to bar little children from school in defiance of the Supreme Court of the land, a nation in which mobs beat and kick and stone and spit upon those who happen not to be white. It asks: "Is this the vaunted democracy? Is this freedom, human dignity and equality of opportunity? Is this fair play? Is this better than Communism?" No, the assertion that Little Rock has damaged America abroad does not call for sneers. Our national security might well hang in the balance.

Governor Faubus of Arkansas precipitated the Little Rock defiance of a Federal Court order by citing state sovereignty and states' rights, as opposed to federal authority. He and his supporters cry out that the South is a hapless minority, subjected to the rule of a ruthless majority. They ask recognition of their minority status in the nation. However, they remain strangely silent about human rights or about the rights of the Negro minority in their midst.

The state sovereignty idea has been distorted beyond all reason. A sovereign state is one which reserves unto itself all authority and independence. Such states enter into treaties with other states; they coin money; they make war upon one another; today they have a seat in the United Nations. The states of this country have none of this power or authority. All such resides in the federal union governed by a national Constitution. No state has a right to secede from this union. This question was settled finally and forever by the Civil War.

There cannot be one law for the South and another for the remainder of the nation. What is constitutional in California is likewise constitutional in South Carolina. Our Constitution makes it clear that the states are prohibited, as states, from imposing any sort of racial restrictions upon those of its citizens who, as citizens of the United States of America, are thus constitutionally entitled to equal and identical rights with all other citizens.

It has been argued that the federal government is the creation of the states.

Even if we accept this thesis, it would apply only to the thirteen original colonies and to the State of Texas. All the other states were created by the federal government—their boundaries delimited, their powers bestowed, their form of government assured. Whatever validity state sovereignty may have had in 1787, it is now a sentimental myth. Any other interpretation would lead to disunion and anarchy.

What of states' rights? Of course the states have certain rights. They also have responsibilities. But these rights and these responsibilities are encompassed within the framework of the Constitution of the United States of America. No state has a right to select the laws which it will observe and reject those which it does not like, any more than an individual has such a right. No state has a right to abridge the constitutional rights of any citizen or group of citizens on the basis of race or color. The rights that inhere in statehood are rights which must be extended equally to all citizens of the respective states. And it is the responsibility of the states to see that these individual rights are safeguarded.

This responsibility the southern advocates of states' rights shirk. They demand for themselves minority rights which in turn they deny to their own minorities. While protesting loudly and vigorously alleged restrictions upon their liberties, they consistently restrict the freedom of Negro citizens in their states.

To justify their discrimination, they point in scorn to the relatively small property taxes paid by Negro citizens of their states, conveniently overlooking the indirect taxes Negroes pay in the form of rent and in the purchase of consumer goods.

Yesterday's *New York Times* tells of the sale of 10 million dollars in school bonds by Mississippi and the account contains the significant statement:

"They are full-faith-and-credit obligations of the state *and have special claim to revenue from a state sales tax."*

Who pays for whose schools? Likewise they disregard the fact that the southern states generally pay into the federal treasury far less in taxes than do the northern and western states. Moreover, the former get back in federal contributions far greater per capita returns than do typical northern states.

Because we believe in the principle of taxation according to ability to pay, we do not begrudge the South this extra share of federal benefits. We would not discriminate against the South because the region is poor. Nor do we believe the South is justified in discriminating against its Negro citizens because they are poor.

In further justification of defiance of the Court's opinion, the segregationists charge that the standards of education would be lowered for all children if schools were desegregated, because Negro children are incapable of attaining the mental achievement of whites. This contention is based upon the comparative records of white and Negro children in scholastic tests, and upon the comparative scores of white and Negro adults in military classification tests.

It is perfectly true that, *on the average,* the Negro scores have been lower than the white scores. It is quite another matter, however, how these differences are to be interpreted. To the rational observer, there is no mystery in the fact that the group averages of people who have had several generations of deficient and sometimes nonexistent education are poorer than those of their more favored fellow citizens.

Actually, the same data show that there is a great difference in achievement on these tests when there has been even a modest step toward equality of opportunity. Northern Negro scores are much superior to those of southern Negroes, in fact, in some instances, they have been found superior to those of southern whites.

Moreover, all of this evidence deals with averages; those who would use it as an excuse for not desegregating schools conveniently forget that many Negroes, despite the disadvantages, score just as high as whites. For these, obviously, poor group achievement is no excuse for continued segregation.

The news pictures from Little Rock, and Nashville, and Charlotte these past months provided some wordless commentaries on the relative quality of the white and Negro children involved.

We hear much, also, of the fear that a "Second Reconstruction" will ensue if Negro Southerners are given free access to the ballot and to equal opportunity. But there are few periods in our history which have left such a heritage of misinformation and distortion. The Reconstruction years are spoken of as the "Tragic Era" of American history, and have been pretty thoroughly sold as such to the nation as a whole. The fact is, however, Reconstruction was not imposed until all-white legislatures of the South's own choosing had proceeded within two years of the War's end, to reinstate Negro slavery by means of the so-called Black Codes.

There is, in fact, considerable justification for regarding the true "Tragic Era" as that in which, a dozen years after the principles of unity and freedom were so bloodily vindicated, the rest of the country turned its back on what it chose to call "the South's" racial problem. The Negro was left, virtually unaided, to work out his own salvation on terms dictated to him in complete disregard of his constitutional status as a citizen of the United States. The bitter consequences of this disregard for what was then, as now, the whole nation's concern, are only too apparent in today's integration crisis.

The proponents of segregation have made much of the "separate-but-equal" doctrine of the *Plessy v. Ferguson* decision of the Supreme Court in 1896. They are bemoaning its reversal by the Supreme Court on May 17, 1954, in the public school segregation cases. In this time of shrill shouting and instigated violence, they choose to forget the prophetic dissenting opinion of Mr. Justice Harlan in the Plessy case. Said the sole dissenter:

If laws of like character should be enacted in the several states of the union, the effect would be in the highest degree mischievous. Slavery as an institution tolerated by law would, it is true, have disappeared from our country, but there would remain a power in the states, by sinister legislation, to interfere with the full enjoyment of the blessings of freedom; to regulate civil rights common to all citizens upon the basis of race; and to place in a condition of legal inferiority a large body of American citizens. . . .

This is precisely what the Southern states have done. This is what they mean by states' rights. This is segregation. This is what is now so feverishly and so fanatically defended as necessary to what has been called in this forum "a precious and sacred custom." Stripped of all rhetoric and emotion, that custom, I submit, embodies the ignoble objective of keeping down, by any means, a whole race on the basis of mere skin color. An intervening hundred years have meant nothing. In 1957, as in 1857 in the Dred Scott debate, the embattled racists are maintaining that a black man has no rights which a white man is bound to respect.

The Negro citizens of our common country, a country they have sweated to build and died to defend, are determined that the verdict at Appomattox will not be renounced, that the clock will not be turned back, that they shall enjoy what is justly theirs.

They are prepared to sacrifice today as they have sacrificed in the past. They are willing and eager to pay the price for freedom so long overdue. Neither punitive legislation, nor harassing regulations, nor threats, nor economic freeze-outs, nor insult, nor humiliation, nor mobs, nor death will halt them in their quest.

Their little children, begotten of parents of faith and courage, have shown by their fearlessness and their dignity that a people will not be denied their heritage. Complex as the problem is and hostile as the climate of opinion may be in certain areas, Negro Americans are determined to press for not only a beginning, but a middle and a final solution, in good faith and with American democratic speed.

The Negro position is clear. Three years of intimidation on the meanest and most brutal of levels have not broken their ranks or shaken their conviction.

What of the rest of our nation? It must make a decision for morality and legality and move in support of it, not merely for the good of the Negroes, but for the destiny of the nation itself.

Already I have indicated that this is a new and dangerous world. This cold war is a test of survival for the West. The Soviet sputnik, now silent and barely visible, casts a shadow not lightly to be brushed aside. Can we meet the challenge of Moscow in the sciences and in war with a country divided upon race and color? Can we afford to deny to any boy or girl the maximum of education, that education which may mean the difference between democratic life and totalitarian death?

One of the lessons of the sputnik is that we dare not persist with segregated education, or with second-class citizenship. It is plain now that we do not have the exclusive "know-how" and that we need every brain and every man and woman who can be mustered for the campaign of survival. In common sense we must train and employ our maximum potential.

Finally, of course, we are impelled by our glorious traditions to take the high road, though hard, rather than the low road, though easy. It is easy for some to employ naked power against those who are partly shackled. It is easy for others to turn aside and to leave the sticky and unpleasant tasks for time to heal or for someone, somewhere, to "work out."

But this has never been the American way when human rights are at stake. It has never been so as we have leaped to the aid of the oppressed across the seas of the world; it cannot be so with our own, within our own borders.

To deny our ability to achieve a just solution within the framework of our Declaration of Independence and our Bill of Rights is to deny the genius of Americans. To reject our moral precepts is to renounce our partnership with God in bringing the kingdom of righteousness into being here on earth.

We may falter and stumble, but we cannot fail.

OUR UNFINISHED BUSINESS

CONTEMPORARY FORUM is an issue-centered compendium of American public discourse in the twentieth century—a record of business transacted within various public forums. It is premature to adjudicate much of the record, yet the evidence is impressive that by and large Americans have succeeded—at considerable cost in lives and treasure—in coming to terms with this "terrible twentieth century," as Churchill once called it, while holding fast to historic freedoms. But no record can guarantee the future. What then of tomorrow, with its haunting paradox "full of peril—bright with hope?" To dismiss the question as anybody's guess consigns the future to fateful chance. If people are to act wisely and bravely, they must sort out and identify those critical matters of unfinished business on which they will be called to negotiate, and ascertain the terms.

Nations often have been sustained and guided in passages from darkness into light by the sagacity of eloquent men. During the crucial decade of the 1950s, one man above others qualified for the office of speaker-at-large to America. As both candidate for high public office and as private citizen, Adlai E. Stevenson devoted himself through travel, speeches, and writing to interpreting the world to America and America to the world. By common consent, at home and abroad, his speeches have exhibited the attributes of the civilized mind and heart—a vision for the future defined by a sense of history and a perceptive acquaintance with contemporary life; faith in ideas as instruments of progress; concern for nuances of thought and expression; appreciation for wit that confers perspective. For these reasons, the closing unit of this volume departs from earlier sections by presenting only one speaker and a single speech: Adlai E. Stevenson's "The Political Relevance of Moral Principle." This speech, delivered near the end of the sixth decade of the century, comes as close as a single speech can to capturing the quality of Stevenson's eloquence in behalf of a new America quickened by a sense of its rendezvous with a world in revolution.

On July 26, 1952, at the unseemly hour of 3:00 A.M., something new happened to political discourse. In his address accepting the Democratic nomination for President, Adlai Stevenson flung open the windows of smoke-filled rooms to wash out the gaseous language of conventional politics. "What does concern me," he remarked, "in common with thinking partisans of both parties is not just winning this election, but how it is won, how well we can take advantage of this great quadrennial opportunity to debate issues sensibly and soberly." Stevenson lost the election, but the quality of his speeches made the 1952 campaign memorable. Stevenson lost again in 1956, but even in defeat his concern for the public consequences of his speeches transcended interest in private misfortune. Interviewed shortly after his second unsuccessful campaign, he reflected on the durable values. "What endures out of all this . . . is the extent to which one can penetrate the minds of people and influence our generation. If I can't win, I at least want to impress some ideas on the thinking of our times; and if I succeed in doing that, it's compensation enough."[1]

In a shrinking world where misery is the rule and insurrection the hope, Stevenson has been profoundly troubled by the moral and intellectual sloth of a fat civilization at home. In season and out he has spoken to stir the conscience and reason of Americans, urging them to abandon false gods and to take up God's work on earth. In his own aphorism, "Only a people who can achieve the moral mastery of themselves can hope to win the moral leadership of others." Our success in coping with this revolutionary age depends on whether we view democracy "as a means of hanging on to yesterday or a way of meeting tomorrow." Hence, the political relevance of moral principle finds its realization in the continuous engagement of a forward-looking citizenry in the on-going, unfinished business of our dynamic world. But better tomorrows, in the final analysis, demand minds informed by the discourse of inquiry and criticism. In Stevenson's own words:

> The tradition of critical inquiry and discussion informs our entire civilization. Our scientific progress is based upon a final belief in rational order coupled with trial and error in establishing that order. At its finest, our religious tolerance is based not on a denial of a spiritual order but upon the belief that man's dignity demands that he should make his own search and find, through freedom to know and to see, the truth which he has it in him to find. And in the field to which fate seems particularly to have assigned me—the field of

[1] John B. Oakes, "Visit with Private Citizen Stevenson," *The New York Times Magazine,* November 25, 1956, p. 12.

politics—I claim that our political institutions reflect, profoundly and
dynamically, the critical view of life. As Walter Bagehot said: "It
was government by discussion that broke the bond of ages and set
free the originality of mankind."[2]

In July, 1959, Stevenson was asked on a London television program what he
would emphasize if he were able to write his own epitaph. He replied: "I would
like most to be remembered as having contributed to a higher level of political
dialogue in the United States."

[2] Adlai E. Stevenson, *What I Think* (New York: Harper & Brothers, 1956), p. xiii.

The Political Relevance of
Moral Principle

ADLAI EWING STEVENSON

(*For biographical sketch, see p. 277.*)

". . . The quality of our moral response has become the decisive issue in politics. . . ."

I have been profoundly flattered by your invitation to inaugurate these annual lectures in memory of A. Powell Davies. Profoundly flattered, also, by the recitation of my qualifications for this inauguration. There have been some other inaugurations for which I was not qualified. I count it a great honor to be asked to help in any way in commemoration of a man so eminently worthy of being remembered, and it is hard indeed to pay adequate homage to a man whose own words were so fresh, so apt, so fitting to the important issues of the day. So I confess my uneasiness.

I must also confess my uneasiness on another count. Not that I am the least bit uncomfortable in the presence of so many Unitarians, but because, not far from this place in this building, hang the portraits of my grandmother and my great-aunt, both of whom were devout Presbyterians. Indeed, I used to say that my father was a Presbyterian and a Democrat and my mother a Republican and a Unitarian; that evidently they made a deal and I took his political party and

The First A. Powell Davies Memorial Address, Constitution Hall, Washington, D.C., January 18, 1959. The text reproduced here was supplied by All Souls Church (Unitarian), who sponsored the address. Reprinted by courtesy of All Souls Church, Washington, D.C.

her religion. I was a compromise to begin with and therefore a natural politician.

Telling that story to political audiences I used to put special emphasis on my father's Democracy; I am very happy at last to be able to put some emphasis on my mother's Unitarianism.

But I am encouraged by one fact. Dr. Davies did not feel that his office as a minister of religion debarred him from comment upon contemporary problems. On the contrary, he saw that he could make his message relevant to his people only by showing it at work in the concrete issues of their daily life.

I think of a story my grandfather told about the preacher who was driving along a back road when he espied a parishioner who was wearily clearing up a rocky field. "That's a fine job you and the Lord have done cleaning up that rocky field," he shouted. "Thank you, parson," the man replied. "I wish you could have seen it when the Lord had it all to himself."

Dr. Davies believed that God is dependent on man, as man is on God. He believed that the clergy above all were responsible for making a reality of the bond between God and man, and he was fearless in letting his congregation and the world know the truth as he saw it. He had a sensitive awareness of peril to the individual in our day of bigness, of statism and conformity. Therefore he was impelled to fight for the oppressed and the persecuted; to fight for equal justice for all and the rights inherent in our citizenship. Ardently he defended freedom of the mind, free speech, the right of the dissenter to speak, the duty of the conformist to listen. And his compassion was boundless.

It was the tardiness of the American social conscience in understanding the severity of its ordeal, its contest with authoritarianism that made Dr. Davies impatient, that made him work so hard to awaken us to the peril. He literally wore himself out trying to mobilize public opinion, trying to induce every American to hold himself personally responsible for the preservation of what we call freedom.

From the mountain of his vision, Dr. Davies constantly proclaimed the political relevance of moral principle and of religion as a "judgment of righteousness." From the dusty plain of politics I would like in my turn to reaffirm this political relevance. I like to believe that there may be some value in echoing testimony from a layman who has spent his middle life in the press and confusion of great events in government service, in diplomacy and in politics.

I was, by the way, inaugurated as Governor of Illinois just ten years ago this week and since then there has never been a dull moment—I was about to say there has never been a moment. As you know, my career was just a series of triumphs! Yet I feel myself blessed like few others, for few of my generation have participated in as many aspects of our national life or seen as much of our world or known as many of its leaders. It has been an exciting, joyous decade of unremitting toil and high adventure, sustained by pride in my great country and by certain confidence in its democratic institutions. Latterly, however, I have been troubled and less sure and it is of these feelings, or at least of some of them, that

I wanted to talk here. I like to think that Dr. Davies shared some of this anxiety. Well, I remember, too, that one of the Gracchi said more than 2000 years ago that political success required three talents and no virtues. The first talent, he said, was the ability to choose the winning side. Failing that, the second talent was the ability to extricate oneself from the losing side. And the third talent was never to make an enemy. After reading that, I understood better how I had succeeded so dramatically!

All politics is made up of many things—economic pressures, personal ambitions, the desire to exercise power, the overriding issues of national need and of national aspiration. But if it is nothing more, it is without roots. It is built on shifting sands of emotion and of interest. When challenged, it can give no account of itself. When threatened, it is in danger of collapse.

Today, when the threat and the challenge to free society seem more total and powerful than ever before, it is not a political luxury nor is it fruitless pedantry to re-examine our fundamental principles. I think it more likely indeed to be the very condition of survival.

There is a phrase of Dr. Davies that stays in my mind. I do not know when I have heard a more terse and pregnant summing up of our predicament. "The world," he said, "is now too dangerous for anything but the truth, too small for anything but brotherhood." This I believe to be in broad measure a correct estimate of the condition of human society, which is now capable, with a few hydrogen bombs, of extinguishing itself. Today we can all be killed by the same bombs or atomic fallout. In that sense we have attained a desperate physical solidarity. But moral and social solidarity in the family of man is still to be found.

Not so long ago I visited Dr. Albert Schweitzer in his primitive jungle hospital in French Equatorial Africa, and he told me that he considered this the most dangerous period in history. I said, "In contemporary history?" "No," he said, "in all human history." "Why?" "Because," he said, "heretofore nature has controlled man in the last analysis, but now man has learned to control elemental forces of nature, before he has learned to control himself."

Many of us seem, here in our country, to rely on some mythical God-given superiority of the white Western world to save us. And my concern is that there is more evidence that the Communists accept the reality of the human condition than we do.

It is impossible to spend weeks traveling around the Soviet Union, as I did this summer, without taking away an overwhelming impression of thrust and purpose in most aspects of Soviet life. The revolutionary ardor of the early days to be sure has cooled with time but even the very pragmatic political leaders seem to believe profoundly in the truth of their way of life and are quietly confident that it will sweep the whole world in time. I think they sincerely believe that their methods, their aspirations, their dreams, make up the final truth about the nature of man and society; that collective man in the collective state is the ultimate unfolding of human destiny, the end of history, the "far off divine event" for which mankind has been in long travail, the vision of "all things made new" that has haunted men's minds ever since Christianity thrust into human thought the intoxicating ideal of a perfected humanity.

From this conviction, if I have not overstated it, flow two consequences. The first is that no effort, no dedication, no sacrifice is too great that may help to realize the Communist party's goals in Soviet society. The second is that no corner of humanity can be a matter of indifference to the Communist state, because the whole human race is destined to become in time one communist brotherhood.

These are not abstract generalizations. Russia is a vast powerhouse of energy, all harnessed to the communal task of building this dream. The thrust of economic growth which adds a nine or ten percent increase each year to industrial expansion is one aspect of this restless energy. The vast sums available for science and research are another. The self-discipline and long hours put in by school children to train themselves as the scientists, the technicians, the administrators, the linguists of the new world order are perhaps the most significant measure of the resources of energy, work and skill upon which the leaders hope to draw. And what one sees and feels in the Soviet Union I am told is dwarfed by China. One night in Moscow I talked with Serge Obraztsov, the brilliant director of the famous Puppet Theatre. Among other things, he said to me: "I visited China five years ago. It was the most extraordinary experience of my life. People in China have had nothing—nothing! Now for several hundred million people there are new dreams. They are dreaming of tomorrow. I cannot describe to you the feeling of excitement there—much, much more even than here in the Soviet Union."

I don't know about China, but the energy, the drive, the dedication in the USSR spill over into international affairs in ways that we are only now beginning to realize. In part, of course, this is the restless concern which all imperial powers must exercise, especially when the peoples they control are as restive and unreliable as the captive peoples in Russia's European empire. But communist activity, planning and efforts in trade and aid are not confined to areas of communist control. They are worldwide, and there is no corner of the earth's surface which they think too insignificant for their attention, none. While trade missions are busy in Latin America, academic representatives are touring West Africa, Arab and Asian students are being trained in Moscow, technical advisers are dispatched to India and Burma, Indonesia, and the glossy flood of propaganda depicting the Soviet millennium of bumper harvests and happy workers is pumped out all around the world.

All this we know—or begin to know. But I wonder how often we try to grasp the scale of dedication that lies behind it. Why should they be so busy? Why so much work and thought? Why such diversion of precious resources? Why such patience through every setback, such forward thrusts through every point of Western weakness? Heaven knows, we only want to stay home. Why don't they? Why do we never meet an isolationist Communist? These are some of the questions that haunted me when I confronted that first time this iron, forceful, formidable way of life.

And I do not think that there is any doubt about the answer. Part of it is simply needed foreign trade. Part is fear, the search for security through friends. And part is the historical centrifugal forces in Russia which have been pressing outward for two hundred years—to the Pacific, the Balkans, the Middle East, the Straits, and so on. But the important thing is that the Soviet Russians believe in their truth, as the men of the Western world once believed in theirs. They, not we, are firing the shots that are heard around the world—and also the satellites that orbit above it. The fact that their faith is in many ways an evil perversion of the great propositions that once made the blood course in Western veins does not alter the fact that their tempo is dynamic and rapid, ours sluggish—even, I think, to ourselves.

Surely, the reason cannot be that we Americans have lost our vision of truth and brotherhood. No country on earth owes the sense of community more explicitly to the fact that it is united not by race or nationality but by fidelity to an idea. We were born "dedicated to a proposition" and our greatest leaders—the Jeffersons, the Lincolns, the Wilsons—were not great because they achieved purely American purposes, but because they were able to speak for humanity at large and extend their vision to the whole family of man.

Nor, I believe, can we find fault with the substance of what we have endearingly called the American dream. Its truths are still "self-evident." The possession of liberty and the pursuit of happiness—rightly understood—these have not been overthrown as the highest goods of human society. Indeed, the ferment of our freedom works inexorably and dangerously in the communist world. No one can have visited Poland without seeing how little the Polish people really accept their servitude and how they look beyond their neighbors to the free world as the reservoir of power and of hope.

But, alas, on the basis of the record, one would hardly suspect that the Western world possessed so powerful a weapon. All our talk—in diplomacy, in strategy, in aid and trade, in all of the intricacies of our worldwide relations—has been to a depressing degree purely defensive. We have offered aid not to help others but to shield ourselves. We have reacted to countless Soviet initiatives; acted on our own initiative barely at all. We watch the skies for other people's sputniks and listen to the telegraph wires for other people's moves. Yet we are the free men of this universe; we are the children of liberty, the beneficiaries of unequalled abundance, and heirs of the highest, proudest political tradition ever known to man!

Why is this lack of initiative? Why this paralysis of will? What have we done to our truth, our brotherhood—the supreme truth of freedom, the Christian truth of brotherly love? Have they failed? Or have we?

There is no more urgent duty than to discover why we have failed, if we have, and I think we have, and to get back into the arena, aspiring, striving, fighting, if you please, once more for what we believe. An examination of what you might call our collective conscience is to my mind far more important than particular projects or programs. You can have a perfect assembly of pieces in your watch, but they are worthless if the mainspring is broken. I am not worried about our various pieces—our technology, our science, our machines, our resources. But I am concerned, desperately concerned, about our mainspring. That it has run down, we know. But is it broken; is it broken beyond repair? In the last analysis, no question is worth more consideration in America today.

And I would like to suggest some of the ways in which it seems to me we have enfeebled the great central pulse of our freedom, the great truth of liberty, which, more than any other nation, we first set working in the modern world.

Goethe, who also lived through a crisis of freedom, said of his generation: "What you have inherited from your fathers, earn over again for yourselves or it will not be yours." We inherited this freedom we talk about so glibly. We seem unaware that it has to be remade and re-earned in each generation of man. One reason for this failure is, I believe, passing at last. In recent years we were stifled with complacent self-confidence. We believed ourselves dominant in every field. We talked of "the American Century." We forgot the ardors and the efforts that had given us a measure of pre-eminence. Complacency made us impervious to ideas, even the obvious idea that we are in danger. So we assumed that all we needed was to sit still to enjoy the "peace and prosperity" that was our right.

I believe that phase is now passing. Our foolish languor has been shaken, if not shattered. We are more ready to examine ourselves and our record. And it is a privilege of our society that every citizen should make his own inquiry. If I stress one or the other aspect of the problem, this is simply my angle of vision. You will have yours. The urgent thing is to feel the need for re-thinking and to set to work these ultimate energies of a free society—which cannot be done by the fiat of government but only by the troubled conscience of responsible men and women.

It is simply as a citizen as concerned as you are that I should like to suggest what seem to me the obstacles to a full understanding of our great mission in this time of testing.

I believe—as I have said before—that we have confused the free with the free and easy. If freedom had been the happy, simple, relaxed state of ordinary humanity, man would have everywhere been free—whereas through most of time and space he has been in chains. Do not let us make any mistake about this. The natural government of man is servitude. Tyranny is the normal pattern of government. It is only by intense thought, by great effort, by burning idealism and unlimited sacrifice that freedom has prevailed as a system of government. And the efforts which were first necessary to create it are fully as necessary to sustain it in our own day.

He who offers this thing that we call freedom as the soft option is a deceiver or himself deceived. He who sells it cheap or offers it as the by-product of this or that economic system is knave or fool. For freedom demands infinitely more care and devotion than any other political system. It puts consent and personal initiative in the place of command and obedience. By relying upon the devotion and initiative of ordinary citizens, it gives up the harsh but effective disciplines that underpin all the tyrannies which over the millennia have stunted the full stature of man.

But of what use is escape from external restraint if, given the opportunity, man simply stunts himself? If freedom means ease alone, if it means shirking the hard disciplines of learning, if it means evading the rigors and rewards of creative activity, if it means more expenditure on advertising than on education, if it means "bachelor cooking" and "life adjustment" courses in the schools, and the steady cult of the trivial and the mediocre, if it means—worst of all—indifference, even contempt for all but athletic excellence in our educational system, we may keep for a time the forms of free society, but its spirit will be dead.

I believe we have had enough of adjustment, of conformity, of easy options and the least common denominator in our system. We need instead to see the "pursuit of happiness" in terms which are historically proven and psychologically correct. The dreary failure in history of all classes committed to pleasure and profit alone, the vacuity and misery accompanying the sole pursuit of ease—the collapse of the French aristocracy, the corruption of imperial Rome, the decline and fall of the resplendent Manchus—all these facts of history do not lose their point because the pleasures of today are mass pleasures and no longer the enjoyments of an elite. If we become a nation of Bourbons, numbers will not save us. We shall go their way, too. Vacuity and indifference are not redeemed by the fact that everyone can share in them. They merely restrict the circle from which regeneration can come.

I say this—I hope you will believe me—in no Puritan or pleasure-hating spirit. On the contrary, there is no boredom, no misery to equal the pursuit of distraction alone. We do not slip into happiness. It is strenuously sought and earned. A nation glued to recreation, to the television screen is not simply at a loss before the iron pioneers of the new collective society. It is not even having a good time. No society has ever spent as much as we do on drink and tranquilizers. Can one argue that this is evidence of universal fun? I ran across a quotation from La-Bruyère on the court of Louis XIV which struck me as relevant: "Les joies sont visibles, mais fausses, et les chagrins cachés, mais réels"—its joys are visible, but artificial, and its sorrows hidden, but real.

But perhaps this misunderstanding of the true nature of happiness and of the conditions of its pursuit is simply an aspect of something else—our misunderstanding of the real nature of freedom. I recall the words of the wise Judge Learned Hand, who warned us that freedom would not survive in our Constitution if it had already died in the hearts of the people. We shall not have a free society unless we have free men.

And how often do we reflect upon what this inner freedom entails? "Give me the man," cries Hamlet, "who is not passion's slave." But this is what we are in danger of becoming, slaves to a tyranny more intimate and inescapable than any that Stalin or Mao Tse-tung could impose. We can be made slaves simply by the clutter and complexity of modern living—which notoriously leaves no time for serious thought and offers every means of distraction so that we can avoid such thought. Between aircraft that take us everywhere more rapidly, newspapers that grow in weight and coverage, news that flashes round the globe, ceaseless and competitive entertainment, fashions—God help us!—that change from sack to trapeze and back again, we can fill up every "unforgiving minute" with enough trash and preoccupation to still forever the deeper voices of the soul. Like Matthew Arnold, we can

> . . . see all sights from pole to pole,
> And glance and nod and hustle by,
> And never once possess our soul
> Before we die.

How are we to defend freedom if, for the tyranny of external control, we substitute the clattering, cluttering tyranny of internal aimlessness and fuss? This freedom of our souls, freedom at the profoundest level of our being, is not a gift to us by our contemporary way of life. On the contrary, much of this life is a direct conspiracy against it. And if we cannot—by a certain discipline, by readiness for reflection and quiet, by determination to do the difficult and aim at a lasting good—rediscover the real purpose and direction of our existence, we shall not be free. Our society will not be free. And between a chaotic, selfish, indifferent, commercial society and the iron discipline of the communist world, I would not like to predict the outcome. Outer tyranny with purpose may well triumph over the inner, purposeless tyranny of a confused and aimless way of life.

I doubt if any society in history has faced so great a moral challenge as ours, or needed more desperately to draw on the deepest sources of courage and responsibility. Ours is the first human community in which resources are so abundant that almost no policies lie beyond our capacity for purely physical reasons. What we decide to do, we can do. The inhibitions of poverty—lack of resources, lack of capital, lack of power—do not hold us back. We can accomplish what we aim at. Thus, perhaps for the first time in the world, choice, not means, ends, not instruments, are decisive.

Then again we have proved—drably and dangerously—over the last decade that defensiveness is not a sufficient reason for action. All the policies we have pursued in self-defense have left us still on the defensive. But if we do not act from fear, we must find some other motivation. In free society there is no other alternative but to tap the vigor, the faith, the imagination of the people themselves. We must find out once more who we are, as the psychologists say. And

I would earnestly appeal especially to the women of our country to help lead the way to this new self-examination and self-discipline.

But perhaps the most urgent reason why the quality of our moral response has become the decisive issue in politics is quite simply that most of the major problems of our day present themselves in moral terms, and are probably insoluble without some stirring of generosity, some measure of vision. Let me give you three instances. In the wealthiest nation in the world, at least five million families still live in squalid but remediable poverty. They are a minority. They do not have the votes to force the issue of their misfortune into the front rank of public issues. They depend, for remedies, upon the alert conscience of the majority. But how do we keep the conscience sensitive and alert? By concentrating on our own concerns? By adding the dishwasher to the television set to the air conditioner? By griping over taxes and attacking that great bogey we call "the welfare state"? By closing our minds every time our shiny car takes us through a slum? No— we shall have the dedication, the drive to wipe poverty out of this rich land only if the well-to-do majority of today do not repeat the selfish indifference which, in many communities, has been the epitaph of the well-to-do of yesterday.

Or take the issue of the rights and status of our colored citizens. This is our small share of a world-wide problem. The four hundred years of dominance of men of white skin is ending. The vast colored majority of mankind are seeking the opportunity and the respect which white people have been lucky enough to enjoy for so long—sometimes at the colored people's expense. But, within this world-wide crisis, we in America, with our colored minority, have a major role to play—for good or evil. "The unfinished work" which Lincoln left us, of creating a society in which all men can hold up their heads as equals and self-respecting citizens, can never be accomplished unless there are enough white men and women who resist to the core of their being the moral evil of treating any of God's children as essentially inferior.

Nor is this simply a question of our own national community. I come back to the painful fact that the Communists show a world-wide concern which is largely lacking among the men of the West. The whole human race is their horizon. Their "brotherhood" is materialist, collectivist, atheist, and we dislike it, but it embraces everybody, and it is the framework of policies which take the missionaries of their new order to the ends of the earth. I say with all the emphasis that I can command that we have no corresponding commitment to our fellowman. For hundreds of years, we have preached the Christian promise of brotherhood, but today, when vanishing space and scientific revolution have turned our planet into a single neighborhood, the ideal means little in terms of concern or conviction, in terms of policy or of action.

Here we are in the Atlantic world, 16 percent of the world's peoples consuming 70 percent of the world's wealth. We cannot be indifferent to the moral implications of this gigantic gap. I do not know how we can gain a new perspective about the narrow world of plenty and of poverty in which we live unless moral insights of justice and compassion stir us to understand the privileged position in which we live.

We are not going to be stirred to action by our own needs. We are the cushioned, the protected, the fortunate minority. It is not the measure of our morals or the lesson of our history to be spurred on only by fear of Russian encroachment. What we have done has largely been from this motivation, and it has left us on the defensive. Our hope is to accept the implications of our own faith, to make concrete the image of brotherhood which we profess, to set to work to express our dedication in whatever effort or sacrifice the world's needs may dictate. And, if we must always think in terms of contest with the Soviets, let us bear in mind that the ability to create the good life for the greatest numbers will be decisive.

This age has been defined in many ways—as a time of conflict in ideology, as a time of ferment in technology, as a period of revolution in science, as an era when at last the means lie at hand to free mankind from the ancient shackles of pain and of hunger. It is all these things—but I believe the true crisis of our time lies at a deeper level. We have indeed conquered means and resources unknown at earlier ages. We have had thrown open to us frontiers of choice which would leave earlier ages stupefied by their scale and their scope.

But all this freedom and elbow room only thrusts onto us with more force the fundamental issue of the truth that is within us. We can use our wealth, our capacity for some vision of truth, some ideal of brotherhood, or we can imprison ourselves within the selfishness of our own concerns and the limitations of a narrow nationhood. This is the dimension of our crisis.

You may argue that these qualities of dedication, of selflessness, are pretty remote from the realities of politics. They are all very well for private life, but what part can they play in the rough and tumble game of partisanship, of primaries, conventions and election campaigns? Ambition, drive, material interests, political skills, the arts of maneuver—all these, you say, have their part, but do not let us pretend that the democratic process is primarily a school of virtue or an arena of moral combat.

And yet, I wonder. It has been the view of great philosophers and great statesmen that our system of free government depends in the first instance upon the virtue of its citizens. Montesquieu made virtue the condition of republican government; Washington declared that it could not survive without it. We have had a hundred and seventy-five years of it and no one can deny that the system has survived a remarkable amount of skulduggery. In fact, it is probably a tougher system than its founders imagined. Yet I believe they are right. For no democratic system can survive without at least a large and an active leaven of citizens in whom dedication and selflessness are not confined to private life but are the fundamental principles of their activity in the public sphere.

Naked interest and ambition will carry a lot of people naturally and inevitably into politics. We do not need societies for the promotion of lobbies. Interests, good and bad, will promote themselves. Nor, in any generation do we lack politicians whose only principle of action is the advancement of their own career—the starry-eyed opportunists and all the other eager men in a hurry to the top. But into what state must politics degenerate if that is all we find active in the political arena? That and sectional interests played upon by personal ambitions? There have been such periods, but our democratic system survived them because such epochs were followed and cleansed by periods of disinterested reform.

But there has never been any disinterested reform without disinterested reformers. And here we come to the essential contribution made by dedication and selflessness to the public good. No one ever did any good in politics without readiness for endless hard work—for the grinding, boring, tedious work, as well as the glamorous, high sounding, headline hitting work. The painstaking hours collecting the facts, the hours in committee and conference, the hours in persuasion and argument, the hours of defeat and disappointment, the hours of disgust and revulsion at the darker sides of human behavior—these cannot be supported without energy and devotion. No reforms come easy; even the most obvious will have its entrenched enemies. Each one is carried to us on the bent and the weary backs of patient, dedicated men and women.

They are not only dedicated in their readiness to give energy and work to the cause; they must also have sufficiently clear sight and open minds and hearts to see the need for reform in the first place. But clear sight and an open heart for the needs of others is again something that hardly "comes naturally." We have so many needs of our own—our families, our jobs, our homes, our fortunes, our prospects. We are hemmed in with needs and interests, weighty, urgent, honorable, human needs and interests, even if they are exclusively our own. It takes an extra dimension of vision to see beyond our inner circle of personal interest. Most people, most of the time, do not possess it, that extra dimension of vision, which is one reason why self-regarding interests make up so much of the stuff of politics. And this, I suppose, is why the men and women of genuine, imperturbable public spirit seem so few and far between.

I sometimes think there is a danger of this element of vision vanishing almost wholly from our political life. In the main we are so comfortable; so many evils of the past have shrunk in size and almost out of sight. At the same time, people marry much younger; they have larger families and are profoundly involved in earning a living, making careers and safe-guarding the future of their children. It is more difficult, they say, to give time to public affairs when private life is so urgent and so absorbing.

Yet is it, I wonder, more urgent and absorbing than a hundred years ago when young men not only married young, had large families, built up careers, but also opened up the new frontiers, created new cities out of the wilderness and gave to new states and communities the framework of active political life?

If one reads the story of young Abraham Lincoln, it is hard to believe that his struggles as a young lawyer, his difficulties as a young parent were less than those of young men today. Yet there was no time when the deepest issues of the day did not occupy his mind or the call of statecraft make itself heard above the claims and clamor of everyday life. Nor was he alone or exceptional. Stephen Douglas' life was no different. The prairie towns were filled with earnest, active citizens deeply, profoundly concerned with the great issues of a nation "half slave, half free." When the multitudes gathered, a hundred years ago, to listen in rapt attention for hours to the Lincoln-Douglas debates, had they fewer responsibilities and duties than the citizens of today to many of whom the great issues of politics seem to be most usefully conveyed in a 15-second television flash of subliminal advertising?

Is it not possible that the pressures of personal responsibilities are not greater but that the dedication and selflessness needed to discern and to influence public issues have shrunk? In a century in which so many of the mentors of the public mind—from the psychiatrists to the ad-men—speak to us in terms of "what we owe ourselves," may there not indeed have been a slackening of devotion compared with those days, not so long distant, when what man owes to God and his neighbor was a common theme of public discourse?

If so, this is a dangerous hour for our politics and for government by consent of the governed. For at no time have so many of the great issues of the day demanded clear, real moral vision to bring them into focus—the vision, if you please, of A. Powell Davies, who loved the truth and believed in man's capacity and right to govern himself.

Notes on Sources and Supplementary Readings

These brief bibliographical notes are supplied to suggest particularly helpful sources of further information on the topics of this volume. General American histories are omitted, as are unpublished studies and other materials not readily available in most libraries. The items included fall into four categories: (1) biographies and memoirs of speakers; (2) special studies that furnish background for issues and speeches; (3) sources of additional speeches; and (4) commercially produced recordings of speakers and speeches. Only a few selected items are listed in each category. For several of the speakers represented in this anthology no biographies are yet available. Omissions in the notes that follow may be taken as our judgment that no satisfactory biography exists.

THE PROGRESSIVE ERA

For full-length biographies, see Paul Glad, *The Trumpet Soundeth: William Jennings Bryan and His Democracy, 1896–1912* (1960); Ray Ginger, *The Bending Cross, A Biography of Eugene Victor Debs* (1949); Henry F. Pringle, *Theodore Roosevelt* (1931); Arthur S. Link, *Woodrow Wilson and the Progressive Era* (1954); Belle Case La Follette and Fola La Follette, *Robert M. La Follette, 1855–1925* (2 vols., 1953); Richard W. Leopold, *Elihu Root and the Conservative Tradition* (1954); Henry F. Pringle, *The Life and Times of William Howard Taft* (2 vols., 1939). For excellent critical essays on Bryan, Wilson, and Roosevelt, see Richard Hofstadter, *The American Political Tradition* (1948). For studies of leading Progressives as public speakers, see W. N. Brigance, ed., *A History and Criticism of American Public Address* (2 vols., 1943): Myron G. Phillips, "William Jennings Bryan"; Herold T. Ross, "Albert J. Beveridge"; Carroll P. Lahman, "Robert M. La Follette"; Dayton D. McKean, "Woodrow Wilson." See also Richard Murphy's essay, "Theodore Roosevelt," in Marie K. Hochmuth, ed., *A History and Criticism of American Public Address* (1955), III.

For background, consult John Chamberlain, *Farewell to Reform* (1932); Russell B. Nye, *Midwestern Progressive Politics* (1951); Eric F. Goldman, *Rendezvous with Destiny* (1952); Richard Hofstadter, *The Age of Reform* (1955); George E. Mowry, *The Era of Theodore Roosevelt* (1958).

Debs' speeches are well represented in the *Writings and Speeches of Eugene V. Debs* (1948). Theodore Roosevelt's most important speeches given during his years of advanced Progressivism are contained in Hermann Hagedorn, ed., *The Works of Theodore Roosevelt, Memorial Edition* (24 vols., 1923–1926), XIX. John Wells Davidson, ed., *A Crossroads of Freedom* (1956) is a splendid edition of Wilson's 1912 campaign speeches; see also Ray Stannard Baker and William E. Dodd, eds., *The Public Papers of Woodrow Wilson* (6 vols., 1925). A bibliography of Root's speeches is included in Philip C. Jessup, *Elihu Root* (2 vols., 1938), II, pp. 521–552. For additional speeches upholding the conservative tradition, see Nicholas Murray Butler's address of the same title as the volume in which it appears, *Why Should We Change Our Form of Government?* (1912); William Howard Taft's 1914 speech, "Getting the Best Out of Life," in *Great Orations Delivered at Peirce Commencements* (1922).

THE LEAGUE OF NATIONS DEBATE

Arthur S. Link, *Wilson the Diplomatist* (1957); Herbert C. Hoover, *The Ordeal of Woodrow Wilson* (1958), particularly the final chapter; Joseph P. Tumulty, *Woodrow Wilson As I Knew Him* (1921), gives personal glimpses not found elsewhere. For a treatment of Wilson as a speaker see Dayton D. McKean, "Woodrow Wilson," in *A History and Criticism of American Public Address*, William N. Brigance, ed. (2 vols., 1943), II. Karl Schriftgiesser, *The Gentleman from Massachusetts* (1945), is a highly unfriendly portrait of Lodge; John A. Garraty's *Henry Cabot Lodge* (1953) is the best biography.

For background, see D. F. Fleming, *The United States and the League of Nations, 1918–1920* (1932); Thomas A. Bailey, *Woodrow Wilson and the Lost Peace* (1944), and *Woodrow Wilson and the Great Betrayal* (1945). For Lodge's account of the League debate see Henry Cabot Lodge, *The Senate and the League of Nations* (1925). Hamilton Foley, ed., *Woodrow Wilson's Case for the League of Nations* (1923), is a compilation of excerpts from Wilson's speeches and writings.

There are numerous collections of Wilson speeches. The Government Printing Office published his western tour speeches, September 4–25, 1919, under the title *Addresses of President Wilson* (1919). Other collections are *International Ideals* (1919), addresses made during his European visit, December 14, 1918–February 14, 1919; and *The Hope of the World* (1920), speeches July 10–December 9, 1919. Henry Cabot Lodge and A. Lawrence Lowell, "Joint Debate on the Covenant of Paris," in *League of Nations*, vol. II, no. 2 (April, 1919). Appendix of Lodge's *The Senate and the League of Nations* contains speeches and a verbatim transcript of the August 19, 1919, White House conference between the President and the Senate Foreign Relations Committee. *The People Shall Judge,* ed. by Social Sciences Staff of University of Chicago (2 vols., 1949), II, contains Wilson's "Peace Without Victory" speech and excerpts from Senate debate, November 19, 1919. The entire debate in the United States Senate can, of course, be found in the *Congressional Record* (1919–1920).

MODERNISM VS. FUNDAMENTALISM IN RELIGION

Harry Emerson Fosdick, *The Living of These Days* (1956) is autobiographical; Chapter 7 deals with the fundamentalist controversy. See also Paxton Hibben, *The Peerless Leader: William Jennings Bryan* (1929); and J. C. Long, *Bryan, the Great Commoner*

(1928). For the speaking careers of Fosdick and Bryan, see Robert D. Clark, "Harry Emerson Fosdick," in *A History and Criticism of American Public Address,* Marie K. Hochmuth, ed. (1955), III; and Myron G. Phillips, "William Jennings Bryan," in *A History and Criticism of American Public Address,* William N. Brigance, ed. (2 vols., 1943), II.

Norman F. Furniss, *The Fundamentalist Controversy, 1918–1931* (1954), is the best monographic treatment; contains useful bibliography. Stewart G. Cole, *The History of Fundamentalism* (1931), also has a good bibliography, particularly of periodical and pamphlet material. Gail Kennedy, ed., *Evolution and Religion* (1957), is an excellent book of readings selected by the Department of American Studies at Amherst College; Eldred C. Vanderlaan, ed., *Fundamentalism vs. Modernism* (1925), is a source book of essays and articles representing both sides of the controversy. For the Scopes trial, see Ray Ginger, *Six Days or Forever?* (1958), and Walter Lippmann, *American Inquisitors, A Commentary on Dayton and Chicago* (1928). J. Gresham Machen, *Christianity and Liberalism* (1924), gives a fuller treatment of the subject discussed in his "Christianity vs. Modern Liberalism."

Clarence E. Macartney, *Things Most Surely Believed* (1930), is a series of sermons on the Apostles' Creed by one of the leading fundamentalist ministers. Mark A. Matthews, *Gospel Sword Thrusts* (1924), presents fundamentalist sermons on doctrinal matters. *The Moody Bible Institute Monthly* published numerous articles and sermons during the twenties; some are available in pamphlet form. *The World's Most Famous Court Trial* (1925) is a stenographic report of the Scopes trial; Bryan's last undelivered speech is included as an appendix to W. J. Bryan and Mary B. Bryan, *The Memoirs of William Jennings Bryan* (1925).

POLEMICS OF THE NEW DEAL ERA

Hoover defends his policies in *The Memoirs of Herbert Hoover: The Great Depression, 1929–41* (1952). James MacGregor Burns, *Roosevelt: The Lion and the Fox* (1956) is the best single-volume biography of Roosevelt. Frank B. Freidel, *Franklin D. Roosevelt: The Triumph* (1956), which is volume 3 of a definitive biography, carries Roosevelt from 1928 through the 1932 election. Harnett T. Kane, *Louisiana Hayride* (1941) is one of many books on the Longs and their political satrapy. Oscar Handlin, *Al Smith and His America* (1958) interprets Smith in his setting. On Willkie as a transition figure in his party, see Donald Bruce Johnson, *The Republican Party and Wendell Willkie* (1960). Richard Hofstadter has written splendid critical essays on Hoover and Roosevelt in *The American Political Tradition* (1948). For a study of Roosevelt as a speaker, see an essay by Earnest Brandenburg and Waldo W. Braden in Marie K. Hochmuth, ed., *A History and Criticism of American Public Address* (1955), III. Three books written by men who worked on Roosevelt's speeches are particularly informative on his speech-making activities: Samuel I. Rosenman, *Working with Roosevelt* (1952); Raymond Moley, *After Seven Years* (1939); Robert Sherwood, *Roosevelt and Hopkins* (1948).

Frederick Lewis Allen, *Only Yesterday* (1931) is a brisk chronicle of the 1920's. Karl Schriftgiesser, *This Was Normalcy* (1948) provides a useful but biting account of political life in the 1920s. Dixon Wecter, *The Age of the Great Depression* (1948) is judicious. For a Socialist's analysis of the era, see Norman Thomas, *The Choice Before Us*

(1934) and *After the New Deal, What?* (1936). Moley's book, cited above, is hostile to Roosevelt and the New Deal. Arthur M. Schlesinger, Jr., *The Age of Roosevelt* (3 vols., 1957–1960) is both brilliant and highly readable: the first volume, *The Crisis of the Old Order,* covers 1919–1933; the second, *The Coming of the New Deal,* takes up the first two years of the Roosevelt Administration; volume three, *The Politics of Upheaval,* runs through the 1936 election, and is indispensable for studying the polemics of the era. For studies on demagogues, see Raymond Gram Swing, *Forerunners of American Fascism* (1935) and Reinhard Luthin, *American Demagogues: Twentieth Century* (1954).

On the campaign of 1928, see *The New Day: Campaign Speeches of Herbert Hoover* (1928), and Alfred E. Smith, *Campaign Addresses* (1929). Hoover's *Addresses Upon the American Road, 1933–1938* (1938) is valuable. For Roosevelt's speeches, see Samuel I. Rosenman, ed., *The Public Papers and Addresses of Franklin D. Roosevelt* (13 vols., 1938–1950). *This Is Wendell Willkie* (1940) contains articles and speeches by Willkie. *Vital Speeches of the Day* (1934–   ), a biweekly publication of contemporary speeches, is abundant in speeches by New Dealers and anti-New Dealers. Charles E. Coughlin, *A Series of Lectures on Social Justice* (1935) is a fair representation of his radio talks. Texts of speeches by 1936 Presidential candidates, both major and minor parties, are contained in *Report of the Sixth Annual New York Herald-Tribune Forum on Current Problems* (1936). Topics of the day are discussed in pamphlets entitled, *America's Town Meeting of the Air* (1935–1956), based on a popular radio forum featuring spokesmen in the public eye. *The New York Times* frequently prints full texts of speeches. The *Congressional Record* not only reports remarks and debates in Congress, but often contains speeches made by Congressmen outside of Congress and subsequently read into the *Record.* Many of Huey Long's radio speeches in 1934–1935 may be found here.

Recorded portions of speeches are available in various commercial albums. Edward R. Murrow and Fred W. Friendly, "I Can Hear It Now, 1933–1945," Columbia Masterworks ML 4095, is a chronicle of sounds and voices of the era with narrative background by Murrow. "Rendezvous with Destiny, 1933–1945," NBC Documentary Records, is a representative sampling of Roosevelt's speeches. "F.D.R. Speaks," Washington Records W-FDR, is the most complete collection of Roosevelt's speeches yet produced. "Norman Thomas Reminisces," Spoken Arts 759, is an autobiographical review of Thomas' public career drawing richly on his speeches.

HIGHER EDUCATION AND SOCIAL CHANGE

Sidney Hook, *John Dewey, An Intellectual Portrait* (1939); G. R. Geiger, *John Dewey in Perspective* (1959); Merle Curti, *The Social Ideas of American Educators* (1935), ch. 15, "John Dewey."

For background on competing theories of education, see: John S. Brubacher, *Modern Philosophies of Education* (1939), ch. 14; Theodore Brameld, *Ends and Means in Education* (1950), especially part I, "Philosophic Foundations of Education." R. Freeman Butts, *The College Charts Its Course* (1939), part IV, contrasts the conservative and progressive positions; see also his *A Cultural History of Education* (1947), chs. 21 and 22. Oscar Handlin, *John Dewey's Challenge to Education* (1959), and George P. Schmidt, *The Liberal Arts College* (1957), ch. 10, "Dewey vs. Hutchins," are good brief discussions. Dewey's *My Pedagogic Creed* (1897) is reprinted in his *Education Today* (1940). See the special John Dewey Centennial section, *Saturday Review*, XLII (November 21, 1959), pp. 16–26.

Vital Speeches of the Day, vols. I to VII, contains numerous speeches on education at commencements, conferences, inaugurations, etc. Paul A. Schilpp, ed., *Higher Education Faces the Future* (1930), is a symposium on American college education; several of the items are speeches. Robert Hutchins' Storrs Lectures at Yale were published as *The Higher Learning in America* (1936); other Hutchins addresses, 1930–1936, in *No Friendly Voice* (1936); more recent speeches, 1946–1956, in *Freedom, Education, and the Fund* (1956). John Dewey, *The Way Out of Educational Confusion* (1931), is his Inglis Lecture.

ISOLATIONISM VS. ONE WORLD

Robert E. Sherwood, *Roosevelt and Hopkins* (1948) is particularly good on this point. There is no published biography of Wheeler. Valuable for an understanding of men and the era are Virginia Cowles, *Winston Churchill* (1953); Alan Bullock, *Hitler: A Study in Tyranny* (1952); William L. Shirer, *The Rise and Fall of the Third Reich* (1960); Eric Sevareid, *Not So Wild a Dream* (1946).

Selig Adler, *The Isolationist Impulse* (1957) focuses on the twentieth century. Edwin Borchard and William Potter Lage, *Neutrality for the United States* (1937) makes a case for basing United States foreign policy on neutrality. Charles A. Beard, *American Foreign Policy in the Making, 1932–1940* (1946), and *President Roosevelt and the Coming of the War* (1948) are severely critical of Roosevelt's diplomacy. Herbert Feis, *The Road to Pearl Harbor* (1950) is a defense of American policies. Two books of high value covering the two sides of organized controversy over the intervention-isolation issue are Walter Johnson, *The Battle Against Isolation* (1944) and Wayne S. Cole, *America First, the Battle Against Intervention* (1953).

The controversy unfolds in successive volumes of *Vital Speeches of the Day* (1934–   ), which makes available speeches by political figures such as Roosevelt, Nye, Borah, Wheeler, Taft, Vandenberg, Mussolini, Hitler, and Churchill, and by opinion makers such as Charles Lindbergh, William Allen White, Robert Maynard Hutchins, Harry Emerson Fosdick, and Robert McCormick. The annual volumes of A. Craig Baird, ed., *Representative American Speeches* (1938–   ) have a fair number of speeches on the issue. There are several valuable individual collections, among which are: Bernardo di San Severino, ed., *Mussolini as Revealed in His Political Speeches* (1923); Raoul de Roussy de Sales, ed., *Adolf Hitler, My New Order* (1941); Winston Churchill, *While England Slept* (1938) and *Blood, Sweat, and Tears* (1941); Edward R. Murrow, *This Is London* (1941); Samuel I. Rosenman, ed., *The Public Papers and Addresses of Franklin D. Roosevelt* (13 vols., 1938–1950); Arthur H. Vandenberg, ed., *The Private Papers of Senator Vandenberg* (1952).

Several commercial recordings of speakers and their speeches are cited on p. 372. A valuable addition to this list is Edward R. Murrow and Fred W. Friendly, eds., "I Can Hear It Now: Winston Churchill," Columbia Masterworks KL5066, a record devoted solely to excerpts from Churchill's speeches with Murrow as narrator.

The Cold War Era

Satisfactory biographies on recent political figures are yet to be written. The best biography of Truman is Jonathan Daniels, *The Man of Independence* (1950). Russel Lord, *The Wallaces of Iowa* (1947) has an account of difficulties between Truman and Wallace over foreign policy. For biographies of Adlai Stevenson, see p. 375. The best book on Robert A. Taft is William S. White, *The Taft Story* (1954). McCarthy is treated critically by Jack Anderson and R. W. May, *McCarthy: the Man, the Senator, the "Ism"* (1952), and by Richard Rovere, *Senator Joe McCarthy* (1959). In his *Senator from Vermont* (1961), Ralph Flanders recounts his role in deposing McCarthy. Marquis Childs, *Eisenhower: Captive Hero* (1958) is mildly critical. James MacGregor Burns, *John Kennedy, A Political Profile* (1960) is the best of several campaign biographies.

For contemporary reactions to threats of the postwar world, see tracts such as Norman Cousins, *Modern Man Is Obsolete* (1945); Emery Reves, *The Anatomy of Peace* (1946); David V. Bradley, *No Place to Hide* (1948); Stringfellow Barr, *Let's Join the Human Race* (1950). Useful first-hand accounts of the diplomacy of the cold war are contained in *Memoirs of Harry S. Truman* (2 vols., 1955); James F. Byrnes, *All in One Lifetime* (1958); Arthur H. Vandenberg, ed., *The Private Papers of Senator Vandenberg* (1952); McGeorge Bundy, ed., *The Pattern of Responsibility* (1952), which is drawn from the public statements and speeches of Dean Acheson. Walter Lippmann, *The Cold War* (1947) is critical of the doctrine of containment. Robert A. Taft, *A Foreign Policy for Americans* (1951) was issued as a campaign document. Roscoe Drummond and Gaston Coblentz, *Duel at the Brink* (1960) deals with John Foster Dulles' years as Secretary of State in the Eisenhower Cabinet. Norman Thomas, *The Prerequisites of Peace* (1959) sets forth imperatives of the age, as he sees them.

Eric Goldman, *The Crucial Decade: America, 1945–1955* (1956) is a readable and interpretative account of the decade. Joseph McCarthy, *McCarthyism, the Fight for America* (1952) presses some of his principal accusations. William E. Buckley, Jr., and L. Brent Bozell, *McCarthy and His Enemies* (1954) is a defense of McCarthy. Reinhard Luthin, *American Demagogues* (1954) gives an account of McCarthy as a demagogue. Owen Lattimore, *Ordeal by Slander* (1950) is a personal document by one who experienced the full impact of McCarthy's accusations. Michael Straight, *Trial by Television* (1954) is a fascinating account of the fateful Army-McCarthy hearings.

For Stevenson's speeches, see p. 375. Hoover's speeches between 1948 and 1960 appear in a series of volumes under the general title *Addresses Upon the American Road* (1951–1961). Some of McCarthy's anti-Communist career is portrayed in *Major Speeches and Debates of Senator Joe McCarthy Delivered in the United States Senate, 1950–1951* (n.d.); other speeches for later years may be found in the *Congressional Record*, and in *The New York Times*. Elmer Davis, *But We Were Born Free* (1953) is a collection of public lectures by a distinguished radio journalist reacting to the McCarthy era. George F. Kennan, *Russia, the Atom and the West* (1957) is a collection of lectures he gave over the BBC. Dwight D. Eisenhower, *Peace with Justice: Selected Addresses* (1961) consists of thirty notable speeches made by the former President. Allan Nevins, ed., *The Strategy of Peace* (1960) is a compilation of Kennedy's speeches on foreign policy during his years as Senator.

Vital Speeches of the Day, and *Representative American Speeches*, edited by Baird, have been cited previously as general collections of speeches. Harold F. Harding, ed.,

The Age of Danger (1952) contains speeches on sundry problems of the postwar world.

Edward R. Murrow and Fred W. Friendly, eds., "I Can Hear It Now, 1945–1949," Columbia Masterworks ML 4261, is a recording of voices and sounds with narrative by Murrow. Portions of the Churchill and Thomas records, previously cited, are also pertinent.

To Secure These Rights

There are no biographies of Wilkins and Brady. Useful autobiographies for background on this issue are: Booker T. Washington, *Up from Slavery* (1901); and W. E. B. DuBois, *Dusk of Dawn: An Essay Toward an Autobiography of a Race Concept* (1940).

For background, Gunnar Myrdahl, *An American Dilemma* (2 vols., 1944); Herbert Apthaker, ed., *A Documentary History of the Negro People in the United States* (1951); Herbert J. Seligmann, "Twenty Years of Negro Progress," *Current History,* XXIX (January, 1929), pp. 614–621. For the N.A.A.C.P., Robert L. Jack, *History of the National Association for the Advancement of Colored People* (1943); Mary White Ovington, *The Walls Came Tumbling Down* (1947). For the Negro in World War II, Walter White, *A Rising Wind* (1945); Margaret Halsey, *Color Blind* (1946). More recent publications are: *To Secure These Rights: The Report of the President's Committee on Civil Rights* (1947); Lillian Smith, *Killers of the Dream* (1949); Harry Ashmore, *The Negro and the Schools* (1954); Don Shoemaker, ed., *With All Deliberate Speed* (1957); Benjamin M. Ziegler, ed., *Desegregation and the Supreme Court* (1958), readings selected by the Department of American Studies, Amherst College.

Many of Roy Wilkins' speeches are available in pamphlet form from the N.A.A.C.P. For speeches of a Southern moderate, see Brooks Hays, *This World: A Christian's Workshop* (1958). Other recent speeches are Eugene Cook, "The Southern View of Segregation," *Vital Speeches of the Day,* XXII (January 15, 1956), pp. 209–214; Jessie P. Guzman, "The Southern Race Problem in Retrospect," *Vital Speeches of the Day,* XXV (July 1, 1959), pp. 566–568. For earlier speeches, see Carter G. Woodson, *Negro Orators and Their Orations* (1925); *Selected Speeches of Booker T. Washington* (1932); Mordecai Johnson, "The Faith of the American Negro," *The Nation,* CXV (July 19, 1922), pp. 64–65. Alice Moore Dunbar, ed., *Masterpieces of Negro Eloquence* (1914), contains one of the few DuBois speeches extant. Booker T. Washington's Atlanta speech (1896) is in his *Up From Slavery* (1901), pp. 218–225.

Our Unfinished Business

Books on Stevenson: Noel F. Busch, *Adlai E. Stevenson of Illinois, A Portrait* (1952); John B. Martin, *Adlai Stevenson* (1952); Walter Johnson, *How We Drafted Adlai Stevenson* (1955); Elizabeth Stevenson Ives, and Hildegarde Dolson, *My Brother Adlai* (1956); Kenneth S. Davis, *A Prophet in His Own Country* (1957); Stuart Gerry Brown, *Conscience in Politics: Adlai E. Stevenson in the 1950s* (1961).

Books by Stevenson: *Major Campaign Speeches* (1952); *Call to Greatness* (1954)— the Godkin lectures at Harvard given in March, 1954; *What I Think* (1956)—selected speeches and writings since the 1952 campaign; *The New America* (1957)—includes selected speeches from the 1956 campaign; *Friends and Enemies: What I Learned in*

Russia (1959)—a collection of brief reports on a 1958 journey. *Putting First Things First* (1960)—recent essays and speeches.

Recordings: James Fleming, ed., "Adlai Stevenson Speaks," RCA Victor Red Seal Records LM 1769—recorded portions of Stevenson's 1952 campaign speeches with narrative by Fleming; Howard R. Lamar and Charles S. Blitzer, ed., "Sounds of an Election Year: Campaign '56," an unnumbered and undated record produced at the Yale University Audio Visual Center.